IS ANYONE LISTENING?

Is Anyone Listening?

Women, Work, and Society

EDITED BY

Merle Jacobs

Women's Press

Toronto

Is Anyone Listening?: Women, Work, and Society
Edited by Merle Jacobs

The first paperback edition published in 2002 by
Women's Press
180 Bloor Street West, Suite 801
Toronto, Ontario
M5S 2V6

www.womenspress.ca

Women's Press gratefully acknowledges financial assistance for our publishing activities from the Ontario Arts Council, the Canada Council for the Arts, and the Government of Canada through the Book Publishing Industry Development Program.

National Library of Canada Cataloguing in Publication Data

Is anyone listening? : women, work, and society / edited by Merle Jacobs.

Includes bibliographical references.
ISBN 0-88961-409-1

1. Women—Employment. 2. Discrimination in employment. 3. Sex discrimination against women. I. Jacobs, Merle

HD6054.2.C3I8 2002   305.43   C2002-903476-0

Page design and layout by Brad Horning
Cover design by Zack Taylor

05   06   07   08   6   5   4   3

Printed and bound in Canada by AGMV Marquis

ONTARIO ARTS COUNCIL
CONSEIL DES ARTS DE L'ONTARIO

The Canada Council | Le Conseil des Arts
for the Arts | du Canada
since 1957 | depuis 1957

This book is dedicated to my mother, Doreen Jacobs
A woman of courage

Copyright Acknowledgements

Acknowledgements

First of all, I wish to acknowledge my three brothers, Patrick, Winston, and Richard, who did not practise sexism and helped me understand gender equality through ideas and actions. My father gave me boxing lessons along with "the boys." He would not allow stereotypes and gender roles to stop his only daughter from achieving whatever she wanted to accomplish. It was from him that I learned to fight injustice. My mother, who was my role model, always saw the need for social change. She taught me that everyone is equal and I thank her for the support she provided over the years. I especially thank her for the lessons of not giving up, even in the face of adversities.

To Malo, Aloma, and Robynne, thank you for all your support and encouragement in this project. Each of you hold distinctive ideas about life. Together the three of you provide balance that helps me understand life's difficulties; for this I am indebted to you.

Apart from family socialization, I want to acknowledge the people of Burma, the country of my youth. As a Buddhist country, it contained equality when it came to gender, religion, and ethnicity. Class as a barrier was less visible. Today, although state oppression exists, there are individuals fighting for justice and equity who are led by a woman, Aung San Su Kyi. I feel at this time that it is important to acknowledge the past when reviewing the issues of the day.

Acknowledgements are owed to friends and colleagues in whose stories I heard about discrimination and hardships due to gender, race, and ethnicity. Your descriptions of workplace discrimination and treatment due to race, gender, and age provoked questions that I hope this reader addresses. I am deeply indebted to you for your insights; they have helped me understand justice, injustice, and the need for social change. I want to thank my cousin Barbara for managing our household, thus allowing me time to write, eat home-cooked meals, and play with Benji and Molly.

Finally, I wish to acknowledge the superb editorial work and the support provided by Women's Press. I would like to thank all of the individuals involved, particularly Althea Prince, for her support and counsel.

Table of Contents

Section Four: Promoting Social Change

Introduction:
Is Anyone Listening?

Merle Jacobs

In constructing this text, it is essential to examine theoretical questions that focus on gender, multiculturalism, and the status of women in society. The relationship between gender and sexism has long been a subject of discussion in Canada, and there is a rich body of feminist scholarship in this area. In this text, examining racialized sexism is another way of understanding power and the politics of gender.

Since the 1970s, the area of multiculturalism has provided us with scholarly discussion of how peoples from other ethnic and racial groups form part of the Canadian fabric. Although our politicians claim that we have an appreciation for Canada's multicultural society, diversity and differences are not, in fact, well accepted. For example, since September 11, 2001, we have found evidence of discrimination and targeting against men of Middle Eastern origin and their organizations. Canada's multicultural policy has created second-class Canadians and left power in the hands of the "two founding peoples."[1]

The position I hold in this society is based on my gender, age, race, ethnicity, and class as well as my years of education. Each of these indicators has a way of creating barriers that can prevent me from achieving desired goals at work within my profession and as a member of society, although at times the same indicators can also provide opportunity when organizations need minorities for their ethnic mix and seek out candidates of colour. However, many qualified individuals are blocked or sidelined due to their gender, race, or ethnicity. Those who are not rewarded are seldom recognized and never achieve their potential. Minority voices have to compete with those from the dominant groups (in Canada, they are the "two founding peoples") for time and space to express their concerns about equity.

Women and racial and ethnic minorities make up a large part of our society. We need to create a safe environment for them to discuss their oppression. Understanding how the world operates for women in a racialized and ethnicized society can make those of us who want social change find ways to reduce discrimination.

Kirby and McKenna (1989) claim that too often researchers, well trained in patterns of thinking, explain and justify a world that few are interested in changing. For them, research and knowledge are used as instruments of power to impose form and order for the purpose of control, thus maintaining oppressive relations. Information is interpreted and organized in such a way that the views of a small group of people are presented as objective knowledge (Kirby and McKenna, 1989:15). Kirby and McKenna acquaint us with the social context of women "from the margins," and how to enable their voices to be heard when we present their needs and views. From my point of view, when we regard these individuals as "from the margins," it focuses on those at the edge of the circle while leaving researchers in the centre with power and prominence. Even those researchers who use their skills to enable the marginalized to be heard are usually from the privileged classes of society. For many scholars, white privilege is treated as everyday behaviour while racialized sexism is "at the margins" and needs to be explained and understood. Therefore, when we look at the circle of power, we may need new vocabulary to be more inclusive when describing differences. We who are placed "at the margins" due to race and class by those currently in power positions do not identify with this marginal position or any other language of discrimination. Recently, when I used the word "marginalized" when referring to myself, it was suggested that I look at where I was positioning myself. It was pointed out that I should instead put the responsibility for marginalization on those who were in positions of power and who were engaged in discriminatory social discourse. These ideas and relationships are socially constructed, and the discussions concerning discrimination need to be engaged in the public domain. This moves the discourse from the margins to become part of the discourse of the whole.

What needs to be addressed is the construction of policy, the language of inclusion and exclusion, and how the group that holds power constructs discrimination. It is through research for social change that we can describe the context of marginalization, disseminate the findings so that wide-ranging debate can occur, and critically assess the directions in which women are controlled through sexism, race, and class in our society. New understandings have to be advanced so that we do not create new boundaries or fences but make the discussion inclusive and build bridges with people from different backgrounds. I edited this book because I considered the available texts seldom conveyed to students the extent of inequalities that women encounter in Canada.

I hope this book will spark a debate not only about women in the workplace, but about how society relegates them to certain positions based on their class, age, race, and ethnicity, thus creating a hostile environment. This book brings together key essays and articles that seek to understand women's place in society. The collection is designed so that familiar features of inequality that are often difficult to comprehend are traced through the different aspects of women's lives and through particular theories.

This book is not an impersonal source of information; it reflects the experiences of women in relation to work, health, education, and society. It is not an attempt at male bashing or exclusion. It is meant to make all of us aware of society's institutions where women's encounters occur, and where unconscious processes, identification, and internalization of dominant values are part of everyday life. *Is Anyone Listening?* is the result of my experience over the last several years when I tried to explain that race, ethnicity, and class matter in women's lives. I encountered societal obstacles, such as harassment in the workplace, but I gained insights from these experiences. It has been suggested in an article in a community newspaper[2] that even the Ontario Human Rights Commission does not deal with racism in real terms and that it does not understand how systemic racism operates in the workplace. The article stated that "filing a human rights complaint takes close to five years to go through the system and in addition less than *one percent of complaints* reaches a Board of Inquiry." If a powerful institutional structure such as the Ontario Human Rights Commission does not listen, then is *anyone* listening?

During the last year, my experiences of working as a primary caregiver, as well as listening to the experiences of older women, prompted questions about the role of the caregivers and seniors in our society. These questions required investigation. I also found myself listening to female physicians and nurses of colour who were having difficulty in the workplace. Sensitivity to the subject matter of sexism, ageism, classism, and what it means to be a person of colour in a white society influences how we communicate with each other. Sometimes the word "communicate" is overused. However, communication is the process of sharing information and has to do with how individuals interact with each other. The words we speak or hear trigger images or messages and reinforce our experiences and understanding of our lived relationships. Communication is important in facilitating shared meanings between individuals, groups, and whole communities. On the other hand, when there are power differences, unshared meanings and a lack of understanding of problems occur in relationships and in society. These conflicts arise both at the individual and systemic level. Communication is a two-way street, and if one party is not listening or does not understand the issues, then communication does not occur and both parties are prevented from interacting with each other. I hope this book will help students understand ageism, sexism, classism, and racialized sexism, and communicate these issues in a way that will help facilitate social change.

In Section One, theoretical perspectives on gender and diversity provide observations and understanding of the issues discussed in the rest of this book. Reflections on feminist methodology make available to us arguments regarding research and the traditions of social science techniques. The scholars point out that theory and method are intimately connected and that we do not merely add women to the relationship. It is important to go beyond the traditional notions reflected in the methods used and acknowledge the differences among women of different ages, ethnicities, races, and classes.

The use of gender as a category constructs differences, which show that gender is not neutral but contributes to power relations. Like gender, race and ethnicity as well as class are categories in our society that construct differences. The authors of the first three articles review how gender and/or race and ethnicity are areas that predefine and place the individual or group in their permitted space within the social world. The discussion also deals with how racialization and ethnicization affect full citizenship rights. The ongoing debate about multiculturalism leads us to the discourse of diversity and how the issue of "race" in particular becomes one issue of contention. There are no easy answers to the issues addressed in this section.

In discussing theories and methods in Section One, I included a reference to how qualitative research can identify racialist discourse. Chapter Three allows the student to view curricula as a means for reviewing equity and white privilege. Students will find out how research, method, and theory in this section view women's experiences in their full complexity based on our racialized society. Gender provides a common ground. Nevertheless, race, ethnicity, and class are barriers between groups of women.

In Section Two, we look at the range and complexity of women's professional lives in which sex-linked occupations are seen as central to femaleness. Most of the articles chosen for this section are based on the traditional professions that women have entered. Even in these traditional professions, we find discrimination, racism, and evidence of the distribution of power among women within society. By looking at the variety and complexity of women's lives across these professions, we can ask if there is a "sisterhood of women." Perhaps race, ethnicity, and class play an important role in dividing women and erode women's claim to be sisters in a common struggle against patriarchy. As feminists, we see the state as a product of a patriarchal society and the needs of capitalism. However, when we examine professions that are predominantly female, we gain insights into the relationships among women and the role of sexist racism in the stratification of the workplace.

The reasons why unfair behaviours are allowed to continue within these professions are not complex. Each of the articles provides us with different insights. The forces of ideology and power that divide women, combined with the obstacles for the integration of women of colour, make it clear that oppression is within the structures of female-dominated professions. As with racialized sexism, women in professions (such as stripping) who are deemed by society to be outside the boundaries of acceptable occupations are considered either deviant or as needing psychological help.

The unorganized sector of work (such as emotional work or erotica) is often discounted and regarded as providing traditional roles that belong to women. While some women talk about power, social change, and professionalism, others are left behind and lack power as well as institutional support to speak as a group to advance their own interests. It is naïve to think that all women are equal and that women are not victimized by other women in Canada.

While the scholars in Section Two provide us with terminology and discuss the position of women in the workplace, they also help us understand subordination as defined in terms of access and control within professions. As well, we come to appreciate how these belief systems are social aspects of everyday life. To varying degrees these scholars have been influenced by the discourse of gender, race, ethnicity, and class. Whatever their theoretical leanings, it is fair to say that they recognize the differences and the differential access that women have within professional structures.

Section Three introduces women we meet in our everyday lives and whose work is hidden from view because of how society values the roles they occupy. The articles examining their lives fall broadly under the theme of exploitation. These scholars look at society's economic base and how economic relations may underlie social relations, domestic interactions, and other practices. The issue of how women internalize the role of caring, and how particular jobs establish them in the underclass is discussed by scholars in terms of equity and oppression. The topics of economics and gender, as well as the domestic domain, are presented in terms of inequality and exclusion. Professional women in the public domain who are regarded as role models, as compared with the women discussed in this section, have greater access to the sources of economic, political, and social power. Illuminating the hidden

— women in low-status, undervalued jobs — may help in the redistribution of economic and social power.

Society ignores the contributions of the domestic worker, who is taken advantage of by the state and the employer, and of the caregiver who works for her family or significant other. Many of these women, when they become senior citizens, continue to be at a disadvantage. Each group is exploited, but in different ways. There are economic reasons why our society has relegated women to maternal roles. Women have internalized the responsibility of "taking care of others" and living a life that includes "giving to others." We rarely see males in caregiving roles, which points to a gender division of labour as well as to socialization.

Women's experiences and perceptions in different professions and in different social and racial groups are quite different from those of women in the dominant group who have achieved a level of success. There are crucial differences in the status of these women as compared with women in the upper classes. Although all women find themselves in oppressive situations, women with less wealth, women whose work is not valued, and women who find themselves as caregivers due to illness are more restricted in terms of time and money. They may not have the energy to reflect and act in their own interests.

The articles in Section Three describe women's limitations in job opportunities and the lack of support for their roles within the larger society. The analysis of the condition of women who volunteer or who provide domestic work for other women lies within a larger debate about the origin of the exploitation of labour. The exploitation of women by organizations and by other women directs us to an analysis of the determinants of exploitation and social inequality. The women in this section who are wageless workers experience specific forms of oppression that marginalize their position in society.

The complex dynamics of how these women live, as well as how society exploits and alters their lives, can be examined. Despite the obstacles confronting this group of women, they provide us with insights to how social decisions are made in Canada. The scholars in these articles show how social and economic positions affect women's position in both absolute and relative terms and limit the opportunities available to them.

Section Four deals with promoting social change. We move from understanding the issues to seeing how change occurs. The scholars use research to focus on practical means of improving or understanding the lives of women. This section helps us understand the interrelated nature of method, theory, research, and social change. Social research can become a vehicle for political critique and social change. Provided in this section are some practical tools that students can use to organize activities for political action. When reviewing the actions we want to take, first understanding current research enables us to express our message. Second, we need to develop strategies to achieve equity and provide an opportunity for those unheard voices. Finally, we need to take action based on the best strategy, relating it to the relationships that currently exist among women and society.

Becoming aware of inequalities in social life may provide us with material to criticize practices, which some people in Canada dismiss as unjustified complaining and whining. We need to call attention to attitudes and practices that disadvantage women. The need to change the experience of women in general is apparent. However, our sisters who are oppressed within female-dominated professions, as well as those who are disadvantaged due to age, race, ethnicity, and class, are excluded in current discussions. Like many other scholars, I depend on research and facts to argue for social change. However, if action for social change does not occur, then we will continue to suffer discrimination and limitation of opportunities. Therefore, action is necessary at every level.

Those students who do not wish to deal with social change may find that this section is not pertinent to them. On the other hand, if students are ready to wrestle with serious matters related to women, work, and society, then this section will help them understand why these issues are not just personal but political. The last article provides examples of how to deal with policy-makers.

In the past decade, Canada has become more intolerant and less respectful of differences. A small but vocal group of thinkers and talking heads have hijacked our societal agenda while we have remained silent due to a lack of access to media outlets and to power brokers. As well, right-of-centre policies have come into government thinking. To challenge this type of thinking, we need to take action as individuals and as a group to keep the issues of oppression front and centre and make politicians accountable for their inaction on issues concerning discrimination. In taking action, especially at the government level, we can transform the agenda of the day to a commitment of equity for all and not just to free-market economic issues that enhance the lives of the powerful. In putting this book together I have transformed my feelings of despair into a commitment for social change, not so much for myself as a woman of colour but for everyone, so that we can have intergrated communities with equal participation.

Notes

1   Native peoples resent the "founding peoples" mythology that pervades the development of the Canadian nation-state because the "founding peoples" refers to the French and English and does not acknowledge the presence or contribution of Native peoples in North America (Elliott, 1983:5).

2   *Share* is a West Indian newspaper that is distributed widely in Toronto. The quotation regarding the Ontario Human Rights Commissions ("However, I do not think that filing a human rights complaint is a good strategy. It will take close to five years to go through the system. In addition, less than one percent of complaints to a Board or Inquiry ...") was in response to students' fee increases, which would make it unaffordable for black youths who wish to study law (Ron Fanfair, *Share* ethnic newspaper, March 14, 2002).

References

Elliott, Jean L. 1983. *Two Nations, Many Cultures: Ethnic Groups in Canada*, 2nd ed. Toronto: Prentice Hall of Canada.

Kirby, S., and K. McKenna. 1989. *Methods from the Margins*. Toronto: Garamond Press.

Section One

THEORIZING GENDER, RACE, ETHNICITY, AND CLASS

Chapter One

Theorizing Women's Work: Feminist Methodology

Pat Armstrong
Hugh Armstrong

Introduction

From the beginning of the current wave of feminism, questions about what should be studied, how it should be studied, and how theory should be related to empirical research have been central. These questions are still crucial issues in feminist debates.

The Subject

As Dorothy Smith (1974) forcefully argued, women have often been invisible in social science literature. But as Meg Luxton (1984:61) has more recently pointed out, social science has not ignored women, but rather it has treated them in ways that fail to make them the subjects of history. Male criteria were assumed to be universal criteria in what Mary O'Brien (1976) called "malestream thought." "Women's oppression is qualitatively different from class oppression, and the qualitative differentiation which must be made in the first instance in theoretical terms simply does not emerge from Marx's work in a direct way" (O'Brien, 1979:100). In addition, what Margrit Eichler (1980) called the double standard meant that identical behaviour was differently evaluated according to whether it was exhibited by women or by men.

In her introduction to *The Effects of Feminist Approaches on Research Methodologies*, Winnie Tomm (1989:2) has offered a concise summary of the feminist critique:

The so-called objectivity of male defined rationality was found to be replete with unexamined pervasive prejudice against women's interests, especially with regard to academic research. The topics were defined by male interests, the methods used to illuminate the topics were devised by men, the messages communicated to the public were those which reflected the interests of the powerful who were usually men.

Research reflecting feminist perspectives was seldom funded. Even when feminists managed to conduct their research, it was unlikely to be published in the traditional academic outlets. New strategies were required (Andrew, 1989).

In response to such criticisms and to pressures from feminists, mainstream books about families, about work, and about inequality began to include chapters on women. Journals were pushed to publish the odd article on women. However, the dominant texts continued to assume a sexless universal person — a person whose likeness was more male than female — and the chapters on women were confined to narrowly defined "women's issues." Today, we still get unemployment figures and female unemployment figures, and a chapter on workers and then one on female workers, as if there were a norm and then an aberration. Within the more radical political economy publications, the materialist analysis of women's subordination ran parallel to, but seldom integrated with, other theoretical developments. Women, and a few men, were left to deal with that stuff. Here, too, women's work was relegated to a secondary position outside the main task of theorizing production.

Increasingly, women become a more prominent category, integrated in the text. In the manner of Canadian versions of American texts, however, publications devoted to examining women all too often merely inserted women in place of men, without transforming the concepts to make them sex-conscious. All too frequently, sex was simply added in, as one more variable among many. Alternatively, as Ruth Pierson and Alison Prentice (1982:110) observed of historical writing, authors assigned "importance to women only insofar as they have contributed to or supplemented the work or achievements of men."

These strategies for including women reflected the definition of what constituted a women's issue. The earliest writing of both historical materialists and radical feminists viewed the subordination of women as embedded in the entire fabric of society, although one group identified production and the other human reproduction as the primary basis for this subordination. Marlene Dixon (1972:230), for example, argued that "class and property relations are the source of the oppression of women," whereas Jane Likely (1972:158–159) insisted that "women's liberation demands that liberation pre-empt revolution." For theorists from both perspectives, the subject matter of feminist theory was the organization of the social structure. It was not restricted to some finite, clearly demarcated area of women's issues, as it had been in early liberal feminist theory. Materialist and radical arguments implied that women's subordination had to be central to all social theory and research, that all questions were women's questions.

As research has increasingly exposed the pervasiveness of segregation and subordination, and as more women have entered and become vocal in the public sphere, it has become more and more difficult for theorists concerned with the position of women to restrict their focus to a narrow range of women's issues. Here feminists from all persuasions, including liberal feminists, have tended to converge.

A key recommendation of the Royal Commission on the Status of Women (Canada, 1970) illustrates this development (see Armstrong and Armstrong, 1982). When the Royal Commission recommended the establishment of a council to "advise on matters pertaining to women," the objective seemed clear. "We want for women no special status, only equal status; no separate realm, only full acceptance in the present human world" (1970:390). However, as the resulting Canadian Advisory Council on the Status of Women conducted research, responded to feminists' demands, and evaluated state programs, equal status was revealed as a complex and difficult goal. And the definition of "matters pertaining to women" expanded enormously. It quickly became clear that women would have to be treated differently in many circumstances if they were not to suffer from their sex. As Judge Rosalie Abella would later explain in her Royal Commission report *Equality in Employment* (Canada, 1984:2), "to treat everyone the same may be to offend the notion of equality. Ignoring differences may mean ignoring legitimate needs." Each time a particular area was investigated, it became clear that it could not be separated from the entire organization of the social structure. It became clear that all questions were women's questions.

For us, this kind of progression meant rethinking theory, and involved us in yet another debate about the appropriate level of analysis for the theorization of gender. We argued that, in materialist analysis,

> to insist on distinguishing a highest level of abstraction that entirely excludes consideration of a sexual division of labour is to be sexist — to reinforce the notion of women being hidden from history, or more accurately, from theory. It is also to guarantee an inadequate understanding of capitalism, given that the split between the public and the private, and thus a sexual division of labour, is essential to this mode of production, at the highest level of abstraction. (Armstrong and Armstrong, 1983b:28)

Patricia Connelly (1983:157–58) has rejected this argument, agreeing with Wally Seccombe that there is a "sexless and epochal abstraction of the capitalist mode of production" and that it is at the level of the social formation that "the relations of production intersect, combine and conflict with the relations of gender in different classes and in different historical periods within one society, and in different societies." The issue remains a central one because its theoretical and political implications are significant. We contend that our position implies that the subordination of women's work cannot be completely eliminated under capitalism, and that it will be eliminated under whatever succeeds capitalism only if the different reproductive capacities of women and men are adequately taken into account.

Method

The emphasis on the techniques used in and the legitimacy given to the so-called "hard" data of quantitative analysis ran counter to the "personal is political" assumption at the core of feminist thinking. In her introduction to the first edition of *Women in Canada*, Marylee Stephenson (1973:xv) explained that, in the women's movement, "every woman's life experience provides valid information about certain aspects of women's situation in general." Although she then offered the qualification that such information provides "a valuable resource area outside the strictly academic field," this observation became increasingly outdated as more and more feminist research focused on recording women's daily lives.

Whatever feminists' position on the appropriate level of analysis, most would agree that all issues are women's issues. Women must be acknowledged as subjects different from men, making all research a concern for women. This means rethinking categories and approaches, not just "fitting women in."

Like dual systems theorists who developed new approaches to human reproduction but left old theories of production virtually untouched (Armstrong, 1984:36–38), researchers who relied on interviews, diaries, personal reminiscences, and group discussions as a means of examining women's work left statistical analytical techniques untransformed.

Those who argued for the exclusive use of qualitative techniques maintained that quantitative techniques both failed to capture many aspects of women's lives and objectified women. As these feminists worked with qualitative techniques and transformed them into what was increasingly called a feminist methodology, they also developed a more thorough critique of old approaches, both qualitative and quantitative. They rejected the idea of researchers who stood "outside" the work being studied and who assumed that they knew more than those actually doing the work. They rejected the tendency to fit women into preconceived categories or theories. And they rejected the pretense as well as the ideal of "value-free" research. They sought to develop, as Thelma McCormack (1989:15) has so cogently explained,

> A new kind of knowledge which did not attempt to be objective, and was no longer attempting to 'predict and control', knowledge without social causation and without looking for regularities that might lead to 'laws', would obliterate the line between subject and object and create both a richer knowledge and a more ethical one. Knowledge would be consciousness-raising for both the people who carried out the studies and those who were studied.

Many of those who argued for this approach held that research on women could only be done by women, because research required not only a commitment to feminist principles and an empathy with those who were studied, but also a shared history. Some argued that this meant that only immigrants could study immigrants, and only people of colour could study people of colour.

Many of the materialists and liberal feminists examining women's work had tended to rely on traditional social science techniques to analyze quantitative data, establishing the segregation of the labour market with these tools. Radical feminists in particular, however, preferred qualitative approaches to the investigation of the commonalities of women's work, establishing women's shared experiences, particularly in the work of mothering and in relations with men. Indeed, as McCormack (1981) pointed out, many feminists rejected the whole notion of scientific investigation, arguing that the rationality it assumed reflected a male way of thinking. They argued instead for collections of women's personal experiences, letting women speak for themselves.

It was important to emphasize that women often had a very clear understanding of their situation; that they frequently understood more than researchers. Moreover, it was important to recognize that how women understood the world and their place in it had an important impact on their behaviour and relations. However, many of those making these arguments seemed to suggest that the woman recording women's experiences was objective and value-free — a mere cipher. Yet this was precisely what they had accused male researchers of doing with their "objective" research. These female researchers still selected the lives to be recorded and the parts of lives to be reported. Equally important, the presentation of researcher as recorder denied what was at the core of feminism — the connecting of the personal and the political and the commitment to change. These connections required theoretical assumptions and an articulated framework, not an invisible researcher. As Linda Briskin (1989:91) has pointed out,

An anti-theory emphasis on personal experience can individualize difference (each experience as unique) to such a degree that the deep-rooted processes by which experience is socially constructed are concealed. As a result, the complex patterning of women's experiences of class, race, gender, and sexual orientation is masked; even the interconnectedness between different aspects of an individual woman's experience (for example, the links between household and workplace), can be made less accessible, thus exacerbating the fragmentation of everyday life within patriarchal capitalism.

In our early work (Armstrong and Armstrong, 1975), we used quantitative data to investigate women's paid employment. As is the case with many other feminist researchers, our purpose was political. We wanted to use evidence that would be both academically acceptable as rigorous research and readily comprehensible to a wide audience. We developed two measures of segregation to explore the changes over time in the allocation of jobs to women and to men. The degree of sex-typing — the proportion of jobs that go to women — was measured by calculating the percentage of all workers in an industry or occupation who were women. The degree of concentration — the proportion of all women who worked in a particular industry or occupation — was measured by calculating the percentage of female workers employed in an industry or occupation. Percentages allowed us to indicate relative change over time and between women and men without resorting to often incomprehensible statistical measures.

But the experience of working with available quantitative data was extremely frustrating. The concepts and techniques used in data collection often excluded women's experience, even when the data were tabulated by sex. Household work was invisible. Moreover, these data could tell us nothing about the nature and conditions of work in either the public or the private sphere. Influenced by these frustrations and by feminist critiques of mainstream methodology, we tried to combine the use of qualitative and quantitative techniques, using statistical data to establish the broad outlines of the segregation, and long, partially structured interviews to examine the nature and conditions of women's work. With other feminists, we rejected the view that social science research is entirely objective, and that the researcher is uncommitted and omniscient, able to understand far better than those being studied what was really happening in their lives. "We are seeking information both on how the work was structured, and on women's approaches to their work and perceptions of it. Obviously the objective and subjective are intimately connected, indeed often inseparable" (Armstrong and Armstrong, 1983c:224). The interviewers were committed feminists with experience in feminist research, teaching, and organizations. Although we "arranged their responses to fit into an ordered framework, and abbreviated some for the sake of pertinence and clarity, we ... tried to let the women speak for themselves" (Armstrong and Armstrong, 1983c:iv). Our theory had developed along with the research and been altered by the research.

We explicitly rejected the temptation to gain traditional legitimacy by transforming our sixty-five interviews into numbers (although, interestingly, at least one feminist reviewer saw this as the major problem with the study). Instead we argued that

> the statistical representativity of the sample survey is lost, but what is gained is much more than a collection of anecdotes. The consistent patterns emerging from the 65 interviews used in this study suggest that we have found many of the common threads in women's work. The women who read this book will provide the real test of its validity. If it resonates well with their own experiences, if it both reflects their daily lives and sheds new light on them, then it will have fulfilled its most important requirement. We believe that the analysis of these interviews provides much more than a string of examples. It contributes to the task of exposing the nature and conditions of women's work. (Armstrong and Armstrong, 1983c:222)

This research served to increase our frustration with the available statistics and statistical techniques, but we were still convinced that some statistical analysis was essential in order to draw out long-term and national trends, and to set the stage for other, qualitative research. Although we agreed with Margaret Benston (1982:56) that "what is needed is a methodology that does not, in fact, relegate the nonquantifiable aspects of a problem to secondary status but instead attempts some kind of integration of this into scientific practice," we also felt that feminists had to transform the quantifiable data and their techniques of analysis. When we were asked, along with other researchers, to participate in a 1982 conference on data requirements to support research into women and the Canadian economy, we tried to put some of these concerns into writing, arguing that

> statistics are not all they are cracked up to be. The way data are collected and tabulated, the way questions are asked and not asked, the way government programmes and policies are structured and the way in which history is considered, all influence the data and in the process often leave out and sometimes misrepresent the position of women. Qualitative data, while not free of faults, can provide an effective complement to quantitative techniques, checking the results, suggesting alternative areas and methods for research and filling in the numbers with the actual experiences of women. (Armstrong and Armstrong, 1983a:37)

Because theory and method are intimately connected, an appropriate methodology involves more than simply adding women in. It involves a transformation of both quantitative and qualitative techniques. It involves examining different processes in different ways because the different work of women and men means that they experience the world in different ways. We were arguing the need for alternative techniques rather than outlining what these techniques would be. We would now argue, however, that they should involve methods that could get at dialectical processes, and that standard mathematical measures, however sophisticated, can only measure linear or partial relationships, not contradictory ones.

Of course, we were not alone in our critiques of traditional academic research methods, or in our search for alternative approaches. The ongoing Luxton, Seccombe, Livingston, and Corman study of Hamilton households combines large-scale survey techniques with intensive interviews. Jennifer Penney's (1983) study of women's work allowed women in the labour force to define the nature and conditions of their work. The papers brought together by Kinnear and Mason in *Women and Work* (1982) testified to the lacunae in existing data bases. Papers from conferences of the Canadian Research Institute for the Advancement of Women (CRIAW) published in *Knowledge Reconsidered: A Feminist Overview* (CRIAW:1984), and by Jill Vickers in *Taking Sex into Account* (1984) collectively demonstrated "the need for new and different questions, focusing on new themes, researched through new methods, and offering new answers" (Gow and Leo, 1984:x); the need to learn "how and when to take sex 'into account' as a variable" (Vickers, 1984:4). In *Feminism in Canada* (Miles and Finn, 1982), the articles by Vickers and by Benston argued for a committed feminist scholarship; those by Cohen, Wine, Pierson, and Prentice and Finn exposed problems for feminist scholarship within their disciplines, and Levine's established the importance of personal experience in social science research. In *On the Treatment of the Sexes in Research,* Eichler and Lapointe (1985) offered specific criteria for determining sexism in research and suggested means for developing a sex-conscious research strategy. Most recently, the twelve authors included in Thom's (1989) *The Effects of Feminist Approaches on Research Methodologies* have emphasized that "research originates from an individual's particular set of interests and is invariably tied to the historical location of that individual" and that "women's location in history is as important as that of men" (11). All these critiques have contributed to the development of a new feminist methodology.

There has been convergence on questions of methodology and subject. Although participants at the 1985 United Nations conference in Nairobi may still have disagreed about whether certain issues are political or are women's issues, and although some women objected to the scope of the party leaders' TV debate on women during the 1984 Canadian election campaign, few feminists in Canada would limit the range of issues to a narrowly prescribed, finite area. And most would agree that new qualitative methods are needed for investigation into women's work. More and more feminists are combining qualitative and quantitative techniques, and, in the process, are transforming these techniques. The old dichotomies between qualitative and quantitative research and between women's issues and people's issues appear less frequently.

Relating Theory and Empirical Research

Although some debates about methodology have disappeared, there are still frequent disagreements about the importance of theory and its relationship to empirical research. Two quite different approaches have been evident and both have come under attack.

An exclusive focus on theory was evident in much of the domestic labour debate. In her review of the articles brought together by Bonnie Fox (1980) in *Hidden in the Household*, Roberta Hamilton (1981:115) criticized the authors for concentrating on developing "a theory which can be appealed to for answers without having to engage in the untidy and painstaking process of encountering the social world." Cerise Morris (1987:121) went much further, criticizing all marxist-feminists for trying "'to fit women in' to a male-centered world view in which the personal gets lost in the realm of 'ideas' and 'structures'."

While some have focused on theory, others have rejected the use of theory, arguing instead for an exclusive concentration on women's experiences. Women were to speak for themselves, providing their own explanations for their work. This approach, too, has encountered its share of criticism. Briskin (1989:91) has argued that this

> tendency to anti-intellectualism and anti-theory in the women's movement which accompanies the emphasis on experience promotes individualism, on the one hand, and on the other, promotes identification of women, not with reason, but with nature — both of which are ideologies of patriarchal capitalism.

Although Dawn Currie (1988:233) agreed that "feminist theory should not become 'expert's theory', rejecting other women's experiences," she disagreed "with the notion that structures and institutions are not oppressive forces and that they are constructed entirely out of everyday life."

Although both these tendencies can be found in the Canadian feminist literature, most feminists have combined the development of theory with empirical research. Most would agree that women should speak for themselves and not be squeezed into predetermined theoretical categories. But the relationship between theory and research is constantly being worked out in the process of conducting empirical research.

Dorothy Smith (1987:153) has argued for a "method beginning from where women are as subjects" rather than one that begins with theoretical constructs. "It is the individual's working knowledge of her everyday world that provides the beginning of the inquiry" (154). Her approach, which she calls "institutional ethnography," is intended to "explicate ... institutional relations determining everyday worlds and hence how the local organization of the latter may be explored to uncover their ordinary invisible determinations in relations that generalize and are generalized" (160). Theory has a place, but it grows out of knitting together these various "standpoints of women."

By contrast, we argued that it is necessary to begin with an explicit theoretical framework because theory is what guides us to select the area and people of concern (Armstrong and Armstrong, 1983a). Women never do simply speak for themselves in empirical research, because as researchers we have already chosen to record what some women say, prompted them to talk about particular aspects of their lives, and edited parts of their representations and interpretations. This does not mean that we should shape the people to fit the theory. Rather, we needed a clear theoretical framework that could be altered or transformed both by the research and by the women's descriptions and analyses of their daily lives.

More recently, Dawn Currie (1988:235, emphasis in original) has argued for "grounded theory." By this she meant an approach in which "*generating the explanation cannot be separated from the process of conducting research.*" The emphasis is on "*theory as process*: that is, theory as an ever-developing entity rather than a perfect product."

Most feminists would now agree that theory building is a continuous process that remains dynamic because it is challenged by research on women's and men's experiences in, actions on, and perceptions of the real world. Increasingly, feminists are "grounding" their research in the way Currie suggests. But "the untidy and painstaking process of encountering the social world" has seldom been absent from Canadian feminist theory.

Conclusion

There are still crucial debates within and between various perspectives on what should be studied and how it should be studied. Materialists continue to begin their analyses with an explicit theoretical framework, as well as a focus on work and how that work is structured by the search for profit. Many use quantitative means to examine structural constraints and qualitative techniques to provide details about historically specific and concrete situations. But what has been defined as work has been expanded to include women's particular part in reproduction, and the boundaries of what can be properly addressed only in sex-conscious fashion have expanded enormously. That the theoretical and methodological interests of materialists have expanded does not mean agreement on how to proceed; rather, it means greater scope for materialist debate.

Radical feminists, on the other hand, continue to focus on the origins of domination and on the "basis for unique feminist values and a feminist vision" (Miles, 1985:16), relying primarily on qualitative techniques for their evidence. What this unique vision entails and how the origins of domination can be related to its elimination are matters of debate among theorists working from this perspective. What is clear, at least to us, is that, "the justification of feminist scholarship must rest not on a special domain (women) or a special kind of empathy (sexual affinity) but on a set of principles of inquiry: a feminist philosophy of science" (McCormack, 1981:3).

References

Andrew, Caroline, *Getting the Word Out*. Ottawa: University of Ottawa Press, 1989.

Armstrong, Pat, *Labour Pains: Women's Work in Crisis*. Toronto: Women's Press, 1984.

Armstrong, Pat and Hugh Armstrong, "The Segregated Participation of Women in the Canadian Labour Force 1941–71," *The Canadian Review of Sociology and Anthropology*. 12 (4, Part 1, November 1975): 370–384.

———, "A Framework for Policy Recommendations on Labour Force Work Flowing from *A Working Majority*," Paper presented to the Canadian Advisory Council on the Status of Women, 1982.

———, "Beyond Numbers: Problems with Quantitative Data," *Alternate Routes*. 1983a, 6:1–40.

———, "Beyond Sexless Class and Classless Sex: Towards Feminist Marxism," *Studies in Political Economy*. 10 (Winter 1983b): 7–43.

———, *A Working Majority: What Women Must Do for Pay*. Ottawa: Supply and Services for the Canadian Advisory Council on the Status of Women, 1983c.

Benston, Margaret, "Feminism and the Critique of Scientific Method," in Angela Miles and Geraldine Finn, eds. *Feminism in Canada*. Montreal: Black Rose, 1982.

Briskin, Linda, "Socialist Feminism: From the Standpoint of Practice," *Studies in Political Economy*. 30 (Fall 1989).

Canada, Royal Commission on the Status of Women, *Report*. Ottawa: Information Canada, 1970.

Canada, Royal Commission on Equality in Employment, *Equality in Employment*. Ottawa: Supply and Services Canada, 1984.

Canadian Institute for the Advancement of Women/Institut canadien de recherches pour l'avancement de la femme, *Knowledge Reconsidered: A Feminist Overview*. Ottawa: CRIAW/ICRAF, 1984.

Connelly, M. Patricia, "On Marxism and Feminism," *Studies in Political Economy*. 12 (Fall 1983): 153–161.

Currie, Dawn, "Re-thinking What We Do and How We Do It: A Study of Reproductive Decisions," *Canadian Review of Sociology and Anthropology*. 25 (2, May 1988): 231–253.

Dixon, Marlene, "Ideology, Class and Liberation," in Margaret Andersen, ed. *Mother Was Not a Person*. Montreal: Black Rose Books, 1972.

Eichler, Margrit, *The Double Standard: A Feminist Critique of Feminist Social Science*. London: Croon Helm, 1980.

Eichler, Margit and Jeanne Lapointe, *On the Treatment of the Sexes in Research*. Ottawa: Supply and Services Canada, for the Social Science and Humanities Research Council of Canada, 1985.

Fox, Bonnie, ed. *Hidden in the Household: Women's Domestic Labour Under Capitalism*. Toronto: Women's Press, 1980.

Gow, June and Willadean Leo, "Preface," in CRIAW/ICRAF, ed. *Knowledge Reconsidered: A Feminist Overview*. Ottawa: CRIAW/ICRAF, 1984.

Hamilton, Roberta, "Working at Home," *Atlantis*. 7 (1, Fall 1981): 114–126.

Kinnear, Mary and Greg Mason, eds. *Women and Work*. Winnipeg: The Institute for Social and Economic Research, University of Manitoba, 1982.

Likely, Jane, "Women and the Revolution," in *Women Unite!* Toronto: Women's Press, 1972.

Luxton, Meg, "Conceptualizing Women in Anthropology and Sociology," in CRIAW/ICRAF, ed. *Knowledge Reconsidered: A Feminist Overview*. Ottawa: CRIAW/ICRAF, 1984.

McCormack, Thelma, "Good Theory or Just Theory? Toward a Feminist Philosophy of Social Science," *Women's Studies International Quarterly*. 4 (1, 1981): 1–12.

——, "Feminism and the New Crisis in Methodology," in Winnie Tomm, ed. *The Effects of Feminist Approaches on Research Methodologies*. Waterloo: Wilfrid Laurier Press, 1989.

Miles, Angela, "Feminist Radicalism in the 1980s," *Canadian Journal of Political and Social Theory*. IX (1–2, 1985): 16–39.

Miles, Angela and Geraldine Finn, eds. *Feminism in Canada*. Montreal: Black Rose Books, 1982.

Morris, Cerise, "Against Determinism: The Case for Women's Liberation," in Greta Hofman Nemiroff, ed. *Women and Men*. Toronto: Fitzhenry and Whiteside, 1987.

O'Brien, Mary, "The Dialectics of Reproduction," in J. King-Farlow and W. Shea, eds. *Contemporary Issues in Political Philosophy*. New York: Watson, 1976.

Penny, Jennifer, *Hard Earned Wages: Women Fighting for Better Work*. Toronto: Women's Press, 1983.

Pierson, Ruth and Alison Prentice, "Feminism and the Writing and Teaching of History," in Angela Miles and Geraldine Finn, eds. *Feminism in Canada*. Montreal: Black Rose Books, 1982.

——, "Reproducing Marxist Man" in Loraine Clark and Lynda Lange, eds. *The Sexism of Social and Political Theory*. Toronto: University of Toronto Press, 1979.

Smith, Dorothy E., "Women's Perspective as a Radical Critique of Sociology," *Sociological Inquiry*. 44 (1974): 7–13.

——, *The Everyday World as Problematic: A Feminist Sociology*. Toronto: University of Toronto Press, 1987.

Stephenson, Marylee, ed. *Women in Canada*. Toronto: New Press, 1973.

Tomm, Winnie, ed. *The Effects of Feminist Approaches on Research Methodologies*. Waterloo, Wilfrid Laurier Press, 1989.

Vickers, Jill McCalla, *Taking Sex into Account*. Ottawa: Carleton University Press, 1984.

Chapter Two

The Paradox of Diversity:
The Construction of a Multicultural
Canada and "Women of Colour"

Himani Bannerji

> Multiculturalism has acquired a quality akin to spectacle. The metaphor that has displaced the melting pot is the salad. A salad consists of many ingredients, is colourful and beautiful, and it is to be consumed by someone. Who consumes multiculturalism is a question begging to be asked.
>
> Angela Y. Davis (1996, p. 45)

Introduction: Comparing Multiculturalisms

Women of colour, diversity, difference and multiculturalism — concepts and discourses explored in this essay — are now so familiar that we are startled when reminded about their relatively recent appearance on the stage of politics and theory. Current political theorization in the West happens very often about and through them, especially when we speak of representational subjectivities and identities and political agencies. My acquaintance with the use of multicultural discourse, which implicates concepts such as women of colour, diversity and difference, among others, is restricted to anglophone western countries. And even among is restricted to anglophone western countries. And even among these I am most familiar with Canada and the United States, and for this last group the discourse of multiculturalism has meant an entry point into an oppositional, or at least an alternative, way of contesting the dominant culture and making participatory space for the nation's others. This other in the multicultural context referred less to African Americans, who are linked more directly with the issue of "race," than to

Hispanic or Asian American and white radical democrats, though of late increasingly it turned to African Americans as well.

To go from these general observations to more specific ones which support my claims, we need only to look at Gordon and Newfield's introduction to *Mapping Multiculturalism*. Dating the arrival of multicultural discourse to the very early 1990s, they carefully weigh out its pros and cons. They point out the discourse's potential (under certain circumstances) for providing "a major framework for analyzing intergroup relations in the United States" (Gordon & Newfield, 1996, p. 1), and its ability to confront racism and connect to "race relations" which are in need of major changes. Seen thus, multiculturalism becomes the heir to the deceased civil rights movement, and helps to disclose what Omi and Winnant call "dispersed projects" of racism (Gordon & Newfield, 1996, p. 3). But the perceived downside to multiculturalism was that in the 1980s it "replaced the emphasis on race and racism with an emphasis on cultural diversity ... and allowed the aura of free play to suggest a creative power to racial groups that lacked political and economic power" (Gordon & Newfield, 1996, p. 3). What Gordon and Newfield do not mention, but imply, is that this "aura of free play," this culturalization of politics, hides the hard realities of profit and class making in the U.S., and also establishes the centrality of an American culture by simultaneously designating other cultures as both autonomous and subcultures. A scathing criticism of multiculturalism as a tool for corporate America, both in terms of its internal diversity management and international capitalism or globalization, features in the essays. One of the strongest of these is the piece by Angela Davis.

Angela Davis's attempt to link social and economic relations of a racialized U.S. (international) capitalism to a critique of multiculturalism is partially offset by those who seek to use it for the creation of a coalitional subject, especially in the feminine. Here the concept of cultural hybridity, construed as integral to multiculturalism, gives it a populist or a radical face, as for example, in Norma Alarcon's (1996) conjugated subjects. For Alarcon, and other such as Chela Sandoval or Michelle Wallace, multiculturalism with its possibilities for cultural hybridity becomes a freeing discourse for subject construction which goes beyond the masculinized rhetoric of cultural nationalism or the fixity of a national identity (Sandoval, 1991). For Michelle Wallace (1994), as for Hazel Carby (1998) in *Race Men*, this is a conscious politics signalling a paradigm of multiple determinations and incommensurability.[1] This is where notions such as "border" identity, a new public sphere and so on become central.[2] For Peter McLaren (1997, pp. 13–14) multiculturalism can be revolutionary by giving him "a sense of atopy, indeterminacy, liminalities, out of overlapping cultural identifications and social practices," while Anzaldúa (1990) speaks to a multicultural subject and the importance of "making face" and "making soul."

It is interesting to note the relative absence of enthusiasm for multiculturalism among those critics who hold a political economic perspective and see it as an ideology for local and global capitalism and cross-border domination by the U.S. economy. Gomez-Peña (1996, p. 66), speaking about Mexican immigrants to the U.S. rendered into "illegal aliens," illustrates how neo-liberalism "under the banner of diversity," and thus of multiculturalism, renders "service to capitalist accumulation" (McLaren, 1997, p. 8). Michael Parenti (1966), in the same critical vein characterizes the U.S. as fascist, and speaks to the use of a multicultural discourse to create identities which McLaren terms (1997, p. 8) as forms of "ideological trafficking between nationality and ethnicity," while Jon Cruz (1996) speaks of multiculturalism's role in negotiating between global capitalism and the fiscal crisis of the state. This radical political economy perspective emphasizing exploitation, dispossession and survival takes the issues of multiculturalism and diversity beyond questions of conscious identity such as culture and ideology, or of a paradigm of homogeneity and heterogeneity as used by D.T. Goldberg (1994), or of ethical imperatives with respect to the "other."

The use of the discourse of multiculturalism in Britain is, as in the U.S., a complicated and voluntary affair. Unlike Canada, the British state has not put forward definitive legislation on this basis. Modes of governance regarding "race" relations or adjudication of racism do not seem to be conducted through a discourse of multiculturalism. Nor has multiculturalism or diversity management yet become an active instrument for the U.K.'s corporate culture in regulating or handling class or labour-capital relations. There may be some symptoms of multiculturalism emerging in the state and economy for management or containment of racialized class relations and exploitation, but they are far from being prominent.

As regards speaking from below, British antiracism is not primarily culturalist. It appears to have its roots in direct political organization against the British state and the economy — particularly regarding importation of labour through immigration and refugee laws and policies, as well as in the tradition of British labour politics (Centre for Cultural Studies, 1982; Gilroy, 1987). The struggle in Britain, it seems, has been much more structural than cultural, some cultural issues around the Bangladeshi and Pakistani muslim immigrants and citizens notwithstanding. The centrality of the dominant English culture, with its colonial self-importance dating back from the days of the empire, has not yielded to any talk of adjustment under the pressure of "other" cultures, though the large presence of immigrants from South Asia and the Caribbean has made some difference in literary and everyday cultural life — in novels, cinema, music or food habits, for example. In an official sense the state of Britain and its political ideology do not respond to diversity by gestures of inclusivity, but rather continue the "Englishness" that the era of the empire has created. Stuart Hall, Erol Lawrence or Paul Gilroy have all spoken extensively to this phenomenon, stressing the racist practices and cultural commonsense of the English national imaginary in books such as *The Empire Strikes Back*, while the journal *Race and Class*, edited from London by A. Shivanandan, or his book *A Different Hunger* (1982), speak to the racist imperialist capitalism of Britain and its highly racialized class formation.

Speaking of political subjectivities and identities, antiracist politics in Britain has largely developed under the umbrella of black and class politics. The notion "black," disarticulated from a biologistic connotation, has codified an oppositional political stance, and this is what Julia Sudbury, for example in *Other Kinds of Dreams* (1998), speaks to as she develops her thesis on black womanist politics of coalition in Britain. She tells us that, avoiding the British government's divisive naming of local non-white population as "black" and "Asian," women of the third world in Britain — i.e. non-white women — have called themselves "black." The term "black," therefore, is not a correlate of being African in this usage.[3] But Sudbury also points out that there have been and are contestations around this term, and we see that recently there are some direct allusions to U.S. popular multiculturalism by black British intellectuals. In this connection they speak positively of multiculturalism regarding possible alliances and coalitions among women and men of different ethnic groups living in Britain.[4] A similar left liberal stance on the question of political identity and agency has emerged in the works of Stuart Hall, for example "New Ethnicities" in *'Race,' Culture and Difference* (Hall, 1992). Hall's antiracist multiculturalism has drawn attention to "a self-representation, a conscious and strategic doubling of oneself and each other, a way of affecting not only the content but also the relations and politics of representation" (1992, p. 270). Similarly, Kobena Mercer spoke of "Thatcherite tillering through the shoals of minority demands" (Gordon & Newfield, 1996, p. 5), in contrast to the U.S. in the 1980s, where multicultural discourse had arisen, suggesting "a breakdown in the management of ethnic pluralism" (p. 5). Likewise Paul Gilroy, in *Black Atlantic* (1993), has been careful to move away from what Cedric Robinson (1996), denying "specular imagining[s]" black and white (p. 116), has called the manichaeism of black and white fixed identities. This emphasis on changing, opening and hybridized identities of black enlightenment thought, which in Gilroy's case also speaks to modernism among black intellectuals, has probably also been evolved to keep a distance from black cultural nationalism, such as that of Louis Farakhan, or even the growing Afrocentric perspective of black American intellectuals such as Molefi Asante.

Whatever these complex reasons for different positions on multiculturalism may be, it is evident that black British use of multiculturalism, which has been both anticolonial and cultural in terms of political identities and agencies, generally came out of an antiracist and anti-empire struggle mounted from a class perspective. We will be hard put to find in it much of a statist multiculturalism. Instead we may find what we have called multiculturalism from below or popular multiculturalism. It is through the door of the notions of hybridity, openness and fluidity of identities, rather than strong state or ethnic nationalism, that a multiculturalist approach has marked "black" politics in Britain.

This same situation is evident in non-white women's politics in Britain. It encompasses intergroup politics, for example between African, Caribbean, Indian and Bangladeshi women, as well as politics between them, the white women's movement and the state. Here too we have the dialectic of universalism or sameness and particularism or difference as in the U.S., and sometimes this is left as an insoluble contradiction. New black women's politics, more womanist than feminist, moved away from the earlier, mainly white, women's liberation movement, to one where there was sought, if not always realized, a cohesion of different women. But the politics of grassroots non-white women's activism which Julia Sudbury records and analyzes has a strong antiracist component, and also a greater attachment to prevalent politics and political culture of the third world countries from which the women come.

This seems to have created a few important responses speaking to problems and divisiveness among non-white women themselves. Amina Mama (Anthias et al., 1992) has seen this type of womanist black women's politics as a façade for identity/authenticity politics, while Pratibha Parmar (1990) and Floya Anthias (Anthias et al., 1992) have spoken to both the divisiveness and points of identity among women. Others have spoken to the resentment among Asian women, who seem to feel that in spite of politicization of the term "black," it has meant African leadership in antiracist women's struggles (T. Modood, 1990). On the other side, there has been also a resentment among Afrocentric women who question the move away from Africa as a point of departure for antiracist politics, and resent the extension of this term to include others (see Sudbury, 1998, pp. 128–131). A very different take on all of this has been put forward by those who, excited by the notion of a post-modern, hybrid (feminine) subject of multiple and shifting subject positions, have approached questions of political subjectivity and agency from a radical multicultural position, similar to those in the United States. I shall mention two anthologies and a book in this respect, which try to go away from the language of blackness/whiteness: Floya Anthias, N. Yuval-Davis and H. Cain, *Racialized Boundaries*; K. Bhabnani and A. Phoenix (eds.) (1994), *Shifting Identities, Shifting Racisms*; and A. Brah (1996), *Cartographies of Diaspora: Contesting Identities.*

This discussion on the variations of the themes of multiculturalism and women of colour should make it evident to what extent they are dependent on context and location in terms of whether they serve the status quo or the opposition. Particularly in the United States, feminists have variously named themselves as women of colour, black women or third world women — often interchangeably — and wrote and organized towards the forging of a social politics in connection with coalition building towards social democracy, radical democracy and a multiculturalist, anti-imperialist feminism. I would like to draw attention especially to women of colour politics with regard to fashioning selves, social subjectivities and agencies, all of which touch the boundaries of identity. The two influential anthologies edited by Chandra Mohanty, Ann Russo and Lourdes Torres (1991) and Jacquie Alexander and Mohanty (1997) give us powerful versions of a radical, or even revolutionary, use of this term. Not unlike Britain, where feminist organizing has sought to create a space "by offering a form of affiliation that has shifted from sameness and commonality [with white or generic women] to the recognition of distinct social histories" (Sudbury, 1998, p. 11), non-white U.S. feminists have also used the notion of women of colour interchangeably with that of black women. Angela Davis, in her preface to Sudbury's book, does so quite unselfconsciously, indicating a routine practice.

Such unselfconsciousness is possible because of the radicalization of this term, women of colour, by anthologies such as *Third World Women and the Politics of Feminism*. The introduction of this book directly signals the radical political use of this term by equating women of colour with third world women as a mode for creating a "viable oppositional alliance" (Mohanty et al, 1991, p.7). The authors claim that this "is a common context of struggle rather than color and racial identification" (p.7). This "common context" is the same as "relations of inequality" which mark the entry of women of colour into the U.S. labour force, for example (p. 24). Mohanty, in her essay "Under Western Eyes," also makes it clear that "woman" is not a found meaning, but is a social subject and agent, a constructed category, and this construction takes place "in a variety of political contexts" (p. 65). This same oppositional antiracist position is clarified in Ann Russo's "Race, Identity and Feminist Struggles: We Cannot Live without Our Lives" (Mohanty et al., 1991). She too does not problematize the category women of colour, but contexts it to antiracist feminist organizing. As she puts it: "Simply adding women of colour to a list of women's issues, I would agree, actually leads to guilt and condescension, as well as to a partial and limiting politics and vision" (p. 301). The result of such add-ons is not an oppositional antiracist subjectivity for women of colour, but one of being constructed as "problems," "victims" and "special cases" (p. 301).

The same oppositional use is further developed in *Feminist Genealogies, Colonial Legacies, Democratic Futures*. Here the woman subject-agent is again called woman of colour or third world woman, with "aim(s) to provide a comparative, relational and historically based conception of feminism, one that differs markedly from the liberal pluralist understanding of feminism. ..." (Alexander & Mohanty, 1997, p. xvi). This political-theoretical position which redeems the term woman of colour from liberal pluralism is expressed by Paula M. L. Moya in explicating and building on Cherríe Moraga's stance in *This Bridge Called My Back* (Anzaldúa & Moraga, 1983). Moya (with Moraga) rids the notion of its cultural pluralism by associating it with non-white, third world women's "flesh and blood experiences" in the U.S., and by extension other western capitalist democracies (Alexander & Mohanty, 1997, p. 23). She quotes Moraga about this "theory in the flesh" which "emphasizes the materiality of the body by conceptualizing 'flesh' as the site on or with which the woman of color experiences the painful material effects of living in a particular social location" (p. 23). Thus Moya builds out of Moraga a realist theory of identity, distinct from identity as projected by cultural nationalism, under the name of women of colour. Moya bares the nature of political identity advocated by Alexander and Mohanty and the opposition against which it is advanced. It needs to be quoted at some length to show her and their take on identity as both a socially grounded and a multifaceted affair:

> The problem posed by postmodernism is particularly acute for U.S. feminist scholars and activists of color, for whom "experience" and "identity" continue to be primary organizing principles around which they theorize and mobilize. Even women of color who readily acknowledge the nonessentialist nature of their political or theoretical commitments persist in referring to themselves as, for instance, "Chicana" or "Black" feminists ... For example, Moraga acknowledges that women of color are not "a 'natural' affinity group" even as she works to build a movement around and for people who identify as women of color. She can do this, without contradiction, because her understanding of the identity "women of color" reconceptualizes the notion of "identity" itself. Unlike postmodernist feminists who understand the concept of "identity" as inherently and perniciously "foundational", Moraga understands "identity" as relational and grounded in the historically produced social facts which constitute social locations. (p. 127)

This radical/oppositional take on the issue of identity obviously stems from what I have earlier called multiculturalism from below. It speaks to the forging of an oppositional/coalitional identity, to becoming rather than being born as a woman of colour as a process of an anti-imperialist political conscientization takes place among feminists. Alexander and Mohanty and the writers of the *Genealogies* anthology are explicitly critical of any subscription to racist imperialist social relations and forms of consciousness, especially by feminists who claim to engage in counter-hegemonic politics.

This discussion of women of colour is incomplete without a reference to Patricia Hill Collins, who in her two books *Black Feminist Thought* (1990) and *Fighting Words: Black Women and the Search for Justice* (1998), has tried to create an epistemology of resistance, while also speaking of black or Afrocentric identities. Since the second book is a further development of the first, we will look at both her epistemological and agency theorizing projects. Her theorization of black feminist thought is one of specialized knowledge created in rejection of and opposition to the claim to universality of standard European academic knowledge. This universality actually turns out to be nothing other than the "interests of their creators" (Collins 1990, p. 15). The issue of social ontology or who produces any thought, then is material for Collins, and she says: "At the core of Black feminist thought lie theories created by African-American women which *clarify* a Black women's standpoint — in essence an interpretation of black women's experiences and ideas by those who participate in them" (p. 15). This position vindicates non-academic knowledge as experts' knowledge, thus reclaiming black women's intellectual tradition, generated from their everyday ideas. In this way black women — "mothers, teachers, church members and cultural creators" — become intellectuals (p. 15). Not just written sources but spoken word, oral tradition, and interactions of the community produce knowledge, and this knowledge, infused with "Afrocentric feminist sensibility" becomes the heart and body of black feminist thought (p. 16). At this point we might ask the questions about identity and political agency that Collins brings to us. It seems to be different from a coalitional approach in the use of women of colour or third world women (Alexander & Mohanty, 1997; Mohanty et al., 1990), especially as Afro-American social ontologies or experiences are sources for black feminist thought. As Collins says, not anyone can produce black feminist thought. Can women from non-African descent be producers of black feminist thought? Interestingly Collins comes up with an inclusive and positive answer. She tries to disarticulate this notion from biology or even possibly from African history in the United States. "Separation of biology from ideology," she says, "must be made" (p. 20). You don't have to be African American to be a black feminist and produce that type of knowledge.

By nature, Collins says, black feminist thought is deconstructive. Its task is "exposing a concept as ideological and culturally constructed rather than as natural or a simple rejection of reality" (p. 14). In this she signals to Linda Alcoff's position of 1988; her example of deconstructive knowledge is Sojourner Truth's problematization of the category "woman" in her "Ain't I a woman" speech. Collins continues her work of resistance epistemology in *Fighting Words,* and in this book explicitly speaks to black feminist thought's contribution to critical social theory (1998, p. xviii). In this test, written particularly to create an ethical-political agency for activists looking for social rather than sectarian justice, Collins does not resort to the category women of colour. To a large extent her radicalization of the term "black women" signals to the strand of British antiracist activism written about by Sudbury. Though still interested in Afro-centrism, Collins seeks to void that notion of its cultural nationalist and particularist context, thus leaving us with an interesting text full of tensions between a general ethical politics and a strong emphasis on the African diaspora's history of domination and resistance.

One could go on much longer on antiracist, anti-imperialist feminism in the U.S. One could also speak at length of the slide of multiculturalist discourse, with its core terms of diversity, difference and women of colour, into liberal culturalism, into its co-optation as a tool for what Angela Davis (1996, p. 41) calls "diversity management," that salad bowl corporate view of difference. But I will stop here, using this introduction as a broadly sketched background for my more limited project, consisting of an exploration of the term "women of colour" as a part of a constellation of ideological agentic and identity terms constituting multiculturalism in the Canadian context. The most salient aspect of this context is that multiculturalism is a state sanctioned, state organized ideological affair in Canada. Not just in Orwell's ideologically constructed communist dystopia, but in actual mundane granting/funding, in electoral policies and outcomes, in ethnic cultural fairs and religious celebrations, in court legal defences, this particular variant of multiculturalism organizes the socio-cultural, legal-economic space of Canada. This paper attempts to critically examine the particular meaning such a conjuncture provides to the notion of women of colour and its home space of the discourse of diversity and multiculturalism. In this, radical potentials spoken of above are substantially diminished.

Canada: Constructing "The Woman of Colour" through Multiculturalism and Diversity

People who are not familiar with North American political and cultural, especially feminist, language are both puzzled and repelled by the expression "woman of colour." I know this because this expression has become a part of my ordinary vocabulary in recent years, and often when I have used it in India my interlocutors, even feminist ones, looked puzzled or annoyed. Most remarked on what a strange expression that was, and others reminded me that I had reverted to a racist, segregational language of apartheid and the American South — a "coloured woman." Even when I tried to insist on the difference between these two expressions, these women were reluctant to relinquish this association. Their reaction reminded me of a time, my early years in Canada during the early seventies, when I learned and evolved my antiracist feminist politics without this word anywhere in sight. At some point it travelled to us from below the 49th parallel, and found a congenial home on our tongue.

The Indian women's response was similar to my own long years of reluctance to use this notion for any purpose of social analysis and critique. I speak of this in my introduction to the anthology *Returning the Gaze* (1993, pp. ix–xv) and in my essays in *Thinking Through* (1995). There I use the notion "non-white" for the purpose of creating an antiracist critique, maintaining that in the context of analyzing racialized social organization and relations, what needs to be stressed is the non-whiteness of this woman social subject of oppression. After all, it is on this basis that she is being oppressed or discriminated against, and others (white women) comparatively privileged. Every other particularity about this subject is built on this binary conceptualization and politics. But having said this, I have to admit that of late the expression woman of colour has crept up on me, especially when I am speaking in common language in my daily interchange with other non-white women who are doing antiracist work. They use it, as do their U.S. counterparts, as a term of alterity, or even of opposition to the status quo in spite of the statist nature of this concept in Canada, and so do I. The question is, how or why did this happen? What necessities or circumstances drew me into this orbit?

To answer this question I have to move back in time. I remember that one of the earliest occasions when I heard this expression was when I was invited to read poetry in a cultural festival. It was called something like Rainbow Women: Multicultural Women in Concert. It was organized by Faith Nolan, now a well-known black Canadian singer. I was struck by the notion of rainbow women, which, I was told, had to do with my being a woman of colour and bringing this colour to join others in a rainbow combination. I was not taken by this exercise. I found woman of colour to be both a coy and an offensive notion and, like many others, thought of the expression "coloured." I did not want to call myself this. Nor did I feel convinced of the capacity for resistance attributed to this notion, which encoded a multicultural unity, cherishing diversity, through promulgating a generic or homogenizing term which would cover all non-white others, mostly those who were not black. So there I had it, two groups of non-white women — black and of colour — arranged in a gradually paling hierarchy, with one end of the spectrum touching the darkest shade of colour. This colour hierarchy struck me then, as it does now, as an offensive way of creating social subjects and political agents. It falls back, even if unconsciously, on the hegemonic common sense of social culture and politics of slavery and apartheid. What colour are you, it asks: are you black, white, yellow, or brown? Shades of negative differences, of being considered mulatto, quadroons, octoroons (ideologies and social relations of plantation societies) lie behind this formulation. They are presumable promulgated in good faith, to fight racist-sexism and white privilege. It is also significant that most of the time this term does not refer to black women, or those of the First Nations. I was quite determined not to use it, but as the '80s rolled by woman of colour was Canadianized. She had, as they say in Canada about immigrants, "landed." And her I am using it every once in a while, for the purpose of intelligibility, to keep in step with my fellow antiracist feminists!

So what discursive revolution, paradigm shift, occurred in Canada during the 1980s and the '90s which could have been hospitable to, or indeed embraced, this woman of colour? In my view, there are two broad political areas which need to be problematized. One could be called, following Louis Althusser (1971), the ideological apparatuses of the state, including its political and civil administration; and the other, the civil society (Gramsci, 1971), the everyday world of common social relations, values and practices of culture and power. We may begin first by speaking of the state, not because it was the first to name us as political agents in terms of being women of colour. It did not, as the term had a U.S. origin. But it provided the political culture for accepting, using and naturalizing a colour-based notion of subjectivity and agency, which in continuity with Canada's colonial formation came to dominate the cultural politics of Canada's other women. Canadians have been living in an historical and current environment of political colour coding, even, or mainly, when forging a liberal democratic politics for the country as a whole.

My claim may be more clear if I were to draw attention to the entry of official multiculturalism onto the Canadian political stage. The open door policy of immigration, especially attributed to the Liberal party and its charismatic leader, Pierre Trudeau, throughout the 1960s and '70s, had brought many people of colour, other "races," into the country. [5] The reason for this was the expectation of capitalist industrial growth in Canada and the aspiration to the creation of a liberal democratic nationhood. The former British colonies in particular provided cheap labour, both skilled and unskilled, as well as the democratic grounds for converging otherness. Thus colour, the cognate of race, refracted into indirect notions of multiculture and ethnicity, was much on the mind of the Canadian state, just as much as in the nineteenth or early twentieth centuries.[6] Unlike the radical alternative political-cultural activists, the Canadian state was careful not to directly use the notion of colour in the way it designated the newcomers. But colour was translated into the language of visibility. The new Canadian social and political subject was appellated "visible minority," stressing both the features of being non-white and therefore visible in a way whites are not, and of being politically minor players. It is at this time, at the urging of the National Directorate of Women and the Secretary of State, that non-white women made a niche for themselves in the mainstream politics by creating a representational organization, the National Coalition of Visible Minority Women.[7] This status of visible minority was not felt by a large number of women to be problematic or compromising, since they shared political values with the mainstream. Minor as their part was, set apart by their visibility, which was also the only ground of their political eligibility, they were content. Until then they were covered under the umbrella of immigrant women, a category that included and expanded beyond non-white women, who were also called third world women. All these expressions have remained in our political-cultural language, but visible minority women has become the strongest. A categorical child of the state, cradled by the Ministry of Multiculturalism and the Secretary of State, this expression underpins and is the mainstream counterpart of the more grassroots notion of the woman of colour. This popular feminist term actually relied for its political meaning and vitality upon the mainstream analogue and the same discourse of multiculturalism pertaining to visible minority women embedded in both state and society for its existential environment. With no interest in class politics, and no real analysis of or resistance to racialization or ethnicization, chiefly preoccupied with bureaucratic representation or inclusion for a very limited power sharing within the status quo, these political terminologies became current usages. The multi-ethnic, multinational state, with its history of racilized class formation and political ideology, discovering multiculturalism as a way of both hiding and enshrining power relations, provided a naturalized political language even to the others of the Canadian society. Not surprisingly, these expressions found their way into general feminist academic and activist discourse and into NGOs for women and into the political discourse of International Women's Day. In particular, visible minority women translated well into women of colour and that became the name chosen by alternative politics of Canada. This practice followed the United States, and it solved the problem of finding a name for building coalition among all women. It vaguely and pleasantly gestured to race as colour and, of course, to gender/patriarchy by evoking woman. But the concept of race lost its hard edges of criticality, class disappeared entirely, and colour gave a feeling of brightness, brilliance or vividness, of a celebration of a difference which was disconnected from social relations of power, but instead perceived as diversity, as existing socio-cultural ontologies or facts.

The suitability of woman of colour for Canadian political culture was such that no one did then, or does now, speak about the absurdity of calling white women colourless or invisible. As for the degeneration of powered difference into diversity, class analysis was, after all, not the main interest of the North American women's movement, while race was accepted by most as an existential, cultural fact, if not always a biological one. This political stance has led to the seeking for better race relations, in which feminists aspiring to diversity have participated. So the term unproblematically combined within itself both the common sense of race and the antidote of liberal pluralism. The apartheid notion of coloured woman stood behind and cast a long shadow over her modern sister, since it was the subliminal principle of intelligibility of this recent coinage, no matter how radically aimed.

Common sense of skin and colour, particularly in the colonial context, is old. Bodies — skin, facial features, height, build, and so forth — had been morally and politically signified for centuries in North America and Europe (see Gillman, 1985). Reducing Africans to "negroes" was an ideological and semantic normalcy for centuries in European and English languages. The "yellow peril" had resulted in the dispersion of the Japanese people into concentration camps. Colour, ethnicity and bodies had long been conflated with moral/cultural ontologies. It is not an exaggeration to say that it was within the context and content of these practices, meanings and political possibilities that the liberal multicultural construction of woman of colour took place. Its epistemological pivot rests on the seemingly benign concept of diversity, a re-named version of plurality, so central to the concept of diversity, a re-named version of plurality, so central to the concept and politics of liberalism. This positivity which is implied in the ideology of diversity mitigates the revulsion that women might feel towards calling themselves or others women of colour. A colour coded self-perception, an identity declared on the semiological basis of one's skin colour, was rendered palatable through this ideology of diversity. Our colour provided the sovereign mark, significant enough to be used as a counter in the political discourse of liberalism. As with all liberal pluralist projects, this constituent element of political identities of others did not come up for scrutiny or a critique, but rather became a given, common sensical category of representation, as though always already there. Moreover, the word "colour" became an associational and connotative path to diverse histories and cultures of the nations of other women. They themselves summoned it to convey their colourfulness through it, thereby quickly slipping into the cultural discourse of tradition versus modernity. Their colour signalled traditional cultures, in a constellation of invented traditions.[8] Culturally integrated colour was thus seemingly divested of its racist undertones, and lost its location in power relations. This erasure indicates the epistemological possibilities of the notion of multicultural diversity. If this desocialized and ahistorical notion of diversity were not a naturalized form of political culture and discourse in Canada, and in the West as a whole, such a coinage or neologism would not have been so easily adopted by women who see themselves as practitioners of politics of opposition. The formal equality of liberal pluralism encoded by diversity also helped to allay anxieties and suspicions.

It may be objected that I am making a mountain out of a mole hill by focusing so much on one single political and cultural expression. Does a name, it may be asked, make so much difference? Would not a rose by any other name smell as sweet? If we had instead called ourselves non-white women, for example, what different political task would we have accomplished? My answer to these anticipated objections or questions would be that the language with which we build or express our political agency has to be taken very seriously. An expression in that context, even when it seems innocuous and solitary, has to be treated as a bit of ideology, and as a part of a broader ideological semantics called discourse. Thus we have to treat woman of colour as a name for a particular type of political agency and examine its ability to disclose our lives and experiences as lived within an organization of social relations of power. It is only then that we can attend to the political direction to which this agency points us. Treated thus, we can safely say that the notion woman of colour does not direct us to examine crucial social relations within which we live, to histories and forms of consciousness of power that mark our presence in the U.S. or Canada. Instead this, as a naturalized reworking of coloured woman, performs an ideological accommodation of "race," while erasing class. Also, in thus equating our political identities with a racialized cultural construction, a second level of reality is created which is far from the actualities of our lives. Yet these social actualities are the realities that need to be daily addressed and changed through our politics. If, at least in the course of our antiracist feminist politics, we call ourselves non-white women, we can gesture towards white privilege. The use of a negative prefix automatically raises issues and questions. But a substitution through the language of diversity and colour distracts us from what actually happens to us in our raced and gendered class existence and culturalizes our politics. In other words, it depoliticizes us.[9]

Since the responsibility for this depoliticization falls upon the epistemology and ideology of diversity, the cornerstone of a pluralist liberal politics and its legitimation, we need to explore extensively and critically the workings of the concept of diversity. Official multiculturalism, which has also become the politics of Canadian civil society, our daily political common sense, cannot be challenged otherwise. The political culture generated by the state in its reflexive dependence on everyday social culture cannot be kept insulated from the ongoing life of the civil society, and if that realm itself is saturated with an historical and official political culture of domination, then that politics of resistance itself can become a part of the state's ideological apparatus. The dangers inherent in constructing a multicultural Canada, with a reified and racialized political agency called woman of colour, calls for a critique of the epistemology and ideology of diversity. The next section of this paper, therefore, engages in this critique, and takes up diversity which endows its discursive affiliates, such as woman of colour, with the power to erase or empty out actual social relations and forms of power — "race," gender and class — while creating an aura of concreteness or meaning whose actual relevances or coordinates are located within the state's discourse of ruling.

The Name of the Rose, or
What Difference Does It Make What I Call It

Diversity has become a commonplace word in our political and cultural world. This seems to have happened in the last decade or so — it has sort of crept up on us. So much so that even businesses have adapted their talk about profit and productivity to the language of diversity, while governments and public institutions set up bureaucracies in its name. On our side, that is, on the side of the people, from below, organizations have been created merging notions of community with diversity — speaking to ethno-cultural pluralities and collective cultural identities. We have versions of this in our everyday language, and in that of scholarship. We have critical feminist anthologies of the politics of diversity,[10] while political theorists have used the term in their communitarian and liberal ways (Eliott & Fleras, 1992; Kymlicka, 1995; Taylor, 1992, 1993; Trudeau, 1968).

So it seems that the time has come to take this rather banal notion of diversity and explore its current popularity in terms of what it does for us politically. To begin with, this word has been used to signify a multiplicity of socio-cultural presences, as a cornucopia of differences of all sorts, that mark the Canadian social space. But this purely descriptive use of the term, signalling heterogeneity without implied power relations, ulterior aim or use, is not the only, or the main, use that has been made of it. This simple descriptive, at most designatory use has been a device for constructing an ideological cultural language or discourse that allows for an instant jump from description to political meanings and practices.

This discourse of diversity is a fusion of a cultural classification, or an empirical/descriptive gesture, with politics. That is, our empirically being from various countries, with our particular looks, languages and cultures, has become an occasion for interpreting, constructing and ascribing differences with connotations of power relations. This process and its conceptual products combine into a political discourse and related ideological practices. In this political deployment the notion of diversity escapes from its denotative function and dictionary meaning and emerges as a value-free, power neutral indicator of difference and multiplicity. But this very character and claim of neutrality allows it to become the governing concept of a complex discourse of social power with its own and related webs of concept. There is a process of surpassing as well as of subsumption involved in this creation of an ideology from the notion of diversity. Conceived as discourse diversity is not a simple descriptive affair. As a centre piece of a discourse of power and as a device for social management of inequality, it is simultaneously interpretive or meaning-making and actively practical. It creates and mediates practices, both conceptual and actual, of power — of ruling or governing.[11] In this discursive mode the concept of diversity entails two functions, which together allow it to be articulated or bonded with other political notions and practices already in place. Together with them, such as with feminism or antiracism, they form a conceptual network and signal to ideological practices of socio-political administration which are certainly not value neutral.

The two ways in which the neutral appearance of the notion of diversity becomes a useful ideology to practices of power are quite simple. On the one hand, the use of such a concept with a reference to simple multiplicity allows the reading of all social and cultural forms or differences in terms of descriptive plurality. On the other, in its relationship to description it introduces the need to put in or retain a concrete, particular content for each of these seemingly neutral differences. The social relations of power that create the difference implied in sexist-racism, for example, just drop out of sight, and social being becomes a matter of a cultural essence (Bannerji, 1991). This is its paradox — that the concept of diversity simultaneously allows for an emptying out of actual social relations and suggests a concreteness of cultural description, and through this process obscures any understanding of difference as a construction of power. Thus there is a construction of a collective cultural essence and a conflation of this, or what we are culturally supposed to be, and what we are ascribed with, in the context of social organization of inequality. We cannot then make a distinction between racist stereotypes and ordinary historical/cultural differences of everyday life and practices of people from difference parts of the world. Cultural traits that come, let us say, from different parts of the third world as used to both create and eclipse racism, and we are discouraged from reading them in terms of relations and symbolic forms of power. The result is also an erasure of class and patriarchy among the immigrant multicultures of others, as they too fall within this paradox of essentialization and multiplicity signified by cultural diversity of official multiculturalism. In fact, it is this uncritical, de-materialized, seemingly de-politicized reading of culture through which culture becomes a political tool, an ideology of power which is expressed in racist-sexist or heterosexist differences. One can only conclude from all this that the discourse of diversity, as a complex systemically interpretive language of governing, cannot be read as an innocent pluralism.[12]

The ideological nature of this language of diversity is evident from its frequent use and efficacy in the public and official, that is, institutional realms. In these contexts its function has been to provide a conceptual apparatus in keeping with needs which the presence of heterogeneous peoples and cultures has created in the Canadian state and public sphere. This has both offset and, thus, stabilized the Canadian national imaginary[13] and its manifestation as the state apparatus, which is built on core assumptions of cultural and political homogeneity of a Canadianness. This language of diversity is a copying mechanism for dealing with an actually conflicting heterogeneity, seeking to incorporate it into an ideological binary which is predicated upon the existence of a homogeneous national, that is, a Canadian cultural self with its multiple and different others (see Bannerji, 1997). These multiple other cultural presences in Canada, interpreted as a threat to national culture which called for a coping, and therefore for an incorporating and interpretive mechanism, produced the situation summed up as the challenge of multiculturalism. This has compelled administrative, political and ideological innovations which will help to maintain the status quo. This is where the discourse of diversity has been of crucial importance because this new language of ruling and administration protects ideologies and practices already in place. It is postulated upon pluralist premises of a liberal democratic state, which Canada aspires to be, but also adds specific dimensions of legitimation to particular administrative functions.[14]

The usefulness of the discourse of diversity as a device for managing public or social relations and spaces, of serving as a form of moral regulation of happy co-existence, is obvious. The Canadian government and other public institutions, the media, and the ideological projection of the Canadian nation (and its unity) are marked by this discourse. In the universities, both in pedagogic and administrative spheres, this language is prominent. It is the staple discourse of arts and community projects, conditioning their working agendas as well as the politics of the funding bodies. In workplaces, diversity sensitization or training has largely displaced talk about and/or resistance to racism and sexism. Even law appeals to diversity in using cultural and religious defences, suppressing contradictions and violences of patriarchy, for example, while fulfilling the state's pluralist obligations (see Volpp, 1994). In the context of making the Canadian nation, unity is posited in terms of diversity, with pictures of many facial types, languages and cultures — "together we are. ..."[15] It is not surprising that Benetton produces a diversity slogan of "united colours" to capture its multicultural markets.

The discourse of diversity has also inscribed our social movements — the women's movement or the trade union movement, for example — where again it helps to obscure deeper/structural relations of power, such as of racism and sexism or racist heterosexism,[16] both among women and the working class, and reduces the problem of social justice into questions of curry and turban. Thus social movements share crucial ideological assumptions of those whom they seek to fight and supposedly have political differences with. In this regard it is important to do a brief retrospective on the issue of difference within feminist theorization and the women's movement. The issue of "race" in particular became one issue of contention.

Many years ago Elizabeth Spelman (1988) wrote a book criticizing North American liberal/bourgeois feminism for its Eurocentrism. Her book, entitled *Inessential Woman: Problems of Exclusion in Feminist Thought*, created disturbing resonances in the world of North American anglophone feminist theories, and many of us used her critique to get a clarity on our own dissatisfaction about mainstream feminism. This critique of essentialism and Eurocentrism, which I addressed in "But Who Speaks for Us" (Bannerji, 1991), developed into a critique of an ideological and identity stance known as whiteness. The most well-known form of this notion is in Ruth Frankenberg's *White Women, Race Matters: The Social Construction of Whiteness* (1993). Though various critiques and adjustments were made of Spelman's and Frankenberg's theorizations and politics, their articulations remain powerful even as they, as white women, confront other white women and speak as insiders to that social ontology. Many others, including Ann Laura Stoler (1995), wrote on various ideological and political aspects of whiteness. However, as Leslie Roman (1993, p. 72) says:

> ... to say that white is a color does not rescue the concept of "race" from similar forms of empty pluralism and dangerous relativism invoked by the larger essentialist discourse of "race". Try as I might to recognize whiteness as a structural power relation that confers cultural and economic privileges, the phrase, spoken declaratively by the racially privileged, can also become a form of white defensiveness.

But of more immediate importance for us are the critiques made by black and third world feminists, such as Collins, Mohanty and Alexander, regarding the politically exclusionary, debilitating and epistemologically occlusive effects of such theorization as conducted within the academy. In their anthology Alexander and Mohanty especially take to task women's studies within U.S. academies. Even among those who claim oppositional knowledge and practices, they declared, "the color of our gender mattered" (Alexander & Mohanty, 1997, p. xiv). They were, they stated, neither "the right color" nor gender, nor nationality in terms of self-definition of the U.S. academy, and by extension of the women's studies establishment (p. xiv). Alexander and Mohanty broaden their critical outreach and compare this outsider status in institutions of learning to the citizenship machinery and ideology deployed in the U.S. The outsider or the alien is born both within the U.S. and outside of its national territories. As they put it (p. xiv): "Our experience makes sense only in analogy to African-American women." The authors in this anthology also question the political and epistemological impact that postmodernism is having within women's studies. As Mohanty and Alexander see it (p. xvii), "... in its haste to dissociate itself from all forms of essentialism, [this impact] has generated a series of epistemological confusions regarding the interconnections between location, identity and construction of knowledge." This refusal of experience, history, and identity in its broadest sense of self-recovery, often found in the curricula of women's studies, has delegitimized the type of grounded social knowledge spoken of by Collins in her two books. The organic intellectuals of the oppressed become invalid by definition if they can not claim their lives as sources for learning and theorizing, as exemplars for the unjust relations within which they live. As Mohanty and Alexander put it (p. xvii): "... localized questions of experience, identity, culture and history, which enable us to understand specific processes of domination and subordination, are often dismissed by postmodern theories as reiteration of cultural 'essences,' or unified stable identity." These current critiques were anticipated as early as 1982 by Hazel Carby (1982).

This discourse of diversity in its comprehensive ideological and political form is materialzed and extended as the discourse of multiculturalism, with its linguistic constellation of visible minority, women of colour and so on. Cultural sensitivity towards and tolerance of others (to the core/national culture and agency) are two behavioural imperatives of this multicultural politics, both at the level of state and society. The all-pervasive presence of diversity in our public discourse has created a situation where even those who are not entirely comfortable with its discursive constellation use it in its various guises in an unconscious submission to what is around, and for reasons of intelligibility. Being effective with funding proposals means translating our needs and concerns into the discourses of multiculturalism. This means speaking in the language of cultural communities and their diversities, of ethnicities and women of colour and visible minorities — both male and female. Otherwise our funders or the state do not hear us.

So, it would seem that there is much invested in the fact of naming, in the words we use to express our socio-political understandings, because they are more than just words, they are ideological concepts. They imply intentions and political and organizational practices. Calling people by different names, in different political contexts, has always produced significantly different results. These names are, after all, not just names to call people by, but rather codes for political subjectivities and agencies. Naming ourselves in terms of class, for example as the proletariat, assuming class as the basis of our political identity, would imply a different political ideology, practice and goal, than if we constructed our political agency with names such as women/ people of colour or visible minorities. Contrary to Shakespeare's assertion that a rose by any other name would smell as sweet, we see that not to be the case in political-ideological matters. In politics the essence of the flower lies in the name by which it is called. In fact it is the naming that decides what flower we have at hand. To say this is to say explicitly that discourse is more than a linguistic manoeuvre. It is a matter of putting in words, mediating and organizing social relations of ruling, of meanings organized through power. It is best to remind ourselves of the title of Dionne Brand's poetry book, *No Language is Neutral* (1990).

The Essence of the Name, or
What Is to Be Gained by Calling Something Diversity

In order to understand how the concept of diversity works ideologically, we have to feed into it the notion of difference constructed through social relations of power and read it in terms of the binaries of homogeneity and heterogeneity already referred to in our discussion on multiculturalism. It does not require much effort to realize that diversity is not equal to multiplied sameness, rather it presumes a distinct difference in each instance. But this makes us ask, distinctly different from what? The answer is, obviously, from each other and from whatever it is that is homogeneous — which is an identified and multiplied sameness, serving as the distinguishing element at the core in relation to which difference is primarily measured. The difference that produces heterogeneity suggests otherness in relation to that core, and in social politics this otherness is more than an existential, ontological fact. It is a socially constructed otherness or heterogeneity, its difference signifying both social value and power. It is not just another cultural self floating non-relationally in a socio-historical vacuum. In the historical context of the creation of Canada, of its growth into an uneasy amalgam of a white settler colony with liberal democracy, with its internally colonized or peripheral economies, the definitions and relations between a national self and its other, between homogeneity and heterogeneity, sameness and diversity, become deeply power ridden.[17] From the days of colonial capitalism to the present-day global imperialism, there has emerged an ideologically homogeneous identity dubbed Canadian whose nation and state Canada is supposed to be.

This core community is synthesized into a national we, and it decides on the terms of multiculturalism and the degree to which multicultural others should be tolerated or accommodated. This "we" is an essentialized version of a colonial European turned into Canadian and the subject or the agent of Canadian nationalism. It is this essence, extended to the notion of a community, that provides the point of departure for the ideological deployment of diversity. The practice is clearly exclusive, not only of third world or non-white ethnic immigrants, but also of the aboriginal population.[18] Though often described in cultural linguistic terms as the two nations of anglophones and francophones, the two nations theory does not include non-whites of these same language groups. So the identity of the Canadian "we" does not reside in language, religion or other aspects of culture, but rather in the European/North American physical origin — in the body and the colour of skin. Colour of skin is elevated here beyond its contingent status and becomes an essential quality called whiteness, and this becomes the ideological signifier of a unified non-diversity.[19] The others outside of this moral and cultural whiteness are targets for either assimilation or toleration. These diverse or multicultural elements, who are also called newcomers, introducing notions of territoriality and politicized time, create accommodational difficulties for white Canadians, both at the level of the civil society, of culture and economy, and also for the ruling practices of the state. An ideological coping mechanism becomes urgent in view of a substantial third world immigration allowed by Canada through the 1960s up to recent years (see Eliott & Fleras, 1992). This new practical and discursive/ideological venture, or an extension of what Althusser has called an ideological state apparatus, indicates both the crisis and its management. After all, the importation of Chinese or South Asian indentured labour, or the legally restricted presence of the Japanese since the last century, did not pose the same problems which the newly arrived immigrants do (see Bolaria & Li, 1988). As landed residents or apprentice citizens, or as actual citizens of Canada, they cannot be left in the same limbo of legal and political non-personhood as their predecessors were until the 1950s. Yet they are not authentic Canadians in the ideological sense, in their physical identity and culture. What is more, so-called authentic Canadians are unhappy with their presence, even though they enhance Canada's economic growth. Blue ribbon Hong Kong immigrants, for example, bring investments which may be needed for the growth of British Columbia, but they themselves are not wanted.[20] But they, among other third world immigrants, are here, and this calls for the creation of an ideology and apparatus of multiculturalism (with its discourse of a special kind of plurality called diversity) as strategies of containment and management.

If this statement seems to be unfounded, we need only note the time around which multiculturalism and the diversity discourse is invented in Canada. Multi-ethnic European immigrations of the past did not inspire it, nor are the present-day European immigrants the target of this discourse, even though cultural, religious, and linguistic differences are very high between them and the two nations of anglo- and francophone communities. An unspoken but active melting pot stance pretty much seems to have been in place. We began to hear of the notion of diversity from the time of allowing citizenship to the previously indentured Chinese and South Asians, from the time of Canada's open door policy in relation to its plans for capitalist growth. The metaphor of Canadian society as the vertical mosaic is an early intimation of the complexities of evolution of a political ideology involving otherness in a liberal democratic context. The open door policy not only allowed but actively pursued immigration from ex-colonized third world countries. Along with that came political refugees. This is when diversity came to be seen as really diverse, in spite of the fact that many came from French and English speaking countries, many were christians, and a large number had more than a passing acquaintance with cultures of Europe and North America. But as they were not indentured workers, or for the most part not illegals, their presence as workers, taxpayers and electoral constituencies was a force to be reckoned with and a problem to be managed. The multicultural policy had to be evolved and put in place for them.

The Canadian state had to deal with a labour importation policy which was primarily meant to create a working class, but not guest workers as in Germany. This involved resistance from white Canadians, from the so-called Canadian worker. It also had to contain the mobility drives of immigrants who were otherwise compliant, but wanted to get a secure economic niche in the country's labour and consumer markets. In the very early 1980s Prime Minister Pierre Trudeau enunciated his multicultural policy, and a discourse of nation, community and diversity began to be cobbled together. There were no strong multicultural demands on the part of third world immigrants themselves to force such a policy. The issues raised by them were about racism, legal discrimination involving immigration and family reunification, about job discrimination on the basis of Canadian experience, and various adjustment difficulties, mainly of child care and language. In short, they were difficulties that are endemic to migration, and especially that of people coming in to low income jobs or with few assets. Immigrant demands were not then, or even now, primarily cultural, nor was multiculturalism initially their formulation of the solution to their problems. It began as a state or an official/ institutional discourse, and it involved the translation of issues of social and economic injustice into issues and quandaries *vis a vis* the response of the so-called Canadians that prompted justificatory gestures by the state. These legitimation gestures were more directed at the discontented Canadians than the discriminated others. Multiculturalism was therefore not a demand from below, but an ideological elaboration from above in which the third world immigrants found themselves. This was an apparatus which rearranged questions of social justice, of unemployment and racism, into issues of cultural diversity and focused on symbols of religion, on so-called tradition. Thus immigrants were ethnicized, culturalized and mapped into traditional/ethnic communities. Gradually a political and administrative framework came into being where structural inequalities could be less and less seen or spoken about. Antiracism and class politics could not keep pace with constantly proliferating ideological state or institutional apparatuses which identified people in terms of their cultural identity, and converted or conflated racist ascriptions of difference within the Canadian space into the power neutral notion of diversity. An increase in threats against third world immigrants, the rise of neo-nazi white supremacist groups and ultra conservative politics, along with a systemic or structural racism and anti-immigration and anti-immigrant stances of political parties, could now be buried or displaced as the immigrants' own cultural problem. Politics in Canada were reshaped and routed through this culturalization or ethnicization, and a politics of identity was constructed which the immigrants themselves embraced as the only venue for social and political agency.

Now it was projected to the world at large that what the incoming third world population of Canada primarily wanted was the same religious, linguistic and cultural life they had in their countries of origin. They were frozen into being seen as traditional cultures and thus socially conservative in entirely. They were bringing down the standards of Canadian modernity and criminalizing the country. The problem for the Canadian state and society then became one of considering what or how much they could retain in Canada of their previous cultures without compromising the national character. The fact that their demands came in many types, and the most important ones pertained to discrimination by the state and the economy which threatened worthwhile employment opportunities, family re-unification for refugees, facilities for women, and so forth, became political non-issues. This emphasis on culture, on immigrants' ethnic self-definition and fundamentalist cultural survivalism, deflected proper publicization of criticism of police violence or general safety issues for non-white people, especially for black youth.[21] In almost every case of police shooting, the police were given immunity, and immigration laws became tighter while deportations increasingly became a threat. De-skilling, not just through underemployment or unemployment, but through state/institutional decertification of professionals, is also a basic fact of third world immigrant lives (see Bolaria & Li, 1988, p. 18; Government of Canada, 1986; Government of Canada, 1984). No third world immigrant is left in doubt that he/she is in Canada on public and official sufferance and is to be grateful for being allowed into the country. They are made to feel that otherness is of an antagonistic variety to Canadians, and they also know that this otherness is not in them, but in how they are perceived, what ascriptions pre-exist their arrival into the country, how racialization and ethnicization have already put a white Canada in place. They come to know that they are seen as virtually invading this Canada. It becomes quickly evident that in a society that preaches the gospel of wealth, they would not and are not expected to go very far. They judge by their presences and absences in the social and economic spaces that they are here to primarily reproduce the under classes.

Through the decades from the 1960s political developments took place in Canada which show the twists and turns in the relationship between third world immigrants and the state.[22] With the disarray of left politics in the country and growth of multicultural ideology, all political consciousness regarding their world immigrants has been multiculturalized. These cultural/ethnicized formulations were like chemical probes into a test tube of solution around which dissatisfactions and mobility drives of the others began to coalesce. Wearing or not wearing of turbans, publicly funded heritage language classes, state supported islamic schools modelled on the existence and patterns of catholic schools, for example, provided the profile of their politics. They themselves often forgot how much less important these were than their full citizenship rights, their demand for jobs, non-discriminatory schools and work places, and a generally non-racist society. Differentiated second or third class citizenships evolved, as a non-white sub-working class continued to develop. Their initial willingness to work twice are hard to get a little never materialized into much. Instead a mythology developed around their lack of success, which spoke of their shifty, lazy work habits and their scamming and unscrupulous use of the welfare system. This is especially ironic since they often came from countries, such as those in the West Indies, from which Canada continues to bring substantial profits. But this story of neo-colonialism, of exploitation, racism, discrimination and hierarchical citizenship never gains much credibility or publicity with the Canadian state, the public or the media. This reality is what the cultural language and politics of diversity obscures, displaces and erases. It is obvious that the third world or non-white immigrants are not the beneficiaries of the discourse of diversity.

The state of Canada wants its differentiated inferior citizens to speak in the state's own language of multicultural identity, of ethnicity and community. This is mainly the language of representation permitted to them. Ethnic or racialized cultural community, not political community organized on the basis of class, gender and racialization, is what the state is willing to acknowledge in their case. Continuous struggles involving issues of "race" and class have created something called "race" relations in some institutions, which, if it becomes antiracist in any real way, is descaled or defunded. Human Rights Commissions, treating cases individually, with no proper powers of enforcement, often act as pawns of the state and capital, adjudicate very few cases and rule rarely in favour of the complainant. Ritualistic non-discrimination clauses that are at times present in state documents to mediate "race" relations often create the impression that "races" actually exist as biological social entities determining behaviour and culture, and only need to relate better. There is not even a language within the state's redress apparatus to capture or describe the racist sexism towards third world or non-white women or men. By simultaneously blocking the politico-social process of racialization from view while organizing people as raced ethnicities, the state of multiculturalism seeks to obscure issues of class and patriarchy as actionable, and therefore the possibility of discovering intercommunity commonalities — for example between third world immigrants and aboriginal peoples, or among the different strands of working classes — diminishes considerably.

Multiculturalism as an official practice and discourse has worked actively to create the notion and practices of insulated communities. Under its political guidance and funding a political-social space was organized. Politically constructed homogenized communities, with their increasingly fundamentalist boundaries of cultures, traditions and religions, emerged from where there were immigrants from different parts of the world with different cultures and values. They developed leaders or spokespersons, usually men, who liaised with the state on their behalf, and their organizational behaviour fulfilled the expectations of the Canadian state. New political agents and constituencies thus came to life, as people sought to be politically active in these new cultural identity terms. So they became interpellated by the state under certain religious and ethnically named agencies. Hardheaded businessmen, who had never thought of culture in their lives before, now, upon entering Canada, began using this notion and spoke to the powers that be in terms of culture and welfare of their community. But this was the new and only political playing field for "others" in Canada, a slim opportunity of mobility, so they were/are willing to run through the multicultural maze. What is more, this new cultural politics, leaving out problems of class and patriarchy, appealed to the conservative elements in the immigrant population, since religion could be made to overdetermine these uncomfortable actualities, and concentrated on the so-called culture and morality of the community. Official multiculturalism, which gave the conservative male self-styled representatives *carte blanche* to do this, also empowered the same male leaders as patriarchs and enhanced their sexism and masculinism. In the name of culture and god, within the high walls of community and ethnicity, women and children could be dominated and acted against violently because the religions or culture and tradition of others supposedly sanctioned this oppression and brutality. And as politically and ideologically constituted homogenized cultural essences which are typed as traditional, such as muslim or sikh or hindu communities, violence against women could go on without any significant or effective state intervention.

For these newly constructed communities, which came to life from scattered populations of the world and based their tenuous cohesion on a minimal doctrinaire affiliation (such as the hindu religion, for example), a heterosexist world view and mistrust of class politics, the multicultural dispensations of the state were a fortunate intervention. Their ethnic self-appellations, born of their long familiarity with colonial and imperialist discourse, were perfectly in keeping with colonial-racist stereotypes used by the Canadian state and culture. It was and is not noted either by the multicultural state or its clients, the so-called communities, that back in their so-called home countries, in whose names their multiculture is fabricated, the contestation that is going on bears little resemblance to these monolithic identities that they project in Canada. Being real countries, lived historical political spaces, these countries were and are going through many political spaces, these countries were and are going through many political and social struggles, changing their forms, none of which were in a position to be petrified into immutable cultural identities.[23] The genealogies of these reified cultural identities which are mobilized in Canada are entirely colonial, though they are being constantly re-worked in the modern context of state formation and capital's transformation. In fact the earlier European orientalist racist perceptions of India, for example, perfectly tally with the Canadian state's and the media's perception of the Indian communities in Canada.[24] The concept of tradition is the principle of continuity and serves as the interpretive and constructive category in both cases. A simple binary of cultural stereotyping of tradition and modernity stands for India and Canada, respectively. The problem of multiculturalism, then, is how much tradition can be accommodated by Canadian modernity without affecting in any real way the overall political and cultural hegemony of Europeans. It is also assumed by both the state and the media, as well as the male representatives of the communities, that Indians or South Asians are essentially traditional and as such patriarchy is congenital to their cultural identity, while class conflict is a modern or non-traditional aberration.

The result of this convergence between the Canadian state and conservative male representatives or community agents has been very distressing for women in particular. Between the multicultural paradigm and the actuality of a migrant citizen's life in Canada, the gap is immense. Among multiculturalists of both the communitarian and the liberal persuasion Canada is a nation space which contains different "races" and ethnicities, and this presence demands either a "politics of recognition" (Taylor, 1992) or a modified set of individual and group rights. But for both groups this diversity of others or difference between Canadian self and other has no political dimension. It speaks to nothing like class formation or class struggle, of the existence of active and deep racism, or of a social organization entailing racialized class production of gender. The history of colonization is also not brought to bear on the notions of diversity and difference. So, the answer to my original question — what is to be gained from a discourse of diversity and its politics of multiculturalism? — lies in just what has actually happened in Canadian politics and its theorization, what I have been describing so far, namely in the erasure and occlusion of social relations of power and ruling. This diversified reification of cultures and culturalization of politics allows for both the practice and occlusion of heterosexism and racism of a narrow bourgeois nationalism. This means the maintenance of a status quo of domination. Many hard socio-political questions and basic structural changes may now be avoided. People can be blamed for bringing on their own misfortunes, while rule of capital and class can continue their violence of racism, sexism and homophobia.

Conclusion

It should be obvious by now that diversity discourse portrays society as a horizontal space, in which there is no theoretical or analytical room for social relations of power and ruling, of socio-economic contradictions that construct and regulate Canadian political economy and its ideological culture. Yet the very need to formulate notions of multiculturalism and diversity, and their introjection into politics and state formation, into the very modes of governance, indicates that all is not as harmonious as it should be. The presence of certain peoples in the Canadian socio-economic and cultural spaces has obviously been considered exceptional, unusual or irregular. Yet their presence has also called into question much of what has been considered usual or regular. This has meant initiating a degree of adjustment for the majority communities and their state which, while sidestepping existing ideological practices, has meant the invention of this ideological state apparatus and cultural language of multiculturalism.

But the discourse of diversity is not new or *sui generis*. As I mentioned before, it is derived from and is in keeping with a language of plurality that has existed in liberal democracy. It relies, as we saw, on reading the notion of difference in a socially abstract manner, which also wipes away its location in history, thus obscuring colonialism, capital and slavery. It displaces these political and historical readings by presenting a complex interpretive code which encapsulates a few particularities of people's cultures, adding a touch of reality, and averts our gaze from power relations or differences which continue to organize the Canadian public life and culture. They assert themselves as perceptions of otherness encoding a hegemonic European-Canadianness.

As I have shown above, by obscuring or deflecting from historical and present power relations, perceptions and systematized ideologies, the deployment of diversity reduces to and manages difference as ethnic cultural issues. It then becomes a matter of co-existence of value-free, power-neutral plurality, of cultural differences where modernity and tradition, so-called white and black cultures, supposedly hold the same value. That is, diversity discourse tries to set up a sphere which claims to be outside of hegemony. It does so uncritically, unreflexively, and yet cannot escape the role of being an instrument of designation of some cultures as *real* culture, while others fall into the category of subculture and multiculture, cultures of the peripheries. This is not dissonant with colonial anthropology's way of assigning non-European cultures a special, hyphenated and bracketed status.[25] This way of thinking accomplishes depoliticization at deeply complex conceptual and political levels. Simultaneously as it disarticulates culture from hegemony, it reduces all political issues into cultural ones and converts culture into a private matter. This removes the civil society — its politically charged expressions, ways of being and seeing, what Gramsci called social common sense — from being considered as the soil and the material for political formations and articulation. This process in effect transforms the category culture into a practical device which both erases and stands in for the social. Any materialist dialectic of culture is dispensed with.[26]

This conceptual feat of emptying out difference of its actual political and cultural content, and thus presenting it as neutral diversity, can only be done by relying on the wholly artificial separation of the public and the private — as parallels of the political and the personal. It is possible because the concept of diversity is much more hospitable to an abstract notion of plurality than that of difference, which instantly summons questions of comparison to others with regard to whom any difference is postulated. A socialization, and therefore politicization, of this concept of difference is far more likely than diversity to lend itself to content saturated with social relations of class, gender, "race," sexuality and so on. This makes difference a much better heuristic device, if not exactly an analytical concept, for understanding situations which both imply and call for politics. We might at this point ask, how we should name ourselves, or what would be an effective name for capturing the oppositional thrust of our political agency? Though it is not possible for me to provide an answer which would satisfy all feminists, nor is it my intention to so do, this topic of named agency and its subjectivity demands a greater clarification. I am content to call myself an antiracist and marxist feminist. It is a distinctly political and socially grounded cultural identity. It does not rely solely on the culture of community at birth, but also speaks to what we have become as political subjects and agents in our own adult political and cultural efforts. This striving for a political self-definition, a self-conscious anti-oppression task of historical recovery, is not a matter of essentialized cultural diversities, but rather, as Paula Moya says (Alexander & Mohanty, 1997, p. 141), it involves an act of "deconstruction of difference." With class, "race" and gender and sexuality seen as components of this difference, we admit of both solidarities and relations of opposition. We can unite, as coalition is a basic prerequisite of organizing for change, with others inhabiting similar socio-cultural locations, and see that unity in political terms. This seeing of common social conditions produced through oppressive relations, rather than an essentialized version of cultures, is an act and task of political conscientization. This admits of asymmetrical social and cultural locations and power relations (for example, between straight and lesbian non-white women in North America), while also moving toward a new level of political consciousness and a culture of resistance. This culture also exists historically with us, as our legacy.

   This same question of political naming, or agency, has been discussed by many feminists, white and non-white. For Mohanty and Alexander, the answer lies in democracy, but not of the capitalist liberal type. They evolve the notion of feminist democracy, but feminist distinct from radical feminism. They speak (1997, pp. xxix–xxxi) to a "transborder, transnational participatory democracy" which resists hegemonic democracy of our times, and to "universal citizenship," to "anticapitalist, anticolonial feminist democracy" in a very similar way to my proposal. This is not radical democracy without class, class struggle or anti-imperialism. Thus it is different from the projects for new social movements as enunciated by Ernesto Laclau and Chantal Mouffe and their followers, who believe that they can make democracy real without fighting racialized gendered, local, national and global capitalism. Alexander and Mohanty eschew cultural relativism encouraged by multiculturalism from above, and seek a redefinition of justice. They want to see a "critical application of feminist praxis in global contexts" which insists on "responsibility, accountability, engagement and solidarity," and advance in their anthology "a paradigm of decolonization which stresses power, history, memory, relational analysis, justice (not just representation), and ethics as the issues central to [their] analysis of globalization" (1997, p. xix). I would say this is a proposal which we should support as the most extensively liberatory one.

But as things are at present, people are not doing a politics consistent with my proposal. We continue to subscribe to the discourse of diversity or liberal plurality, forgetting both its depoliticizing capacity and its ability to perform a most powerful political function. We might remind ourselves what the political cognates of diversity are. We might ask what is its home discourse, for concepts do have homes in a general discursive constellation, and what are their ideological-political imports? The discursive home and political cognates of diversity lie in liberal democracy, whose particular ways of constructing a self-enclosed, self-sustaining polity through the mechanism of installing a separation between the state and the civil society, and the reduction of equality into a formal gesture, have long been noted (see McPherson, 1977). This is the meaning of the concept of citizenship in liberal or bourgeois democracy, which rests on divesting the political from the social, the equality of citizenship from the inequality of class and other power relations. The so-called diverse cultural or ethnic communities are also constructed on this model as equal to each other and to the dominant Canadian culture of Euro-Americans. Diversity relies on the postulation of an abstracted, non-social ground zero.

Diversity as discourse, with its constellation of concepts such as multiculturalism, ethnicity, community, and so forth, becomes an important way in which the abstract or formal equality of liberal democracy, its empty pluralism, can gain a concreteness or an embodiment. Through it the concept of citizenship rids itself of its emptiness and takes on signals of a particularized social being or a cultural personhood. The sameness implied in the liberal notion citizenship is then stencilled onto a so-called diverse culture, and offers a sense of concrete specificity. This purported plurality with pseudo-concreteness rescues class democracy, and does not let the question of power relations get out of hand. Differences or diversities are then seen as inherent, as ontological or cultural traits of the individuals of particular cultural communities, rather than as racist ascriptions or stereotypes. This helps the cause of the status quo and maintains ascribed and invented ethnicities, or their displaced and intensified communal forms. The discourse of diversity makes it impossible to understand or name systemic and cultural racism, and its implication in gender and class.

When concreteness or embodiment is thus ideologically depoliticized and dehistoricized by its articulation to the discourse of diversity, we are presented with many ontological cultural particularities which serve as markers of ethnicity and group entities, and there is no recognition of a core cultural-power group boundaries. Since these ethnic communities are conceived as discrete entities, and there is no recognition of a core cultural-power group, a dispersion effect is introduced through the discourse of diversity which occludes its own presumption of otherness, of being diverse, and which is predicated upon a homogeneous Canadian identity. It is with regard to this that diversity is measured, and hides its assumptions of homogeneity under the cover of a value and power neutral heterogeneity. Thus it banishes from view a process of homogenization or essentialization which underpins the project of liberal pluralism.

Ultimately then, the discourse of diversity is an ideology. It has its own political imperatives in what is called multiculturalism elaborated within the precincts of the state. It translates out into different political possibilities within the framework of capitalism and bourgeois democracy, and both communitarian liberals and liberals for individual rights may find it congenial to their own goals. Politics of recognition, an ideology of tolerance, advocacy of limited group rights, may all result from adopting the discourse of diversity, but what difference they would actually make to those people's lives which are objects of multicultural politics, is another story.

Notes

This is a reworked version of a paper given at Southeastern Women's Studies Association Annual Conference, Athens, Georgia, April 1997. Thanks are due to the Faculty of Educational Studies, University of British Columbia, for time given to do research for my work as a visiting scholar. I would especially like to thank Professors Leslie Roman and Patricia Vertinsky for their encouragement and support.

1   Wallace is aware of the problems associated with multiculturalism, but supports it in general from a psychoanalytic perspective involving many aspects of self-formation.

2   See in this context Peter McLaren's introduction to *Revolutionary Multiculturalism* (1997), but also Connolly (1995).

3   Regarding the term "black women" in political usage, see Sudbury (1998, p. 20, fn 1).

4   Sudbury outlines in her introduction the history of these different bids at political identities and their shifts.

5   For a history of immigration in Canada, see Law Union of Ontario (1981).

6   On "race," colour and the Canadian state's immigration policies in the late 19th/early 20th century, see Government of Canada (1974, 1986).

7   See Brand and Carty (1993); also Ng (1993). For an uncritical liberal view, see Government of Canada (1986).

8   On invention of tradition see Hobsbawm and Ranger (1983); also Mani (1989), and Ismail and Jeganathan (1995).
9   On culturalizing politics, see Benjamin (1969).
10 For an example of feminist anthologies using "diversity" in the title, see Hamilton (1986), especially the introduction.
11 On ideological categories and conceptual practices of power and relations of ruling, see the first two chapters of Smith (1990).
12 For the ground of a theoretical critique of diversity, see Roman (1993).
13 On the Canadian national imaginary see Bannerji (1996).
14 For diversity language in administration, see Davis (1996) on the language of corporate multiculturalism.
15 Common slogan of several government advertising campaigns, to be filled in with "Ontario" or "Canada."
16 For homophobia and racist heterosexism in cultural nationalism or ethnic communitarianism, see, in the U.S. context, Collins (1998) and Carby (1998), to name two texts. In the Canadian context very little has been written about this phenomenon, probably due to the deeply social and economic involvement of the so-called communities in the state's policies of multiculturalism. See Dua and Robertson (1999), especially my paper (Bannerji, 1999).
17 On the racialized nature of Canada's political economy as a white settler colony, and its attempts to retain features of this while installing itself as a liberal democracy, see Bolaria and Li (1988).
18 It is redundant really to speak of the exclusion/marginalization of the aboriginal people in Canada, both in terms of their claim to land and livelihood as well as culture, but the following books are interesting as examples of discussions on these issues. See Kulchyski (1994) and Monture-Angus (1995).
19 On reading the skin as whiteness, as an ideological/political construction, see Frankenburg (1993).
20 On immigration to Canada from Hong Kong, and recent Chinese immigration, see Wong (1997), Li (1993); also Skeldon (1995).
21 Between 1988 and 1992 three unarmed black young men were killed by police in Toronto and one in Montreal, and one young woman permanently paralysed in a police shooting.
22 For example, the change in immigration policy from the "family reunification" programme to a primarily skills based one shifts the demography of Canada. It brings a kind of immigrant, perhaps from Eastern Europe, who does not pose the problem of "race."
23 See Butalia and Sarkar (1997). The essays in this anthology show the intensity of the political struggle between secular, left feminist forces and the hindu right.
24 An India or South Asia has been invented, with befitting identities or cultural stereotypes for people of the subcontinent living in the diaspora. A production of orientalism and a more forthright racism, these stereotypes rest on the use of the concept of tradition.

25 For examples of colonial anthropology, see Radcliffe-Brown (1965) or Evans-Pritchard (1965); also for its more postmodernist, radical versions, see Geertz (1988) or (1988) or Comaroff and Comaroff (1991).
26 For a materialist view of culture, see Williams (1980).

References

Alarcón, Norma. "Conjugating Subjects in the Age of Multiculturalism." In Avery Gordon and Christopher Newfield, eds. *Mapping Multiculturalism*, 40–48. Minnesota: University of Minnesota Press, 1996.

Alcoff, Linda. "Cultural Feminism versus Post-structuralism: The Identity Crisis in Feminist Theory." *Signs* 13, no. 3 (1988), 405–436.

Alexander, Jacqui, and Chandra Mohanty, eds. *Feminist Genealogies, Colonial Legacies, Democratic Futures.* London and New York: Routledge, 1997.

Althusser, Louis. *Lenin and Philosophy,* trans., Ben Brewster. London: Verso, 1971.

Anthias, Floya, Nira Yuval-Davis, and Harriet Cain, eds. *Racialized Boundaries.* London and New York: Routledge, 1992.

Anzaldúa, Gloria, ed. *Making Face, Making Soul/haciendo caras: Creative and Critical Perspectives by Women of Color.* San Francisco: an aunt lute foundations book, 1990.

Anzaldúa, Gloria, and Cherrie Moraga, eds. *This Bridge Called My Back: Writings by Radical Women of Color.* New York: Kitchen Table Women of Color Press, 1983.

Bannerji, Himani. "But Who Speaks for Us?" In Himani Bannerji, Linda Carty, Kari Dehli, Susan Heald and Kate McKenna, *Unsettling Relations: The University as a Site of Feminist Struggles,* 67–108. Toronto: Women's Press, 1991.

_____, ed. *Returning the Gaze: Essays on Racism, Feminism and Politics.* Toronto: Sister Vision Press, 1993.

_____. *Thinking Through: Essays on Feminism, Marxism and Antiracism.* Toronto: Women's Press, 1995.

_____. "On the Dark Side of the Nation: Politics of Multiculturalism and the State in Canada." *Journal of Canadian Studies* 31, no. 3 (1996), 103–128.

_____. "Geography Lessons: On Being an Insider/Outsider to the Canadian Nation." In Leslie Roman and Linda Eyre, eds. *Dangerous Territories: Struggles for Difference and Equality in Education,* 23–42. New York and London: Routledge, 1997.

_____. "A Question of Silence: Reflections on Violence against Women in Communities of Colour." In Enakshi Dua and Angela Robertson, eds. *Scratching the Surface: Canadian Anti-racist Feminist Thought,* 261–277. Toronto: Women's Press, 1999.

Benjamin, Walter. "The Work of Art in the Age of Mechanical Reproduction." In *Illuminations*, 217–252. Trans. Harry Zohn. New York: Schocken Books, 1969.

Bhabnani, Kumkum and Ann Phoenix, eds. *Shifting Identities, Shifting Racisms*. London: Sage, 1994.

Bolaria, B. Singh and Peter S. Li. *Racial Oppression in Canada*. Toronto: Garamond Press, 1988.

Brah, Avtar. *Cartographies of Diaspora: Contesting Identities*. London and New York: Routledge, 1996.

Brand, Dionne. *No Language Is Neutral*. Toronto: McClelland and Stewart, 1990.

Brand, Dionne and Linda Carty. "Visible Minority Women: A Creation of the Colonial State." In Himani Bannerji, ed. *Returning the Gaze: Essays on Racism, Feminism and Politics*, 207–222. Toronto: Sister Vision Press, 1993.

Butalia, Urvashi and Tanika Sarkar, eds. *Women of the Hindu Right*. New Delhi: Kali for Women, 1997.

Carby, Hazel V. *Race Men*. Cambridge: Harvard University Press, 1998.

_____. "White Women Listen! Black Feminism and the Boundaries of Sisterhood." In Centre for Contemporary Cultural Studies, *The Empire Strikes Back*, 212–235. London: Hutchinson, 1982.

Centre for Contemporary Cultural Studies. *The Empire Strikes Back*. London: Hutchinson, 1982.

Collins, Patricia Hill. *Black Feminist Thought: Knowledge, Consciousness and the Politics of Empowerment*. London: Harper Collins, 1990.

_____. *Fighting Words: Black Women and the Search for Justice*. Minneapolis, Minnesota: University of Minnesota Press, 1998.

Comaroff, Jean, and John Comaroff. *Of Revelation and Revolution*. Chicago: University of Chicago Press, 1991.

Connolly, William. *The Ethos of Pluralization*. Minneapolis, Minnesota: University of Minnesota Press, 1995.

Cruz, Jon. "From Farce to Tragedy: Reflections on the Reification of Race at Century's End." In Avery Gordon and Christopher Newfield, eds. *Mapping Multiculturalism*, 19–39. Minneapolis, Minnesota: University of Minnesota Press, 1996.

Davis, Angela Y. "Gender, Class and Multiculturalism: Rethinking 'Race' Politics." In Avery Gordon and Christopher Newfield, eds. *Mapping Multiculturalism,*, 40–48. Minnesota: University of Minnesota Press, 1996.

Dua, Ena and Angela Robertson, eds. *Scratching the Surface*. Toronto: Women's Press, 1999.

Eliott, Jean L. and Augie Fleras. *Multiculturalism in Canada: The Challenge of Diversity*. Toronto: Nelson, 1992.

Evans-Pritchard, Edward E. *Theories of Primitive Religion*. Oxford: Clarendon Press, 1965.

Frankenburg, Ruth. *White Women, Race Matters: The Social Construction of Whiteness*. Minneapolis, Minnesota: University of Minnesota Press, 1993.

Geertz, Clifford. *Works and Lives: The Anthropologist as Author.* Stanford, California: Stanford University Press, 1988.

Gilman, Sander. "Black Bodies, White Bodies: Toward an Iconography of Female Sexuality in Late Nineteenth Century Art, Medicine and Literature." In Henry Louis Gates Jr., ed. *"Race" Writing and Difference,* 223–261. Chicago: University of Chicago Press, 1985.

Gilroy, Paul. *Ain't No Black in the Union Jack: The Cultural Politics of Race and Nation.* London: Hutchinson, 1987.

_____. *Black Atlantic: Modernity's Double Consciousness.* London: Verso, 1993.

Goldberg, David T., ed. *Multiculturalism: A Critical Reader.* Oxford: Blackwell, 1994.

Gomez-Peña, Guillermo. *The New World Border.* San Francisco: City Lights Books, 1996.

Gordon, Avery and Christopher Newfield, eds. *Mapping Multiculturalism.* Minnesota: University of Minnesota Press, 1996.

Government of Canada. *A Report of the Canadian Immigration and Population Study: Immigration Policy Perspective.* Ottawa: Department of Manpower and Immigration and Information Canada, 1974.

_____. *Royal Commission Report on Equality in Employment.* Ottawa: Ministry of Supply and Services, 1984.

_____. *Equality Now: Report of the Special Committee on Visible Minorities.* Ottawa: House of Commons, 1986.

Gramsci, Antonio. "State and Civil Society." In Quentin Hoare and Geoffrey Smith, eds. and trans. *Selections from the Prison Notebooks,* 210–276. New York: International Publishers, 1971.

Hall, Stuart. "New Ethnicities." In James Donald and Ali Ratansi, eds. *'Race', Culture and Difference,* 252–260. London: Sage, 1992.

Hamilton, Roberta, ed. *The Politics of Diversity.* Boston: Beacon Press, 1986.

Hobsbawm, Eric and Terence Ranger, eds. *The Invention of Tradition.* Cambridge: Cambridge University Press, 1984.

Ismail, Qadri and Pradeep Jeganathan, eds. *Unmaking the Nation: The Politics of Identity and History in Modern Sri Lanka.* Colombo: Social Scientists' Association, 1995.

Kulchyski, Peter, ed. *Unjust Relations: Aboriginal Rights in Canadian Courts.* Toronto: University of Toronto Press, 1994.

Kymlicka, Will. *Multicultural Citizenship: A Liberal Theory of Minority Rights.* Oxford: Clarendon Press, 1995.

Law Union of Ontario. *The Immigrants Handbook.* Montreal: Black Rose Books, 1981.

Li, Peter S. "Chinese Investment and Business in Canada: Ethnic Entrepreneurship Reconsidered." *Pacific Affairs* 66, no. 2 (1993), 219–243.

Mani, Lata. "Contentious Traditions: The Debate on *Sati* in Colonial India." In Kumkum Sangari and Sudesh Vaid, eds. *Recasting Women: Essays in Indian*

Colonial History, 88–126. New Brunswick, New Jersey: Rutgers University Press, 1989.

McLaren, Peter, ed. *Revolutionary Multiculturalism: Pedagogies of Dissent in the New Millennium.* Boulder, Colorado: Westview Press, 1997.

McPherson, C.B. *The Life and Times of Liberal Democracy.* Oxford: Oxford University Press, 1977.

Modood, Tariq. "Political Blackness and British Asians." *Sociology* 28, no. 2 (1990), 859–876.

Mohanty, Chandra, Ann Russo, and Lourdes Torres, eds. *Third World Women and the Politics of Feminism.* Bloomington, Indiana: Indiana University Press, 1991.

Monture-Angus, Patricia. *Thunder in My Soul: A Mohawk Woman Speaks.* Halifax, Nova Scotia: Fernwood Press, 1995.

Ng, Roxana. "Sexism, Racism, Canadian Nationalism." In Himani Bannerji, ed. *Returning the Gaze: Essays on Racism, Feminism and Politics,* 223–241. Toronto: Sister Vision Press, 1993.

Parenti, Michael. *Dirty Truths.* San Francisco: City Lights Books, 1996.

Parmar, Pratibha. "Black Feminism: The Politics of Articulation." In Jonathan Rutherford, ed. *Identity, Community, Culture, Difference,* 101–126. London: Lawrence and Wishart, 1990.

Porter, John. *The Vertical Mosaic.* Toronto: University of Toronto Press, 1965.

Radcliffe-Brown, Alfred R. *Structure and Function in Primitive Society.* New York: The Free Press, 1965.

Robinson, Cedric. "Manichaeism and Multiculturalism." In Avery Gordon and Christopher Newfield, eds. *Mapping Multiculturalism,* 116–124. Minneapolis, Minnesota: University of Minnesota Press, 1996.

Roman, Leslie. "White is a Color! White Defensiveness, Postmodernism and Anti-Racist Pedagogy." In Warren Crichlow and Cameron McCarthy, eds. *Race, Identity and Representation in Education,* 71–88. New York and London: Routledge, 1993.

Sandoval, Chela. "U.S. Third World Feminism: The Theory and Method of Oppositional Consciousness in the Postmodern World." *Genders* 10 (1991), 1–24.

Sheldon, Ronald, ed. *Emigration from Hong Kong: Tendencies and Impacts.* Hong Kong: Chinese University Press, 1995.

Shivanandan. *A Different Hunger: Writings on Black Resistance.* London: Pluto Press, 1982.

Smith, Dorothy E. *The Conceptual Practices of Power: A Feminist Sociology of Knowledge.* Toronto: University of Toronto Press, 1990.

Spelman, Elizabeth. *Inessential Woman: Problems of Exclusion in Feminist Thought.* Boston: Beacon Press, 1988.

Stoler, Ann Laura. *Race and the Education of Desire.* Durham, N.C. and London: Duke University Press, 1995.

Sudbury, Julia. *'Other Kinds of Dreams': Black Women's Organizations and the Politics of Transformation.* London and New York: Routledge, 1998.

Taylor, Charles. *Multiculturalism and 'the Politics of Recognition.'* Princeton: Princeton University Press, 1992.

_____. *Reconciling the Solitudes: Essays on Canadian Federalism and Nationalism.* Montreal: McGill-Queen's University Press, 1993.

Trudeau, Pierre. *Federalism and the French Canadians,* trans. Patricia Claxton. Toronto: MacMillan, 1968.

Volpp, Leti. "Misidentifying Culture: Asian Women and the Cultural Defense." *Harvard Women's Law Journal* (1994), 57–101.

Wallace, Michelle. "The Search for the 'Good Enough' Mammy: Multiculturalism, Popular Culture and Psychoanalysis." In Theo Goldberg, ed. *Multiculturalism: A Critical Reader,* 259–268. Oxford: Blackwell, 1994.

Williams, Raymond. *Problems in Materialism and Culture.* London: Verso, 1980.

Wong, Lloyd. "Globalization and Transnational Migration: A Study of Recent Chinese Capitalist Migration from the Asian Pacific to Canada." *International Sociology* 12, no. 3 (1997), 329–351.

Chapter Three

Qualitative Research to Identify Racialist Discourse: Towards Equity in Nursing Curricula

Rebecca Hagey
Robert W. MacKay

Introduction

> We have racialized our society and our individual lives to such a degree that the problem of the colour line, as W.E.B. Dubois warned many years ago, is not only the central problem of the twentieth century, but will be of the twenty-first as well. Like any black person I have ever known, I now perceive both obvious and subtle racism in the immediate world around me every single day. (Lazarre, 1996, pp. x–xxi)

> The 'white eye' is always outside the frame but seeing and positioning everything within it." (Hall, 1982)

This study reports the first phase of an ongoing initiative in a university school — preparing nurses from undergraduate to doctoral level — to address the curriculum with respect to antiracism. We present an overview of the research, and a synthesis of theoretical and methodological principles for discourse analysis, briefly reflecting on the context of doing research in a microcosm of our own students and colleagues. We discuss selected findings in relation to a discourse approach to antiracism, which begins with interpretive readings to identify racialist talk. We provide a vision for integrating equity into curricula and into professional life and beyond where the goal is improvement of the benefits we share and offer as professionals toward building an equitable, healthy society.

Background and overview of the research

The initiative was an in-house funded research project to address learning needs regarding culture in the curriculum that Papadopoulos et al. (1994) call a need "to challenge racism and avoid approached that merely reify culture" (p. 635). This was especially problematic for addressing racism in the context of our Faculty, where there is still talk about the 'R'-word and where millions of dollars were spent on research on the quality of work life without any attention to the problem of racism during a period of highly publicized legal settlements awarding substantial monetary compensation to nurses filing complaints of racism (Calliste, 1993, 1995, 1996).

Policy in Canada is beginning to advise explicit anti-racism initiatives for all health professional curricula (Joint Committee, 1995). The hesitation felt within our project appears to be consistent with trends in nursing, where curriculum planning lacks an emphasis on race, despite Burrows' (1983) excellent early work. For recent articles on curriculum and culture which do not explicitly name racism or other equity issues (see for example, Smith et al., 1993; Spitzer et al., 1996).

The study was commissioned by the curriculum committee after one Faculty member proposed a plan for integrating culture into the curriculum as a member of a national committee, Committee for Cultural Integration into Education in Professional Schools (CCIEPS) in Canada under the aegis of the federal Heritage Program (see Yoshida, 1994). The plan attempted to address racism in the curriculum. It was felt by the curriculum committee that the evaluation component of the plan was problematic and a research approach could address that weakness. A research committee was formed and decided to first conduct qualitative research to identify issues and perceptions which could then be used both in faculty development and in devising an evaluation tool. It was felt that a tool would provide 'research leverage' to generate accountability and make change see-able. The tool can be used to assess progress toward the goal of integrating culture and antiracism in the curriculum. Findings from a pilot of the tool have already been presented as a report to the curriculum committee in our Faculty.

Statements from the faculty calendar:
formal display of values

Under the heading of Undergraduate Program, the official vision of nursing is provided in the Faculty calendar. "Nursing is the deliberate caring practice of promoting, restoring and maintaining individual, family and community integrity. Caring is the act of 'being with' people in a special way which acknowledges the uniqueness of individuals in their particular context.

Nursing's perspective is characterized by an emphasis on the well-being and optimal functioning of persons, whether sick or well. Nursing as a practice profession must be politically knowledgeable and instrumental in the promotion of public policy which fosters health. As part of our commitment to the advancement of knowledge in nursing, we fundamentally encourage the ethos of enquiry and critique and a reflective stance towards knowledge. Learning is a shared experience with both teachers and students as learners" (Faculty of Nursing, 1997, p.15).

The calendar goes on to specify an expectation with respect to the culture of clients: "The nursing student should be respectful of client's values, culture and religion" (Faculty of Nursing, 1997, p. 36).

Study curiosities: what are the informal values in the live discourse?

Within this general context, the first phase of the study addressed the undergraduate programs by open-ended interviews and focus groups, of students, faculty, preceptors and staff and the following questions were negotiated within the in-house research committee:

1. What are the student's and faculty's perceptions of how culture is integrated through the curriculum?
2. What are the student's impressions of the environment within the school, including faculty members, with respect to antiracism?
3. How do students feel about methods of evaluation used in the school?
4. What suggestions do students, faculty and staff have to improve racial and cultural sensitivity in the school?

Actual probes which got used included the following:

1. What is your impression of how culture is integrated in the curriculum?
2. How would you like to see culture integrated into the curriculum?
3. What is your impression of the environment within the faculty regarding cultural sensitivity?
4. Do you have any concerns about evaluation process and cultural sensitivity?
5. How could the faculty provide a more culturally sensitive environment?

Within in a research environment committed to positivist science, we decided to use stratified random sampling to obtain the interviews and focus groups, thus deviating from usual qualitative strategies which might have chosen key informant interview or focus groups based on social groupings, or other sampling methods (Thorne et al., 1997). Stratification was by grades A, B, C and D, using aggregate performance records. D is a failing grade in our program. Our proposal called for also interviewing faculty, preceptors and front-line staff in contact with students, however, we found the individuals randomly sampled were reluctant to be interviewed and in the end, most avoided doing so. The sample included 40 students and one staff person interviewed and eight student focus groups with a total of 40 students and one faculty and one preceptor in a small focus group. The study we present concerns only one issue emerging from the qualitative phase; evidence of racialist social cognitions and practices, as reflected in discourse.

Theory supporting the interpretive perspective: racialist effects of marginalization, problematization and containment

Essed (1991, p. 52) outlines how oppression, repression and legitimization are accomplished by everyday racism as follows:

1. Socialized racist notions are *integrated into meanings* that make practices immediately *definable* and *manageable*.
2. Practices with racist implications become in themselves *familiar and repetitive*, underlying racial and ethnic relations are *actualized and reinforced* through these routine or familiar practices in everyday situations.

She goes on to develop inventories of the frequency of the effects of everyday racism in the marginalization, problematization and containment experienced by the 55 women of color in her study (pp. 180–183). Also she establishes that racism is by definition the expression or *activation of group power* (p. 41) and that "specific practices are by definition racist only when they activate existing structural racial inequality in the system" (p. 39).

One type of discourse which contributes to the condoning of racism (and therefore to the activation of structural inequality) is that which Essed calls the "discourse of tolerance" (p. 6). An example of how this works is when the press and academics "openly attack blacks (and whites) who fight against racism. This legitimizes and reinforces indifference to racial oppression and tolerance for racism among the dominant group" (p. 7). At the same time within this type of discourse, talk can be managed to give the impression that nobody is excluding anyone; within this discourse practice, the individual is seen as accountable only to the self and how much motivation he/she has for advancement. Hence, the inadvertant (or advertant) disadvantaging of 'others' is simply something to be *defined* and *managed.* We will show how the definitions used in managing advancement through professional school do not *name* or *mark* racial disadvantage or white privilege (Frankenberg, 1993). Hence racial dominance is managed guilt-free.

Henry et al. (1995, p. 312) argue that within a reassuring environment of ideals about equity, justice, democracy and so on, racial discrimination and disadvantaging flourish so that "in the midst of a society that professes racial equality, there is racial inequality; instead of fairness, there is unfairness; instead of freedom of speech, there is the silencing of voices advocating change; instead of impartiality, bias; instead of multiculturalism, ethnocentrism. Diversity becomes assimilation, the rule of law results in injustice, service means lack of access, and protection increases the vulnerability of racial-minority communities." This is the paradox of what they call *democratic racism.* We are interested in showing how racial effects are accomplished through discourse. To do this we provide the following synthesis of work on a non-essentialist approach which can be applied to make racism as a process, see-able.

Equity as inclusivity: essential categories as problematic

All inequalities can be seen as problems of essentialist cognitions. An essentialist approach would identify people as belonging to a category which can be both social and biological, and would assign traits to that category. We avoid this approach since we know for example that what we are calling *dominant discourse* can be voiced by members of disadvantaged groups who may or may not choose to oppose their oppression. We also know that members of elite groups who access and execute powerful decisions can advocate for and organize new structures and relations, which improve the lives of members of oppressed groups. In this formulation we do not ear tag anyone as belonging to either of the former groups.

We are examining the entire corpus of discourse of our sample of interviews and focus groups, in relation to particular surface structure and process features, (see below) that can provide evidence of the use of particular discourse strategies, arguments and ideologies drawing on theory about discourse logic, and how it organizes real relations and social patterns. Specifically, we invite the reader to ponder how the signaling of the rule of advantage or disadvantage is reproduced in the discourse and how the ingroup/outgroup dynamic segregates the possibility of relations in the lived curriculum; to consider how group based power and exclusionary practices are being perpetuated in the student population; to consider how the identity of whiteness carries with it particular capacities for engaging in ruling relations.

Representations of whiteness and otherness

Studies of the discursive reproduction of racism are made possible by application of the discipline of discourse analysis of text and talk, the microanalysis of speech which constructs whiteness as an identity, from which 'others' are excluded.

We are theorizing a category of whiteness, which is distinct from a category of otherness. Whiteness carries certain privileges of a normality, authority or dominance, freedoms for flexibility, capacity for voicing and likelihood of being heard, opportunity for being in control, events being orderly, having information about the correct means and channels, etc. By contrast, otherness carries, respectively, difference and marginalization, subordination, disadvantaging, restriction, being silenced, lacking information or cooperation for control, events being in chaos, lacking information about correct means and channels and so on, which are consistently disadvantages in comparison to the privileges associated with whiteness. Evidence of potential racialist effects then requires orienting to the segmenting possibility of sets of opposites created by the social cognitions or implicit arguments present in the discourse milieu: whiteness/otherness; normality/marginalization; dominance/subordination; privilege/disadvantaging; freedom/restriction; voicing/being silenced; controlling/lacking the power to control.

We invite you, the reader, to inspect the transcripts for evidence of whiteness and the privileges associated with it, and for evidence of how white privilege is reproduced in discourse which by default constructs 'others' and implies their subordination. See Hagey et al. (in preparation) for a demonstration of how the default message works. We report an interface of discourse where there is a power struggle to maintain white privilege, to discipline 'others' and to resist any expectation they might have for normality, and hence to push them to the margins. We provide evidence of discourse in this milieu, where the identity is that of being marginalized, of being silenced. We show as well, the identity of having the correct means and channels to engage in power ... associated with the known privileges of whiteness which constitute default rules for success and access.

Van Dijk's method (1993b, pp. 102–119) allows the inspection of racialist discourse through the examination of processes. For example, a command can be directed to someone who does not belong to the majority group, with no excuse for violating norms of courtesy and then manifests as a form of everyday racism (Essed, 1991).

Implicit meaning in van Dijk's approach, is examined through varying perspectives, possible implications, presence of pre-suppositions, and coherence, level of description and degree of completeness, global coherence or whole text themes. These are the main techniques used in reading the data for this study. However it is worth pointing out that data from the study could be further validated in an ethnographic approach which would focus on *action, interaction and speech acts* studied for turn taking, interruptions, impression formation, politeness and deference and the use and abuse of the norms of courtesy and recognition — one of the more active ways that whiteness is constructed and that disadvantaging is accomplished in the lived curriculum.

However, the passive way that whiteness is constructed is by far the more pernicious. Woodward (1997) points out that "discourse and systems of representation construct places from which individuals can position themselves and from which they can speak" (p. 14).

This property of discourse, of specifying one platform of speech in relation to others, offers a way of passively announcing status, articulating complex messages through body language, of maintaining the pecking order, of implicitly enacting group dynamics to carry our ritual dramas which announce who has power and who does not; who is defining the reality of the situation and so on.

In all of the above properties of text or talk, what is of interest for van Dijk, is the *argument* that comes through in the ideology or the *social implication* that effects alliances and partnerships versus exclusion, marginalization, censorship, discrediting, inferiorizing, problematizing, accusing, etc., in the negative construction and ruling of 'others' and the positive construction and advantaging of 'whiteness'. The generic form of this process which we found to be pervasive in the discourse of our participants, is the ruling that real Canadians have 'whiteness' and as we shall see, 'whiteness' comes in gradients of purity which discounts 'non-standard' English, itself a construction of otherness. These constructions through text and talk operate on an ingroup/outgroup dynamic where racial identity is both constructed and reproduced, signaling the inclusion and exclusion of particular individuals identified as members of particular groups (Fanon, 1961; Hall et al., 1978; Frankenberg, 1993; van Dijk, 1993a,b, 1998). Where the rule of whiteness is applied, where there is an implicit message of "this rules" or "I deserve advantage," or where there is an open disclosure that the rule of white privilege is acceptable, we call this the discourse of *dominance*. We turn now to highlight this signaling in action, in the talk of students interviewed which has been converted to transcript text.

Some dialogue and interpretive analysis: us and the discourse of other

We have limited the presentation of perspectives emerging from the data to student perspectives on other students, and student perceptions of faculty/

preceptors. Specifically, we invite the reader to ponder the perceptions of the rules of privilege reflected in the reported speech, and how the embedded ingroup/outgroup dynamic can create at least an initial segregation or barrier for the possibility of relations in the lived curriculum.

We invite you, the reader to join in the interpretive reading process.

The indication of a pause by the speaker is "—" (or a dash); and where we have omitted segments of dialogue for the purpose of brevity, we use "..." There are spots where the speaker was inaudible, which appear in the transcript as "unclear", and we are confident that none we present compromise the integrity of our data or argument. We let you be the judge of the interpretation we provide for each example we have selected, to begin to flesh out the 'whiteness/otherness' discourse dynamic.

Example 1: whiteness is unnamed and unmarked

Interviewer: Now what's your impression of how culture is integrated in the curriculum in the (unclear)

Student 1: I think they — I find it very basic. Like they make it known that you should be aware of different cultures and when you're with a client, depending on what their culture is, it could affect the caring of that client. And, ahm, they tell you to be, you know, increase your awareness of your own values and their values. But I think that's as far as it goes when it comes to culture. Like they don't really get into any specifics, and I find like mostly with somebody like me, I come from a Canadian background, like I don't really know any type of culture, not to say that Canadian is a culture, but I mean it's very hard to define the Canadian culture compared to like if you talk about Italian culture or the Chinese. And I just find okay, you told us to be aware, but that's as far as they've gone.

Interviewer: Okay. So they haven't really — you'd like them to find you some type of guidelines or —

Student 1: Yeah, I'd just like to — like there's a couple main cultures within Canada. Like there's obviously diverse amount, but you've got the main like the Jewish, the Italian, you know, the Negro, ahm, and I think it would just be helpful if maybe they give us like you know, a little bit about the religious background, you know, about the different cultural practices so then when we do enter the field we do have some sort of knowledge base instead of going in there blind-sided. I don't know if they involve that in the later years or not, I don't know. But I mean as far as I know from what I've learned this year, like I haven't really gotten much out of the culture bit. So —

Interpretive reading of Example 1: whiteness as normality and responsibility for ordering; the term culture is about subordinating others

In following the argument, "I come from a Canadian background ... very hard to define the Canadian culture ... like there's a couple main cultures within Canada. Like there's obviously diverse amount, but you've got the main like Jewish, the Italian, you know the Negro, ahm, and I think it would be helpful if may be they give us like you know, a little bit about the religious background ...," we view a stance that is separated according to the logic: whiteness is to normal Canadian, as other is to Italian, Chinese, Jewish, Negro (in the order of their appearance in the text).

In saying "not to say that Canadian is a culture," the speaker tips us off to a categorization which has been reported by Hall for Britain (1978). Whites say ethnics have culture, and deny their own ethnicity by denying English (small c) culture. In this Canadian version, the term culture does not have to apply, — "It's very hard to define the Canadian culture" — while for backgrounds of Italian, Chinese, Jewish and Negro, the term culture applies.

Of course everyone has an ethnic heritage and culture, but the assertion spoken by the student can carry with it the privilege her own background is normal while particular others are marginal to that normality.

However, the logic gets expanded to add, whiteness is to responsibility for knowledge of culture and religion, as other is to "the culture bit." The argument that emerges from the implicit put down is that other cultures provide the data which one learns to achieve whiteness. That is, "I haven't really gotten much out of the culture bit" can be seen as somewhat of an imperious stance, either towards the content, or towards what was delivered to her in comparison to what she expected. Either way, her self positioning is elevated in relation to the otherness of the subject and we should be looking for ways she will take command of the subject in the future. The scenario she describes, is not, for example, to be working with nurses who are leaders in a particular community, and being guided by them. Rather, the program is to take charge of the field situation, despite lack of knowledge: but, "it would just be helpful if maybe they give us like you know, a little bit about the religious background, you know, about the different cultural practices ... instead of going in there blind-sided." The community leaders are marginal to this program. Counting this as evidence of the dominance/subordination paradigm, we would have concern about how this student would relate to the student in the next example, especially given the category Italian, she uses when culturalizing some Canadians, and not herself.

Example 2: discourse provides the
position from which individuals can speak

> Interviewer: Do you feel like — have you ever had an instance maybe a situation where you might have felt uncomfortable because of maybe something an instructor said or a preceptor said? Have you ever come across a situation like that?

> Student 2: Well, yeah, there was one time, ahm, actually this was — think I heard it from a couple of the instructors where they kinda said to me, you know, "What kind of accent is that?" You know. And I said, I don't have an accent, right? I didn't think I had one. I have an Italian background but I was born in this country. But it's just that I don't want to say the word, but (giggling) we have an Italian way of saying this, but I guess I don't know the Canadian way of speaking English, it's different from the way other people speak English if you come from a different background, right? So I don't know, I guess I kind of felt like —

> Interviewer: That they were kind of —

> Student 2: They were putting me down, I felt like, that's what — I honestly did feel that you know. Kind of like why, you know, where did you get that accept from? Weren't you born here? And I said yes, you know. So it was kind of like — I guess because I wasn't speaking a lot of the other, I don't know ...

> Interviewer: Can you think of maybe why they're like that, or why they come across like that?

> Student 2: "Ahm, you know, like I was saying at first, you know I was telling you about the way I was speaking English and that kind o' thing? I guess it as almost like there are certain people that they fit in with, you know, that they fit into their — I don't know the way they think. And I guess the way I am doesn't fit into the way, you know, the way they think or whatever. So it kind of pushes me out a little."

Interpretive reading of Example 2: marginalized and silent about it

The literature on racism abounds with examples of various ethnic groups coming under the rubric of whiteness or falling from the grace of whiteness, with the white Anglo Saxon Protestant being at the core of the privilege to dominate. Just as whites who support antiracism get expelled from the inner sanctum, entire populations of people with white skin may not qualify for the lime light of whiteness for particular historical reasons, including immigration. This student links her Italian background as the source of her treatment as other, at the hands of instructors, "so it kind of pushes me out a little." Notice she is silent about her feelings, not discussing them with the instructors who constructed her marginality. Thus she remains marginalized by these encounters, expressing no means to correct the situation and establish herself as normal or feeling included.

In the hierarchical scheme of whiteness and otherness there is a continuum, of lesser and lesser privilege and more domination/subordination and exclusion from resources and power. In the next example, the student names more discrimination issues such as a very small inclusion of Blacks, the perception of unfair grading, interference when speaking, being looked at with no eye contact, etc. Such consequences give credence to a continuum model where being further from the center of power, potentiates increased vulnerability and disadvantage.

Example 3: essentialism can be expressed as whiteness or otherness

Interviewer: So what's your impression of the atmosphere at the University of (name) or in the Faculty of Nursing?

Student 3: From a cultural perspective or my own personal?

Interviewer: Your own perception plus like as your own culture type of thing perspectively, the way you see it.

Student 3: First of all, I think we could have greater representation of people from my own culture. I don't see that around and it's very hard for me to see someone.

Interviewer: And what's your cul — what background are you?

Student 3: Ahm, well, a black person.

Interviewer: Okay, right!!

Student 3: It's very when you look around you have to look really hard to see one. We have a greater representation like from the Chinese community or from — white or other cultures. But I would just like to see more. I don't know the reason why, but it would be good, at least you know that you are represented in that area and if anything should come up, at least you have your own behind you supporting you. And my perception of my preceptors, ahm, some of them are okay; I've had experiences with a few that weren't all that positive. I wouldn't call names or anything (chuckles).

Interviewer: Well, it's fine because everything is being deleted.

Student 3: But I've had experiences where with my assignments, ... But I don't get the marks that I deserve from certain people. And sometimes I find, too, that you don't get the opportunity to express yourself. Fine if you start talking, for instance in nursing we tend to have a lot of open discussion and communication, you find that people tend to cut you off when you try to express yourself. And sometimes, too, I find not only for myself, but for other students from different backgrounds, that if they — when they try to explain themselves and if they are not coming across quite clearly or if they don't speak English like the way all Canadians speak, they ahm, they get cut off too. Sometimes people are talking to you and they don't look at you, they look otherwise, you know, and I think that's discrimination.

Interpretive reading of Example 3: insiders speak otherness; speaking otherness from a marginal position

"If they don't speak English the way all Canadians speak ..." is an example of a person, identifying herself as a black person, using the similar logic as we saw in example one: Canadians have normal English; marginal Canadians have non-standard English. This is an example of the reproduction of the essentialist categories falling under our paradigm normal versus other. The student is speaking otherness. A well known response to such talk in many black communities admonishing this reproduction would be "how white of you," thus linking the idea of normal with whiteness and with the perpetuation of dominance in such discourse.

This student expresses how she gets the feeling of being one of perhaps a very few of her people who are admitted. Even though she may be an insider, she is subject to being subordinated, dominated, marginalized and silenced as her experiences illustrate. Yet, even in being critical of such experiences, her language reinforces the otherizing of people who speak non-standard English, which she suggests is not the way "all Canadians speak."

Example 4: white privilege offered as a reason for freedom from dominance

> Interviewer: ... do you find that they help foster maybe a cultural sense of the environment, that you're able to meet your own need? Do you have any problems with any of the faculty?

> Student 4: No, I've never had a problem with that.

> Interviewer: So you've never had a problem where anybody said, you know, who said you can't do such and such and such.

> Student 4: No, I've never had that. I mean, I don't know, you know, I mean, I'm White, I'm very Canadian, kind of thing, I don't — maybe other people might find that to be a problem, but I never had that (unclear).

Interpretive reading of Example 4: "no, I've never had a problem with that ... I'm White, I'm very Canadian"

This student volunteered the idea of whiteness being associated with freedom from some problems. What she does not lament, is that the privilege she gains necessarily implies a logic of disadvantaging for others.

Example 5: being silenced: violation of privacy and confidentiality

> Student 5: Ahm, so she's a little bit like, ahm, biased. So not only for me, she gave, ahm, a hard time to people from other origins as well who are not from her origin. So that was one instance that I could remember.

> Interviewer: Can you give like — expand on it. What did she do?

> Student 5: Ahm, she would probably like say — I told you it's a clinical instructor — so she would probably come and pick on

you in a clinical setting. Or she would probably say — or she would embarrass you in front of people, saying that, ahm, what you did was wrong, or "you should have done that before," but she would never like take you and talk to you privately or individually.

Interviewer: So you find she was only doing it to specific individuals?

Student 5: To specific, yeah, I find that. But then I didn't see that same, ahm, same thing in other instructors, so like (unclear).

Interviewer: So what made you feel that that had to do with culture? Did you kind of see the way she was targeting certain people? Is that what made you think?

Student 5: Yeah. Um-hm so only towards some people ...

Interviewer: You think it has to do with maybe prejudice or racism or?

Student 5: Ahm, I don't know how the difference between like racism and, ahm, you know what I mean? Like it could be a racist and it could be culture, I don't know. But it's — certainly the color difference is there.

Interviewer: So you've seen some students that have complained about some of the preceptors?

Student 5: Yeah.

Interpretive reading of Example 5: silencing practiced by the instructor: public display of monitoring the other

The student talks about an instructor: "... A little bit, ahm, biased. So not only for me, she gave, ahm, a hard time to people from other origins as well who were not from her origin ... she would embarrass you in front of people ... she would like never take you and talk to you privately or individually."

She describes the instructor as not being concerned with her work but with marking people of color as marginal by embarrassing them in a public display.

Like a number of other students, this student's perception is that less care for confidentiality or privacy is taken when reviewing a student's knowledge and practice, if the student happens to be a person of color: "she would embarrass you in front of people."

Notice the student hesitates to resort to the discourse of race, but having been given permission to say what she thinks, she articulates the issue in terms of color: "certainly the color difference is there." This difference is actually in keeping with the suggestion of the previous student, that freedom from admonishment is an expectation of white students, while infringement on autonomy and integrity is reported for persons of color. This duality suggests an ingroup/outgroup dynamic may exist in assigning the privileges of respect, autonomy and integrity to students.

Example 6: containing the borders and maintaining the ingroup/outgroup duality

Interviewer: So you think there is some work that needs to be done in the curriculum?

Student 6: In this city in a big way, yeah. I had that experience last term in (names place). I mean I didn't have to open my mouth and it's already — somebody was — well you see, I was on the receiving end of another, of a kind of, ahm, kind of a discrimination and I hadn't even opened my mouth; but I walk in with my nice little white face and automatically I'm receiving this, ahm well, discriminate against me and I haven't even done anything yet. I'm labeled already, right. That is — so it's a two-part process here, I don't know how you go about that one, but —

Interviewer: And how do you think students can be helped to deal with situations —

Student 6: I think they have to be perhaps, ahm, discrimination isn't just — it's definitely a two-way stress. And it's not even discrimination, it's misunderstandings a lot of times but it's a two-way street and I mean it exists in everybody ...

Interviewer: Right. You think it's a hush-hush type of issue where people kind of keep it to themselves and they don't really like to share it as a group and deal with it?

Student 6: No, I did actually, in an informal way of speaking in a class of Chinese students and they were talking to me about their experiences being what my convention was and I turned it around and told them about mine being virtually labeled to being. So it's kind of strange, 'cause they're being, I mean I've been — my family's been in North America since 1785, I mean that's all we are, so I mean I'm kind of a mainstream Canadian and I've never — and I never thought about it as, you know, I mean I just am. And to be discriminated or feeling that reverse was quite different...

Interviewer: Okay. Now if you had a problem with say, you felt the teacher was really unfair for some reason, you weren't sure why, do you feel that you've enough support within the Faculty to go and talk to somebody about this?

Student 6: The situation has never arisen. Ah, well I would use my chain of command, yeah. (laughs) Wouldn't have a problem.

Interpretive reading of Example 6: "I would use my chain of command"

Student: "Kind of discrimination ... I haven't done anything yet. I'm labeled already ..." My family has been in North America since 1785 ... Ah, well I would use my chain of command ..."

The congregation of numerous others in a group appears to be a threatening situation for preserving white privilege and dominance. The student provides no evidence of the others feeling the tension or threat that she clearly felt. It is unclear what was done to her to "be discriminated." It does seem apparent that she intervened: "I turned it around and told them about mine being virtually labeled to being."

"Feeling that reverse was quite different" indicates a past tense so her intervention apparently worked to make the situation normal. The rule of the 'settlers of Canada have priority' seems to be in place. Her "chain of command" is intact. The problem of the majority of others versus the minority of whites has been contained. The others will not take control and perpetrate 'reverse' racism. It is worth nothing that "feeling that reverse" was not constructed as an experience providing insight and empathy, but as an occasion for challenge and resistance.

Van Dijk comments on the discourse of reverse discrimination as one of resisting the knowledge that there exists a hierarchy of power and the face to face tension is likely to acknowledge the continued, unchallenged, unaccountable dominance in decision making by the white group where there is only token input from minorities in all the major institutions in western society (van Dijk, 1993a,b). Nursing being a microcosm of society, would be expected to reproduce the relations of dominance where the white students feel they have access to decision making to take care of their own interests, and others while not barred, would experience barriers. We turn now to present some examples of minority students' perceptions of barriers in addressing their interest with preceptors or faculty where racism is not seen as an issue, therefore is not on the agenda for discussion.

Example 7: the problem of the denial of racism

Student 7: You know, that's the major problem I've had with this faculty, is they will tell you all these wonderful things of what's gonna happen when you get out into the work force or things to expect and it's not — doesn't seem anywhere close to what you actually get; and nobody talks about the victim blaming that goes on, nobody really addresses the racism that you might encounter, nobody addresses any of the issues, from other professionals.

Interviewer: So it doesn't really seem to be in touch with reality?

Student 7: No. It doesn't. It doesn't ... It doesn't seem that we — even in clinical groups, it doesn't seem there's ever an instance where you really feel comfortable to talk about those kind of issues. Or talk about issues where you believe that there might be a nurse that may be racist and I'd just like hear about because I don't really feel — and I don't think myself would ever feel comfortable to bring that up in a clinical group. It would be a difficult thing. Because I mean to — to suspect that somebody is like that is hard enough, because you can't really prove it. But to also bring it up that this is your feeling, I mean it would be so hard. And I don't know myself I don't think I would bring it up to a faculty (unclear).

Interviewer: Why do you think it would be hard? Like what's your sense and why? Is it because — ?

Student 7: Well you — for me — it'd be hard because you don't know what kind of interaction the instructor and that particular nurse would have and you don't know how that's gonna affect

your practice when you go in. I think that's my main — no matter
kind of — even if it's racism or it's just that you don't get along,
there's always a sense that well she goes back to my instructor,
you know, what's gonna be said and how this person will treat
me when I get back into the —

Interviewer: So that fear of retaliation?

Student 7: Yeah. And it might not be, it might not be intentional;
like the instructor could go in there with your best interest, but
the person may perceive this as a threat and it will come back
on you in different ways, you know, that's oh yeah, that's been
a — at one point in particular that was a concern.

Interviewer: That was a concern.

Student 7: Yeah.

Interpretive reading of Example 7:
owning the denial of racism

The student says "I don't think I would bring it up to a faculty."

The student is indicating an adaptive response to a state of denial about
the relevance or importance of the issue of racism suggesting the environment
may not be safe enough for her to topicalized the issue.

On reflection, we own the fact that our probes were silent about racism.
Our interviewer topicalized only culture in opening up the dialogues. The
issue of racism may have been muffled in such an approach, and the disclosure
of this student would indicate there are many issues to be discussed: for
example, "it might not be intentional; like the instructor could go in there
with your best interest, but the person may perceive this as a threat and it
will come back on you in different ways ..."

We believe that as faculty, we need to care if students are not having
equitable learning experiences and we need to care that health care is not
organized equitably. Dr. Martin Luther King said there is nothing more shocking
or inhumane than injustice in health.

The larger political context of
race relations in Canadian nursing

The ingroup/outgroup phenomena and the denial of racism we report here
is very evident in the larger context of Canadian nursing, where "visible
minorities" (a Census Canada term), have been invisible. For example a

recent publication by the former director of the Nursing Human Resource Data Base for Ontario, on career mobility in nursing (Hiscott, 1998), completely ignores ethnoracial status in nursing. On the cover depicting nurses in varied roles, are white-only faces. This absence of nurses of color is an 'out of sight out of mind' mentality that is curious because of the massive demographic shifts in the last few decades which have impacted on the intake into the profession especially in the large urban centres. A nurse historian recently wrote that responding to diversity has been "a major challenge facing nurses in this century" (MacPherson, 1996, p. 23). This challenge has been partly the denial of racial discrimination and abhorrence toward charges of racism by those in key positions within the profession (Calliste, 1996).

Studies done in Toronto report that visible minority nurses are overrepresented in "lower paid, lower status jobs" in comparison to white nurses and underrepresented in management positions. The Ontario Human Rights Commission found evidence of widespread individual, institutional and systemic racism at the North Western General Hospital confirmed by independent studies by the Doris Marshall Institute (1993) and Arnold Minors and Associates (1993), OHRC (1994). Calliste (1995, pp. 11–12) reports that "in May 1994, seven black nurses won a landmark settlement of $320,000.00. The NWGH also agreed to adopt and implement policies and practices that would transform it into an institution free of racism."

Practices which rely on the essentialist social cognitions and racialist discourse we have been describing were exemplified at the North Western Hospital coming to light during the above mentioned investigation. The Ontario Human Rights Commission found that there was streaming based on racism. White nurses applying for jobs, were asked for their preferred clinical specialty areas. Nurses of color were not asked this and were told that there were openings in long-term care only. This way of organizing the intake reflects a duality of whiteness/otherness: whites can have the privilege of performing in a variety of clinical specialty areas while nurses of color as a group warrant denial of this privilege and can be streamed, subordinated, managed, in short, taken advantage of.

Out of the experiences of nurses filing grievances and complaints alleging racism, grew the Coalition for Black Nurses linking with the Congress of Black Women of Canada, the Black Action Defense Committee, Black Women for Progress, the Coalition of Visible Minority Women of Ontario (Inc.) in coalition with the National Action Committee on the Status of Women. Other organizations have rallied support for grieving visible minority nurses, such as Nurses and Friends Against Discrimination, Ontario Association of Black Health Care Providers and the Culture Care Nursing Interest Group. The first author is the co-chair of the Culture Care Nursing Research Council of the latter group.

The attitude of denial of the problem of racism in health care employment and delivery is captured in the phrase, "minority problems do not exist here." People of color who get caught in the effects of white/other organizing concepts or blueprints for management, are actually blamed for bringing attention to the issue. They become the problem. As Essed (1991) points out in her study, marginalization, problematization, and containment are the main effects of racialist society cognitions and discourse. The containment efforts are related to trying to manage the problems constructed by management in the first place, in the problematization phase, although as we have seen, containment is also a general tendency in managing the other.

What is missing in these responses of denial, is explicit accountability for racialist practices. This accountability should be written into anti-harassment policies, curriculum guidelines, human resource audits, statements of eligibility for accreditation, faculty calendars, etc. Such policy implementation can begin opening up the normalization of accountability for equity, the promotion of choices of those currently marginalized, the freedom from containment and problematization of those currently segmented off as 'other', the acceptability of discussing issues and conducting constructive problem solving and so on.

In the Canadian province of Ontario, the nursing regulatory body is currently implementing standards for cultural sensitivity in practice. Many nurses of color fear this tool will be used to harass them as it does not address their plight of being constructed as other, different, marginalized, problematized, excluded and contained.

An explication of the underlying values practiced in the enactment of the white/other paradigm

We already presented the dualities of dominance/subordination, normality/marginalization, privilege/disadvantage, voicing/silence, freedom/restriction, access to correct means/lacking correct means and, finally, order/disorder. This last set of oppositions we believe is pivotal in the reproduction of the ideology and the persistence of the practices which emanate from these social cognitions.

However, stronger than mere passive reproduction of otherness, is the promotion of images of threat. Hall et al. (1978, pp. 46–48) discuss this problem and note that the media continually reproduce images of threat or danger in relation to those with African heritage. Canada has absorbed the British ideas of European imperialism and this set of practices holds so that immigrants who are not from Europe carry an image of risk, authorizing maltreatment with no accountability. We have seen for example this xenophobic pattern in the incarceration of Canadians of Japanese ancestry during the Second World War, confiscating their property and not returning it to them when the war was over. Canadians of German ancestry while not having a happy time, experienced no such abuse. The charge of threat, together with the suspension of property rights consistently experienced by first nations people, was applied to non-European *others.*

Bringing the discussion back to the lived curriculum as we have reported it, we see a microcosm of the larger society and its values. Practices are going to reflect widespread language use which normalizes essential categories and assigns positive or negative values, justifying advantage as well as dominance and disadvantage, reproducing ingroup/outgroup patterns through the practices of marginalization, exclusion, and the ready contingency perogative of problematization and containment of *others.* The production of an image of risk authorizes mistreatment as a management strategy when labour or resource contingencies require conserving privileges for the whiteness camp by operationalizing the concept of otherness.

Summary of conclusions

We have presented an overview of a research project that was interested in establishing a baseline of qualitative research, and then developing a tool for implementing and evaluating antiracism programming. We found discomfort within the faculty during the course of our research and have since dropped the idea of measuring change, but are planning instead to simply proceed with faculty development workshops inviting shifts within our institution, profession and personal life, toward equity. We are nevertheless going forward with the tool development.

We presented a synthesis of theory and method for reading and interpreting discourse in order to make racialist talk or text, see-able. We applied this approach to analyze discourse in transcripts of interviews and focus groups of undergraduate students. We selected segments of discourse from the entire corpus to capture students' speech that would highlight the effects of racism and begin to make racialist discourse see-able. One of our techniques was to juxtapose one transcript after another, thereby illuminating the different perspectives of students who volunteered information about being privileged related to their being white versus students who linked their marginalization or other detrimental treatment with their identity as someone who doesn't fit the dominant norm. We indicated the dominant paradigm as that of whiteness/otherness which segments groupings into ingroup/outgroup. We used transcripts to show how the reality of ingroup versus outgroup is activated and conveyed by students' and instructors' use of language.

We indicated there is denial of racism in the profession, despite widely publicized grievances, law suits and rallies organized by various professional support groups. Such denial is reflected in a curriculum that doesn't support either theory about racialist phenomena or the open discussion of issues that may come up clinically and has no commitment to ensuring that all graduates have some understanding of these phenomena. We also acknowledged that our research probes reflected some denial of racism, too.

We tried to speculate on how the white/other paradigm remains so entrenched in the everyday practices of people engaging in nursing. We pointed to the characteristic of maintaining order and the propensity for risk ideation (xenophobia) about particular groups to reinforce the perception of order.

Such logic accommodates the irrational questioning of a student about her accent or publicly embarrassing a student in reviewing course content. By contrast, a number of students volunteered the explanation of their privilege as being related to their whiteness or the way they spoke English.

We did not set out to divide the sample into white versus people of color, because we noted that the ideology whiteness/otherness can be used or critiqued, independently of skin color. Such essentialist categorizations are hidden in the perpetuation of inequality, and need to be named, reflected upon and bracketed in the new agenda of bringing about accountability for racialized disadvantaging. The goal of making racism and its effects see-able is to further equity in health professions, in health and in society.

Acknowledgments

For supportive commentary for our work: Evelyn Brody, Pushpa Butani, Gail Donner, Ruth Gallop, Kate Hardie, Diane Irvine, Pamela Khan, Hilary Lewellyn-Thomas, Souraya Sidani, Rani Srivastava, Jane Turrittin. For able assistance: Noreen Choudhry, Julia Kim.

References

Burrows, A., 1983. "Patient-centred nursing care in a multiracial society." The relevance of ethnographic perspectives in nursing curricula. *J. Adv. Nurs.* 8 (6), 477–485.

Calliste, A., 1995. End the silence on racism in health care. Build a movement against discrimination, harassment and reprisals. Canadian Congress of Black Women Conference Report. A conference for black nurses and other health care workers. Ontario Institute for Studies in Education. Toronto, Ontario, May 25–26.

——, 1996. "Antiracism organizing and resistance in nursing: African Canadian women." *Can. Rev. Soc. Anth./RCSA* 33 (3), 362–390.

Doris Marshall Institute (DMI), Arnold Minors and Associates (AMA), 1993. Ethno-racial Equality: A Distant Goal.

Essed, P., 1991. Understanding everyday racism: an interdisciplinary theory. Sage Publications, London.

Faculty of Nursing, 1997. Calendar, 1996-1997. University of Toronto.

Fanon, F., 1961. Black Skin, White Masks. Grove Press, New York.

Frankenberg, R., 1993. The Social Construction of Whiteness: White Women, Race Matters. University of Minnesota Press, Minneapolis.

Hagey, R., Turrittin, J., Collins, E. (in preparation). Experiences of women of colour in the context of professional nursing: cosmopolitan citizenship or democratic racism?

Hall, S., Critcher, C., Jefferson, T., Clarke, J., Roberts, B., 1978. Policing the Crisis: Mugging, the State, and Law and Order. Macmillan, London.

Hall, S., 1982. "The whites of their eyes: racist ideologies and the media." In: Bridges, G., Brundt, R. (Eds.), Silver Linings: Some Strategies for the Eighties. Lawrence and Wishart, London.

Henry, F., Tator, C., Mattis, W., Rees, T., 1995. The Colour of Democracy: Racism in Canadian Society. Harcourt Brace & Co, Toronto, Canada.

Hiscott, R.D., 1998. Career Paths of Nursing Professionals. Carleton University Press, Ottawa.

Joint Policy and Planning Committee of the Ontario Hospital Association and the Ministry of Health, 1995. Draft antiracism policy guidelines. Toronto.

Lazarre, J., 1996. Beyond the Whiteness of Whiteness: Memoir of a White Mother of Black Sons. Duke University Press, Durham and London.

McPherson, K., 1996. Bedside Matters: The Transformation of Canadian Nursing, 1900–1990. Oxford University Press, Don Mills.

Ontario Human Rights Commission (OHRC), 1994, Minutes of Settlement.

Papadopoulos, I., Tilki, M., Alleyne, J., 1994. "Transcultural nursing and nurse education." Br. J. Nurs. 3 (11), 583–586.

Smith, B.E., Colling, K., Elander, E., Latham, C., 1993. "A model for multicultural curriculum development in baccalaureate nursing education." J. Nurs. Ed. 32 (5).

Spitzer, A., Kesselring, A., Ravid, C., Tamir, B., Granot, M., Noam, R., 1996. "Learning about another culture: project and curricular reflections." J. Nurs. Ed. 35 (7), 322.

Thorne, S., Reimer, Kirkham, S., MacDonald-Emes, J., 1997. Focus on qualitative methods: interpretive description: a non-categorical qualitative alternative for developing nursing knowledge. Res. Nurs. Health 20, 169–177.

Van Dijk, T., 1993b. "Analyzing racism through discourse analysis: some methodological reflections." In: Stanfield II, J.H., Dennis, R.M. (Eds.), Race and Ethnicity in Research Methods. Sage Publications, Newbury Park, CA, pp. 92–134.

——, 1993a. Elite Discourse and Racism. Sage Publications, Newbury Park.

——, 1998. Ideology: a Multidisciplinary Approach. Cromwell Press, Trowbridge.

Woodward, K., 1997. "Concept of identity and difference." In: Woodward, K. (Ed), Identity and Difference. Sage Publications, One Thousand Oaks.

Yoshida, M., 1994. The integration of cultural content into an undergraduate nursing curriculum: a model at the University of Toronto. In: Educating professionals for diversity, Report of the Committee for Intercultural and Interracial Education of Professionals. Toronto.

Section Two

PROFESSIONAL WORK SPACES

Chapter Four

Teaching Against the Grain: Contradictions and Possibilities

Roxana Ng

I began this chapter with the notion of writing about anti-racist and anti-sexist education from a critical pedagogy perspective. As my thinking developed, however, I found myself turning to my own and other minority teachers' teaching experiences in postsecondary educational settings and our trials and tribulations in implementing alternative classroom practices that are both contradictory and exciting. At first, this troubled me; I feared I was getting off topic, especially when the deadline for submitting the first draft of this chapter drew near. But the anguish and desire with which I have been grappling since I began teaching almost ten years ago would no longer be subordinated to professional discipline. So I found myself writing about the contradictions and possibilities of critical teaching in the academy from a rather personal perspective.

As my writing progressed, I turned increasingly to the writings on feminist pedagogy, to other women writers who have spoken of their own pains, trials, and tribulations as teachers attempting to subvert an enterprise that is both oppressive and liberating. It is their writings that have given me the inspiration and courage to write about my experience and to continue the search for alternative ways of thinking, writing, learning, and teaching that have transformative potentials.

Thus, I begin this chapter with a deep gratitude to all the writers whose work I have consulted, to the students and colleagues with whom I have shared my own thinking and earlier drafts of this chapter, and to members of this writing project who have offered encouragement and support for my tentative effort. In particular, I thank Bob Regnier, who was the project's discussant for an earlier version of this chapter, for reminding me that I am indeed on track in terms of the project we undertook. He wrote in his discussion of October 19, 1990, when the contributors of *Anti-Racism, Feminism, and Cultural Approaches to Education* congregated to discuss the chapter manuscripts:

> You offer a way to grieve and lament the limitations and contradictions in our pedagogies without carrying them as guilt. Your example, of acknowledging "the pains, the trials and tribulations" of yourself as a critical pedagogue ... centres consideration about the critical pedagogue as "subject." You expose the heart of commitments that critical pedagogues often write about in abstract terms even though they feel them deeply and personally. At the same time, you reveal the personal tentativeness, vulnerability, uncertainty and contradictions of searching and re-searching for a way of teaching that is truly emancipatory.

Introduction: Concepts And Method

This chapter unfolds, then, as an exploration into the contradictions and possibilities of critical teaching from the standpoint of the minority teacher. I am using the term "minority" in its standard sociological usage; it refers to people who are relatively powerless in the hierarchy of power and authority. Thus, although women as a group and blacks in South Africa are numerically the majority, in power terms they are minorities. As I am both a woman and an ethnic minority (i.e., nonwhite, non-British in Canada), I use the term "minority teacher" to refer to both minority statuses. The term "minority," then, is applied broadly to members of subordinate groups vis-à-vis the dominant group, and includes women and ethnic and racial minorities.

I am using the term "critical teaching" to include the discourses that question and challenge existing knowledge base and power relations. These discourses include critical pedagogy, anti-racist education, and feminist pedagogy. I make no claim here to provide a systematic review of these burgeoning bodies of work. Throughout this chapter, I draw on writings in the literature to throw light on and guide my own pedagogical beliefs and practices.

Although it is true that each of these discourses is substantively different and ridden with internal debates, one common feature is that they are all concerned with power and inequality. In the words of Peter McLaren, a major proponent of critical pedagogy, critical theorists "begin with the premise that men and women [and I would add people belonging to ethnic and racial minority groups] are essentially unfree and inhabit a world rife with contradictions and asymmetries of power and privilege" (McLaren, 1989: 166).[1]

Barbara Thomas, in spelling out the differences between multicultural and anti-racist education,[2] also points out that the recognition of unequal power between groups is the salient feature of anti-racist education. She writes:

> Anti-racist education posits that diversity *per se* is not the problem. ... It is the significance that is attached to the differences, and more importantly, the way that differences are used to justify unequal treatment that is the problem — i.e. racism. It is unequal power that limits the dimensions of one's ability to earn a living, meet basic needs, make one's voice heard. It is unequal power that makes the struggle for self-respect ... a formidable task. (Thomas, 1987:105)

Certainly, feminist pedagogy, growing out of feminist theory and women's studies, begins with the premise that men and women are unequal and have differential access to power structures. This has led to a distortion in the construction of knowledge itself, so that what counts as knowledge as much of what we learn is the formal educational process are one-sided and biased.[3]

Thus, one of the major aims of these critical approaches to education, diverse though they are, is to develop critical consciousness among the students/learners and to empower them (for example by reducing the power differential between teachers and students, or by involving students in curriculum development). The long-term goal implicit in these pedagogical approaches is the belief that democratizing the classroom and empowering students will lead to changes in structures of inequality. Jargon such as "emancipatory teaching," "student empowerment," "pedagogy for radical democracy," and so on are the leading principles of critical teaching.[4]

The assumption is that critical teaching is by definition subversive. The role of the critical teacher is to bring into sharp relief the historical inequalities that have been entrenched in social structures and to facilitate the radicalization of students. With the exception of feminist pedagogy, the power differential between the teacher and students is rarely problematized. While the literature on feminist pedagogy is attentive to issues of power, there is a tendency to treat power differential as existing merely between teachers and students.[5] There is little examination of power as a dynamic relation that permeates classroom interactions. In exploring the contradictions of critical teaching, I wish to examine the way in which power, embodied in and enacted by all participants in educational settings, operates to sustain existing forms of inequality, in order to discover how to alter these relations. I will discuss how "power" is conceptualized next.

On Power and Authority

In sociology, power is viewed frequently in macro terms, as a property of social structures and institutions. For example, the police have the power and authority to charge and arrest people who are seen to be breaking the law; policemen are empowered by law to keep order and arrest those deemed to be disrupting the social order. Men have power over women by virtue of their control over major societal institutions and structures. This is a common way to understand power sociologically.

Here, I want to put forward the notion of power as a dynamic relation that is enacted in interactions. My understanding is derived from theorization and empirical investigations in interpretive sociology, beginning with the work of Weber and more recently in ethnomethodology.[6]

In particular, Pamela Fishman's analysis of conversations between intimate couples illustrates succinctly how unequal power between women and men is enacted, established, and maintained in interactional settings. In her study, Fishman analyzed the conversational patterns and strategies of five heterosexual couples by tape-recording their conversations in their homes. The couples had the right to turn off the tape recorder or edit out conversations as they liked. On the whole, Fishman felt that the tape recordings represented conversations that occurred in natural settings. In analyzing these mundane conversations, she found marked differences in women's and men's conversational strategies and patterns. Men tended to make more statements and control the topics of conversations. Women tended to support conversations by using minimal responses such as "hmm," whereas men used such responses to end conversations. In conclusion, Fishman argued that gender relations are not givens; they are negotiated on an ongoing basis (Fisherman,1978). Her analyses, as well as those of other researchers, demonstrate that power and hierarchical relations are not abstract forces operating on people. Power is a human accomplishment, situated in everyday interaction; thus, both structural forces and interactional activities are vital to the maintenance and construction of social reality.

It is this notion of power as a dynamic relation, which is negotiated continuously in interactional settings, that I want to draw attention to here. I am making a distinction between "authority" and "power." In the context of this chapter, "power," however derived, is a more individual property which is subject to negotiation interactionally. "Authority," on the other hand, is formal power granted to individuals through institutional structures and relations. Thus, the police have legal authority to take certain courses of action. Teachers have authority over students as a consequence of their ascribed role in the educational system. But in an interactional setting, this authority can be challenged by those without formal power.

On Commonsense Sexism and Racism

In addition, I want to explicate how sexism and racism, as relations of domination and subordination that have developed over time and saturate all interactional contexts, are operative in educational settings. I use the term "commonsense sexism and racism" to refer to those unintentional and unconscious acts that result in the silencing, exclusion, subordination, and exploitation of minority group members — that is, what people generally refer to as sexist and racist attitudes. In an earlier work, I argued and showed that gender, race, and class are relations, not just analytical categories that are sutured[7] into the development of Canada as a nation; activities such as the building of the railway for the nation's westward expansion, exploiting Chinese men through a system of indentured labor, and at the same time forbidding the immigration of Chinese women constitute an example of the conjunction of race, gender, and class in nation building (Ng, 1989).

It is through the process of colonization and nation building that we see how racism and sexism became crystallized as systems of domination and subordination. In this chapter, as in my earlier writings, I want to get away from the notion that sexism and racism are merely products of individuals' attitudes (of course they cannot be separated from people's attitudes) by emphasizing that they are systems of oppression giving rise to structural inequality over time. Indeed, certain norms and forms of action are so entrenched that they have become the "normal" and taken-for-granted ways of doing things. Pamela Fishman's story, quoted above, can be seen as an example of how commonsense sexism operates, when men unconsciously and automatically control and direct topics of conversations. The other side of the coin is that women, all too often, actively perpetuate their own subordination by not only deferring to men, but actually doing the work of supporting conversations in which their centrality is minimized.

Himani Bannerji (1987) was among the first Canadian writers to introduce the concept of "commonsense racism." The term "common sense," used in the everyday vernacular, denotes ordinary good sense. The present usage is derived from Gramsci's work, and refers to the incoherent and at times contradictory assumptions and beliefs held by the mass of population (see Sasson, 1982:13). Commonsense racism and sexism can refer to the norms and forms of action that have become ordinary ways of doing things of which people have little consciousness, so that certain things, to use Bannerji's term, "disappear from the social surface" (Bannerji, 1987:11). Sexism and racism *are* normal ways of seeing, thinking, and acting.[8]

I want to add that if we treat sexism and racism as commonsense features of the world (in the way in which I use the term, following Gramsci and others), then we can see that none of us are immune to or separated from these features of society. Educationally, it is the responsibility of critical teachers to begin to explicate them, so that we can confront our own racism and sexism, and to work towards eradicating them in all spheres of social life.

Methodological Issues

In addition to making use of secondary sources, this chapter includes my own teaching experience in a university setting over the past ten years, especially my experience in the last five years teaching in a graduate school of education. Putting my commitment to democratic pedagogy into practice, I have always experimented with unorthodox teaching techniques. Since 1989, when I asked students to keep a journal on their own progress in an advanced graduate seminar, Feminist Theory and Methodology, I began to record my own and the students' responses in this and other classes. These records enter in various ways into the writing of this chapter, as data, reflections, and analytical remarks.

As well, I am including as data anecdotal remarks I collected over the years. While the use of anecdotes is not normally accorded scientific status in scholarly writings, I am advocating their use in explicating the taken-for-granted features of everyday life — in explicating commonsense sexism and racism. These mundane, offhand remarks are used to illustrate how power is enacted interactionally and how commonsense sexism and racism operate as part of the relations that constitute our educational experience. That is, rather than dismissing them as anecdotal, they are treated as essential features of a larger social organization. My assumption is that analyzing them will tell us something about the social organization in which these remarks are embedded. This is similar to the way in which Dorothy Smith treats individual experience:

> If you've located an individual experience in the social relations which determine it, then although that individual experience might be idiosyncratic, the social relations are not idiosyncratic. [All experiences] are generated out of, and are aspects of the social relations of our time, of corporate capitalism. These social relations are discernible, although not fully present or explicable, in the experiences of people whose lives, by reason of their membership in a capitalist society, are organized by capitalism. (Campbell, n.d.)[9]

In this chapter, I write as a teacher — as a middle-class woman and a member of the intelligentsia with some authority and privileges; as a woman of color who is marginal in the overall system of authority and privilege; as a social scientist who is supposed to be rational, analytical, and detached; and as a sensuous, living individual (to borrow Marx's phrase) who has emotions and feelings. These positions and identities do not sit well together. They give rise to contradictions and dilemmas that I, and every human being in her or his multiple locations and subjectivities, experience and must deal with continuously. It is nevertheless in these contradictions that I exist, and therefore think, speak, and write.

In writing this chapter, therefore, I do away with the false notion that the knower/writer can be "objective," as is commonly assumed in social scientific writing, that she can occupy a position that transcends all viewpoints. I attempt to preserve the knower/writer as an active subject in the text, grappling with her own multiple locations and contradictions. I believe that it is in confronting these contradictions and dilemmas that all of us may come to grips with what haunts us and propels us to work towards a better world. As Cynthia Cockburn writes: "It is precisely out of the process of bringing such contradictions to consciousness and facing up to illogicality or inconsistency, that a person takes a grip on his or her own fate. Politically, it is of vital importance that we understand how we change" (Cockburn, 1983:13).

Power and Authority:
Contradictions for the Minority Teacher

Although there has been an increasing recognition among progressive academics, including critical teachers, to assert the importance of gender, race, and class in social analyses, in actual fact how relations of gender, race and class operate in educational settings remains unexplicated. In this section, I will explore how commonsense sexism and racism penetrate the power dynamics between minority teachers and students.

In the discourses of critical teaching, feminists are among the first educators to describe and analyze problems encountered by female teachers in the classroom. Based on her own teaching experience, Friedman observes: "Any kind of authority is incompatible with the feminine" (Friedman, 1985:206). This sexist and patriarchal assumption denies the woman teacher her right to speak as a figure of authority. "To be 'woman,' she has no authority to think; to think, she has made herself 'masculine' at the cost of her womanhood" (ibid.:206). The fact that female professors are sometimes addressed as "Mrs.," rather than "Professor" or "Dr." like their male counterparts, is an example of the denial of female teachers' authority at a superficial but telling level.[10]

To be a woman and a university teacher, one's power and authority are undermined constantly by existing gender relations that operate in society at large. In examining ninety-four student evaluations she received from a sociology course, Susan Heald found that only three mentioned content on women and feminist issues as positive. Most students considered her approach problematic and the issues she raised digressing from the formal curriculum: "A slightly opinionated personality emerged on feminist issues which is all right but sometimes took the topic under discussion astray. Perhaps a less biased approach to certain issues. I feel her feminist attitudes, at times, interfered with the understanding of some course content" (Heald, 1989:23).

A feminist perspective, then, is seen to be biased knowledge, vis-à-vis pure knowledge. Teaching from this critical perspective further undermines the credibility of a female teacher. Interestingly, the positive qualities of Heald's classroom, such as students having space to voice their opinions, small group discussions, and cooperative learning, were not treated by the students as part of her pedagogical approach. Rather, they were seen to be features of her personality. If a teacher is female and/or a member of a racial minority and engages in critical teaching, she is in a position of double jeopardy.

Minimally, then, sexism manifests itself in the classroom in terms of students' challenge to the female teacher's authority and credibility. More endemically, women's presence in institutions of higher learning is met with overt hostility. This hostility manifests itself in minor incidents such as sexist jokes and graffiti, traumatic events (for women) such as campus rapes, and the shattering tragedy of the Montreal massacre in the fall of 1990.[11] The following illustration from the *Toronto Star* brings sexism as a systemic property in higher educational institutions into focus:

> An outgoing woman attending a big-city university is unaware that a male classmate has an abnormal interest in her. During a class, she expresses views counter to his idea of how she should feel about the issue being discussed. After class, in front of witnesses, he slams her against a wall, calls her names and verbally abuses her. She complains to the administration, asking that he be charged with assault, but is persuaded that the matter should be handled internally. A conviction, she is told, would perhaps destroy the future of a good student. The university is to make arrangements for the man to continue his education under individual tuition. (Quinn, 1990)

While this example concerns the experience of a female student, female professors' experiences are not drastically different. For example, Sheila McIntyre, a law professor at Queen's University, detailed in a memorandum to her faculty dated July 26, 1986, the hostile incidents directed at her by law students, especially male students. She received no support from her colleagues and the administration until she resigned and took her case to the press and the Canadian Association of University Teachers (CAUT). Even though CAUT took up her case, with the final result that she was offered a tenure-track position at Queen's (as opposed to the two-year term appointed into which she was originally hired), some of her male colleagues both at Queen's and at CAUT felt that she "had jumped the gun" and mishandled the whole situation.[12] The fact that these comments were made and received as being perfectly sensible pinpoints precisely the embeddedness of sexism in our collective consciousness. Her case is not unique, but is an example of what female faculty face as part of their lives on campus.[13]

For a racial minority female teacher, the devaluation of her authority and credibility is compounded by her race and ethnicity. Her presumed inferiority has its roots in the history of the colonization of Canada, which resulted in the vertical mosaic (Porter, 1967), and in the inequality between the developed countries and the Third World as a result of the imperialist expansion of the West. Speaking from my own experience as a Chinese woman, I have frequently been called "cute" by my students and occasionally by colleagues. (Yes, it is meant to be a compliment, but why do I think of Suzie Wong when people say that?)[14] Many comment on my accent, either as practically flawless or as needing improvement. In one university where I taught, a group of female students expressed the concern that my voice (with the accent) was too soft, and therefore the other students laughed at me after class. They wondered whether I could increase my volume or behave more authoritatively (or both). Ironically, I once overheard a comment between two male professors regarding a woman in a sessional appointment who had applied for the tenure-track job in the department. They were not in favor of this candidate because her voice was too strident: "You can hear her all the way down the hall when she is lecturing."

To be a minority teacher in a higher educational institution is to be continuously at risk. The risk increases when minority teachers attempt to instill critical consciousness among the students, as the experience of Susan Heald shows. Over the years of my teaching, I have had students complain both about the content of my courses and my teaching methods. On one occasion, when I taught a course called Cross-Cultural Education, a male student complained to the department chair about the content of my course halfway through the academic year. Although it was clear from the course outline that I had included gender relations as an integral part of cross-cultural education, he maintained that there was no reason why this should be part of the curriculum. He had come to the course wanting to learn about multicultural education and techniques of controlling a multiracial classroom. Instead, he argued that he only received materials on how schooling produced and maintained social inequality. He conducted an analysis of the course contents and concluded that 35 percent of the material dealt with gender (in addition to race) relations; if he added the number of times "women" were mentioned in the lectures, the percentage increased to 50 percent. He felt that he was being shortchanged and demanded that I change the course content or be fired. The department chair supported the student and requested that I change the course halfway through the year, in spite of the fact that this was the only complaint. He did not want the student complaining to the administration, and cautioned me about giving this student a bad grade, in case he appealed his grade. In this example, we see how men collude with other intentionally or unwittingly to assert male dominance (Ng, 1993).

The kinds of experiences reported here are experiences that I and other minority professors encounter on a regular basis. Thus, even when they have been granted formal institutional power, other practices are at work in the university setting that strip minority teachers of their right to speak and act as figures of authority (see Hoodfar, 1992; Ng, 1993). The preceding examples illustrate how commonsense sexism and racism operate to disempower minority professors of the legitimate power they may have earned.

In describing the sexist encounters of female and feminist teachers, I do not mean to suggest that men are the only instigators of these practices. Women, both students and university staff, including secretaries and peers, collude and participate in the denigration of female authority. In other words, women's presumed inferiority and lack of authority are internalized by *both men and women*.

Because gender and racial lines are so clearly drawn in the hierarchy of the academy, in which the power holders and power brokers are primarily white men, minority professors are marginalized even when they have gained entry to the academy. It is no longer curious to me that in some universities where I have taught, female students interested in gender relations and women's studies asked white male professors to supervise their work, while calling upon me to give them references and feedback on a regular basis and to complain about their supervisors. Similarly, I am a member on several thesis committees on minority students who are working in race and ethnic relations (one of my specializations) chaired by my (white) male colleagues, who may be working in other fields altogether. As Friedman observes, women are called upon to play "the role of the all-for-giving, nurturing mother whose approval is unconditional" (Friedman, 1985:206), but they cannot be granted intellectual leadership. And when indeed female professors act in their professorial role, as a number of my senior colleagues do, they are the recipients of intense resentment and hostility from students, ironically including feminist students.

In exploring the experience of feminist academics and how feminist pedagogical discourse informed their practice, Ilona Miner discovered that feminist faculty were subject to excessive criticisms by female students. (She did not interview male students in her study.) For critical teachers, especially feminist teachers, attempts at critical teaching can be acutely painful experiences, as one informant revealed:

> If you are a feminist you are very exposed, particularly because you have to have this moral commitment to the women's movement, and to what feminists share. Therefore the criticisms that students make, they're often made very harshly, and they're often made as though as a teacher you have no insides and they can hurt you as much as they want, and you're not seen as someone who feels pain. It would be nice to see another version of feminist pedagogy that called on students to see that teachers are also human, are also women. ... I think of one or two people here ... who went through absolute fucking hell from groups of feminists, who if you heard them talking you think, yes, ... wonderful, open, free, etc. And then you'd hear the other side of it. You'd see this person in awful pain and in tears, and I don't know how to put those two things together. I think there is some real problem with feminist pedagogy as an orthodoxy. (Miner, 1990:16)

Ironically, Miner found that when male teachers incorporated feminist principles in their classrooms, they got more praise and a warmer reception from female students (Miner, 1990). This is another aspect of commonsense sexism that manifests itself in the classroom.

Thus, a major contradiction for minority teachers implementing critical teaching is that as they attempt to humanize the classroom, as figures of authority, their own humanity is taken away. There is a fundamental tension in the notion of empowerment: as they attempt to empower students, minority teachers are disempowered.

In the next section, I explore the power professors, including minority professors, do have over students, and the contradictions for critical reaching therein.

Institutional Power and Student Resistance

Minority status notwithstanding, professors do possess real authority over students conferred by the institutional structure(s) of which they are a part. One of the major criticisms by Elizabeth Ellsworth of theories of critical pedagogy is that they have left this fundamental power relation between teacher and student unproblematized (Ellsworth, 1989). While the literature on anti-racist education tells of the silencing of minority students, it does not address this power issue directly. Again, it is feminist teachers who have undertaken to explore this tension, perhaps because their own marginality in the power structure is such a poignant part of their work process. Thus, Barbara Roberts writes: "I personally think that such a relation [between professor and student] is inherently abusive, and that exercising this type of power over another person is by definition abusive, even if not *done* abusively (emphasis in the original) (Roberts, 1988:3). In exploring the paradox of the feminist professor as a "bearded mother" (Morgan, 1988), Kathryn Morgan writes, "If the feminist teacher actively assumes any of the forms of power available to her — expert, reward, legitimate, maternal/referent — she eliminates the possibility of educational democracy in the feminist classroom" (Morgan, 1988:50).[15]

Their views paint a pretty grim picture of the possibility of critical teaching; indeed, they suggest the impossibility of education as an empowering tool in a patriarchal and hierarchical society. Furthermore, in implying that the adoption of any form of power by women professors is oppressive and potentially abusive to students, they unwittingly deny women the right to be experts and intellectual leaders, in much the same way that students deny minority teachers these rights (see Friedman, 1985). However, I do think that they point out an important issue for the critical teacher to explore, and that is that institutional authority *is* an embodied and oppressive feature in a pedagogical setting *regardless of the intention of the teacher.* These analysts point the way for examining how commonsense sexism and racism enter our consciousness and practice in insidious ways. Here, I wish to explore two ways in which commonsense sexism and racism operated in the classroom.

First, professors do have control over the forms and content of knowledge, a control they take completely for granted, irrespective of their own race and gender. This authority is conferred by their formal position in the class structure and the hierarchy of the academy. It is part of the institutional relation into which we enter and over which we have some, but never total, control. We can be more or less open about student input, but we cannot go into the class without a course outline and have the students design it. This is especially true for those of us in marginal positions (e.g., part-time, sessional, untenured position) in the university hierarchy.[16]

More fundamentally, the learning environment in postsecondary institutions is organized in such a way that the student must learn whatever the course offers and "*display* what she has learned, *that* she has learned" (emphasis in the original) (Roberts, 1988:5) to the teacher. Roberts points out correctly that this is the basic contradiction of feminist, and I would add other, forms of critical teaching. I want to underscore that this is an institutional feature of the work process of teaching, and not an attribute of individuals.

The crucial point is not deny the existence of such constraint(s) and assume that somehow, with good intentions and skills, the critical teacher can reverse this process and turn the classroom into a democratic place (as theorists of various forms of critical pedagogies, including Kathryn Morgan imply). The university classroom is *not*, by definition, a democratic place. To pretend it can be is to deny that hierarchy and institutional power exist. It is to delude ourselves that democracy and empowerment can be achieved by goodwill alone. I will explore the possibility of working within the constraints of institutional power later.

Second, and more insidious, what we know how to do well, that is teach students how to construct rational arguments and conduct objective analyses, is also shot through with gender, racial, and class subtexts. In her critique of critical pedagogy, Elizabeth Ellsworth insightfully points out that forms of rational thinking and arguing, with we develop and refine through the educational process, are already racist and sexist because they set up as opposite an irrational "Other" (Ellsworth, 1989:301; see also de Beauvoir, 1952).

Another realm in which people's taken-for-granted assumptions operate at a completely spontaneous level is through the routine accomplishment of classroom interactions. Similar to the way in which minority teachers' authority is routinely challenged in the classroom, teachers also enforce their authority by controlling topics and forms of discussion. It is in analyzing interactional, including conversational, strategies that we begin to unpack the depth of commonsense sexism and racism.

Examining interactions between professors and students in a feminist classroom by means of conversational analysis, Stockwood (1990), writing from the position of a student, describes how feminist professors exercise their authority to control topics of discussion. In the documented case, the professor used interruptions and questioning, among other strategies, to curtail disagreements and redirect the topic(s) of discussion. But this is not a game played by the professor alone. Students reinforce their own subordinate position by *allowing* themselves to be interrupted or by using comments such as "I don't know" to soften potential confrontation and disagreement and disagreement between themselves and the professor. Analyzing a segment of the dialogue between herself and the professor, Stockwood writes:

> What is interesting is that I was, in my mind, very clear about my position, a position that I would not have retreated from under different circumstances where I felt an equal in the discussion. I was, in effect, structuring talk in order to elicit agreement from the professor. What is also interesting is that I chose not to, or was unable

to[,] articulate my position. Somehow the location of the professor as judge, tutor, critic, and evaluator of the students' scholastic abilities set up a relationship between us that was not only locally produced through talk, but also extra-locally managed through the normative requirements regulating teacher-student interaction. ... While the professor was speaking, I chose not to self-select a turn to talk to rectify the understanding [between herself and the professor] even though I could have theoretically regained the floor by ... an interruption, or by introducing a repair at the next available transition-relevancy place. ... I felt it was inappropriate to interrupt the professor. Given the public nature of the dialogue and my own preconceived notions that the professor's right to the floor ultimately takes precedence over mine, I did not attempt to interject at the next available transition-relevancy place, rather I waited until the professor clearly signalled turn completion. My waiting, based on my interpretation, serves to illustrate how I effectively contributed to reinforcing dominant-subordinate relations. (Stockwood, 1990:11, 12–13)

Stockwood's analysis shows clearly that power is a relation that has to be negotiated continuously in the classroom between teacher and students. Professors, including feminist teachers, use a number of dialogic strategies to assert the authority conferred on them by the institution. Students participate by either cooperating with the professor, as the above example shows, or refusing to grant her such authority by confrontational and other strategies.

For those of us who have taught undergraduate classes, especially first-year classes, we are well aware of the tactics used to disrupt the classroom dynamic and challenge teacher authority. These tactics include chattering among classmates, passing notes, and creating other disturbances that disrupt the flow of the lesson, not to mention direct confrontation by questioning and forcefully disagreeing with the professor in change. Ultimately, in most situations, the professor's authority prevails due to the position she occupies in the educational hierarchy vis-à-vis the student. While she has formal authority in the classroom, her *power* is subject to challenge. In the case of the minority teacher, her power is challenged more, due to the marginal position occupied by minority groups in the society at large.[17]

In addition to interactional strategies that professors employ consciously to assert their authority in the classroom, sexism and racism operate at a more subliminal level. Since I know of no study of classroom interactions in the university setting with regard to the professor and students based on racial differences, I make use of the work by Sara Michaels on a Grade 1 classroom as an illustration (Michaels, 1986).

Michaels's study focuses on discursive patterns of a racially mixed Grade 1 classroom with half white and half black students. By tape-recording an activity called "sharing time" and conducting classroom ethnography, Michaels discerned two distinct intonation patterns and discourse styles among the black and white students. She noticed that the white students' discourse style tended to be topic centered. That is, the discourse was tightly organized, centering on a single topic or series of closely related topics, "with thematic development accomplished through lexical cohesion, and a linear ordering of events, leading quickly to a punch line resolution" (Michaels, 1986:102). By contrast, black students tended to use a topic-associating style. That is, their narrative pattern consisted of a series of segments or episodes that were implicitly linked in highlighting some person or theme (Michaels, 1986:103). Michaels further noted that Mrs. Jones, the teacher, who was presumable white, was much more successful at picking up on the white students' topics, interjecting at the right moment with questions to help the student develop the theme of his or her narrative. She was less successful at picking up on the black students' stories. In fact, she often mistimed her question and interrupted the child in midclause.

> Moreover, the teacher appeared to have difficulty discerning the topic of discourse and anticipating the direction of thematic development. As a results, her questions were often thematically inappropriate and seemed to throw the child off-balance, interrupting his or her train of thought. In cases where the child continued to talk, undaunted, these turns were often cut short by the teacher, who jokingly referred to them as "filibusters" on occasion. (Michaels, 1986:108)[18]

From a liberal perspective, this kind of situation can be interpreted as a problem in cross-cultural communication. More seriously, from the vantage point of critical teaching, we must recognize and acknowledge that this is how students are silenced in the classroom. This example show how the teacher acts unconsciously to reinforce the subordination of black children, and as such constitutes and instance of how commonsense racism operates internationally.

In their reflective paper on their respective experiences as student and professor in a graduate seminar, Magda Lewis and Roger Simon unpacked how the silencing of female students occurred in spite of the intention of the male professor (Lewis & Simon, 1986). With regard to my own teaching experiences, the following incident is telling:

This story concerns a course called Gender Stereotyping that I offered to a group of student teachers around 1985. In an attempt to show how gender hierarchy was routinely established, I used the study by Pamela Fishman of intimate heterosexual couples described previously.

The Fishman study is one of my favorite teaching pieces because it is both illuminating and provocative. Students' standard reaction is to discredit the study by saying, "It's not true." Women, they maintain, are the dominant ones because they talk more. I would then ask them to do some empirical research to determine whether indeed Fishman's observation could be corroborated or rejected.

Similar reactions occurred on this occasion among the eight female and two male students in the class. As the discussion and debate ensued, I noticed another dynamic going on in the classroom. The women started to make faces to each other and giggle. When I asked what was going on, they just giggled more, and started to write and pass each other notes. As the class progressed, I became increasingly frustrated and mystified. Finally, when the class concluded, one student, a young woman who was assertive and maintained that she was definitely the more dominant one in her marriage, came and talked to me.

She told me that the female students noticed, as the class proceeded, that I was giving the men more air space. Indeed, I was interrupting the women more than the men, and they felt I was sexist! I was completely stunned by this revelation, and took the next two classes to discuss, in more depth, the embeddedness of gender hierarchy and sexism in our own consciousness. The group also made a pact that they would take responsibility to remind each other and me when such patterns occurred in the future so that we could change not only our ideas, but our practice.

This example pinpoints precisely the insidiousness of racism and sexism, not only in institutional structures but in our individual and collective consciousness as well. It throws light on the contradictions faced by critical teachers. In spite of our theoretical commitment to a pedagogy of empowerment, as human beings we, too, have internalized the power relations that predominate in society. In our everyday activities, the people to whom we defer and over whom we exercise our power and authority are all constitutive and reflective of the patriarchal and racist ordering of the society of which we are a part. We show, not so much through theory, but more significantly through practice, what critical teaching is all about. We, too, participate in the systems of oppression of the very members of society whom we want to empower.

Power Relations Among Students and the Role of the Critical Teacher

There is an additional dimension of power dynamics operative in the classroom that goes beyond the realm of critical teaching, and that is the power relations that exist among students. Again, these relations are in place outside the classroom, and are brought into the classroom by all members who are its constituents. Commonsense sexism and racism, as well as other features that permeate institutions of higher learning, frequently find their liveliest manifestations in the classroom.

In "A Discourse Not Intended for Her: Learning and Teaching within Patriarchy," Magda Lewis wrote eloquently of the silencing that she and other female students experienced in a graduate seminar that explored the relation between language and power (Lewis & Simon, 1986). Roger Simon, as a critical teacher in this seminar setting, attempted to open up space for female students to participate actively and equally in discussion. He used Janice Radway's *Reading the Romance* (1984) as a major text to organize discussions around the relationship between subjectivity and forms of social practice (Lewis & Simon, 1986:463). As the seminar progressed, what emerged was a distinction between the ways that male and female students read the text, and who defined how the text should be treated in the classroom. Increasingly, the women felt unable to participate because the forms of discussion were controlled by the men and their notion of female inferiority. Speaking to each other during class breaks, the women

> uncovered the perspective from which the men in the class discussed Radway's work, ... the subtleties of how they twisted the analysis until the subjects of Radway's study fit the image that was required to sustain the notion of male superiority. We came to understand the oppressive relation within which women become the subjects of male discourse. It became clear that the only difference between us and the women in Radway's study was that as graduate students we lived out and contested the partriarchic social relations under different circumstances. The oppression was no less felt, and the struggle no less difficult. We were the women in Radway's study. The women in Radway's study were us. In a moment of collective insight we understood that we are our history, and our history is laid within patriarchy. (Lewis & Simon, 1986:466)

The classroom, being part of a white male-dominated hierarchy, always confers privilege to those members who are the dominant group. This is true in a "standard" classroom (versus a "critical" classroom in which the teacher is committed to an alternate pedagogy), in the use of mainstream curricular materials and the assumption of traditional power relations. Even in a critical classroom, the interactions among students are frequently organized by forms of discourse that marginalize members of minority groups. In the preceding example, we see that male students take for granted their right to speak and control the contents of classroom discussions. Minority members both defer to and feel silenced by their dominance.

In the years of my teaching, I had observed that it is not uncommon for minority students to interrupt each other more, thereby granting students from the dominant group (usually white males with the "proper" accent and so forth), and occasionally white women, more time and space to make their views known. White male students, especially, face less challenge among their peers, regardless of how unsound their views and opinions may be. (As we saw earlier in this chapter, the threat of male violence, both actual and symbolic, is always present as a check on female insubordination.)

It is worthwhile describing in some detail the interactional dynamics in a course I offered called Sociology of Minority Groups. Unlike other courses in the institution in which I teach, this course had about equal numbers of white students and minority students (as opposed to having predominantly white students). Among them were two extremely vocal young black students, a man and a woman, who took on the role of policing "correct" positions on anti-racism in classroom discussions. Apart from dominating the discussions, they also disrupted discussions, especially when other minority students, notably women from non-European backgrounds, attempted to put their views forward. On one particularly memorable occasion, an older black woman was severely chastised when making a presentation on the lack of representation of black women in educational administration. She was told in no uncertain terms that she had adopted the dominant perspective by suggesting that black women should attempt to seek upward mobility in mainstream power structures. By contrast, the white male students were able to contribute to discussions with few interruptions, and their opinions, no matter how unsound, would be treated jokingly at worst. When I interceded and mediated in these discussions, my authority was challenged and I was accused of attempting to silence the two vocal students because of the minority position they represented.

This example is interesting on several dimensions. Regardless of whether the older black woman's analysis or position was correct, a classroom that adopts the principles of critical teaching should enable the airing of multiple voices. In this classroom, principles of anti-racist education were used by some students as a control mechanism to suppress other voices that deviated from their own. It is interesting to observe that in this class, the relatively large number of minority students interrupted students from the dominant group. This phenomenon suggests a form of internalized colonialism whereby members of minority groups treat as less credible and authoritative the opinions of their own members, while deferring to members of the dominant group.

In adopting theories of critical pedagogy to teach a course entitled Media and Anti-racist Pedagogies, Elizabeth Ellsworth came to the conclusion that "students' and my own narratives about experiences of racism, ableism, elitism, fat oppression, sexism, anti-Semitism, heterosexism, and so on are partial — partial in the sense that they are unfinished, imperfect, limited; and partial in the sense that they project the interests of 'one side' over others" (Ellsworth, 1989:305). Based on this experience, she challenged the principle of critical pedagogy that assumes the unity of "the student voice." She observed that this voice is itself fragmented, that people speak from their "multiple and contradictory social positionings" (ibid.:312).

In a standard classroom, the mode of discourse characterized by debate and winning arguments is highly valued and therefore unproblematic. It became problematic in my, and other critical teachers', classrooms, which employ a different set of pedagogical principles and assumptions. Students, including minority students, have learned ways of displaying to the professor what counts as learning and as being a good student (see Roberts, 1988), which in part involves conforming to the standard mode of discourse, such as winning an argument. My approach, on the other hand, negates this mode of exchange and renders it invalid. In so doing, I, as the figure of authority, devalue what the students know how to do. In the eyes of the students, my minority status in the larger society makes my authority questionable, especially when my teaching methods deviate from the normal ways of doing things.

It is also interesting that by utilizing these alternate principles, I implicitly give students permission to interrupt each other and challenge me in the name of critical teaching, however interpreted. This occurred in the preceding example that I gave, and also in an advanced seminar, Feminist Theory, Methodology and Education, which I offer yearly. The first year I taught this graduate seminar I asked students to use the class as a forum to share research of theirs that they wished to improve. I had used this method in senior undergraduate seminars before and found it highly effective in encouraging cooperative learning among the students. Usually, even an academically marginal student would improve her or his presentation and writing skills over time and by the end of the course.

In this particular seminar, we developed a format where the student who wished to have her research worked on by the class would circulate her written work at least one week prior to the class; she also gave us some idea of what she found problematic so far and how she wanted her work to be discussed. The next seminar would be organized as a working session on this particular piece of research. To my horror, some of these discussions became not only heated but downright nasty, as class members held onto their respective brands of politically (and therefore theoretically) correct positions and criticized the presenter and each other in frequently destructive ways. In one poignant case, a lesbian student who was exploring the relationship between obesity and lesbianism became completely devastated. My own intervention was met with hostility from some members of the seminar. As I later discovered when I read the journals students submitted, they felt that I was silencing them contrary to my promise to implement feminist pedagogical principles in the classroom (see also Miner, 1990).

Leaving aside the real authority a teacher can and indeed does command, I want to draw attention here to how the rhetorics and ideology of feminism, anti-racism, and critical pedagogy are used as ideals against which members of the class are measured — and frequently found lacking. In this way, these critical approaches can and do become new forms of orthodoxy that are themselves oppressive (Miner, 1990). Meanwhile, students to whom the interventions are directed do feel rejection and pain, and their feelings must not be minimized. It is in this kind of situation that we confront fully the contradiction of classroom democracy, which is so much part of the rhetoric, if not the practice, of alternative pedagogies. At the same time, I would maintain that it is also through facing up to these contradictions that we come to grips with the limits and boundaries of critical teaching within a hierarchical structure and begin to explore the possibilities therein.

To being, then, critical teaching must recognize that the university, as do other institutions of learning under contemporary forms of capitalism, operates with a meritocratic system (see Bowles & Gintis, 1976). Rewards in this structure are given to those who can demonstrate that they are more meritorious than others. There is a hierarchy of merits according to which faulty, as well as students, are rewarded differentially by getting grants, scholarships, or good references to enable them to compete successfully both within the university and outside it. Students survive, therefore, by excelling and competing with one another for the few positions at the pinnacle of this system. Indeed, competition is the very basis of university education.

This system does not present itself as a problem in the standard classroom because it is set up in conformity to the same system of merit and reward. However, it presents a dilemma for the critical teacher because critical teaching explicitly or implicitly challenges the system and attempts to transform what we have come to identify as oppressive features of the educational process. But ultimately, the critical classroom, too, is located within this award system. To survive, students have to get good grades by competing with one another. The systemic nature of this dynamic penetrates a critical classroom. Among other oppressive forms of social life, sexism, and racism, themselves systems of domination and oppression, are the ingredients that constitute the cornerstone of our meritocratic educational system.

But the curriculum, testing instruments, and rules for competition and excellence are not neutral. Feminist scholars have shown that what is treated as natural and objective knowledge is in fact one-sided and biased. Knowledge in ideological structures, including universities, is developed by men — I would add white, ruling-class men — for men based on the experiences of men (see Smith, 1975). Examining educational materials on aboriginal people and multiculturalism in Canada, Lewis (1987) and Manicom (1987) found that they are written from a white supremacist standpoint even when information on other (than British and French) cultures is incorporated into the school curriculum. In her exploration and analysis of skills-oriented versus process-oriented teaching and their differential effects on black and white children, Lisa Delpit has identified "a culture of power" at work in the classroom that operates to disadvantage black students who live outside that culture (Delpit, 1988). Thus, this system of competition for excellence tends to be more advantageous to the individuals who share the same premise, perspective, and code of exchange as those in power. These individuals tend to be white men from particular class backgrounds.[19] If minority students wish to compete and excel in this system, they must learn to internalize the standpoint and code of the "culture of power" and operate within it. This is one way that internalized colonialism expresses itself in the classroom. Furthermore, as we move up and through the educational hierarchy, the competition becomes keener. As competition intensifies, the possibilities of promoting critical and cooperative teaching become increasingly curtailed.[20]

In sum, a number of oppressive social forms are constitutive of and operative in the academy. I have tried to explicate how commonsense sexism and racism are manifested in the classroom through the silencing and devaluation of minority students, both by male students and by each other, because of the cycle of competition and excellence in which they and we are caught. Sexism and racism are among the multifaceted ways in which power relations organize classroom dynamics.[21] As critical teachers, unless we seriously analyze and confront the changing contours of these relations, critical teaching will remain a purely theoretical exercise.

Possiblities of Critical Teaching

The literature on critical teaching has addressed variously curricular and pedagogical issues. For example, theorists of both critical pedagogy and anti-racist education are concerned with a critique of existing forms and content of the curriculum, which negate the experiences of minority groups (racial minority and working class students). Together with feminist pedagogy, they are also concerned with classroom process: the airing of multiple voices and experiences. The contradictions I examined above in part arise out of the insistence of allowing previously oppressed members to speak out (frequently at the expense of suppressing other voices), and attempts by critical teachers to democratize the classroom (I myself have taken this for granted).

In an article in the *Harvard Educational Review*, Lisa Delpit examines the implications of a skills-oriented approach versus a process-oriented approach for black students. She makes clear that she is not favoring one approach over another (although there is a tendency for critical teachers to indeed do this). Rather, based on her and others' experiences as black teachers, she suggests that a process-oriented approach works well for students who already know the code and rules of the subject matter. Such code and rules are established by the dominant group, and what operates in the classroom is "the culture of power" (Delpit, 1988:282). Since black students are outside the culture of power, they are ignorant of the code that operates in the classroom, and thus a process-oriented approach in fact disadvantages them from competing within the educational hierarchy. To empower students who are not already participating in the culture of power, teachers can explicitly state the rules of that culture, making acquiring power easier for these students (ibid.:282). Thus, with regard to teaching writing, she is calling for a skills-oriented approach for black students, who have not learned the code of the culture of power, so that they can survive in that culture.

One of the messages in Delpit's discussion is that the critical teacher must assume his or her authority explicitly and teach students the skills necessary for surviving and competing effectively in the "culture of power." This is an issue about which I have frequent debates with some of my white colleagues. They maintain that students must be free to develop their thinking and writing without being told by the professors the rules of certain scholarly conventions. I am often described as the tough teacher who insists on receiving written materials according to certain scholarly and stylistic formats. As a woman of color who has spent years of my life figuring out what is required of me in order to do acceptable academic work, I realize how important it is to teach these skills explicitly. Reading Delpit's article make realize that for members of the dominant group, this is something that is taken for granted, and thus invisible. What needs to be pointed out is that teachers have different experiences, and therefore different teaching styles, based on our gender, race, and other identities that are developed over time. This informs the way we teach, which falls outside of the process versus skills debate. In every classroom encounter, the strategies we use must be worked out in situ rather than as abstract principles that are used regardless of contexts.

Furthermore, as critical teachers, we must recognize that a classroom is not isolated from the society at large. In our enthusiasm, I think we want to believe that our teaching can change our students, and by extension the world. Indeed, as Linda Briskin has pointed out, no single classroom can "overcome the realities of a racist, heterosexist patriarchal capitalist society. It can only engage with them" (Briskin, 1990:14). Ultimately, we need to link the theoretical understanding derived from the classroom context to the real-life struggles of minority people occurring outside the classroom. In reflecting on the limits of critical pedagogy, Ellsworth (1989) describes how students decided to launch a series of activities on campus to raise awareness of racism and demands for change. In the institute in which I teach, we have formed an anti-racist network of faculty, staff, and students outside of any particular classroom context. In the four years since its formation, it evolved from an informal support group to a pressure group that is pressing for the hiring of more minority faculty and staff, for expanding the existing curriculum to include minority perspectives, and for developing an anti-racism policy. Many members have formed alliances with anti-racist groups and participated in anti-racist activities in the city. It is by encouraging students, not to mention ourselves, to participate in struggles outside of the classroom that we indeed empower students to take control over their lives and change the world, not by eloquent rhetorics that do not stand the test of practice.

Thus, while classroom process is important, it is equally important for the critical teacher to assume the responsibility of directing students to an examination of how systems of inequality have emerged and developed historically and to point out the ways in which different forms of inequality have become part of our collective consciousness. By explicating some of the routine unconscious processes in which we engage, we can begin to confront our own contradictions and work towards change. In the final analysis, critical teaching is not only for the oppressed (i.e., for the students who are deemed to be recipients of our great theories and wisdom). It is for us as human beings, to help us liberate ourselves from the shackles of our own learning, which has been mediated by sexism, racism, and other forms of oppression. It is when we, too, engage in critical learning that we can hope to achieve the possibility of critical teaching.

Notes

1   Critical pedagogy is not a coherent or monolithic body of work with a single theory viewpoint. It is derived from various critical theoretical perspectives notably the critical theory of Habamas and the pedagogical theory of Paulo Freire. The major contemporary proponents of critical pedagogy include Henry Giroux, Roger Simon, Michael Apple, and Peter McLaren, *Life in Schools* (1989).

2   While multicultural education has been in vogue since the promulgation of the multiculturalism policy in 1971, anti-racist education is an emerging and relatively untheorized field of study in Canada. For various attempts to describe and analyze multicultural education, see Masemann (1978/79) and Young (1979). For an excellent comparison of multicultural and anti-racist education, see Thomas (1987).

3   For a critique of knowledge making from a feminist perspective, see Dorothy E. Smith (1975). For one of the earliest collections of feminist pedagogy, see Culley and Portuges (1985).

4   Elizabeth Ellsworth provides a convincing self-critique of the pitfalls of critical pedagogy in her article "Why Doesn't This Feel Empowering? Working through the Repressive Myths of Critical Pedagogy" (Ellsworth, 1989).

5   Issues of power are posed in various ways by feminist teachers. Writing about their own experiences in the classroom, Sheila McIntyre (1986) and Susan Heald (1989) speak poignantly of the sexism directed towards them as teachers from students, especially male students. Barbara Roberts (1988) and Kathryn Morgan (1988), on the other hand, write of the power teachers, including feminist teachers, have over students in the classroom.

6   Max Weber (1969) defines power as the ability and chances of an actor to impose his or her will on another in a social relationship. Berger and Luckman (1967) take this notion further to suggest that particular people have the power to construct and impose their definition of reality on others. More recently, researchers in ethnomethodology and social linguistics have begun to analyze how power is enacted microsociologically. For example, Thorne and Henley's work (1975) mapped how men dominate women through the use of language. Fisherman's (1978) conversational analysis, quoted in this chapter, shows precisely how conversational patterns between intimate heterosexual couples maintain existing power relations between the sexes.

7   I am indebted to Cameron McCarthy for the use of this word. He came up with it when members of this writing project helped me to clarify my conceptualization of gender, race, class, sexism, and racism in the aforementioned symposium.

8   Elsewhere, I have asserted that gender, race, and class are equally important relations to understand and explicate in social analysis (see Ng, 1989). While I have focused on racism and sexism in this chapter, I want to emphasize that class inequality and oppression are equally pervasive and important for us to explicate and eradicate.

9   This is recorded in a report entitled "An Experimental Research Practicum Based on the Wollstonecraft Research Group," by Marie Campbell. See also Smith (1987).

10   While this is not a universal phenomenon, I have observed this in more than one university where I have taught.

11   The Montreal massacre involved the shooting death of fourteen female engineering students by a frustrated young man who felt that his denial of

entry into engineering school was due to the admission of female students. While his act could be interpreted as that of a madman, analyses of the event make it clear that his action, no matter how irrational, had targetted women whom he considered "feminist." This indicates the pervasiveness of sexism, including misogyny, in our culture. Here, I did not distinguish between the experiences of female students and female teachers. Although female students, due to their relatively powerless position in the university hierarchy, experience special problems such as sexual harassment, women as a minority group are marginal to the academy in general. More to the point, their very presence upsets the status quo; it threatens male power and engenders hostility in the way I describe.

12   Even though I know this statement is in some sense scandalous and verges on gossip, I decided to include it because it is precisely the way in which sexism operates effectively as a silencing and disempowering instrument. I was party to some of these comments in a CAUT conference I attended in Toronto in March 1990.

13   See, for example, Nielsen (1979).

14   For the uninformed reader, Suzie Wong was a movie and television character in the fifties and sixties: a high-class prostitute of mixed Chinese and English parentage. As the protagonist of the film, she mesmerized the men, mostly Caucasian, she met by her grace and demure seductiveness, and they fought for the honor to protect and cherish her. At least in Hong Kong — a British colony — and Britain, the film and its sequels captured the hearts of Western and Chinese audiences alike, and led to the stereotype of Chinese women as lovely creatures who are in need of protection and love but who cannot be taken seriously.

15   Whereas I make clear distinction between the terms "power" and "authority," Morgan (1988) does not make such a distinction. I find her discussion problematic because it fails to examine power as a dynamic process in the way that I try to capture in this chapter.

16   Various theorists have reflected on changing the form and content of education. See bell hooks (1988) and Russell (1981), for example. In her paper entitled "Interactive Phases of Curricular Re-Vision: A Feminist Perspective," Peggy McIntosh (1983) describes a four-phase process of change. In the final phase, she envisions that the dichotomy between teacher and student would disappear and everyone would participate in developing and shaping the curriculum. While this kind of vision is important, it is not entirely possible under the existing structural constraints of universities.

17   See, for example, some of the school ethnographies in the symbolic interactionist tradition (Delamont, 1976; Hargreaves & Woods, 1984).

18   I am indebted to Sandra Ingram, who drew my attention to Michaels's work by sharing her own writing with me.

19 For an excellent study on class differences in students' differential educational experiences, see Connell et al. (1982).

20 For an interesting exploration of competition among women in the academy, see Keller and Moglen (1987).

21 Sexism and racism are by no means the only forms of subordination in the academy. Age, ability/disability, sexual orientation, body size, and so forth so constitute ways in which individuals are differentiated and silenced (see also Ellsworth, 1989). In the institution in which I teach, student statuses (part-time, full-time, Canadian and immigrant versus foreign students) are ways that students differentiate and discriminate among themselves. Part-time students, especially, feel marginalized and silenced because they have less access to the decision-making processes open to students who are available to attend meetings or classes during the day. This spills over to class dialogues that are geared towards the development and refinement of certain discourses with which they are less familiar (e.g., the discourse on critical pedagogy).

References

Bannerji, H. (1987, March). Introducing racism: Notes towards an anti-racist feminism. *Resources for Feminist Research*, 16(1), 10–13.

Berger, P., and Luckmann, T. (1967). *The social construction of reality*. New York: Anchor Books.

Bowles, S., and Gintis, H. (1976). *Schooling in capitalist America: Educational reform and the contradictions of economic life*. New York: Basic Books.

Briskin, L. (1990). *Feminist pedagogy: Teaching and learning liberation*. Ottawa: Canadian Research Institute for the Advancement of Women.

Campbell, M. (n.d.). An experimental research practicum based on the Wollstonecraft Research Group. Unpublished report, Department of Sociology, Ontario Institute for Studies in Education.

Cockburn, C. (1983). *Brothers: Male dominance and technological change*. London: Pluto Press.

Connell, R.W., Ashenden, D.J., Kessler, S., and Dowsett, G.W. (1982). *Making the difference: Schools, families and social division*. Sydney: George Allen and Unwin.

Culley, M. and Portuges, C. (Eds.). (1985). *Gendered subjects: The dynamics of feminist teaching*. Boston, London: Routledge and Kegan Paul.

de Beauvoir, S. (1952). *The second sex*. New York: Knopf. Vintage Books Edition, 1974.

Delamont, S. (1976). *Interaction in the classroom* (2nd ed.). London and New York: Methuen.

Delpit, L. (1988, Aug.). The silenced dialogue: Power and pedagogy in educating other people's children. *Harvard Educational Review*, 58(3), 280–98.

Ellsworth, E. (1989, Aug.). Why doesn't this feel empowering? Working through the repressive myths of critical pedagogy. *Harvard Educational Review*, 59(3), 287–324.

Fisherman, P. (1978, April). Interaction: The work women do. *Social Problems*, 25(4), 397–406.

Friedman, S.S. (1985). Authority in the feminist classroom: A contradiction in terms? In M. Culley and C. Portuges (Eds.), *Gendered subjects: The dynamics of feminist teaching*. Boston, London: Routledge and Kegan Paul.

Hargreaves, A., and Woods, P. (Eds.). (1984). *Classrooms and staffrooms: The sociology of teachers and teaching*. Milton Keynes, UK: Open University Press.

Heald, S. (1989, Dec.) The madwoman out of the attic: Feminist teaching in the margins. *Resources for Feminist Research (RFR)*, 18 (4), 22–26.

Hoodfar, H. (1992). Feminist anthropology and critical pedagogy: The anthropology of classrooms' excluded voices. *Canadian Journal of Education*, 17(3), 303–20.

hooks, b. (1988). *Talking back: Think feminist; thinking black*. Toronto: Between the Lines.

Keller, E.F., and Moglen, H. (1987). Competition and feminism: Conflicts for academic women. *Signs: Journal of Women in Culture and Society*, 12(3), 493–511.

Lewis, M. (1987). Native images in children's books. In J. Young (Ed.), *Breaking the mosaic* (pp. 108–144). Toronto: Garamond Press.

Lewis, M., and Simon, R. (1986). A discourse not intended for her: Learning and teaching within patriarchy. *Harvard Educational Review*, 56(4), 457–72.

Manicom, A. (1987). Ideology and multicultural curriculum: Deconstructing elementary school texts. In J. Young (Ed.), *Breaking the mosaic: Ethnic identities in Canadian schooling*. Toronto: Garamond Press.

Masemann, V. (1978/79). Multicultural programs in Toronto schools. *Interchange*, 9(3), 29–44.

McIntosh, P. (1983). Interactive phases of curricular re-vision: A feminist perspective. Unpublished paper, Center for Research on Women, Wellesley College.

McIntyre, S. (1986, July 28). Gender bias within the law school. Memorandum to all members of Faculty Board, Faculty of Law, Queen's University.

McLaren, P. (1989). *Life in Schools*. Toronto: Irwin.

Michaels, S. (1986). Narrative presentations: An oral preparation for literacy with first graders. In J. Cook-Gumperz (Ed.), *The social construction of literacy*. Cambridge: Cambridge University Press.

Miner, I.L. (1990). Women teaching women: A contradiction in terms. Unpublished paper, Department of Sociology, Ontario Institute for Studies in Education.

Morgan, K.P. (1988). The paradox of the bearded mother: The role of authority in feminist pedagogy. Unpublished paper, University of Toronto.

Nielsen, L. (1979, November). Sexism and self-healing in the university. *Harvard Educational Review*, 49(4), 467–76.

Ng, R. (1989). Sexism, racism and Canadian nationalism. In J. Vorst (Ed.), *Race, class, gender: Bonds and barriers*. Toronto: Between the Lines and Society for Socialist Studies.

———. (1993). "A woman out of control": Deconstructing sexism and racism in the university, *Canadian Journal of Education*, 18(3), 189–205.

Porter, J. (1967). *The vertical mosaic: An analysis of social class and power in Canada*. Toronto: University of Toronto Press.

Quinn, P. (1990, Sept. 8). Is life on campus really safe? *The Toronto Star*, p. G1.

Radway, J. (1984). *Reading the romance: Women, patriarchy, and popular literature*. Chapel Hill: University of North Carolina Press.

Roberts, B. (1988, June). Canadian women's studies classrooms as learning sites: Dis-abling double messages. Paper presented at the Canadian Women's Studies Association Annual Meeting, Windsor.

Russell, M. (1981). An open letter to the academy. In *Building feminist theory: Essays from Quest*. New York: Longmans.

Sasson, A.S. (Ed.). (1982). *Approaches to Gramsci*. London: Writers and Readers.

Smith, D.E. (1975). An analysis of ideological structures and how women are excluded: Considerations for academic women. *Canadian Review of Sociology and Anthropology*, 12(4), Part 1, 353–69.

———. (1987). *The everyday world as problematic: A feminist sociology*. Toronto: University of Toronto Press.

Stockwood, P. (1990, March). Out of the fat and into the fire: Confronting patriarchy in a graduate feminist seminar. Paper presented at the Atlantic Association of Sociologists and Anthropologists Annual Meeting, Saint John, New Brunswick.

Thomas, B. (1987). Anti-racist education: A response to Manicom. In J. Young (Ed.), *Breaking the mosaic: Ethnic identities in Canadian schooling*. Toronto: Garamond Press.

Thorne, B., and Henley, N. (1975). *Language and sex: Difference and dominance*. Rowley, Mass.: Newbury House.

Weber, M. (1969). *The theory of social and economic organization*. New York: Free Press.

Young, J. (1979). Education in a multicultural society: What sort of education? What sort of society? *Canadian Journal of Education*, 4(3), 5–21.

Chapter Five

Racism in Nursing

Tania Das Gupta

Introduction and Research Methods

This chapter describes and analyzes the existence of racism in nursing, revealing consistent patterns of covert and overt forms of racism faced by Black nurses in Ontario.

Research on racism in nursing is sparse, even though analyses of gender, sexism and class in this profession are more readily available.[1] I will explore systemic practices of racism as well as document the "everyday culture" of racism in hospitals, particularly in reference to Black female nurses. Even though I dwell on the experience and practices of racism in general, in particular I examine the experiences of women and members of the middle or professional class. I will comment on sexist racism which is apparent in daily interactions between Black nurses and their managers. Therefore, racism, gender and class will all be examined.

The experiences of Black nurses and other healthcare workers illustrate these various forms of racism. In the 1950s, Black women from the Caribbean were granted temporary entry permits to Canada in order to be trained as nursing assistants, and employed in "such unattractive specialties as psychiatric hospitals and sanatoria."[2] A study by Wilson Head[3] reveals that women of colour working in healthcare today are mostly concentrated at the lower levels of nursing, in cooking, cleaning and laundering, and thus create a racially-segmented workforce. There are very few nurses of colour at the supervisory level. Essed[4] also documents racial segregation in nursing in The Netherlands whereby Black nurses are over-represented in non-management positions, in geriatric nursing training, as home helpers and "temps". Lee-

Cunin[5] confirms this pattern by saying that Black nurses in Britain are over-represented in areas where promotional opportunities are extremely limited, for example in geriatrics and psychiatry.

Workers of colour have been excluded from better paid, secure, and more desirable jobs in nursing through systemic practices in the labour market and in other related institutions, such as the educational and immigration systems. Calliste[6] writes that Canadian nursing schools did not admit Canadian-born Black students before the 1940s, apparently because Canadian hospitals would not employ them. It was only after a public campaign against this racist, sexist exclusion was conducted by the Nova Scotia Association for the Advancement of Coloured People and supported by some trade unions and church groups that this policy was challenged. Interestingly, Caribbean students were admitted into nursing schools because the assumption was that they would return to their countries of origin for employment.

Calliste writes that between 1950 and 1962, Canadian immigration authorities admitted limited numbers of Caribbean nurses, urged by groups such as the Negro Citizenship Association. However, they were admitted under differential rules compared to White nurse immigrants. Calliste argues that Black nurses "were required to have nursing 'qualifications over and above' those required for white nurses."[7] Out of the four categories of nurses accepted, one included graduate nurses from the Caribbean as students who were required to finish a three-month obstetrics course, be eligible for registration with the Registered Nurses Association as well as guaranteed employment by a hospital which was "aware of their racial origin." This is a significant point because Canadian hospitals had a "White only staffing" policy at that time. Upon fulfillment of all these requirements, they could apply for landed immigration status. In contrast, White nurse applicants without the obstrectics course were granted landed immigrant status by Order-in-Council. Moreover some graduate nurses from the Caribbean worked as nursing assistants while waiting for entry into the obstetrics program because access to these courses for foreign students was limited. Another category of Black students was given temporary entry permits to enroll in nursing assistant programs offered by hospitals, provided there was a demand for them in these hospitals upon graduation. However, Calliste notes that only some of these graduates gained landed immigration status whilst others continued on temporary work permits.

Lee-Cunin[8] notes how nursing schools in Britain are inaccessible to women of colour, and how reluctant they are to accommodate a change in nurse uniforms, for example, the right of Muslim nurses to wear trousers. Both of these factors have contributed to a decline in the recruitment of Black and Asian nurses at the time of research. Re-grading of nurses also led to the downgrading and underpayment of Black nurses.

Canadian research has revealed that, once hired by hospitals, nurses of colour are subjected to racially-biased performance appraisals or *no* documentation of their performance appraisals, which then disqualifies them from promotions. In the early 1960s, Black nurses with "better qualifications" than White nurses were discriminated against in terms of promotions purely on the basis of racism.[9] In Head's[10] study, the failure rate in promotions was significantly higher for Blacks than for Whites. Many of the Black professionals interviewed, including doctors, clearly attributed this to differential opportunities and to racism. Some talked about being "by-passed" or being told they were "too experienced".[11] Most Black workers felt their qualifications were not being utilized in their jobs, while most White workers felt the opposite. Stereotypes, prejudices, individual discrimination and systemic discrimination are not mutually exclusive. In fact, they are mutually reinforcing and occur as a continuous cultural process.

The Head[12] report documented Black workers being summarily dismissed and unjustly laid-off, healthcare institutions being unable to deal with complaints against Black workers, and those same workers being penalized for disagreeing with their supervisors.

Registered nurses are highly-skilled professionals, given a great deal of discretion and control, unionized, and in most cases well paid. They are not usually considered victims of exploitation and racial oppression in Canada. However, even within this middle-class group, we find evidence of intense and damaging racism, sexism, classism and ageism. Harassment is often the price one has to pay in order to challenge class privilege, which is almost always tied in with white skin and gender privileges. Essed[13] documents the insubordination of Black (Surinamese) nurse supervisors in The Netherlands. Essed[14] tells us that the harassment faced by Black nurses in The Netherlands is often subtle and of an "everyday" nature. For instance, she writes that they are often accused of theft, considered "stupid" when they do not understand a Dutch dialect, stereotyped as being "irresponsible" and not allowed to speak Surinamese[15] in the workplace.

In her study, Essed[16] discussed the fear White nurses have of Black solidarity. The maintenance of a "temporary" and "migrant" pool of Caribbean nursing assistants in Canada in the early 1950s was also a way of ensuring a lack of solidarity and thus vulnerability of these workers.

Research Methodology

Since 1993, I have become aware of a number of cases of human rights violations of Black nurses in their workplaces. In some of them, I served as an expert witness. I have looked in-depth at some of these alleged human rights violations by reviewing various reports of the Ontario Human Rights

Commission (OHRC). I have also found a report by Doris Marshall Institute (DMI) and Arnold Minors and Associates[17] very useful in understanding workplace racism. The two latter organizations were contracted by a hospital in Toronto in 1993 to help develop management and employment strategies to promote and ensure ethno-racial equality in the hospital. Beginning in 1990, seven Black nurses and one Filipino nurse from the hospital had filed complaints with the Ontario Human Rights Commission for being subjected to racial harassment and in some cases being fired or forced to resign. After a period of four years, the nurses won their cases, and a settlement was reached with the hospital.

The consultants hired by the hospital held a number of group interviews, one with the board and one with senior and middle managers. Other interviews were individually conducted. The consultants noted that the interviews were not completely successful:

> "Staff are very reluctant to talk, and take extreme precaution when giving information; have fear of reprisals ..."[18]

The consultants also reviewed the hospital's management manual, its newsletters from September 1992 to September 1993, its philosophy statement, minutes from a variety of meetings in which the hospital was involved, raw data from a survey conducted internally which drew 357 returns, OHRC reports and other related documents.

I have also undertaken an interview with a staff member of Ontario Nurses Association (OHA)[19] to develop a more global view of the problem. Finally, I attended a conference[20] in Toronto, which brought together Black registered nurses and other healthcare workers. In the course of this conference, I heard five healthcare professionals, including four registered nurses, present stories of racial harassment at their hospitals. One of the main purposes of sharing these stories was to establish links and support each other. Following the conference, a meeting was called to plan and organize a Black Nurses and Other Healthcare Workers Association.

In addition, I have relied on an article by Stan Gray[21] referred to earlier where he documents the experience of a senior Black woman who worked as a nurse's aide at a Toronto hospital and who was forced into early retirement. The woman contends that she was subjected to age and racial discrimination.

Overall, I am relying on the personal experiences of ten Black healthcare professionals, nine of them registered nurses in Ontario, apart from the secondary sources that I have already acknowledged. In addition, I draw on an interview with a key informant, a staff person from the Ontario Nurses' Association (ONA). Owing to ethical considerations, I have used fictitious names to identify nurses and hospitals, apart from the ones who are named already in secondary sources. All the hospitals I examined are large in size, based in metropolitan areas in Ontario and have multi-racial or multi-ethnic workforces, but managed overwhelmingly by White personnel.

The Big Picture: Political Economy of Healthcare

As reported by Armstrong et al,[22] the current phase of healthcare policy is marked by cost-cutting through such means as restructuring, privatization and de-institutionalization. This has had profound and mostly negative effects on the nursing profession and on patient care. For instance, in the name of "quality assurance," nurses are now being monitored more through "form filling." Campbell[23] has also discussed this development. Changes in hospital work schedules include laying off full-time nurses while increasing those on part-time shifts and "floating" nurses and volunteers. These changes, all in the name of "employee empowerment," have seriously reduced the continuity and quality of patient care, and adversely affected the "team spirit" so crucial in this profession. Simultaneously, there has been a rise in staff conflicts; there is more management and hierarchy, nurses are being asked to "report on" each other, there is more disciplinary action against nurses, and more harassment in general. Restructuring is being undertaken in hospitals too fast, in the absence of proper training of both staff nurses and nurse managers. Moreover, scientific management principles are being introduced in hospitals without any thought to the impact on patient care, let alone on employees. Wotherspoon[24] discusses the fact that nurses are caught in two contradictory dynamics: 1) their demands for professionalization and a return to community-based healthcare; and, 2) proletarianization and gender subordination. Even though hospitals are arguing that the current economic crises in healthcare has not had any significant negative effect on care,[25] nurses and other healthcare employees insist that "quality care has gone out the window."[26] Some hospitals have implemented American models of healthcare based on the concepts of a low-paid, deskilled and non-unionized staff.[27] National surveys of nurses in Canada reveal dissatisfaction over staff shortages, workload, and quality of patient care.[28]

Restructuring in healthcare has also reduced the importance of "emotional labour" in nursing.[29] The latter is commonly referred to as "bedside manner" and refers to "working through frightening or worrying feelings and helping ill people and their families ... work out a strategy they can live with." This work of emotional management requires skills particular to women congruent to gender ideology. Given the nature of patriarchy, emotional labour and its associated skills are not particularly valued in our society and it is even more devalued under fiscal "crisis." Ironically, it is emotional labour that is most "appreciated," not necessarily "valued," by patients and their families.

Most of the studies on healthcare crises and its effects on patient care and on labour relations have the limitation of being race-blind. It is assumed that the impact of reorganization and increased surveillance of nurses is uniform to *all* nurses. My research reveals that Black nurses, other nurses of colour and in a few instances militant White nurses are being adversely affected and experiencing it in different ways. Stan Gray[30] confirms this in a recent article where he documents the experience of a Black woman who worked as a nurse's aide in a Toronto hospital. She was subjected to harassment, suspended from work for alleged patient abuse and finally forced into early retirement. She believes that her harassment happened because of the "downsizing of healthcare."

The literature is also class-blind in most instances. Nursing managers are generally registered nurses (RNs) as are staff nurses. However, most nurses of colour work as staff nurses, and are the most adversely affected by fiscal constraints and management strategies. White nursing managers are key players in the daily harassment of these nurses. Therefore, by generalizing the impact on *all* nurses, one is also obfuscating class differences among different categories of RNs.

Racism in the Wards

Following are more specific examples of how racism is experienced by mainly African-Canadian nurses on a daily basis. Similar experiences by other women of colour, such as Chinese-Canadian nurses, are also referred to.

Targeting outspoken nurses of colour seems to be a common experience. Typically, a Black nurse is singled out and subjected to differential treatment by management compared to White workers. This often takes the form of negative documentation being obtained from direct supervisors and colleagues on nurses of colour and accumulating this to be used later for discipline. One nurse said:

> "Black nurses are reprimanded from coming late for break-times. All nurses are committing errors, but only nurses of colour are documented and reprimanded ..."[31]

One healthcare worker[32] said that she had been labelled as "incompetent," even though there was no formal complaint filed and her work "performance was great." One nurse argued that she knows of instances where documentation was fabricated in order to "frame" nurses of colour. The following is her description of how this can happen:

> "... camps form on the unit and then war is on ... feel very nervous ... very intimidated, being watched, documented ... they ask the opposition camp to document and they will fabricate ..."[33]

Gray[34] writes of a 61-year-old Black nurse's aide who was allegedly "framed" twice with patient abuse because she was targeted by hospital management for early retirement. When she refused the retirement offer, she was subjected to harassment and charged with patient abuse, along with another senior registered practical nurse who also happens to be Black. That charge was dropped because of "lack of merit." In the second charge, a patient's sitter complained about her. Management immediately suspended her from work, despite a discipline-free work record spanning 26 years. The following describes what happened when she returned to work:

> "Cynthia was told she was no longer qualified to be a nurse's aide. She was immediately shunted to cleaning toilets, beds and floors. ..."[35]

The alleged incompetencies of these nurses are not dealt with in the same manner as most White nurses. A staff member from ONA said:

> "White nurses who've made mistakes have been helped and improved, whereas Black nurses are being set up to fail. ... In remedial programs they are being followed very closely. ..."[36]

She continues:

> "People are disciplined differently and treated differently. ..."

The DMI report confirms this perspective. It notes:

> Disciplinary measures are lenient towards White staff; swift and unbending towards people of colour. For example, tardiness by a White person is ignored, even if it is a frequent occurrence; racial minority staff are immediately warned, even put under surveillance, for tardiness. One was dismissed due to tardiness which was her first offence in three years of employment.[37]

The accusation of incompetency of Black nurses, fabricated or not, immediately leads to summary dismissals or suspensions of the targeted nurses. One nurse[38] was fired within a few days of being first made aware that her performance was lacking, thus violating the policy of progressive discipline in her hospital. She was penalized for deficiencies for which White nurses are seldom disciplined, and rarely dismissed.

Another nurse[39] tells of being suspended from work without pay after an argument with a White colleague. In addition, she was not to be assigned any leadership role for a period of time. On the other hand, the White nurse was not disciplined and was assigned a leadership position, even though she was junior to the Black nurse.

Another nurse said that she was dismissed on grounds of making "several" medication errors. Some minor errors may have been made, but she was, in fact, accused of making many more than were entailed.

> "... the client's well-being is primary ... the College of Nurses says that we should start with systemic problems rather than individual problems. This is not followed in most cases. It mostly leads to disciplinary action. ..."[40]

Scapegoating is a common experience when Black nurses and other nurses of colour are subjected to false accusations, blaming and disciplining for unwanted events or actions in which they were not the sole participants. Nurses of colour are often blamed for conflicts with patients, other colleagues and for faulty nursing practices, e.g. incorrect medication delivery. In situations of staff conflict, scapegoated nurses are often taken to task even though they may actually have been the victims of harassment. In one case, a nurse[41] was given a counselling letter following a patient's complaint letter about her. The latter was subsequently placed in the nurse's file even though the patient's family members had been aggressive towards her to the point of being "physical." She was penalized for the incident and the fact that she had been physically threatened was not mentioned or dealt with anywhere.

Another nurse[42] delivered a baby who died minutes after birth. She reported that she was questioned by hospital officials for months after the event, even though the mother and other family members were completely satisfied with her efforts. She was transferred to another unit and subjected to other forms of harassment.

Excessive monitoring can be a way in which a Black nurse is targeted so that s/he feels constantly watched, judged and threatened with the prospect of being framed for dismissal. The crucial point in this process is that similar monitoring is not happening for White nurses. It contributes to a "poisoned" environment. An ONA staff member describes how this happens:

> "... They (Black) nurses are supervised closely ... you get so nervous ... afraid to make mistakes ... supervisor asks questions or comments to confuse ... not helpful or constructive ... there was one case of a nurse of colour who had to use a piece of equipment that White nurses don't have to do ... the union became involved and the supervisor backed off."[43]

One senior nurse[44] tells of her manager accompanying her and unnecessarily lecturing her on simple and ordinary procedures with patients. A file of negative documentation was also compiled against this nurse, subsequently leading to her termination.

Marginalization is a result of isolation. Isolation can happen for various reasons, but it is more likely to occur if a person of colour is working in a predominantly White environment, or if the employee lacks empathy from managers or co-workers. In cases of alleged racism experienced by Black nurses from White patients and their relatives, it is not unusual for management to deny the possibility of racism and to "lump" in racism with other negative behaviours from patients. It seems that management fails to recognize the differential impact on Black nurses of a patient who is angry because of a "care" issue and one who is angry and racist. The following excerpt from the DMI report is an example of marginalization:

> [The] patient said: "Get your Black hands off me." Or, without being asked, would say: "Yes, I'd like to have a White nurse." Unit managers would not back up staff, when they complain about this abusive language. The result is that patients continue to be abusive, knowing that such behaviour is being tolerated.[45]

Thus, racial incidents are not followed up and investigated. In fact, it is believed that racism does not exist. By denying the existence of racism, Black Nurses are further marginalized and unsupported. In one case, a nurse[46] was issued a formal warning letter after a patient's relative complained about the quality of her patient care. The nurse alleges that the patient's relative had made a racist remark towards Black nurses. The latter allegation was not fully investigated by management, and was, in fact, dismissed.

In another case, a nurse[47] was physically threatened by a patient's relative for alleged neglect and he was heard to make a racist and sexist comment. Although management recognized the physical safety issue brought up by this incident, it did not acknowledge nor address the aggressive racism that was expressed against the nurse.

Solidarity among Black nurses is often seen as a threat by White management. This is ironic since management often systemically segregates Black nurses so that they work in similar floors and departments. The perceived threat of Black nurses' solidarity is sometimes dealt with by management by dispersing and separating them, for example assigning them different break times, or by strongly discouraging their association through threats and intimidation. The following are some testimonies:

"... one nurse of colour will not back up other nurses of colour for fear of retaliation. ..."[48]

"... I became afraid of repercussion on friend ... fear for self and family ... endangering my license, my life, anyone who's close to me. ..."[49]

"... I was transferred to another unit to separate me from my colleagues in the unit who would have supported me. ..."[50]

Infantalization of Black nurses is also prevalent when they are subjected to condescension, belittling, "put downs," and labelled as "not being good enough." For instance, the ONA representative interviewed said there was a general "lack of tolerance" towards nurses for whom English is a second language or a second dialect. They are accused of not having communication skills and of "asking too many questions" if they attempt to clarify terminology with which they may be unfamiliar.[51] Almost every nurse who spoke at the "End the Silence" conference mentioned they had been characterized as having "a communication problem." One nurse related the following case involving a Chinese-Canadian:

"... she was removed from the operating room to do clerical work, housekeeping work, 'Joe' jobs. ..."[52]

The DMI report cities the following testimony:

It was found that Black nurses were censured for speaking in local dialects among themselves, Italian and Portuguese nurses, for example, were freely allowed to speak their first languages to one another.[53]

Black nurses are often unnecessarily criticized for the quality of work. Sometimes they are patronizingly directed to take courses which are far below their actual skills or experienced Black nurses with years of seniority will be lectured unnecessarily on a simple procedure. One nurse[54] who was subjected to racism and to aggressive behaviour by a patient's relatives was referred to a workshop on crisis intervention. This action trivialized the traumatic impact of racial harassment on her, and implied that she was to blame for the handling of the incident.

Blaming the victim is a related practice in these hospitals; management will often blame Black nurses for the nurses' misfortunes, including their experiences of racism. Nurses[55] who have complained about racism have been accused of "using" racism to divert attention from their own deficiencies, thus denying their experience completely. It is implied that these nurses are dishonest, unreliable and have a "chip on their shoulder." The DMI report quotes management's position with regard to the complaints made to the Ontario Human Rights Commission by Black nurses and nurses of colour on account of racial discrimination:

> In the hospital's press release of March 27, 1991, I indicated that dismissals and disciplinary actions against employees are based on their behaviour and compliance with standards of practice, and are not racially motivated. This remains the hospital's position. ...[56]

Bias in work allocation and a segregated workforce is evident in hospitals, where Black nurses and other nurses of colour are assigned to heavier duties in less specialized areas, given less desirable shifts and units, knowing that some of these nurses have considerable experience and skills and some have physical disabilities that are not accomodated. This fact was reiterated by several nurses at the "End the Silence" conference. One nurse[57] also mentioned that nurses of colour are often assigned patients of colour. The DMI report mentions that nurses of colour are commonly streamed into chronic care and away from acute care, such as surgery.[58]

The ONA informant confirmed that there is evidence of over-representation of nurses of colour in "heavier" units which are not considered the pinnacle of nursing. For instance, in a number of large hospitals, 70 per cent of the nurses in the veteran's wing and in the long-term care unit are nurses of colour.[59] She further cited a case where a director of nursing in such an unit issued a memo to nurses just prior to the Caribana[60] weekend saying "if you call in sick this weekend, you have to bring in a doctor's note." This was obviously directed at Black nurses and the ONA was able to challenge this successfully.

In general, Black nurses are also treated differentially and adversely with regard to "good shifts," lunch breaks and vacations.[61]

Most nurses in leadership positions, e.g., head nurses, team leaders and charge nurses, are White and hospitals are overwhelmingly run by White management. An ONA staff person confirmed that there are few Black nurse managers. She estimated that in Ontario there are less than five Black or Filipinos in senior managerial positions, with more of them being Filipino than Black.[62] Often, a junior White nurse will be trained to take on a leadership role while a senior Black nurse will be passed over.

Underemployment and the denial of promotions are also evident among Black nurses in hospitals. They are often discouraged from applying for leadership positions on the basis of "lack of skills" or lack of competence. Several nurses at the "End the Silence" conference spoke about having trained White nurses who subsequently became managers. They also spoke about Black women "not being approached" to be managers. An internal hospital report states:

> It was felt that the chances of advancement and promotion within the hospital are very limited, particularly with respect to Black nurses. Apparently there are no Black managers. Considering the percentage of staff which is Black, this was felt to be unfair and very bad for staff morale.[63]

Many Black nurses find their supervisors are disbelieving and unaccommodating when they complain of a particular disability or illness. These nurses are often asked to bring doctor's notes and medical clearance to prove themselves whereas White nurses are not asked to do the same. In one case, a Black nurse,[64] still recovering from an illness, refused to work at night because she felt she was still not well enough to work that shift given that there is less staffing support. The management concluded that she was lying and she was subsequently fired, partly as result of this incident.

One nurse at the "End the Silence" conference mentioned the following incident:

> "One nurse [of colour] was sick and went home. [The] manager stated that she had "abandoned" her patients and was going to be reported to the college."[65]

Whether or not this nurse had a replacement to take over her shift makes no difference as far as management reactions are concerned. In all the cases of which I am aware, nurses were still disciplined by management, even though a replacement was found in every case.

Co-optation of individual nurses of colour and selective alliances with nursing staff are sometimes used in order to monitor outspoken Black nurses targeted by management for disciplinary action. As mentioned earlier, co-opted nurses may collude in the fabrication of documentation in order to "frame" an outspoken nurse of colour. Some of the testimonies reported in the DMI report address this issue directly:

> "Some nurses were requested by their nurse managers to spy on their co-workers and to report back with information which could later be used against those employees."[66]

"I fell ill because of harassment I received at the hands of my manager. My blood pressure went up, and I was in severe shock; I was intimidated, berated, yelled at and threatened due to my refusal to bear false witness against my supervisor, a woman of colour. When I refused to co-operate, I was told my behaviour is insubordinate. ..."[67]

When accused of racism, management in hospitals and other institutions will point to "token" managers of colour in order to prove their commitment to equality of opportunity. What is downplayed is the fact that management is overwhelmingly White and people of colour are rare exceptions.

Contextualizing Everyday Racism in Hospitals

In the preceding section, I described some of the most common experiences of racism faced by Black nurses in hospitals. These experiences tell us about White management practices and also about the way employment systems operate in these hospitals. Management practices may be standard or differential, conscious or unconscious, but all have an adverse effect on most Black nurses and other nurses of colour. This is systemic racism in the workplace. In other words, individual practices by managers are based on racism evident in the employment systems of these hospitals, including the everyday culture of the workplace. In the next section, I will link management practices with racist employment systems.

As mentioned, leadership in these hospitals is predominantly White. This is a result of subjective promotional procedures. For example, a nursing unit manager, usually White, often will "name" who will fill a particular leadership position. Pre-screening, checking of references, interviews and internal transfers are often left to one person, usually a White female manager. This reliance on one person making choices leaves room for subjectivity and biases which creep into the decision-making structure. For instance, it was reported by Hardill[68] that:

During hiring, one reference check was generally completed for White nurses; three references were commonly checked before hiring Black nurses ... Personnel files and job application forms for Black nurses frequently contained personal and irrelevant information about their families, place of origin and English proficiency.[69]

It is also evident that the selection of nurses for leadership positions is inconsistent. For instance, in one unit, a team leader's position may be rotated; in another unit, nurses with special training may be preferred for these positions. This shows that *ad hoc* methods are used to fill leadership positions based on the style of individual managers. This affects Black nurses adversely, as evident from their testimonies.

Some of these hospitals use word-of-mouth recruitment methods. Various reports on employment equity have pointed out that word-of-mouth recruitment can act as a barrier to the employment of people of colour and women in non-traditional jobs and sectors. It basically reproduces the status quo. Therefore, if the labour force in an establishment is racially segmented and predominantly female, then the word-of-mouth approach will merely reproduce that pattern.

In some hospitals, internal candidates are given first preference at times and, at other times, the competition is opened to those in the external labour market. The inconsistency in the outreach process is a concern from an employment equity perspective. Who decides when the competition will be open and when it will be closed? Biases are sure to operate as such important decisions are often left to one or two management staff.

When job interviews are being conducted by individual managers, it is imperative that training be given in employment equity measures. As there is an overwhelming denial of racism by hospital management, such an approach is not likely to be adopted. It is evident that interviewers often use vague, subjective criteria to select personnel. The suitability of candidates is often judged by the external presentation of the candidate in the interview situation. It is apparent that candidates may be judged on verbal fluency and non-verbal cues, most likely based on cultural, class and gender biases. Effective styles of communication tend to be associated with the styles of people who are already in the organization[70] therefore those who present themselves "differently" may be viewed as "less effective." An interviewer who is unfamiliar with cross-cultural issues such as the ones in these hospitals, can assign negative values to candidates' verbal and non-verbal cues and thus judge their suitability for a job in a biased and an incorrect way.

Similar biases seem to flourish within the employee appraisal systems, where vague and subjective criteria are often used to judge people's job performance. For instance, several nurses reported being judged negatively on "communication skills" or on "personality problems." Frequently, no further specifications are provided on these criteria so that the supervisor conducting the appraisal can interpret these terms in her own way. In other words, vague criteria provide the scope for arbitrary decisions influenced by one's prejudices and power position. Also, employee appraisals are used to determine if an employee should be promoted or granted a permanent position.

It appears that disciplinary measures are also taken in non-standard ways and are therefore prone to supervisory biases. In light of the biases evident in the outreach, recruitment and appraisal processes, suspensions and firings of Black nurses and other nurses of colour need to be questioned. There are several examples of differential disciplinary measures being taken with Black and White nurses. Also, the apparent failure to deal with performance concerns of some Black nurses in a constructive manner that is directed to improvement indicates inconsistent disciplinary procedures.

The handling of medication errors in hospitals creates concerns from an employment equity perspective. It is not surprising that many Black nurses have reported they have been unfairly accused of making "too many medication errors," and disciplined, as a result, in some cases actually being dismissed from their jobs. The purpose of documenting medication errors is not consistently and clearly understood by management and nursing staff in hospitals. Some believe it is there to discipline nurses, or used to periodically review the medication delivery system. Others believe it serves as a safeguard against lawsuits. The policy surrounding this issue seems to be cut and dry, but, in practice a great deal of discretion remains at every level. On what basis are these discretionary decisions taken? Is it based on any set guidelines, or is it subjective? When most head nurses are White, there is cause for concern if the alleged error has been made by a Black nurse.

By and large, these hospitals do not have practical anti-harassment policies and complaints procedures, particularly where it concerns racial harassment. Where a policy exists, it may be unknown to employees and clients, and specific guidelines to deal with racist incidents will be lacking.

The everyday experiences of racism described here, become logical if seen in the context of systemic racism and sexism in the employment systems of hospitals. Scapegoating, targeting and excessive monitoring by management are not surprising given the biases built into the employee performance appraisal and in the disciplinary measures taken. In both of these management functions, the use of vague, subjective, and non-standardized criteria results in differential treatment of Black and White nurses.

The marginalization of Black female workers in a predominately White female workforce is predictable, given the racial segregation which exists. Biased recruitment, outreach and interview processes lead to a racially segregated workforce. Also, a predominantly White management with no training in cross-cultural, anti-racist and anti-sexist issues, and lacking a viable policy on racial harassment, will be ill-equipped to respond to and deal effectively with racist incidents.

Underemployment and the lack of promotions among Black nurses are natural consequences of work environments in which there are no standard and objective procedures for employee performance appraisals.

Co-optation, selective alliances and tokenism have to be viewed in the context of the nature of hospital leadership. As mentioned, the latter is predominantly White, lacking in cross-cultural and anti-racist skills, perceiving Black female workers in stereotypical ways, including feeling threatened by them, and not guided by any policy on racial harassment. The traditional management method of divide and rule is the only one they know, and that is what is often used.

Management actions *vis à vis* Black nurses also betray its entrenched system of stereotypes and prejudices, most of which arose out of slavery and have now become part of the everyday culture of racism. This culture of racism is evident in the culture of hospitals. Stereotypes about Black people as being "childlike," "inferior," "unskilled" and "dishonest," underlie the practices of infantalization, blaming the victim, bias in work allocation, underemployment and lack of accommodation for their disabilities. The following testimonies from White staff members documented by DMI and Minors illustrate common stereotypes and prejudice held about Black nurses:

"Some Black employees are very slow. If they were White, they wouldn't last."

"Nurses trained in Jamaica come with below average standards and need extra training."

"There are some people who don't feel as committed or as integrated; for example, some people from the islands. ..."

"When it came to the work ethic, people in Nigeria didn't grow up with nose to the grindstone; they wanted to be laid back and have fun. But if they come here where we are more disciplined, problems occur because some people here do not understand cultural differences. ..."

"I feel that visible minorities are excessively sensitive and do not take responsibility for their actions. Their lack of self confidence leads them to accuse everyone else, and lay the blame elsewhere. There is no evidence of racism in the hospital."[71]

The daily harassment of Black nurses and other health professionals give us a glimpse of what can happen in a racist, sexist culture where Black women workers with high levels of skill and leadership qualities challenge the status quo. Individuals who have much to gain from the status quo, i.e., those with relative power, White in most instances, struggle to put Black women back in their "ascribed" place. In discussing the sexual harassment of

"X", a Black woman worker in a predominantly male, White workforce, Bannerji[72] writes:

> The expectations from X obviously were that she should fit some common notion of her "natural" inferiority as a black woman and should also "know her place". ...

Bannerji further describes this form of harassment as a "racist sexual harassment." A similar dynamic is apparent in the case of Black nurses in hospitals, except that they are working in predominantly female workforces. The form of harassment is definitely a "classist racial harassment," one in which employees are disciplined and punished by "superiors" for being in the wrong place in terms of class and racially-prescribed roles, and for challenging the stereotypes of "what Black people should be like."

In addition, it is also apparent that these nurses are also challenging the stereotypes of where Black women "should be" within the workplace. Being registered nurses, with seniority, playing leadership roles with junior nurses (frequently White), other nursing personnel and patients (of diverse racial and ethnic backgrounds), these Black women are violating gender norms, which are laced with racism and class ideologies. Interestingly, White female managers often characterize Black nurses in the same way White males have done since the days of slavery. Black nurses are frequently described as "yelling and screaming," "threatening," reducing white colleagues "to tears," intimidating, dangerous, insensitive, and "cruel." Stereotypes about Black women being "troublemakers" and "evil" underlie White, female management paranoia about Black solidarity and the targeting of outspoken nurses. The denial of Black women's experiences of racism, illness and disability by White female managers seems to reproduce assumptions about the former's "toughness" and "Amazon quality," almost to the point of being non-human. With such characterizations, Black female nurses are portrayed as the antithesis of the "feminine," a reversal of the soft-spoken or silent, acquiescing, nurturing, serving, compassionate and kind female figure associated with "White femininity" and with the nursing profession. White female nursing managers who are responsible for evaluating staff nurses, and who have used their privilege to document racist, sexist impressions are in effect saying that Black women should not be in this profession because they are "not qualified." By these characterizations, Black women are being "nullified as women" and therefore rendered unskilled in terms which have traditionally defined this profession as "women's work." "They" are considered unqualified because of the assumed deficiency in their nursing skills but also because of their personalities which are extensions of who they are — Black women!

Notes

1   Pat and Hugh Armstrong, *Take Care: Warning Signals for Canada's Health System,* (Toronto: Garamond Press, 1994); Pat Armstrong, et al. *Vital Signs: Nursing in Transition,* (Toronto: Garamond Press, 1993); Marie Campbell, "Management as 'Ruling': A Class Phenomenon in Nursing," *Studies in Political Economy,* 27 (Autumn, 1988).

2   Agnes Calliste, "Women of 'Exceptional Merit': Immigration of Caribbean Nurses to Canada," *Canadian Journal of Women and the Law,* Vol. 6, No. 1, 1993, p. 95.

3   Wilson Head, *An Exploratory Study of Attitudes and Perceptions of Minority and Majority Group Healthcare Workers,* (Ontario: Ontario Ministry of Labour 1985).

4   Philomena Essed, *Everyday Racism: Reports From Women of Two Cultures,* (California: Hunter House Inc., 1990).

5   Marina Lee-Cunin, *Daughters of Seacole: A Study of Black Nurses in West Yorkshire,* (West Yorkshire: West Yorkshire Low Pay Unit Ltd., 1989).

6   Calliste, "Exceptional Merit," pp. 85–102.

7   Calliste, "Exceptional Merit," p. 95.

8   Lee-Cunin, *Daughters of Seacole.*

9   Calliste, "Exceptional Merit," p. 100.

10 Head, *Exploratory Study.*

11 Head, *Exploratory Study,* p. 59.

12 Head, *Exploratory Study.*

13 Essed, *Everyday Racism.*

14 Essed, *Everyday Racism.*

15 Surinam was Dutch colony for about 400 years. Over 200,000 Surinamese people migrated to The Netherlands in the 1970s and 1980s.

16 Essed, *Everyday Racism.*

17 Doris Marshall Institute and Arnold Minors & Associates, *Ethno-Racial Equality: A Distant Goal? An Interim Report To Northwestern General Hospital,* Toronto, December 1993–January 1994.

18 DMI and Minors, *Ethno-Racial Equality,* p. 34.

19 Valerie MacDonald, Coordinator, Employment Relations Service, ONA, interviewed by phone on October 13, 1993.

20 "End the Silence on Racism in the Health Care Field," A Conference for Black Nurses and Other Health Care Workers, Congress of Black Women of Canada Toronto Chapter, Ontario Institute of Studies in Education, May 26, 1995.

21 Stan Gray, "Hospitals and Human Rights," *Our Times,* Vol. 13, No. 6, December 1994, p. 17–20.

22 Armstrong et al, *Take Care,* p. 53.

23 Campbell, "Management as Ruling."

24 Terry Wotherspoon, "The Impact of Healthcare De-Institutionalization on the Organization and Delivery of Nursing Services," in *Women, Medicine and Health* edited by B. Singh Bolaria and Rosemary Bolaria, (Halifax: Fernwood Publishing, 1994).

25 Lisa Priest, "Hospitals Helping More, Group Says," *The Toronto Star,* May 18, 1995, p. A34; Daniel Tatroff, "Under the Knife in Chilliwack," *Our Times,* Vol. 14, No. 2, May/June 1995.

26 Geoff Meggs, "Quality Caring," *Our Times,* Vol. 14, No. 2, May/June 1995, p. 43.

27 For a case study of the effects of an American model being implemented in a B.C. hospital, see Tatroff, "Under the Knife in Chilliwack."

28 Discussed in Wotherspoon, "Impact of Healthcare," p. 265.

29 Byrad Yyelland, "Structural Constraints, Emotional Labour and Nursing Work," in B. Singh Bolaria and Rosemary Bolaria (eds.), *Women, Medicine and Health,* (Halifax: Fernwood Publishing, 1994), pp. 231–240.

30 Gray, "Hospitals," pp. 17–20.

31 Debbie, "End the Silence" Conference, Toronto, May 26, 1995.

32 Terry, "End the Silence," May 26, 1995.

33 Debbie, "End the Silence," May 26, 1995.

34 Gray, "Hospitals," p. 17.

35 Ibid.

36 MacDonald, October 13, 1993.

37 DMI and Minors, *Report,* p. 39.

38 Joan, OHRC documents.

39 Tracy, OHRC Complaint.

40 Mary, "End the Silence," May 26, 1995.

41 Tracy, OHRC Reports.

42 Wilma, "End the Silence," May 26, 1995.

43 MacDonald, October 13, 1993.

44 Joan, OHRC documents.

45 DMI and Minors, *Report*, p. 33.

46 Tracy, OHRC Reports.

47 Denise, OHRC Reports.

48 Debbie, "End the Silence," May 26, 1995.

49 Rosa, "End the Silence," May 26, 1995.

50 Wilma, "End the Silence," May 26, 1995.

51 MacDonald, October 13, 1993.

52 Debbie, "End the Silence," May 26, 1995.

53 DMI and Minors, *Report,* p. 35.

54 Tracy, OHRC documents.

55 Ibid.

56 DMI and Minors, *Report,* p. 32.

57 Debbie, "End the Silence," May 26, 1995.

58 DMI and Minors, *Report*, p. 34.
59 MacDonald, October 13, 1993.
60 An annual weekend of celebration held each summer, organized by the Caribbean-Canadian community in Toronto.
61 DMI and Minors, *Report*, p. 37.
62 MacDonald, October 13, 1993.
63 DMI and Minors, *Report*, p. 35.
64 Marilyn, OHRC Reports.
65 Debbie, "End the Silence," May 26, 1995.
66 DMI and Minors, *Report*, p. 35.
67 Ibid.
68 Kathy Hardill, *Discovering Fire Where the Smoke Is: Racism in the Healthcare System, Towards Justice in Health,* (Summer, 1993a).
69 DMI and Minors, *Report*, p. 37.
70 City of Toronto, *Equal Opportunity, Detecting Bias: Part One,* (Toronto: City of Toronto, August 1983), p. 40.
71 All the preceding quotes are from DMI and Minors, *Report*, p. 40–41.
72 Himani Bannerji, *Thinking through: Essays on Feminism, Marxism, and Anti-Racism* (Toronto: Women's Press, 1995), p. 142.

References

Armstrong, Pat, Hugh Armstrong, Jacqueline Choiniere, Gina Feldberg, and Jerry White. *Take Care: Warning Signals for Canada's Health System.* Toronto: Garamond Press, 1994.

Armstrong, Pat, Jacqueline Choiniere, and Elaine Day. *Vital Signs: Nursing in Transition.* Toronto: Garamond Press, 1993.

Bannerji, Himani. *Thinking Through: Essays on Feminism, Marxism, and Anti-Racism.* Toronto: Women's Press, 1995.

Calliste, Agnes. "Women of 'Exceptional Merit': Immigration of Caribbean Nurses to Canada." *Canadian Journal of Women and the Law,* Vol. 6(1), 1993, pp. 85–102.

City of Toronto. *Equal Opportunity: Detecting Bias: Part One.* Toronto: City of Toronto, 1983.

Campbell, Marie. "Management as 'Ruling': A Class Phenomenon in Nursing." *Studies in Political Economy,* 27, Autumn 1988.

Doris Marshall Institute and Arnold Minors & Associates. Ethno-Racial Equality: A Distant Goal? An Interim Report to Northwestern General Hospital. Toronto, 1994.

Essed, Philomena. *Everyday Racism: Reports from Women of Two Cultures.* California: Hunter House Inc., 1990.

Gray, Stan. "Hospitals and Human Rights." *Our Times,* Vol. 13(6), December 1994, pp. 17–20.

Hardill, Kathy. "Discovering Fire Where the Smoke Is: Racism in the Healthcare System." *Towards Justice in Health*, Summer 1993.

Head, Wilson. *An Exploratory Study of Attitudes and Perceptions of Minority and Majority Healthcare Workers.* Ontario: Ministry of Labour, 1985.

Lee-Cunin, Marina. *Daughters of Seacole: A Study of Black Nurses in West Yorkshire.* West Yorkshire: West Yorkshire Low Pay Unit Ltd., 1989.

Meggs, Geoff. "Quality Caring." *Our Times*, Vol. 14(2), May/June 1995.

Priest, Lisa. "Hospitals Helping More, Group Says." *Toronto Star*, May 18, 1995, p. A34.

Tatroff, Daniel. "Under the Knife in Chilliwack." *Our Times*, Vol. 14(2), May/June 1995.

Wotherspoon, Terry. "The Impact of Healthcare De-Institutionalization on the Organization and Delivery of Housing Services" in B. Singh Bolaria and Rosemary Bolaria (eds.), *Women, Medicine and Health*. Halifax: Fernwood Publishing, 1994.

Yyelland, Byrad. "Structural Constraints, Emotional Labour and Nursing Work" in B. Singh Bolaria and Rosemary Bolaria (eds.), *Women, Medicine and Health*. Halifax: Fernwood Publishing, 1994.

Chapter Six

Toward Anti-Racism in Social Work in the Canadian Context

Usha George

Recognizing the pervasiveness of racism and the importance of anti-racism in social work practice, this chapter attempts to provide a framework for anti-racist social work practice in Canada. I will begin with a brief overview of the literature on racism at different levels of intervention in social work practice. The second part of the chapter provides an analysis of the Canadian structural context in which social work is practised. The final section of the chapter outlines a framework for anti-racism in social work practice. The framework emphasizes multiple levels of analysis and engagement. At the individual level, this involves layers of understanding, which recognize the discourse of racism, the problem of intersecting oppressions, the historical experiences of different groups in Canadian society and the barriers they face, the role of the state in creating and sustaining oppressions, and the importance of active engagement towards the elimination of racism. At the organizational level, the framework emphasizes the importance of anti-racist organizational change. Anti-racist work at the structural level incorporates coalition building for collective action. The concluding section of the chapter reiterates the importance of white social workers and social workers of colour working together to bring about anti-racism change.

Racism and Social Work Practice

Race and ethnicity are important considerations in social work practice, however, social work has paid inadequate attention to them (Cooper 1973; Casas 1985; Proctor and Davis 1994; Sue, Arredono and McDavis 1992). Racism is inherent in social work practice (Dominelli 1988; Henry, Tator,

Mattis and Rees 1995). In a content analysis of literature on social work practice with minorities, McMahon and Allen-Meares concluded that "most of the literature on social work practice with minorities is naive and superficial and fails to address their social context" (1992:533). The colour-blind approach which prevailed until the late 1960s and the "blame-the-victim" approach which characterized much of the 1970s and part of 1980s (Cooper 1973; Proctor and Davis 1994) shared certain assumptions that racial/ethnic minorities were by nature pathological and, therefore, individual problems were the result of individual group characteristics. This approach encouraged racist practices and provided an excuse for counsellors not to challenge inequities within the system (Sue, Arredono and McDavis 1992). Much of the research during this period focussed on race and ethnicity as client characteristics (Casas 1985; Ponterotto and Sabnani 1989). No attention was paid to variables such as counsellors' attitudes towards minority clients, the power differentials between counsellors and clients or the structural inequalities that limited minority access to services. Later models referred to in the literature as the culturally different model, the multicultural model or the culturally pluralistic or diverse model (Sue et al. 1992) pay attention to the culture, ethnicity and race of the clients, while ignoring the unequal power relations between the client and the social worker and the multiple oppressions that clients of colour experience in a stratified society (Dominelli 1988).

Racism is also rampant at the organizational/agency level. In a review of nearly 400 publications from Canada, the U.S., Britain and Australia, Reitz (1995) concluded that there is considerable evidence that immigrant groups do not use many important health and social services because of barriers related to language, cultural patterns of help-seeking, inadequate information about services, cultural insensitivity on the part of service providers and lack of service availability. In their study of Metropolitan Toronto, Doyle and Visano (1987) identified many barriers faced by racial and ethnic minorities in accessing health and social services. Racism in human services is manifested in "a lack of appropriate programs and services, ethnocentric values and counselling practices, a tendency to devalue the skills and credentials of minority practitioners, inadequate funding for ethno-racial community-based agencies, a lack of minority representation in social agencies, and monocultural or ad hoc multicultural models of service delivery" (Henry et al. 1995:154). "Personal, institutional and systemic racism affect the kinds of service, training and employment opportunities available to members of racial minorities throughout the social and health-care system" (Tator 1996:153).

At the organizational level, racism is manifested in the predominance of assimilationalist and multicultural models of organizations (Jackson and Holvino

1989; Henry et al. 1995; Tator 1996; Minors 1996). The assimilationist, or mono-cultural model, assumes that equality is achieved by treating everyone the same, that too much attention paid to differences will only perpetuate those differences, that the collective history of a group is irrelevant to work with clients for minority cultures, that workers are competent to deal with all issues, that racism is limited to a small number of people and that the values of the organization permeate every facet of the organization's functioning (Tator 1996:155). The multicultural model leads to superficial changes in an organizations' functioning that do not alter their fundamental structure, functioning or culture. These organizations effect cosmetic changes to their operations, such as employing a small number of ethnic staff or translating some of their publications into languages other than English. The low-profile minority workers get very little support in their work and the needs and perspectives of minorities get minimal attention. The culture of the organization is still mainstream and organizational inertia prevents real progress towards creating access and equity for ethno-racial minorities (Henry et al. 1995). "Social work exists in a racist society and, like other services that target minority populations, social work is open to charges of racism" (McMahon and Allen-Meares 1992:53). Moreover, society undergoes changes over time and so does the nature of racism created and perpetuated by the dominant system.

The Structural Context of Racism in Social Work

"The world today is a racial battlefield" (Winant 1994:267). True as it is, this statement and others are being made at a time when the division of human beings on the basis of racial characteristics is generally accepted as invalid as a method of interpreting the complex nature of humankind. An examination of the structural context of social work will further our understanding of the persistence of racism in these times because "demographic shifts, political realignments and economic pressures — both global and national — profoundly affect the nature of racial identity" (Winant 1994:286). Lee, McGrath, Moffatt and George have identified "the critical trends facing geographic, functional and identity-based communities in Canada" (1996:223). Originally developed to examine the context of community practice, their framework is broad enough to provide an understanding of the context of social work practice. Four general trends that impinge communities are the effects of globalization and technological development, ideological impositions upon the concept of community, the devolution of social welfare responsibility to the local community, and the growing diversity of communities (1996:223–27). These trends do not operate in isolation, they interact in complex ways on the lives of individuals and groups. Brief explanations of these trends are given below.

Capitalism has become a global system as a result of the movement of capital and people, enhanced by the development of information technologies. These developments are often seen as historical imperatives and therefore they escape close scrutiny of their impact on communities. However, they contribute to the marginalization and disempowerment of a great number of people, especially immigrants, refugees and poor people in Canada (1996).

The global era has also brought with it a new social contract, in which rationality, technology and corporate power take precedence over community, personal autonomy and humanity. Principles of mutual responsibility, equality and empowerment acquire new meanings within a technological and individualistic paradigm (1996).

Massive changes have taken place in the area of social programs. Under the pretext of deficit reduction, federal and provincial government support for education, health and social programs is being slowly eroded. As a result, local governments and local communities are asked to shoulder the responsibilities of individual and community well-being. The concept of community capacity is promoted to evoke the nostalgic notions of caring neighbours, which masks the real intentions of the political masters (1996).

The demise of geopolitical colonialism, the development of a neocolonial political economic order, and the mass migration of people from former colonies to most Western societies have contributed to the growing diversity of hitherto homogeneous populations. Immigration trends in countries like Canada, Australia and the U.S.A. show an increase in people from non-European countries. Canada's population is becoming more and more diverse in terms of its ethnic composition (Statistics Canada 1996).

Much has been written on racism in Canadian society and how the policies and programs of the government have further marginalized poor people, immigrants and refugees. It is important to recognize the existence of racism in the contemporary Canadian context. For example: Martin Loney

advances the unfashionable point that poverty and wealth, not race or gender, remain the key influences on life chances. The book details the millions of dollars of public money directed to groups like NAC and Alliance for Employment Equity to promote the fiction that, through race and gender, biology dictates destiny. (Loney 1997)

The Ontario Coalition of Agencies Serving Immigrants states that community leaders feel that newspaper articles about immigrants, refugees and people of colour are neither fair nor balanced and that the effect of this imbalance on immigrant communities is substantial. (OCASI 1996)

Although the proportion of visible minorities in the Canadian labour force rose from 5.9 percent in 1986 to 12 percent in 1996, their representation in the public service has increased from 2.7 percent in 1987 to only 4.1 percent in 1995. (Samuel 1997)

A study which examined the impact of funding cuts on community services in Toronto observed: "the people who have lost the most in terms of access to services over the last two years of cuts have been immigrants and refugees." (Social Planning Council of Metropolitan Toronto and City of Toronto 1996:46)

A number of steps by the current provincial government in Ontario including the cancellation of the Employment Equity Policy, the dismantling of the Anti-Racism Secretariat and cuts to many social programs that provided access and equity to minority populations have clearly indicated the lack of political will to address systemic discrimination in our society. Any systemic attempt to counter racism has been abandoned in favour of market-driven approaches. In keeping with the trend of the times, anti-racism as a system-wide strategy to bridge the power and opportunity gaps for minority populations has become decentralized. Racism is micro-managed and dealt with at the individual level even when it is reported.

A Framework for Anti-Racism in Social Work

Anti-racism is integral to the profession of social work. Social justice, the primary goal of social work, cannot be achieved in a racist society; it cannot be achieved through methods of practice that ignore the racialization and marginalization of vulnerable groups in society. Anti-racist social work theory, along with other critical social work theories, combines theory and practice to produce knowledge, interpret and change the world. It also argues for the unity of different levels of practice and policy work in social work (Banes 1998). "Thus, in a general sense, anti-racism refers to measures and mechanisms designed — by state institutions, organizations, groups and individuals — to counteract racism" (Henry et al. 1995:39).

Although researchers and practitioners disagree over the best way to eliminate racism, they all recognize the importance of multiple levels of analysis and engagement. "I concur with those who have called recently for an explicit recognition of the multiple determination of racism, one that draws upon not only historical materialism but also psychoanalysis" (Miles 1994:207). "Any strategy for effectively resisting racism, therefore, cannot be unitary — and probably not even unified" (Anthias and Yuval-Davis 1992:157). According to Dominelli (1988), anti-racist social work focusses on transforming the unequal social relations between Black and white people into egalitarian ones; therefore, deconstructing racism requires changes at both systemic and individual levels. Recent attempt by Bishop (1994), Essed (1996) and Kivel (1996) have also emphasized the importance of multiple levels of anti-racism work.

The model proposed here has three components incorporating individual, organizational and structural levels: (1) anti-racism education and training for social workers, (2) anti-racism organizational change and (3) coalition building for collective action. These components should not be seen in isolation; their interactions are vital to an effective anti-racism strategy. Although a legal and policy framework is an important component of anti-racism work, it is not included in the model because the state is the final source of macro-policies. Social workers can influence the state mainly through collective action. In the following section, I will examine the three components of the propose anti-racism framework in detail.

Anti-Racism Education and Training

At the individual level anti-racism requires that white social workers recognize their relative positions of power and privilege in a hierarchical social system that works in their favour. White social workers need to undergo anti-racism sensitivity training to enable them to unearth and discard avoidance strategies (Dominelli 1988). Social work education should provide the appropriate knowledge, values and skills to practice social work in an anti-racist way. The term "layers of understanding" denotes the convergence of knowledge, values and skills needed for ethnically sensitive social work practice (Devore and Schlesinger 1996). Cultural competence, that is, the ability to work effectively with individuals and groups belonging to different cultures (Green 1995; Lum 1986; Cross, Bazron, Dennis and Isaacs 1989), is also important in anti-racist social work. The layers of understanding which should form the basis of anti-racist social work education and training in the Canadian context are as follows.

Recognition of the Nature of Racism

This requires an understanding of the social construction of race and racism and the changing nature of racism. Although the notion of biological groupings of people on the basis of phenotypical characteristics is "no longer intellectually and politically viable as a public discourse" (Modood 1997:154), new forms of racism have emerged. For example, in a climate of democratic racism policy or practice, initiatives to change oppressive conditions are undermined by the assumptions expressed in statements such as:

- "Racism doesn't exist in a democratic society."
- "Everyone experiences discrimination from time to time."
- "Racial conflicts occur because of diversity."
- "Minority groups refuse to adapt to Canadian society."
- "People of colour have cultural problems."
- "All we need is to treat everyone equally." (Henry et al. 1995:308)

The discourse of cultural racism (Modood 1997) ascribes group differences to differences in culture. Under paternalistic and competitive racism (Essed 1996) the roles of dominated groups are defined by the dominant group's perception of the dominated groups.

Silva, after a thorough review of the existing views on racism (idealist, classical Marxist, neo-Marxist, institutional, internal colonialist and the racial formation perspective), advances a structural interpretation of racism that incorporates elements of the various theories. Silva defines racialized social systems as "societies that allocate differential economic, political, social and even psychological rewards to groups along racial lines; lines that are socially constructed." In a racist society, "a set of social relations and practices on racial distinctions develops at all societal levels." Races "historically are constituted according to a process of racialization" and opposition between racialized groups. This in turn gives rise to a racial ideology, which is not a superstructural phenomenon, but "the organizational map that guides the actions of racial actors in society." Racialized societies also produce racial contestation, which "reveals the different objectives interests of the races in a racialized system" (Silva 1997:10). This framework explains overt and covert racial behaviour as well as the changing nature of racism.

Changes are due to specific struggles at different levels among the races, resulting from differences in interests. Such changes may transform the nature of racialization and the global character of racial relations in the system (the racial structure). Therefore change is viewed as a normal component of the racialized structure (Silva 1997:11). This perspective, however, does not answer the question: how do racialized systems come into existence? It has limited ability to explain the intersections of class and gender in racialized societies. The structural origins of racism demands a structural solution for its elimination and this has important implications for "curing" racism.

Understanding the overlapping relationships of race, ethnicity and culture and the interlocking oppressions of race, ethnicity, class, gender, sexual orientation, age, religion, language and other factors on the experiences of clients and the relationship between clients and social workers.

The overlapping definitions of race, ethnicity and culture complicate efforts to understand racism (Yinger 1994; Berry and Laponce 1994). "We are close to having come full circle. In the nineteenth century, race was used to mean culture as well as race. The twentieth century may well end with culture meaning race as well as culture" (Berry and Laponce 1994:5). Although much work has been done in this area, theories about the complex relationships among race, class, gender and other forms of oppression are still inconclusive (Stasiulus 1990). For example, women of colour experience racism and sexism together. These oppressions interact and influence each other. "Multiple oppression is stressful and draining" (Gerrad 1991:564). "Racism cannot be understood without considering their interconnections with ethnicity, nationalism, class, gender and the state" (Anthias and Yuval-Davis 1992:viii).

The concept of integrative anti-racism represents recent attempts to capture the intricate relationship between race, class, gender and other sources of oppression (Dei 1995, 1996). Integrative anti-racism requires an understanding of the different yet intersecting forms of oppression based on race, gender class, sexual orientation, religion, age, language or other factors, using race as the lens through which varied forms of oppression must be viewed (Dei 1995, 1996). Integrative anti-racism acknowledges the shifting and intersecting experiences caused by socially constructed race, gender and class categories and recognizes the saliency and visibility of certain forms of oppression. Integrative anti-racism draws on six interrelated issues:

1. understanding the process of articulation of social difference,
2. understanding the relevance of personal experience and knowledge,
3. understanding how differentials of power and privilege work in society,
4. understanding the saliency of race,
5. understanding the importance of global political economic issues, and
6. understanding how to engage in social transformation.

"When we also develop a consciousness about the numerous layers of oppression that add up to subordinate the majority of people in society, we can better understand how these various oppressions also have a personal impact on our own lives" (Carniol 1991:118).

Appreciating and understanding the historical experiences of different ethnic groups in Canada and the structural barriers they face in gaining access to services.
The history of Aboriginal peoples in Canada and the experiences of Black Canadians, Chinese-Canadians, Japanese-Canadians and South Asian-Canadians with respect to Canadian immigration policies reveal the extent of exploitation, domination and racism that has characterized the relationship

between the dominant whites and others (Bolaria and Li 1988; Henry et al. 1995). Some of the theories that explain and predict the situation of ethnic groups in a post-industrial society are: assimilation, amalgamation, modified assimilation, modified pluralism and differential incorporation has been applied to the Canadian situation, in relation to Caribbean people in Toronto (Henry 1994). Henry argues that "societal racism," that is, the racism and discrimination in mainstream society, and its reluctance to respond to the needs of newcomers "create the marginal status for the Caribbean people and result in their differential incorporation into Canadian society" (Henry 1994:16).

Acknowledging the role of the state in disempowering some population groups and understanding the impact of "neutral" policies on marginalized communities.
Recognizing the emerging heterogeneity of Canadian society, the government has a number of legislative measures to guarantee equal treatment of ethnic minorities in Canada. The Canadian Charter of Rights and Freedoms, the Canadian Policy on Multiculturalism, the Canadian Immigration Act, the Human Rights Code and federal Employment Equity legislation are examples of such attempts. It is important that social workers have a grasp of the strengths and weaknesses of these policies. Moreover, social workers should be equipped to examine the implications of new policies on minority populations. For example, the proposed recommendations in the current legislative review of the Immigration Act have both economic and social implications for Canada's immigrants.

Working towards the elimination of all forms of oppression through reflective practice, critical thinking and collective action.
Social workers, due to their privileged positions, may not admit their own racism. This may happen through denial, omission, decontextualization, colour-blind approaches, dumping approaches, patronizing approaches and avoidance (Dominelli 1988). Anti-racism awareness training for social workers enables them to examine their individual attitudes and how they shape behaviour. It also helps social workers see the connection between individual and structural elements in racism, and how personal changes can contribute to structural changes through the design of policies and practices that are sensitive to the needs of non-dominant groups. Many of the models developed in cross-cultural training share three characteristics: a recognition of the role of one's own ethnic or cultural identity in determining one's world view, an emphasis on learning about other cultures, and the teaching of intervention and counselling skills for use with members of other ethnic groups (Corvin

and Wiggins 1989). White social workers can become allies with marginalized people to break the cycle of oppression (Bishop 1994).

Feminist ideas have tremendous possibilities for combating racism. "The agreement to hear, see, and know about racism in ourselves is the core of making anti-racism a norm for ethical feminist therapy practice" (Brown 1995:145). The three feminist principles: feminist consciousness and consciousness raising, the principle of integration and the idea that the personal is political are relevant to the development of an interactive perspective on ethnic minority issues (Gould 1987). Consciousness raising has two elements: it searches for dehumanizing social structures and it is oriented towards action to alter these social conditions (Mullaly 1993). The concept is very similar to the conscientization process by which individuals make the connections between the values, behaviours and attitudes they endorse and perpetuate and the social positions they occupy (Freire 1970). Conscientization enables social workers to understand their own privileges and this in turn helps them to change their attitudes and behaviours to treat others with openness and dignity (Dominelli 1988).

Anti-Racism Organizational Change

Social workers can encourage anti-racism organizational change by ending the conspiracy of silence about racism, by establishing equity in the workplace, by initiating discussions about the components of anti-racist social work and by establishing mechanisms to monitor the progress of anti-racism policies and programs within the agency (Dominelli 1988).

Anti-racism organizational change demands a holistic approach, commitment to the eradication of all forms of oppression and the elimination of racial disadvantage within the organization. It requires that social workers acknowledge that the perspectives of people of colour are relevant and real, and that people of colour should be included as full and equal participants in the organization. The organization must make fundamental changes to its policies and practices to be more inclusive. The "integrated multicultural/ anti-racism model" of human service organizations gives high priority to the issues of minority access, participation and equity (Tator 1996).

James (1996) introduces an anti-racist model of service delivery which stands in sharp contrast to the multicultural model. The anti-racist model is characterized by the ongoing analysis of individual experiences in institutional contexts, challenges to existing power relations, the ongoing analysis of social systems in relation to its constituencies, the examination of the values of human service providers and institutions, and the provision of programs of employment equity and access for disadvantaged groups.

The models proposed by Dominelli (1998), Henry (1995), Tator (1996) and James (1996) incorporate both individual and organizational imperatives for change. Minors (1996) examines different models of change within organizations. The transition from "uni-versity" (discrimination) to "poly-versity" (anti-discrimination) represents anti-racism organizational change for the organization. In this process, the organization passes through six stages from an excluding organization, to a passive club, to token acceptance, to symbolic equity, to substantial equity, to an including organization. This is a linear model and actual organizational pathways may differ because of complex institutional patterns of behaviour.

Successful transition to anti-racism requires organizations to identify structures and behaviours that need to be changed, determine training and education needs, sanctions and supports, plan and implement necessary changes, and review, monitor and evaluate the changes (Thomas 1987; United Way 1991). At the organizational level there should be an anti-racism policy with goals, timetables and accountabilities that will promote access and equity for clients and for minority workers in service provision and the management of the organization.

Anti-Racism and Coalition Building

Social workers must help mobilize communities for action against discriminatory practices, policies and legislation. Social work tradition has always emphasized individual change along with social action, social change and community development (Elliott 1993).

Anti-racist social work recognizes the relationship between individual troubles and structural inequalities and works towards connecting the personal and the political. The community development continuum (Jackson, Mitchell and Wright 1989) takes into account the need for individuals to take charge of their lives. Jackson et al. (1989) suggest that this continuum consists of a number of stages: developmental casework, mutual support, issue identification and campaigns, participation in and control of services, and social movements. The goal of developmental casework is to create links between individual service users, so that they can mobilize for change for themselves and others. Developing mutual support involves strengthening families and establishing friendships and other networks. During the stage of issue identification many "natural networks" come together to form coalitions interested in achieving change. The participation and control stage provide opportunities for people to become active in decision making to ensure that services are responsive to local needs. The final stage involves participation in social movements. At this point people become committed to ongoing change. This continuum does not describe an inevitably upward progression. Individuals can enter the continuum at any stage.

When social workers reject the strong push towards a conventional version of casework and act forcefully in favour of clients, they are at least temporarily able to interrupt the top-down flow of power and the associated social relations imposed by the welfare state. Granted such interruptions are by themselves insufficient to change the prevailing structures of society, they nevertheless constitute essential building blocks for basic change (Carniol 1991:116). And unfortunately setbacks may occur.

Two important components of this model are empowerment and advocacy. According to Evans, the literature suggests three processes that facilitate empowerment (1992). These are skill building, the enhancement of feelings of efficacy and awareness of social realities which, taken together, are said to develop a sense of critical consciousness. Advocacy is an important element in anti-racist social work. "Advocacy involves acting as a broker among the community, institutions, and government — identifying unfair and unjust practices, advocating for new policies and programs, supporting external alliances or coalitions, working collaboratively with ethnospecific agencies, and lobbying for changes in education, policing, justice, and employment" (Tator 1996). The essence of anti-racism is to challenge the status quo through political activism. Therefore the anti-racist worker has to be a theorist and a practitioner at the same time (Dei 1996).

Conclusion

In concluding this chapter, I would like to draw attention to three important points. First, all social workers should be involved in anti-racism work. White social workers and social workers of colour should share the responsibility for bringing about change. Commenting on the complex relationship between race, ethnicity and nationalism, Rattansi (1992) points out "that racism and ethnocentrism are not necessarily confined to white groups" (p. 36). Varying levels of ethnocentrism, nationalism and even racism exist among people of colour, and social workers should be aware of the resulting ambivalence and contradictions. Secondly, the state has a major role to play in providing policy and fiscal supports to anti-racism efforts. The state has to create the required institutional framework to eliminate racism that affects the lives of people who are already vulnerable. Third, as discussed in the second part of this chapter, the context of social work practice is changing rapidly. Diminishing resources have promoted the development of short-term interventions and brief service models. In Ontario many programs and services specially designed for immigrant and refugee communities have been eliminated. In an environment of growing insecurity, anti-racism work should not be seen as a nonessential component of social work.

References

Anthias, F. and N. Yuval-Davis. 1992. *Racialized Boundaries: Race, Nation, Gender, Colour and Class and the Anti-Racist Struggle.* New York and London: Routledge.

Banes, D. 1998. *Everyday Practice of Race, Class and Gender.* Unpublished Ph.D. dissertation. Faculty of Social Work: University of Toronto.

Berry, J.W. and J.A. Laponce. 1994. *Ethnicity and Culture in Canada: The Research Landscape.* Toronto: University of Toronto Press.

Bishop, A. 1994. *Becoming an Ally: Breaking the Cycle of Oppression.* Halifax: Fernwood Publishing.

Bolaria, S. and P. Li. 1998. *Racialized Oppression in Canada.* 2nd edition. Toronto: Garamond Press.

Brown, L. 1995. "Anti-Racism as an Ethical Norm in Feminist Therapy Practice." In J. Adelman and G. Enguidanos (eds.), *Racism in the Lives of Women: Testimony, Theory, and Guides to Antiracist Practice.* New York: Haworth Press.

Carniol, B. 1991. *Case Critical: Challenging Social Work in Canada.* 2nd edition. Toronto: Between the Lines.

Casas, J.M. 1985. "A Reflection on the Status of Racial Ethnic Minority Research." *The Counselling Psychologist* 13: 4581–98.

Cooper, S. 1973. "A Look at the Effects of Racism on Clinical Work." *Social Casework*, February.

Corvin, S.A. and F. Wiggins. 1989. "An Anti-Racism Training Model for White Professionals." *Journal of Multicultural Counselling and Development* 17: 105–14.

Cross, T.L., Bazron, B.J., K.W. Dennis and M. Isaacs. 1989. *Towards a Culturally Competent System of Care: A Monograph on Effective Services for Minority Children Who are Severely Emotionally Disturbed.* Washington, D.C.: Georgetown University Child Development Center.

Dei, G.J.S. 1995a. "Integrative Anti-Racism: Intersections of Race, Class and Gender." *Race, Gender and Class: Special Edition* 2(3): 11–30.

———. 1995b. "Examining the Case for African-centred Schools." *McGill Journal of Education* 30(2): 179–98.

———. 1996. *Anti-Racism Education: Theory and Practice.* Halifax: Fernwood Publishing.

Devore, W. and E.G. Schlesinger. 1996. *Ethnic-Sensitive Social Work Practice.* 4th edition. Boston: Allyn and Bacon.

Dominelli, L. 1988. *Anti-Racist Social Work.* London: MacMillan.

Doyle, R. and L. Visano. 1987. *Access to Health and Social Services for Members of Diverse Cultural and Racial Groups, Reports 1 and 2.* Toronto: Social Planning Council of Metropolitan Toronto.

Elliott, D. 1993. "Social Work and Social Development Towards an Integrative Model for Social Work Practice." *International Social Work* 36(1): 21–37.

Essed, P. 1996. *DiVeRSiTY: Gender, Colour and Culture*. Amherst: University of Massachusetts Press.

Evans, E.N. 1992. "Liberation Theology, Empowerment Theory and Social Work Practice with the Oppressed." *International Social Work* 35: 135–47.

Freire, P. 1970. *The Pedagogy of the Oppressed*. Hammondsworth: Penguin.

Gerrad, N. 1991. "Racism and Sexism, Together, in Counselling: Three Women of Colour Tell Their Stories." *Canadian Journal of Counselling* 25(4): 555–66.

Gould, K. 1987. "Feminist Principles and Minority Concerns: Contributions, Problems and Solutions." *Affilia*, Fall: 6–19.

Green, J.W. 1995. *Cultural Awareness in the Human Services*. Boston: Allyn and Bacon.

Henry, F. 1994. *The Caribbean Diaspora in Toronto: Learning to Live with Racism*. Toronto: University of Toronto Press.

Henry, F., Tator, C., W. Mattis and T. Rees. 1995. *The Colour of Democracy: Racism in Canadian Society*. Toronto: Harcourt Brace.

Jackson, B.W. and E. Holvino. 1989. "Working with Multicultural Organizations: Matching Theory to Practice." *Proceedings of a Workshop on Diversity: Implications for Education and Training*, 109–21.

Jackson, T., Mitchell, S. and M. Wright. 1989. "The Community Development Continuum." *Community Health Studies* XIII(1): 66–73.

James, C.E., (ed.). 1996. *Perspectives on Racism and the Human Services Sector: A Case for Change*. Toronto: University of Toronto Press.

Kivel, P. 1996. *Uprooting Racism: How White People Can Work for Racial Justice*. Gabriola Island, B.C.: New Society Publishers.

Lee, B., McGrath, S., K. Moffatt and U. George. 1996. "Community Practice Education in Canadian Schools of Social Work." *Canadian Review of Social Work* 13(2): 221–36.

Loney, M. 1997. Letter to the Editor. *Toronto Star*, November 1.

Lum, D. 1986. *Social Work Practice and People of Colour: A Process-stage Approach*. Monterey, CA: Brooks/Cole.

McMahon, A. and P. Allen-Meares. 1992. "Is Social Work Racist? A Content Analysis of Recent Literature." *Social Work* 37(6): 533–39.

Miles, R. 1994. "Explaining Racism in Contemporary Europe." In A. Rattansi and S. Westwood (eds.), *Racism, Modernity and Identity*. London: Polity Press.

Minors, A. 1996. "From Uni-versity to Poly-versity: Organizations in Transition to Anti-Racism." In C.A. James (ed.), *Perspectives on Racism and the Human Services Sector: A Case for Change*. Toronto: University of Toronto Press.

Modood, T. 1997. "'Difference,' cultural racism and anti-racism." In P. Werbner and T. Modood (eds.), *Debating Cultural Hybridity: Multi-cultural Identities and the Politics of Anti-Racism*. London: Zed Books.

Mullaly, R. 1993. *Structural Social Work, Ideology, Theory and Practice*. Toronto: McClelland and Stewart.

OCASI (Ontario Council of Agencies Serving Immigrants). 1996. "Community agency survey." *A Nation of Immigrants*. Toronto: OCASI.

Ponterotto J. and H. B. Sabnani. 1989. "'Classics' in Multicultural Counselling: A Systematic Five Year Content Analysis." *Journal of Multicultural Counselling and Development* 17: 23–37.

Proctor, E.K. and L.E. Davis. 1994. "The Challenge of Racial Difference: Skills for Clinical Practice." *Social Work* 39(3): 314–23.

Rattansi, A. 1992. "Changing the subject? Racism, culture and education." In J. Donald and A. Rattansi (eds.), *Race, Culture and Difference*. London: Sage Publications with The Open University.

Reitz, J. 1995. *A Review of the Literature on Aspects of Ethno-racial Access, Utilization and Delivery of Social Services*. Report prepared for The Multicultural Coalition for Access to Family Services and Ontario Ministry of Community and Social Services.

Samuel, J. and Associates Inc. 1997. *Visible Minorities and the Public Service of Canada*. Report submitted to the Canadian Human Rights Commission. Ottawa: J. Samuel and Associates Inc.

Silva, E. 1997. "Rethinking Racism: Toward a Structural Interpretation." *American Sociological Review* 62(3): 465–86.

Social Planning Council of Metropolitan Toronto and City of Toronto. 1996. *Profile of a Changing World*.

Stasiulus, D. 1990. "Theorizing Connections: Gender, Race, Ethnicity and Class." In P. Li (ed.), *Race and Ethnic Relations in Canada*.

Statistics Canada. 1996. *Canada's Changing Immigrant Population*. Catalogue 96-311E.

Sue, D., Arrendono, P. and R.J. McDavis. 1992. "Multicultural Counselling Competencies and Standards: A Call to the Profession." *Journal of Multicultural Counselling and Development* 20: 64–88.

Tator, C. 1996. "Anti-Racism and the Human Service Delivery System." In C.A. James (ed.), *Perspectives on Racism and the Human Services Sector: A Case for Change*. Toronto: University of Toronto Press.

Thomas, B. 1987. *Multiculturalism at Work: A Guide to Organizational Change*. Toronto: YWCA of Metropolitan Toronto.

United Way of Greater Toronto. 1991. *Action, Access, Diversity! A Guide to Anti-racist/Multicultural Organizational Change for Social Service Agencies*. Toronto: United Way.

Winant, H. 1994a. *Racial Conditions*. Minneapolis: University of Minnesota Press.

——. 1994b. "Racial Formation and Hegemony: Local and Global Developments." In A. Rattansi and S. Westwood (eds.), *Racism, Modernity and Identity*. London: Polity Press.

Yinger, J. 1994. *Ethnicity: Source of Strength and Source of Conflict*. New York: State University of New York Press.

Chapter Seven

The World of the Professional Stripper

Chris Bruckert

If you wandered into one of the over 200 strip clubs in Ontario, you might notice the dim lighting, the pool tables and video games, the continually running pornographic movies, and the smell of stale beer. You might notice that this is clearly a "male space" that is, somewhat ironically, defined by the presence of (some) women. Women in scant attire "hanging out," women sitting and listening with apparently rapt attention to men, women at some phase of undress dancing on stage, women in champagne rooms[1] dancing for, or talking with, (clothed) men who are sitting only inches away from their naked bodies. At first glance the scene appears so imbued with the markers of gendered oppression, objectification, and exploitation that analysis is hardly necessary. Nonetheless, things are not as straightforward as they seem. From the perspective of the women "deep" in conversation or dancing on the stage, strip clubs are not about entertainment, or immorality, or sex. They are about work.

In this chapter we explore the work of strippers through the lens of feminist labour theory. Using an approach informed by Marxism, symbolic interactionism, and feminism allows us to shift between analytic levels and consider the intersection and tension between market economy, social and gender relations, regulatory frameworks, dominant discourses, labour processes, and work site practices. When we step outside of morally loaded assumptions and attend to the understanding of industry workers, it is quickly apparent that strippers' work is both similar to and markedly different from other working-class women's labour.[2]

From Entertainment to Service

The trajectory of labour of Ontario's strippers over the last three decades speaks to the unique position of strip clubs as both commercial enterprises embedded in the market economy and, at the same time, the product and focus of dynamic social processes including moral and legal regulation. It also illustrates how broader labour market trends and economic shifts not only position clubs to exploit strippers but also condition the nature of that exploitation. In the mid and late 1970s strippers were entertainers who, in exchange for wages,[3] performed five sets of four songs (three fast, one slow floor show) during their six-hour shift. During the 1980s and into the 1990s Canada experienced periods of recession, a general stagnation of fiscal growth, and high rates of unemployment (Phillips, 1997:64). During this period of economic restructuring, manufacturing jobs were displaced, the service sector expanded exponentially, and women's labour market position was destabilized (Luxton and Corman, 2001). For working-class women labour market reorganization resulted in a move into labour-intensive consumer service sector employment characterized by low pay, low capital–labour ratio, limited job security, poor working conditions, and non-standard labour arrangements such as part-time, casual, and seasonal work. In principle protected through labour legislation, in practice marginal, non-unionized workers in this sector have limited recourse to legal protection and are susceptible to a range of exploitive practices (Duffy and Pupo, 1997). In addition, the vanishing social safety net compounded the vulnerability, economic need, and domestic responsibilities of this social strata. As a result, workers were not only, by default, increasingly employed in the service sector but situated to embrace work in the growing non-standard labour market, including casual and flexible self-account work, as an income-generating strategy that allowed them to fulfill their many social and personal obligations.

It was in this context of economic decline and dwindling options for working-class women that the new industry innovation of table dancing[4] was introduced in the early 1980s and used to justify cutting dancers' pay to $30 or $40 a day. At the same time shifts were increased from six to eight hours, and bar fees[5] were implemented. By the early 1990s as the economy continued to spiral downward threatening even the "bad jobs" in the service sector, clubs went from exploiting workers to the full appropriation of their labour. Many dancers found their pay eliminated, as they were offered the option of working for "tips" or not at all. In short, in Ontario between 1980 and 2000 stripping was "deprofessionalized,"[6] dancers were redefined as service providers, wages were reduced, and the labour requirements were substantially increased.

Today, while some dancers continue to work "on-schedule" earning between $35 and $45 for an eight-hour shift, most work as "freelancers"[7] receiving no financial compensation from the club. Under either arrangement dancers are expected to pay the established bar fee of between $10 and $20, follow house rules, remain in the bar for a predetermined period of time — hanging out and "looking like a hooker" (Debbie)[8] — and perform between one and five three-song "sets" on stage. Similar to other subcontracting relations (i.e., electricians) exotic dancers are responsible for furnishing tools, in this case music, costumes, and transportation. In exchange for labour, fees, and compliance with the expectations of the club, the bar provides the labour site — the physical space (bar, chairs, champagne rooms) and other coordinated and necessary labour by disk jockeys, bartenders, servers, and doormen. This setting is, of course, crucial. Without it, a dancer cannot solicit the private dances that constitute her income.[9]

In spite of receiving no, or minimal, pay the workers' labour and general deportment remains under the control of management, who establish the house rules governing attire and behaviour, expectations of stage shows, interactions with customers, and services offered in the champagne rooms. Compliance is realized through economic sanctions in the form of fines and by the club's power to deny access to customers. A dancer who is defined as troublesome, who complains "too much," who doesn't follow the house rules, or who leaves with a customer may be suspended or barred permanently. "Troublesome" dancers also risk being blacklisted. This can have dire consequences, since the marked dancer will be unable to pursue her trade anywhere in the city. Put this way, today strippers are in a contradictory space — on the one hand they are managed like employees and subject to disciplinary regimes if they fail to comply, while on the other hand they are denied the pay and protection generally associated with employment.

The exploitative nature of managerial attempts to extract maximum labour power notwithstanding, there have also been positive implications for workers in the shift from entertainment to service. With de-professionalization and lower labour costs, a new industry standard of continuous stages and lots of "girls" emerged. These changes in turn meant new employment opportunities and an opening up of the labour market as the demand increased. They also conditioned the relationship between management and dancers in new ways. Their limited commitment to a particular labour site affords individual dancers greater levels of autonomy and allows them to determine, within particular confines, where, when, and how much they work. Since the club no longer pays workers but exchanges fees and labour site access for free labour, the ability of management to control labour has been somewhat eroded. This is exacerbated by the managerial need for a stable work force and their subsequent hesitancy to alienate the dancers on whom they rely. This is particularly true for women with considerable organizational assets (i.e., a "sexy" appearance, a client list).

Moreover, the new organization not only conditions labour relations but also interacts with class to shape the labour site itself. In the past, the nature of the entertainment-based industry compelled dancers to work full-time and travel "the circuit." These conditions effectively excluded many women workers who embraced other "respectable" social roles: children, partners, school commitments, other jobs. Today, dancers can opt to work full-time, part-time, or occasionally; and either never, or only periodically, go "on the road" in response to particular financial difficulties. In real terms this, coupled with the impoverishment of women workers in Canada generally, opened up the industry to reputable working-class women and women from middle-class families whose eroding economic position (coupled with ideological changes regarding the meaning of nudity) has rendered morally suspect labour increasingly tenable. Tina, a sole-support mother, started working as a stripper when after years of steady employment she found herself:

> On welfare for seven months. And it was hard and ... I saw those, ah, those ads [in the newspaper]. And one day I decided to, to go, to try it y'know. But it was scary. I was 29 years old and I didn't know what was going on there.

Like Tina, these new workers need to overcome their own stereotypical assumptions about strip clubs; however, those who effectively deconstruct the dominant discourses sometimes remain in the occupation for considerable periods of time. In turn as these new workers bring to the labour site their own class culture and investment in respectability, these values have become embedded in the industry structure itself. Today, the markers of rough working-class culture — practices (partying, drugs), appearance (cut-off jean shorts, tattoos), values (being "solid"), and language (talking tough) — are either absent from strip clubs or are limited to one token "rough bar."[10]

In 1973, amendments to the provincial Liquor Control Act expanded the definition of "theatre" (Ontario, 1973) and made it possible in Ontario to combine alcohol and nudity in a legal commercial endeavour. Since then, the trajectory of strip clubs in the province reveals how the complex interplay between market economy and labour structure shapes the labour process in marginal spheres at the same time as the labour process shapes the class origin of the available employee base. Workers are then positioned in a contradictory class location: they are both independent entrepreneurs who manage their own business — thus, are the bourgeois — and employees who sell (or in this case exchange) their labour power and who rely on, and must comply with the expectations of, an individual capitalist — in this case, the proletariat.

The Job

When we shift our focus and apply the feminist labour lens to the question of labour practices another set of questions emerge. What does the work entail? What skills and competencies are workers expected to bring to the labour site? What strategies do dancers employ to negotiate the occupational hazards? What are the particular challenges of the job? In addition, by retaining the focus on class, we are also positioned to ask: How does strippers' labour compare to that of working-class women more generally?

The Stage

Though frequently ignored in labour theory, sexuality does not operate outside of the labour market. Rather "sexuality is a structuring process of gender" (Adkins, 1992:208), and gender and sexuality are central "to *all* workplace power relations" [emphasis in original] (Pringle, 1988:84). Certainly in the consumer service sector where working-class women are clustered, workers are expected to bring to the labour market not only the ability to assume an attractive "made-up" appearance so that "part of the job for women consists of looking good," but also must offer, explicitly or implicitly, a feminine and sexualized presentation-of-self (Adkins, 1992: 216,218). In fact much of the publicly visible labour (waitressing, flight attendants) that women traditionally undertake has a sexual subtext. Framed in this way, strippers' erotic labour situates them on a continuum of visible sexuality that frequently characterizes working-class women's labour force engagement. What marks the strip club as unique, however, is the self-conscious reliance on women's bodies. While other service industries may use women's bodies to make a product or service more appealing (Adkins, 1992), here the service and the body are conflated so that sexuality appears to define the labour.

A woman working in a strip club as a stripper first and foremost has to *act* like a *stripper*; whether she is on the stage or not, she is always *performing*. This involves both the ceremony common to visible employees of "playing [her] condition to realize it" (Goffman, 1959:76) and the fact that the dancer is allowed some creativity, although, like actors generally, she is required to assume a role that is not her own, nor of her making (Henry and Sims, 1970). To entertain, she has to "do a stage." This public erotic labour involves the ability to perform for, but also interact with, the audience, whose very presence legitimates the work.[11] In addition, a stripper's act requires a degree of comfort with nudity, a willingness to expose herself physically, and a self-assured and confident presentation-of-self. Many strippers develop a strong stage presence and are often competent dancers, proficient not only in the standard stripper "moves" but able to incorporate, and execute (in very high heels) their own eclectic mix of ballet, jazz, acrobatics, aerobics, and posing. On stage a dancer must continue to smile or at least assume the appropriate sexually vacant expression — "I think about doing laundry or watch the TV" (Debbie) — in the face of apathy and, sometimes, taunts. These kinds of verbal comments touch not only on her performance but, in light of the gendered appearance imperative, on her value as a woman. In short, she needs to develop the capacity to distance herself from the negative evaluation of the audience.

Although obscured by the performance component and nudity, stage shows are physically demanding labour. And, like so much physical labour, it can be dangerous.[12] In addition to the risks inherent to dancing in stiletto heels, there is the threat of infectious disease. While many dancers take protective measures,[13] the dressing rooms, washrooms, stage, and pole are, at least in some clubs, not particularly well-maintained. The work is also exhausting and technically difficult: "Pole work is a lot of hanging upside down, it's a lot of balance, muscle technique. It's hard to look sexy when you're upside down and all the blood's rushing to your head!" (Diane). Put another way, the "moves" can only be erotic if they appear effortless and natural, a feat that necessitates practice, skill, and considerable muscle development.[14] In short, constructing sexuality is not natural or easy but hard *work*; however, the more effective the illusion, the more sexual the portrayal, the more the *work* is invisible.

The question becomes: How is erotic labour understood and negotiated by participants? Perhaps the most telling finding was how few comments were made by interviewees about sexuality. It appeared to be largely incidental. While dominating public consciousness, nudity, sexual presentations, and interactions are normalized within the cultural environment of the strip club, so that the erotic nature of the labour is essentially a non-issue for participants. Moreover, unlike other labour sites, in the club sexuality is explicit and monetarily compensated: "it [sexual harassment] was all over, in what I do, *no* that's the place" [emphasis hers] (Tina). In addition, out in the open, sexuality can be managed:

> Wouldn't you say in a restaurant, the owners, the cooks, they're gonna grab you for free at their convenience? But in a bar, first of all they *don't* grab you, they're gonna be thrown out, and whatever happens they're always forking out the bucks for it [emphasis hers]. (Kelly)

Perhaps more important still are the meanings scripted onto the labour. A dancer engages with the indicators of sexuality, and these links to the erotic appear to define her job as a *stripper*. However, this explicitly erotic labour operates at the level of the visible body. It is not about sex but nudity and the visual presentations of the erotic: "You manipulate your body in a certain way and you throw a sexual aspect to it" (Debbie). Put another way, dancers engage in surface acting where "the body not the soul is the main tool of the trade. The actor's body evokes passion in the *audience*, but the actor is only *acting* as if he has the feeling" [emphasis in original] (Hochschild, 1983:37). The eroticized setting, available props, and their own expectations may ensure that the audience defines the entertainers as sexual, but the experience of workers is markedly different:

> At the Blue Lagoon it's a lot easier because there's TVs. So I can't see anyone from the stage, so I watch TV. I'll listen to music, and I'll watch TV, and I'll just dance. I've been doing it, you know when you do it so often you're looking straight at people's eyes but you're going, you're kinda looking over yonder type, looking at the TV there. You're doing your little crawl and you're like giggling inside cause there's some show on. I mean I've lost it completely because I was doing a show and I was trying to talk to someone and *The Simpsons* came on TV and I started pissing myself laughing. I couldn't do it anymore. I walked off the stage. (Debbie)

The Floor
As previously noted, today's dancers must continually negotiate two discrete, and sometimes conflicting, jobs during their work day. The quasi-contractual obligation is to perform strip-tease shows and "hanging out" — tasks for which she receives not a paycheck but attains access to customers. As self-account service workers, all or most of the worker's income is directly paid by customers in fee-for-service arrangements. In order to "make her money" dancers must first solicit and sell their private dances by convincing "a guy that he really wants a dance" (Debbie). Here labour practices are constrained not only by house rules but also by individual inclination. Some dancers flatly refuse to approach customers: "Some girls go around and ask, 'hi baby how you doing' and start shaking their things in front of him. No! I don't like that at all. I just wait for them. If they want me bad enough, they'll come and get me, they'll signal me or tell the waitress" (Rachel). Others "work the floor" — socializing and engaging promising looking customers in conversation. The most aggressive hustlers greet all customers. At a minimum they "give them the eye, just like you would in a bar" (Debbie).

Having "sold" her service, the dancer accompanies the patron to the champagne room where she seeks to maximize her income by employing a variety of special skills. "Once they come and get me, they're screwed. They're stuck with me, and I'm gonna keep them and siphon out every last dime I can get" (Rachel). While this may entail dirty dancing, more frequently dancers employ "straight" strategies to maximize income:

> I don't stop [dancing] until they tell me to stop, and then I tell them how much. I don't do one dance and then sit ... I used to do that, one dance and that's it. Then you don't get another dance. So I just keep dancing. (Sally)

In the champagne room a dancer needs to encourage the customer, retain his attention and good will, and yet remain firmly in control of the situation. The challenges have increased with the media and public discourses throughout the lap-dancing debates. Apparently, customers frequently equate surface presentations of sexuality with actual sexuality, so that dancers are wrongly presumed to be, if not prostitutes, then highly promiscuous. Today "99% by the customers, oh yes, 'You must have a price.' ... the way society is, they're allowed to expect it" (Marie). This means that an individual dancer is required to cope with customers' anticipation of sexual fulfillment while she labours in an environment where she is presumed to be, but cannot be, sexually available.

Not surprisingly given the physical space and discursive parameters, making money also renders dancers vulnerable to physical or sexual aggression. As a result, they must remain vigilantly attentive to clues that identify potentially dangerous patrons (body language, conversation, approach, intoxication). Dancers also routinely rely on each other for protection — "In the champagne room we're all watching each other's back" (Debbie) — and most of the more experienced dancers have perfected strategies that maximize their control of the interaction. One research participant described her atypically candid approach:

> I stand [and] I make them open their legs like this. If they give me a problem, my knees are right here. Ya, I'm serious! Every guy has to sit with their legs open. I want full range. Some of them say "why" — "cause if you get out of line I'll kick you right there." Fucking right, you hurt me, I'll hurt you right back. These are the rules, you don't like them, you get the fuck out, don't ask me to dance. A lot of them [dancers] sit with their legs wide open — he's going to get his hands to your crotch before you get your feet to the floor, 'cause he's got a hold of your legs. (Sally)

Emotional Labour

While erotic labour, either on the public stage or in the relatively private champagne rooms, appears to define strippers' labour, in practice strippers are increasingly required not only to engage in the surface acting essential for the selling and providing of private entertainment services but also to provide an interpersonal social service that necessitates a unique set of skills and strategies. Here Arlie Hochschild's (1983) concept of emotional labour has resonance.[15] Many customers are only marginally interested in nude entertainment whether it is on the public stage or in a private champagne room. Instead these men come to strip clubs because they "want someone to talk to" (Rachel) and will "spend a couple of hundred bucks and they sit there and talk to a girl that's nice to them and makes them feel good for a few hours" (Diane).

For the dancer this parody of social relations necessitates "playing a game. ... It depends on the guy, the drippier you are, the more money you'll make. The more you laugh at his jokes, the more money you'll make" (Sally). In essence the dancer presents a cynical performance (Goffman, 1959:18), instrumentally and consciously playing to the expectations of an audience of one:

> I mean obviously they're going to be nice. They're being paid to be there, so it's not like it's not a good idea to be a bitch or something. Guys aren't gonna spend money on you. And that's what you're there for. (Diane)

Essentially, a dancer's livelihood depends on her ability to recreate social relations and "treat them like they're people. You don't just treat them like they're a ten dollar bill" (Rachel). Interactions are routinized charades where dancers create the illusion of a novel interaction with a "special" person. In short, strippers' daily labour involves not only continual performance — playing the role of a stripper — but also adopting other personas, in effect playing a number of roles, within a particular spectrum of possibilities, consecutively and sometimes concurrently:

> I used to give every guy a different age depending on what they wanted. I also gave different stories, but that's complicated to keep track of. Sometimes I acted really young and walk[ed] around the club in a skirt being cutesie. You don't even have to look that young, just act young. It's really weird. Different guys want different things. (Sarah)

Like other direct service workers, a stripper has to be able to manage her emotions and anger in the face of ignorant and trying customers. However, there is something more — she participates in a financial interaction that masquerades as a social relationship with its sense of reciprocity: "I should probably have my PhD in psychology by now for all the problems I've listened to and all the advice I've given" (Rachel). Social relationships are normally defined by mutual concern. In the strip club, however, the appearance of concern becomes a commodity that is purchased: "I feel guilty when they tell me things. Because personally I don't give a shit. But I have to pretend I do" (Jamie). Notably, unlike the professionals to whom Rachel compares herself, a dancer has neither the language nor the professional training on which to rely to guide them through the interaction; instead, she has to improvise as she continually reinvents herself and adapts her performance.

Although talking to customers appears to be a rather innocuous activity, many dancers express exasperation: "You have to go sit down with the guy and blah blah blah blah blah blah blah blah. I hate that" (Tina). In fact, the most distress was voiced by research participants about this activity. On reflection, this is not surprising. As capitalism expands and the service industry swells to include the supply of emotional and interpersonal services (for men) in a commercial imitation of authentic social relationships,[16] the boundaries are being blurred and the product is not only the service but the server herself. For strip industry workers this means they are alienated not just from their bodies — through their physical capacity to work or their labour power — nor from their surface sexual self-presentation in a way that was normal in burlesque theatres. They are alienated from something more — their social selves:

> Temporarily you're someone you're not, just for this guy, just so you can get his money. If he wants to believe something then you just play right along with it. "Ya I'm from wherever" and make yourself up to be something you're not. (Sally)

The result is a disassociated sense of self, so that "I pretend I'm somebody else and I get all glamorous and I go into work. I'm a completely different person in the club, a completely different person" (Debbie). Workers are very explicit about the need to distance and separate their different selves: "I have a very distinct difference between my job and my life, and I find if I mix the two of them that I can't keep it straight" (Ann). This assumption of separate identity is in part facilitated by the use of stage names so that "on stage I'm Kim so that's not me either" (Alex). It would appear that, as new areas of social and interpersonal life are transformed into services to be bought, the alienation inherent to the labour process in modern capitalist societies is also extended into a new arena.

Stripping is Women's Work

To summarize the discussion so far, when we abandon morally loaded assumptions, explore labour structure and practices, and "normalize" the labour of strippers by making links to the "reputable" work of working-class women, similarities start to emerge. Today strippers are contractual own-account workers who experience the same sorts of issues confronting other working-class women in Canada, including a non-supportive work environment; exploitation and oppression by owners and managers, non-standard labour arrangements, lack of security, and minimal protection by the state. As part of the burgeoning consumer service sector they, like many other direct service workers, do a job that requires erotic and emotional labour. The job itself is physically exhausting, emotionally challenging, and definitely stressful.[17] Success is contingent on the development of complex skills and competencies including performance, construction of sexuality, sales, and finely tuned interpersonal skills. The very existence of these skills belie the customary focus on deviance rather than work process in much of the literature. Of course that these skills are largely dismissed, or rendered invisible, is not unique to the strip trade but characterizes many working-class women's jobs (Gaskell, 1986). It does, however, affirm once again the relative and subjective nature of what is defined as skills.

It is women's work in another way as well. Traditionally women were expected to provide men with nurturance, care, and support. Dancers provide this service for men who "want someone to listen to their problems" (Sarah) on the market on a fee-for-service basis. Suspending momentarily what it says about the state of alienation in advanced capitalist society that men are prepared to pay $10 for every four minutes[18] they spend in the company of a woman ($85 per hour if they take the flat rate[19]), we can appreciate that this is fully consistent with the move of capital into the types of services traditionally performed in the home. In the context of intimate relations this empathetic support is not experienced as particularly challenging; within the labour market it proves to be difficult, emotionally taxing labour that requires both surface and deep acting and the implementation of complex skills. Like so much of the labour women do, it is obscured, even to participants, by the context in which it occurs and the taken-for-granted nature of the competencies. That is to say not only is the labour structured so that work is interspersed with social interaction but emotions do not "fit" into the language of work, so that while the strippers are fully aware that "it's hard on your head after a while" (Diane), they are, nonetheless, sometimes not fully cognizant of this as *labour* activity.

But Not a Job Like Any Other!

Recognizing this work as labour, we must exercise caution. While we can legitimately make links to more reputable labour sites for almost every aspect of the dancer's work, few jobs require this combination of skills and necessitate that the worker operate in such a complex and emotionally taxing labour environment. In this last section we attend to specificity and consider stripping as a *marginal* labour activity and reflect on the implications for workers.

First, we need to consider that stripping is a stigmatized labour location.[20] While participation in the paid labour force is a taken-for-granted imperative for most Canadians, the nature of an individual's work is something they are presumed to choose. "Choosing" a labour market location that is on the margins of legality, morality, or propriety can have profound implications, as the stigma of labour location is transformed into a stigma of the worker (Polsky, 1969). For women working as strippers, this is compounded by the conflation of the skin and sex trades in the dominant discourse that further vilifies strippers and personalizes the whore stigma:

> It's the reputation that goes with it. People — when you tell them what you do, they go "oh — really!" Oh ya. Oh ya. There is, um, to the outside, to the outside world — there is no difference between a prostitute and an exotic dancer. (Debbie)

These workers must contend with moral righteousness and stereotypical assumptions in interpersonal relations and in a range of social and economic areas from housing — "some places don't rent to strippers" (Diane) — to finance — "it's hard to get credit in a bank" (Marie) — that are generally assumed to operate outside of moral consideration. Put another way, *working* as a stripper becomes *being* a stripper, an identity marker with very real implications in the lives of women in the industry and that shapes the worker's experience of the wider world.[21] While most dancers deconstruct the discourses and challenge the assumptions that underlie the stigma (prostitution, drug abuse, immorality) and effectively manage their personal and social identities, they must, nonetheless, continually engage in social and personal exchanges where their labour location is understood to be definitive.

The implications of participating in "disreputable" labour extend beyond questions of identity and social interaction. Dancers must also negotiate a web of state regulatory practices unknown to employees in more "reputable" occupations. Throughout the 1980s and into the early 1990s, in response to claims made by community groups that linked strip clubs to increased crime and vice, municipalities throughout Ontario began to regulate the industry through severe zoning restrictions, banning clubs from residential areas, restricting the clubs to commercial zones, and stipulating no strip-club parameters around churches and schools. They also introduced licencing that required the newly designated "exotic entertainment parlour attendants" to purchase annual licences under threat of fines and even imprisonment.[22] The nature of the licencing is revealing and speaks to the moral subtext of these strategies. For example, in Toronto strippers are categorized along with massage-parlour attendants, while in Ottawa attaining a licence is contingent on dancers' first demonstrating they have not been convicted of indecent acts, procuring, prostitution, or for any offence under the Narcotics Control Act.

In 1995, as part of broader zero-tolerance health initiatives engendered by the fear of HIV/AIDS and Hepatitis C, the Ontario Labour Minister ruled that lap-dancing could expose workers to fatal disease and, therefore, that it constituted a potential health hazard for workers, contrary to the Occupational Health and Safety Act (Ontario Ministry of Labour, 1995). This labour law provided municipalities with a new regulatory tactic. In 1995 and 1996, a number of municipalities implemented bylaws outlawing lap-dancing by citing the newly established health risks associated with the practice. Finally, of course, strippers are at risk of being charged under Criminal Code prohibitions against presenting an indecent stage performance (section 169), public nudity (section 170), and being an inmate of a bawdy house (section 210).[23] In principle, these controls are intended to regulate the industry in the interests of broader society; in practice, they not only stigmatize and marginalize workers but also further restrict the employment options of women workers: some clubs are "zoned" out of existence, while live entertainment ceases to be economically viable for smaller clubs in light of the hefty annual fees.

Conclusion

If I have done my job well, it should be clear to the reader that the work women perform in strip clubs, is *hard* work. In order to be able to practice her trade, a dancer has to appear periodically on stage, dance, and remove her clothes for a roomful (or worse, *not* a roomful) of men "for free." In order to "make her money," she has to present herself as an attractive "sexy" woman, sell her service to an individual patron, and retain his attention by engaging in erotic and/or emotional labour while carefully maintaining physical and psychological boundaries. In the champagne room, her naked body may well be inches from her client, but she is continually being monitored by the manager, the doorman, other dancers, and the police. Like a rape victim, if she is inappropriately touched, she is held responsible and sanctioned. All the while she has to cope with the particular stress of working in a leisure site as well as deal with the chaotic environment and interpersonal conflicts that abound. When she leaves the labour site, she continues to engage with the stigmatized nature of her occupation, managing her social and personal identity as well as coping with the stereotypical assumptions of her friends, intimate partners, and the state agencies with whom she interacts. In other words, while we can legitimately make links to more reputable labour sites for almost every aspect of the dancer's work, there are few jobs that require this combination of skills and necessitate that the worker operate in such a complex and emotionally taxing labour environment. Furthermore, the implication of stigma means that the labour has far-reaching costs in the worker's personal life.

At the same time, the implications of having a "job like no other" are not all bad. Unlike most workers who provide traditional women's work on the open market, a stripper is well compensated for her labour. Furthermore, not only does the job offer her a flexibility and autonomy seldom available to working-class women, it allows her to develop competencies that are useful outside the labour site — assertiveness, boundary maintenance, and interpersonal skills. In addition, although her work may leave her frustrated and angry, it also affords her a broader vision, enhanced self-esteem, good body image, comfort with her sexuality, and confidence — all worthwhile attributes and ones that many women continue to struggle to realize.

Notes

1   These cubicles, measuring perhaps three feet by five feet each, are equipped with two (most often vinyl) chairs facing each other, an ashtray and a ledge to hold drinks. While the cubicles are usually hidden from the general view of the club, they are open to be monitored by anyone passing down the aisle between them.

2   This chapter is based on data gathered during a year of participant observation in a southern Ontario strip club, fifteen in-depth, semi-structured interviews with women working as strippers, and a series of interviews with other industry employees including managers, doormen, bartenders, waitresses, and disk jockeys. For a more detailed description of the methodology or for a further development of the arguments see Bruckert (2002).

3   Wages ranged from $275 to $600 a week in the late 1970s.

4   Table dances are a one-song strip show performed at the patron's table. Today, in spite of the advertised availability of $5 table dances, these are rare. Most dancers simply refuse to remove their clothes in the middle of the bar. At any rate, most patrons are easily persuaded to enjoy the privacy afforded by the champagne rooms, where for $10, the stripper either dances on a stool or sits in close proximity to the customer and moves — a dance in name only.

5   Dancers are required to pay bar fees or "DJ fees" of between $10 and $20 per shift. In practice this means that the dancer must "pay to work there" (Jamie). Depending on the club these fees compensate the disk jockey and sometimes the bartender, who also receive no pay in the traditional sense.

6   This redefining of labour as semi-skilled is consistent with the trend towards deskilling that Braverman (1974) identified as characteristic of twentieth-century capitalism. That deskilling is ideologically and economically useful (for capitalists) is revealed when we realize that throughout the 1980s and 1990s, at the same time as skills were being denied, employers in mainstream sectors of the labour market were establishing inordinate educational requirements (Rinehart, 1996:78). It would appear that labour-dependent personal service industries capitalize on existing age, gender, and racial stratifications by hiring marginal workers and then justify their low wages through reference to their marginal status (Reiter, 1991:148).

7   DERA (Dancer's Equal Rights Association of Ottawa) estimates that one in four Ottawa dancers are "on-schedule" (DERA, 2001).

8   On-schedule dancers are booked for eight-hour shifts, while freelancers must remain for a minimum period — usually four or five hours — established by the bar.

9   To perceive these arrangements as anomalous risks reaffirming marginality by locating it outside of established labour practices. In fact, in the way it is organized, stripping is comparable with the non-stigmatized service occupation of realty. Like strippers, real estate agents are in such a paradoxical relation to their "employers" that the term is hardly appropriate. Realtors are actively recruited by brokers; they are hired, and they can be fired. But since they receive no direct financial remuneration for their labour from their employer, the relationship is nuanced. In exchange for legal protection and access to the necessary legitimizing context (including the use of the name, licence, and insurance), means of production (phone services, office space, and technical support), the realtor commits her/himself to a particular brokerage firm (including providing "free" labour staffing the office).

10   There was a particular irony here. While the dominant discourse increasingly defines stripping as immoral, the clubs and workers are becoming progressively more committed to respectability: "they think of it as a business now, y'know, the newer generation; it's more like a business instead of just the stereotyped thing that people used to do. The girls are keeping their money. A lot less drugs" (Rachel). Furthermore, young women from the rough working-class, who wear the markers with pride, are being marginalized within the industry. It is precisely these women whose employment options are restricted and who are the most exploited population of workers.

11   Her agency is noteworthy. Far from being solely an object of the male gaze, it is the dancer who establishes the interaction with the audience and determines the pace, actions, and movement of the show. The audience's

reading of her sexualized form does not erase her authorship. We see this clearly when a dancer enacts a fine parody as she plays with her own and her audience's sexuality, although she is usually quite careful, given the economic-power dynamic, not to let the audience in on the joke.

12 While not all working-class jobs are manual, physically challenging jobs are overwhelmingly working class. Consequently, the labour sold frequently has a socially unacknowledged (though recognized by the wage-labourers themselves) youth imperative and uncompensated costs in terms of health and well-being (Dunk, 1991; Houtman and Kompier, 1995:221).

13 These include bringing their own towels to sit on and sometimes their own cleaning materials.

14 In addition, creating an erotic persona necessitates countless hours of labour in appearance, clothes, make-up, and sometimes tanning salons or plastic surgeries.

15 Hochschild (1983) argues that rather than simply selling her mental and physical labour, the modern service workers must now engage in emotional labour. This requires the worker, in exchange for a wage, to "induce or suppress feeling in order to sustain the outward countenance that produces the proper state of mind in others" (1983:7) and engage in "deep acting" by re-creating personal experiences in a commercial setting. Such a worker must manage her feelings not just for private social relations (which we all do), but as a commodity to benefit the corporation that pays her wage. The process, which requires her to transform her smile into a *sincere* smile, cannot avoid creating a sense of alienation from feelings (Hochschild, 1983:21).

16 It is possible that capitalism is responding to the market and exploiting men's insecurity in the changing gender relations that characterize the latter half of the twentieth century. With the erosion of male power that "is based on the compliance of women and the economic and emotional services which women provided" (Giddens, 1992:132), men struggle with the new expectations and their own need for intimacy (Giddens, 1992:180).

17 For dancers "role overload," identified as a key contributor to workplace stress (Levi et al., 1986:55) is normal. Dancers have to constantly negotiate two separate, sometimes conflicting, jobs during their work day. The quasi-contractual obligation of the stripper is to perform strip-tease shows and "hang out" — "looking like a hooker" (Debbie) — tasks for which she receives not a paycheck but the opportunity to "make her money"; that is, to take the chance to utilize the profitable skills of soliciting and playing the game. Her job not only requires her to fulfill a number of roles at the same time but also to continually manage the emotional and sexual demands of patrons. She must try to maximize her income while simultaneously engaging in boundary maintenance to protect her emotional and physical space. In addition dancers are subject to the stress shared by other labourers engaged in emotional work (Adelmann, 1995:372) as well as the particular stressors shared by entertainers

— performance anxiety and a fear of even minor physical injury that can effectively curtail their career (Sternbach, 1995): "I can't work with black eyes, I can't work with big scars across my face" (Jessie).

18 These prices were in effect in 1999.

19 These prices were in effect in 1999.

20 Of course other occupations are also stigmatized — morticians, custodians, and used car salespeople, to name a few.

21 It is also a "sticky" stigma infecting those around the dancer as well (Goffman, 1963:30), so that her family may be, or may perceive themselves to be, stigmatized. Certainly, those who share her labour site are. It is also sticky in the sense of enduring even after participation in the industry has ceased. The almost inevitable linguistic designation of *ex*-strippers in the media speaks to an understanding that participation in the trades legitimates continued assumptions of immorality.

22 In 2001 there is considerable provincial disparity. Some municipalities, such as London and Kitchener, require clubs, but not attendants, to purchase licences. In municipalities that continue to licence dancers, costs can be quite high. In Windsor, dancers must pay $225 plus administration and photo fees annually.

23 For a more detailed discussion of this regulation, see Bruckert and Dufresne (2002).

References

Adkins, L. (1992). Sexual work and the employment of women in the service industries. In M. Savage & A. Witz (Eds.), *Gender and bureaucracy*. Oxford: Blackwell.

Adelmann, P. (1995). Emotional labour as a potential source of job stress. In S. Sauter & L. Murphy (Eds.), *Organizational risk factors for job stress*. Washington: American Psychological Association.

Braverman, H. (1974). *Labour and monopoly capital: The degradation of work in the twentieth century*. New York: Monthly Review Press.

Bruckert, C. (2002). *Taking it off, putting it on: Women in the strip trade*. Toronto: Women's Press.

Bruckert, C. & Dufresne, M. (2002). Re-configuring the margins: Tracing the regulatory context of Ottawa strip clubs. *Canadian Journal of Law and Society* (forthcoming).

Canada. (1998). *Pocket criminal code*. Scarborough, ON: Carswell.

DERA. (2001). Mission statement. Ottawa: Dancers Equal Rights Association of Ottawa Carleton. (n.p.)

Duffy, A. & Pupo, N. (1997). *Part-time paradox*. Toronto: McClelland & Stewart.

Dunk, T. (1991). *It's a working man's town: Male working class culture in northwestern Ontario*. Montreal: McGill-Queen's University Press.

Gaskell, J. (1986). Conceptions of skill and work of women: Some historical and political issues. In R. Hamilton & M. Barrett (Eds.), *The politics of diversity: Feminism, Marxism and nationalism*. London: Verso.

Giddens, A. (1992). *The transformation of intimacy*. Palo Alto, CA: Stanford University Press.

Goffman, E. (1959). *The presentation of self in everyday life*. New York: Doubleday.

——. (1963). *Stigma*. Upper Saddle River, NJ: Prentice Hall.

Henry, W. & Sims, J. (1970). Actors' search for a self. *Trans-Action* 7,11.

Hochschild, A. (1983). *The managed heart: Commercialization of human feeling*. Berkeley, CA: University of California Press.

Houtman, I. & Kompier, M. (1995). Risk factors and occupational risk groups for work stress in the Netherlands. In S. Sauter & L. Murphy (Eds.), *Organizational risk factors for job stress*. Washington: American Psychological Association.

Levi, L., Frankenhauser, M. & Gardell, B. (1986). The characteristics of the workplace and the nature of its social demands. In S. Wolf & A. Finestone (Eds.), *Occupational stress: Health and performance at work*. Littleton, MA: PSG Publishing.

Luxton, M. & Corman, J. (2001). *Getting by in hard times: Gendered labour at home and on the job*. Toronto: University of Toronto Press.

Ontario. (1973). An act to amend the Liquor Licence Act. (Chapter 68, 69). *Statutes of the Province of Ontario*. Toronto: Thatcher.

——. (1996). *Occupational Health and Safety Act*. Toronto: Ministry of Labour.

Phillips, P. (1997). Labour in the new Canadian political economy. In W. Clement (Ed.), *Understanding Canada: Building the new Canadian political economy*. Montreal: McGill-Queen's University Press.

Polsky, N. (1969). *Hustlers, beats and others*. Garden City, NJ: Anchor Press.

Pringle, R. (1988). *Secretaries talk*. London: Verso.

Reiter, E. (1991). *Making fast food*. Montreal: McGill-Queen's University Press.

Rinehart, J. (1996). *The tyranny of work: Alienation and the labour process*. 3rd ed. Toronto: Harcourt Brace.

Sternbach, D. (1995). Musicians: A neglected working population in crisis. In S. Sauter & L. Murphy (Eds.), *Organizational risk factors for job stress*. Washington: American Psychological Association.

Sundahl, D. (1987). Stripper. In F. Delacosta & P. Alexander (Eds.) *Sex work*. Pittsburgh, PA: Cleis Press.

Chapter Eight

Gender Inequality and Medical Education

Jo-Anne Kirk

Introduction

Today, we have certain understandings about medicine as an institution — about the experience and climate of medical school, as well as the nature of medical practice. However, this vast body of literature about medicine is incomplete. We have only a limited understanding of the relevant issues because the majority of analyses have either completely excluded women in medicine as subjects of analysis, have discounted women's experiences as insignificant or irrelevant, and/or have assumed that women's experiences are identical to those of male medical students and practitioners.

Clearly then, an accurate account of women's experiences within the institution of medicine is missing from the overall understanding of medicine. What is further absent is experiential interview data, that is, women's own accounts of their experiences as members of the field of medicine. This paper is based on a study (Kirk, 1992) which attempted to address this serious gap in the literature and, therefore, expand the common understandings about medicine. More specifically, the study aimed to identify the effects and consequences of the medical school environment on women medical students' perceptions of the persistence of sexism within their training programs. While the number of quantitative studies on women in medicine is increasing, this study was unique in that it provided a forum for women's voices to be heard. In sum, the emphasis of this research was not merely on women in medicine, but rather on women's experiences within the institution of medicine, which exists within, and is dependent upon, a patriarchal society.

In 1990–91, women comprised 44 percent of the total enrollment in Canadian faculties of medicine, compared with 7 percent in 1957–58, and 18 percent in 1970–71 (Association of Canadian Medical Colleges, 1991). At the University of Manitoba, women comprised 38.8 percent of the total enrollment in the four-year undergraduate medical training program in 1990–91 (Institutional Analysis, 1991). It is clear from these statistics that women are now better represented in medical schools and in the profession that in the past. Yet, the question arises as to whether these numbers actually represent a positive and progressive change in the medical profession's attitudes toward women as students, as physicians and as professionals.

The findings reported here are based upon extensive interviews in 1991 with 21 women who were at various stages of the four-year undergraduate medical training program at the University of Manitoba. Ten of the respondents were women in the preclinical stage of medical training (Med I and II), and eleven were women in the clinical component (Med III and IV). The women ranged in age from 22 to 44 years, and all were Canadian citizens. Five were women of colour, six women were living with partners, two women had children, five lived with their parents, and the remainder lived on their own, with or without roommates. These students were asked if they had experienced differential treatment based on gender and if they had observed similar treatment of classmates and/or faculty. The interview and question format permitted respondents to report both favourable and unfavourable treatment. The interview touched on all aspects of medical school experiences, both during and outside the class. While during interviews each respondent was asked specific questions, participants were encouraged to elaborate on their answers and to comment on issues not directly covered by specific questions. In short, interviews yielded a wide range of data on the "climate" within the medical school.

Medical School: The Climate

The interview data suggest that women still feel, both subtly and overtly, like outsiders in a 'male profession.' Moreover, even though women enter medicine with qualifications and characteristics equal to those of men (Eisenberg, 1989), gender stereotypes still have a prominent place within the working of the medical school environment.

Women students encounter a primarily male dominated environment. This starts with the admissions interview. Most of the women reported that the interview committees were composed mainly of established male physicians from the Faculty of Medicine. The female member of the committee was usually a fourth year student, a resident, or a junior physician within the profession. Next, all of the women revealed that they had been asked themselves, had heard about other women who were asked, and/or had expected to be asked about their intentions to have a family, and their ensuing ability to balance domestic demands with a career in medicine. While there was some disagreement among women on whether such a question was relevant to the admissions process, the concern that most women did express was that their response could be held against them. As one woman explained:

> I was asked whether or not I wanted kids. ... at the time I said 'no I didn't want to' and I believed that at the time, still, I'm not sure. I don't think it's fair to ask anyone if they want to have kids when they're not even married or going out with anyone, it's ridiculous because you can never plan that. I knew they would though, just because I heard from so many students. Now that I'm in, I don't think it's relevant to ask — before I thought it was. And it intimidates you when they do ask you that on the interview because the minute you think they're going to pry into what you want to do — if you said you want kids — then you think immediately that they wouldn't want you in — and really, that's the impression you get because you always have the impression that if you say yes you want children, they're going to think you're not as serious about medicine — that you're not going to be as good.

Furthermore, not one woman had ever heard of a man being asked a similar question during the admissions interview. In fact, many found the very prospect to be amusing.

While such a question reflects the reality that many women in medicine opt to have families, the underlying message is that this is problematic for the profession. Women are aware that they are entering a profession that evolved on the labour of men who could, if they chose to, devote endless hours to developing their skills, while their wives stayed at home and managed the family. One woman even jokingly commented that "probably most women doctors wish they had a wife." Many women referred to medicine as "the Old Boys' Club" and spoke about the strong sense of tradition that prevailed and served as the basis for such attitudes as, "this is the way we did it and we learned and we suffered and we were up for 42 hours — why can't you? If you can't cut it, what are you doing here?" As another woman concluded: "It's a male-dominated, paternalistic old boys' hangout, and they like it that way and they'd like to keep it that way, by and large."

Despite a growing body of evidence to the contrary (cf. Harris & Conley-Muth, 1981; Harward et al., 1981; Brown & Klein, 1982; Altekruse & McDermott, 1988; Kettner, 1988; Martin et al., 1988; Eisenberg, 1989; Wheeler et al., 1990; Dickstein, 1990; Phelan, 1991), the notion still persists that women's career commitment in medicine is not as strong as that of men's. In fact, this belief is so pervasive that some women even express it themselves. As one woman explained:

> [You] have to realize a lot of women who go into medicine end up practicing for awhile and dropping out — or practicing half time — taking it easier. So if they're looking at who to bring in — they get less service for their money — for their education dollar, out of women.

Others stated that at one time or another they heard comments which suggested that "women don't make good doctors because they have kids and work part-time and are not in tune ..." and ultimately that the inclusion of women "is influencing medicine towards a slacker outlook." While some women felt that such sentiments were outweighed by the positive influences they had encountered, including the positive feedback they often received from female patients, most women expressed a strong desire to see real change in the attitudes within medical training. Such change would acknowledge that medical school is "not an endurance course — not only for the toughest of the tough." This change would reflect attitudes that accept and value 'women's life-styles' for encompassing a more balanced and realistic outlook on life and not as reflecting less commitment to the profession. Many women agreed that such changes would not "just help women, but help everybody by making the profession a little bit more humane." However, as one woman reflected, "[I] really think society has to change — when it does, medicine will too."

Virtually every woman spoke of the conflict that they felt existed between their personal goals (which often included having children) and their career options. Most women admitted to leaning towards a career in areas such as Family Medicine, Pediatrics, and Obstetrics and Gynecology, and 'life-style' was identified as the primary reason. Over and over, women explained that their goal of having a balanced life-style was incompatible with the demands of longer, more intense and inflexible residencies — typically Surgery and Internal Medicine. When I asked women how they came to realize this, they responded in various ways. Some had received direct comments from professors and clinicians such as:

> 'Well, you don't want to do that (Orthopedic Surgery). ... You want to go into Family Medicine, that way you can have kids — stay home — don't have to work 120 hours/week.' — and this was done in a condescending manner.

Or heard statements which conveyed the message that:

> 'Well there are no female pediatric cardiologists.' ... His attitude
> was that I couldn't do it simply because I was a woman — simply
> because no women have ever done it.

Several women also stated that they believed that certain specialties
were inherently less appealing to women because of the physical or
psychological nature of the area of specialization. For example, several women
spoke of the perceived requirement of physical strength for Orthopedic
Surgery, which tended to eliminate the pursuit of this option. Relatedly,
while the field of Obstetrics and Gynecology is an acceptable specialty for
both men and women, there is an underlying assumption that Urology (often
focussing on the male uro-genital tract) is off limits to women.

Most women spoke about surgery's reputation for being a male-
dominated, macho and paternalistic boys' club. Horror stories abound
describing why surgery is still perceived as a hostile environment for women.
Women recounted tales about the bad hours and inflexible time commitments,
the lack of maternity leave, the lack of female change rooms, the lack of
respect for and poor treatment of female patients, as well as the lack of
female residents and surgeons to serve as role models. Woman also described
surgery rotations as "a month and a half of them trying to make you cry" and
as "having to work harder to be accepted." Unwelcoming messages about
surgery seem to filter down through the school by osmosis:

> It's (the) old guard protecting its turf — they have to keep the myth
> and magic alive — that such and such a group is the only elite here.
> For some, only 'elite' is guys. It's an undercurrent thing and I don't
> know where I picked that up from, but it seems to be filtering down
> somehow.

As one woman summed it up:

> I know more male students that want to be surgeons than women
> just because they hear from women clerks that surgery was the
> biggest drag. ... surgery especially has the reputation that 'we are
> the workers.' Here at 6 a.m., stay till 7 p.m., and if you can't keep
> up with it, you're just not cut out for it. Definitely a very macho
> image — 'we're really driven' — you have to be as driven if you're
> planning to do this. It's not really conducive if you're planning on
> having children. You KNOW you're going to be really stuck if you

get pregnant during residency. You KNOW that taking maternity leave means you lag behind your classmates and you will not get good appointments. Whether it's overt or covert, you know that. It's definitely harder to be a woman in it than a man.

Consequently, most women are still 'choosing' to go into traditional female fields. Women reported that the demand for female Family Practitioners, as well as the perceived benefits — such as more flexible residencies and work opportunities, maternity leave and on-site daycare, and an overall less hostile environment — were definitely assets that these specialties had to offer. However, the impression that I received from most women was that the perceived curtailment of their career options was not taken lightly nor without regret and disappointment, even frustration and anger. "There's always a niggling feeling of cop-out when you read that there's only one female General Surgeon in Manitoba — that seems a terrible shame." Another woman explained:

> I know I'm pretty good with my hands, but again, the scheduling would bother me and again, the people I'd have to work with. But you've got to penetrate those fields somehow. And another thing would be is that I wouldn't want to 'traditionalize' myself and go into something like Family Medicine and Pediatrics and those things that are female-dominated.

It appears that women face a catch-22 situation: while they recognize the need to make inroads into male-dominated specialties, they also recognize the need to learn and work in a tolerable environment and most were not willing to endure the pitfalls of being token women.

Some reactions were even stronger. Although some women joked that "Family Medicine is where women go and Pediatrics, cause we know about kids and babies — Obs-Gyny is where women go because that's natural, our hormones will just tell us what we're supposed to do," others made the connection between such underlying attitudes, and the lack of control and lack of respect that women encounter. A definite system of hierarchy exists within medicine which ranks everything from medical students and hospital staff, to fields of specialization (Merton et al., 1957; Becker et al., 1961; Shapiro, 1978). While the male-dominated surgical specialties are seen as home to the 'cream of the crop,' traditionally female specialties rank lower. Although most women down-played prestige and money as motivating factors in their medical careers, without doubt, these qualities are valued in society and, at some level, cannot be dismissed as insignificant.

As one woman complained with some sarcasm:

[Such fields are] allowable for women. ... of course, being the nurturing type and stuff, we should be around children and home-making, wives, mothers ... and Family Medicine because it takes so little training and off they go. So ... (I) feel like going into Surgery or something just to prove them wrong because there's only one surgical resident at St. B. that's a woman — ONE and just to be the other one, I'll do it too. And I won't do it because I don't like the lifestyle, but I don't want to go into Peds. just because it's so expected. To be dismissed so easily ... I almost want to do it just so I can get the respect.

Finally, in some cases, women expressed anger and frustration at having to make compromises that their male peers, who were sometimes their partners, were not faced with. As one woman stated:

My boyfriend, who's relatively aware of these things, says 'but I want to be an orthopedic surgeon.' I say, 'but what if your wife does too?' 'Well, it's difficult.' ... and that's after I went digging, 'what about the woman you're going to marry?' I know lots of men that wouldn't even consider that, they'd just go on. And that doesn't mean that they don't do Family Practice, but they don't really consider that.

Female Role Models

Concern expressed by women was the absence of female role models, particularly in some specialties: "I have yet to see a female surgeon — but I know they exist [laughs]."

Overwhelmingly, the women interviewed stated that there were not enough women teaching in medical school. Most women reported that only between 5 and 20 percent of their instructors had been female. All respondents were extremely enthusiastic about having more women occupy positions within the medical school hierarchy — from lecturers and preceptors to department heads and deans. Women were seen as important role models who provided females with a sense of belonging and comradery. As explained by one woman:

I think it would make a difference to me if there were more women, yeah. I think I would feel much more included. I would feel more excited about learning a lot of stuff. It would be exciting to me if more women were teaching more pertinent topics. ... I think if there were more women overall, I would feel more included.

The women also reported that female professors were very approachable, and served as much needed sources of information regarding what it was like to be a woman in medicine. As one woman explained:

> I would like to see more women preceptors because it's nice to have someone to identify with and that's the bottom line. ... When I was on surgery — Neurosurgery — there was a female resident, the only one in Manitoba and one of a handful in Canada. I really wanted to talk to her. Why had she chosen this specialty? Neurosurgery is known to be hectic. I wanted to know if she still wanted to have a family or whether she thought it was still viable — but those kinds of issues you just don't discuss with men. I want to know how she felt it went and that's why it would be nice to talk to some women surgeons at this stage of the game. I want to know what their lives are like. Have they made sacrifices? Was it worth it?

Just as women lauded the benefits of having more women visible in the medical college, they also described the effects of the lack of female role models. The message that several women conveyed was that, by and large, the physician is still seen as male, even in their own eyes. One woman reported that it was "strange to see a woman come in the room, to tell the truth" and another stated "[I] find I just assume that the preceptor is going to be male generally because most are." Another woman stated that,

> Often when a woman comes to the front of the class, people make the assumption — oh, she must be a dietitian or a physiotherapist, or whatever else — or, she can't be a doctor, or we won't listen. Really, women instructors have to work extremely hard to grab the class' attention.

One woman expressed the concern that her male colleagues might not learn to value and respect women, or feel comfortable taking orders from female interns because of the lack of female authority figures. Moreover, she wondered whether she and her female peers would garner the same respect as males, once they got into the system. Another admitted that "a strange thing happened when I actually did get a female lecturer in medicine — once in a blue moon — I didn't take them as seriously as I took men. It was kind of disappointing when I realized ... how much that influenced me."

Finally, some women also made the connection between the lack of female academics and the dearth of women in positions of authority within medical school. The message here was clear: if there are few women in the power structure, the likelihood of change is a lot less promising. One woman summed up the significance of the situation for herself:

> I think it (more women) would make my experience a lot more positive because ... at least I'd know that if I so choose to become an academic doctor, it would just send me the message that there's less barriers, because that's what I thought when I was in undergrad and didn't see any female profs. I thought, there must be something that stops women from doing this, either it's too hard to have children, there's sexism, you're actively discouraged from doing this. That's what the message is that I get from seeing so few women profs, that there are some barriers somewhere that makes it more uncomfortable for women to do this. And if there were more, I wouldn't feel that and would be more likely to consider it.

Relatedly, some women felt that the unequal number of women and men admitted to medical school was not problematic and to illustrate this, they expressed sentiments such as:

> I don't think that it makes any difference. If it was 10/90, then it would make a huge difference. But 40/60 is sort of balanced. If it was a noticeable imbalance, it would make a difference, sure.

However, other women made the connection between the imbalance of females and males in medical school and the ingrained inequities in the ideology and structure of the institution. To illustrate, one woman revealed that to many people, a ratio of 60 percent men to 40 percent women equals 50/50, "at least, it was as 50/50 as it was going to get." Another woman elaborated on the imbalance in an interesting manner:

> Really, it should just be 50/50, of course, some years lower or higher, but it's never higher, never over 50 percent (women). People say, 'oh, it's close to 50 percent,' but it's never above it, there's never that occasional peak. It just seems to me in talking to doctors — male doctors that I had for clinical skills last year said if you became a Family Physician and you're a woman, you could hang up a shingle, and in 6 months you would have a full practice. So obviously, there's a big demand for them. So, if male doctors are taking 3 years to fill up a practice, maybe there's too many men in medicine.

Not surprisingly, most women found organizations such as the Federation of Medical Women of Canada to be vital links to women in medicine, as well as a source of support and community. One woman also spoke of the negative reaction that a few of her peers gave to an announcement of one of this organization's upcoming meetings. She thought that it was disconcerting that some men would have so little sensitivity to the need for such an organization. She added, "the entire medical organization is for medical men, that's why we need something for medical women."

Sexism in Medical School

In a 1983 article on women in medicine which appeared in the magazine *Mother Jones,* David Osborne wrote (1983:22):

> Ten years ago, the profession was notorious for its sexism: the men's club atmosphere of the hospital, the constant barbs aimed at the few women who dared compete, the Playboy centerfolds slipped into lecture slides. Today, men simply cannot get away with that sort of behavior.

If ten years ago the sentiment was that blatant sexism within medical school was no longer tolerable, what are women reporting about their experiences today? One message seems to be, as discussed earlier, that there is a distinct 'maleness' to the medical school environment. One woman attempted to explain her perception in the following way:

> It just felt really isolating. So much of medicine — the concepts — are male somehow. Like you don't really talk about the human aspect of things. ... you don't talk about illnesses in women's language, if you know what I mean. ... And I started to notice that — I don't know if I can explain it to you — sort of, the language used in notes is very static, very fixed — square [laughs]. I don't have the words to describe it, and when I think how would I describe it myself, it's a lot more flowing, more descriptive kind of language. I started noticing that because I thought how would I describe this particular illness? Very, very different. ... So in that way, I'm probably reading too much into it, but I wonder if I've developed almost a male way of thinking? Because I learned in that language for so long, it would take me a number of years to unlearn that particular way of thinking about it.

Women also spoke of the 'natural' use of the generic 'he' in many contexts. While to some women this was seen as a non-issue, one particular example provided a sobering image:

Things like when they wrote up cases for tutorials, the doctors were always male. Even now when I read a case history, if it's a female doctor, it blows my mind. I find out later that all along I was thinking of this person as male and they refer to something that indicates that she's female. I think [laughs] that's impossible. We don't have women doctors. [But you're going to be one.] I know! It's contradictory, that's what I'm saying, but no matter how it happens, when someone refers to the doctor, I immediately bring out a male picture.

Several women also related an incident where an information package on exam stress put out by Psychological Services for medical students addressed the medical student population in a gender specific manner throughout. As one woman articulated:

Another example is the guy in charge of Psych. Services for medical students puts up a little thing for first and second years, an exam stress thing ... but it's always written to male students — always, "you may feel stress because you don't want to disappoint your girlfriend or wife.' We were thinking, what about boyfriends or husbands, or why can't you say that in a gender neutral kind of way? 'You don't want to disappoint important people in your life.' It's specifically written 'he, he, he,' and referring to female partners. Some women do have female partners, but that's obviously not what they're thinking when writing this. There are lots of examples of using male pronouns, gender specific kind of stuff.

Several women also agreed that the male body was often the norm in anatomy diagrams and texts, as well as being the implied norm within the context of lectures and tutorials. As one woman explained:

Just little things that people say don't matter but do. If a patient comes to you, HE has presented with this. Why not just say the patient? People say I'm splitting hairs, but it makes a big difference. If a man comes in with abdominal pains, or a woman, I'm going to be thinking of two completely different systems. No, they definitely do tend to use the male as 'the normal.'

And another woman stated:

The pronoun used was always 'he,' including in gynecology. They wouldn't say 'he,' but would say 'man.' They would say 'the menstrual cycle in man.' That's funny to me, although these people would say 'man' is humankind — but, I can't say that without laughing. And nobody seems to notice that.

Many women also stated that women's health issues were not seen as central and important, but were often tacked on at the end, condensed into one token lecture slot. According to some of the women interviewed, this marginalization and devaluation of women's health appeared in many forms, ranging from learning that the majority of medical research refers to the "35 year old, 70 kilogram male [which] does not take into account women's unique endocrine situations," but is often universally generalized, through to the value-laden clinical skills and diagnostic frameworks that students are taught. An example that illustrates this point particularly well was related by one woman:

Basically, I don't think anyone was sensitive to people as people. We're not appropriately taught how to do a breast exam. I happen to teach this, it's one of the things I do — I've done for four years — I teach medical students how to do 'gyny' exams. I know how to do a good breast exam, and how to judge when a poor breast exam is done. It's an important exam to teach, but it's not really taught except in the small program I'm involved in, once in third year and once in fourth year. ... In second year, we were officially taught how to do a breast exam. My group was taught it by an old surgeon — male — who taught it to us on a rubber breast, which felt nothing like my breast, or any breast I've ever felt, and I've examined many. And it was a joke ... almost obscene to be taught on this rubber breast. In my small group, jokes were made. First of all, we're not taught how to do the exam appropriately on a rubber breast, it didn't feel right, and also, the whole idea that there was that part of the body that was so filled with all connotations of whatever in your head that we have to use a rubber model. We don't use a rubber model on an abdomen exam or anything else, and God knows, they never even teach the genital exam. We don't have genitals. We were taught this exam on a rubber breast and then we went up to the wards to do a real breast exam and I was elected to do the breast exam ... and I did the breast exam the way I always do, and he actually apologized to this woman. He said, 'these students — that was probably the most thorough breast exam you'll ever have and my goodness, you certainly don't need that.' He just kind of 'pooh-poohed' the whole thing as if to say, this isn't an important part of your exam. And I felt, what's he saying to her about breasts — to us students — never mind to me — but to everybody else who's supposed to be a physician, who's supposed to know the importance of these exams. What's he saying about breasts?

Women patients were treated with certain disrespect. For instance, in regard to breast examinations, yet another woman commented on the lack of respect that was shown to a woman within a similar context:

The breast exam was finished ... and he (doctor) had turned away, except her top was left down. And just a little thing like that he just didn't even notice. And as we left I turned to her and said, 'let me put that up for you,' because she didn't know what we wanted to do next. Whether he would have done that with a testicle/penis exam — something like that, I have no idea.

Women also reported encountering inappropriate and insensitive phraseology such as 'the bleeding uterus' and 'curetted a woman.' As one woman responded, "we asked him (the lecturer) when we would ever see a tutorial called 'the pussing penis,' and he said that he didn't think that would be coming up." Another woman stated that:

I was conscious because I was pregnant last year — another text that we use currently referred to a pregnant uterus as something like a 'tumorous mass.' It made it sound just horrible — very bizarre descriptions of female anatomy — really inappropriate. And the male anatomy is simply the norm, that's true.

Relatedly, many women spoke about one senior professor in particular who used non-clinical language to describe female body parts. Several women stated that they were offended and found it an inappropriate double standard that, within a lecture setting, male genitalia was referred to as the penis, while women's breasts were called 'tits.' Women also spoke about a couple of professors who were notorious for "addressing everything in sexual innuendo ... [They] tell dirty jokes as an intro to their lecture." As one woman elaborated:

One prof, in particular, apparently has been making dirty jokes for 30 years, and the first class we had, he didn't say anything directly, but comments made about breast feeding and menstruation were questionable — I always wondered. The first lecture I just didn't get a good feeling from it — wondered if something was going on here. Then the next lecture, it was blatantly sexist jokes, I can't remember exactly, but I remember that I left half way through the class, I said that I was never going to one of his lectures again. And the next lecture that I didn't attend — but I have a friend who was in class. [He] started out with the joke: 'what's the difference between a 3 ring circus and a chorus line? One is a cunning array of stunts' and then he just left it, meaning the other is a stunning array of cunts. This was made in the third lecture in a room full of people.

Similarly, some women found it offensive that issues dealing with breasts and genitalia were often sexualized by both professors and colleagues alike. To illustrate, one woman related this incident which took place in the anatomy lab:

I said, 'now when I'm looking for the vas deferens, which is the tube that you cut during a vasectomy, where do I go?' And I was asking a male doctor, I mean, we were dissecting a male genitalia. ... He says, 'Well, you palpate the spermatic cord ... you've probably done that, haven't you?', like meaning on a live person. I just looked at him 'Are you serious?' and just walked away. It was just so 'nudge, nudge, wink, wink, hey honey.'

As well, one woman stated that:

Apparently the cervix feels like the tip of the nose, and some jokes are made about that among doctors and people doing pelvic exams — and suggestions that women find it pleasurable. I feel like saying, 'yeah, nothing is more pleasurable than having my butt slid down to the end of a table with my knees up, with a complete stranger' — it's not a fun thing. They make it something sexual, when it isn't sexual at all. It's no more sexual than a rectal exam — both are completely uncomfortable and completely disquieting for the person having them done. You'd be hardpressed to find a woman that goes to the gynecologist in the city just for fun. Definitely jokes of that vein, quite often.

Also, as one woman revealed, "even having lectures on STDs and stuff, and professors saying PID is a disease of promiscuous women." And another elaborated on this same issue:

Whether it's a comment from a gynecologist telling us that women with PID should automatically be considered promiscuous ... the act of judging is certainly not the place of physicians ... her partner may have 10,000 partners, and to judge her, to call her promiscuous — to use that word. If you use it in your own mind, that's one thing, but to use it in front of 80 impressionable young doctors-to-be who believe everything you say — I thought, it just felt wrong.

And another woman revealed that while talking to some of her male classmates about specialty choice, one commented that, "well, I'm not going into Gynecology — I couldn't stand to look at another one of those when I came home."

Women also described the many ways that they were made to feel marginal and less or differently valued. Women were called 'girls' or mistaken for nurses — and they pointed out that even senior nurses in their 50s were called 'girls' by male clerks and residents in their 20s.[1] Some women reported feeling invisible or being ignored by male professors and preceptors, sometimes through subtle incidents, such as:

Subliminal messaging ... just in terms of, say there are 8 people working with a physician, when it comes to doing things like putting the robe back on the patient, usually it's a woman singled out to do things like that ... just kind of a different treatment. And then if you're talking about the different cranial nerves emerging from the brain stem, usually there's total eye contact with the male people in the group, it's very subliminal.

Conversely, some women felt that they were judged more harshly than their male peers. Many felt that they had to work harder than their male classmates just to be seen as equally competent. As one woman concluded: "women must look competent, men just look incompetent for themselves, but when women fumble, they sort of give all other female students a bad name."

Women articulated a variety of ways in which they were treated differently and inappropriately by male professors, clinicians, colleagues, and patients. These included being judged on the basis of their appearance, being called a 'skirt,' or being leered at as they walked through the hospital wards. Women heard patronizing comments such as, "it's so nice to have a pretty girl here," and witnessed and experienced inappropriate touching, such as 'bum pinching,' as well as sexual advances — which occurred within both clinical and instructional settings. To illustrate, one woman revealed that, in her opinion, one particular professor "... took advantage of the kind of questions and contact that he had with, I would say, female students in that environment, to touch women. ... I was certainly aware that this was going on and was making people uncomfortable."

Many women mentioned crude, misogynist and offensive humour that surfaced in many places, including 'Beer and Skits.' While some women described 'Beer and Skits' as an appropriate forum for crude jokes which "nobody takes seriously," and/or while "extremely sexist," not "degrading to women in general, because it is not meant in that way," clearly, others were not as convinced.

To many women, 'Beer and Skits' with its occasional displays of pornography and crude sexual humour, simply reflected the sexist attitudes that were all too common within the profession. Women revealed that females were often stereotyped within skits as 'housewives or hookers,' and one woman explained that:

> It was interesting that ... the positions women would take in different skits, this was quite overt, it wasn't just me who noticed ... guys would have the main roles — the women would have the short little skirts, the 'cutesy' back-up signing positions — they wouldn't have equal kinds of positions ... and these are women and men who are supposed to be equals in the same class ... to dress like that — to always act as handmaidens to male doctors, it makes you wonder what kind of role they're going to take in the hospital ... and I think that a lot of them don't see that by behaving like that, that's the kind of position that they may be seen to set themselves into.

Yet another woman explained:

> This is medicine's big social night and this is what we do — why? There are so many things that we could do that are funny about medicine, why pick this? Well, that's what 'Beer and Skits' is, a night where everybody get together and uses the words 'penis' and 'vagina' as much as possible. It's so pathetic — so highschoolish ... and just as bad towards the men, but it's definitely got a tilt towards being anti-woman, definitely. Yet a lot of people don't perceive is as that. A lost of women think I'm just being uptight.

Furthermore, while it is 'comforting' to know that as a result of one particular class that hired a female stripper to help them with their skit a couple of years ago, strippers have been officially banned from 'Beer and

Skits,' some women feel that such measures are not enough. One woman made the connection between the inherent sexual harassment evident in a genre of skits featuring "women in skimpy outfits and men as whistling construction workers," and the spectrum of everyday violence in women's lives. She explained: "Now with the news about women's issues — rape trials on TV. Hey, these attitudes have to be stopped. Just walking down streets and women getting attacked. I started thinking, I have a responsibility too."

Finally, despite Osborne's (1983) optimistic proclamation that blatant sexism was no longer tolerated in medical schools, several women described a recent incident where a pornographic centrefold made its way into a set of lecture slides, to the amusement of many people in attendance. While the professor "initially appeared startled," he then "started describing in great detail the size of her breasts and what he'd like to do with them, which is completely inappropriate for a lecture in any kind of educational forum." Several women described being shocked, stunned, and disoriented by the experience. Although a formal letter of protest was written requesting an apology from the lecturer, several women stated that they were disappointed at the lack of support received by those who complained. As well, many women were shocked by the intensity of the anger projected, mainly by male classmates, who thought that the women were overreacting.

Clearly, though, just as important as the examples of sexism that women spoke about were the reactions such instances got from those within the medical school. Women spoke of male peers and professors who were supportive and understanding. To illustrate, one male professor receptively altered his lecture notes to read 'uterine bleeding' and 'curetted a cervix.' But as many women pointed out, this was not always the case. In one instance, complaints about offensive jokes and inappropriate terminology were trivialized by faculty, administration and students alike. Reactions to the complaints were described as defensive and dismissive. For example, in response to several women's complaints about the sexist and misogynist humour of another professor, women gave various descriptions of how the event was trivialized and dismissed by members of both the faculty and the administration. As one woman explained, referring to the professor in question: "[He] said that if ... the women in class were SO insecure, then they're not suitable as physicians because they're going to run across certain comments that are JOKES in real life, and they're not going to make it." Finally, as one woman reflected:

> There's definitely still some sexist profs out there and the fact that nothing is done to silence them sends the message that it's not that

important. It doesn't really matter. Even if it's offending you and making you uncomfortable, it's your problem, you should get over it because it doesn't bother us ... it was only one person, admittedly, but it sends a pretty strong message.

This message is strong. Several women said that they would not feel comfortable objecting publicly to blatant sexism or harassment because they did not want to be labelled as troublemakers. What appears to be most disquieting is that several women admitted that they would be reluctant to make a visible complaint, or to sign their name to a formal complaint, because they were afraid of the ramifications. As one woman revealed: "I guess I'm pretty reluctant to bring stuff up to the level. ... I think a lot of women end up getting nailed because they go that route — they get people angry. Whether they do or they don't, you still get labelled." As another woman explained:

That's a big issue for women right now. Because I'm in a very touchy point in my education — if I was an intern and already graduated, it's a slightly different situation, but now, I would more than likely jeopardize my situation. It would be more harmful to me than to the person I was accusing, more than likely. And I would have a really hard time deciding whether it was worth it, unless it was so overwhelmingly awful. ... Because even if you are right, are justified, there's a stigma attached to complaining.

Even among their peers, many women stated that when they spoke out against sexism they were told that they were overreacting, they were too sensitive or that they couldn't take a joke. Their complaints were trivialized and dismissed, and they were personally labelled as being 'uptight' or 'bitches.' Moreover, according to several women, the ultimate insult and method of silencing women is to be labelled as feminists and, therefore, as lesbians. In fact, several women that I interviewed emphasized that they were NOT feminists, even though, in my perception, they went on to articulate extremely in-depth, 'feminist' analyses of the discrimination that they encountered in medicine. To many women on the medical campus, feminism is seen as dangerously radical and extremist — a forum for the propagation of man-hating and male-bashing. Furthermore, feminism was often linked to lesbianism, which also highlights the issue of homophobia within the culture of medical school and, indeed within society in general. As one woman stated:

There now seems to be a backlash against the whole feminist things. ... A lot of women I know [have a] 'feminist fear' — [they're] quick to distance themselves from that just in case there's negative ramifications. ... Somebody said, 'oh, well I wouldn't consider myself a feminist.' I said 'oh, why not? 'Well, no, just, I'm not.' The image of the bra burner was definitely what she was referring to.

As another woman reflected:

> There are so many issues you could explore. What about gay women here? This would be the WORST place — how difficult — you can't even begin to image. ... Some of the comments ... just so scary me. ... 'Radical, lesbian, feminist' — that's exactly the words, exactly the words used to silence women.

Not surprisingly, several women spoke of the isolation they felt at being attacked for voicing their opinions. Some began to question whether indeed they had overreacted and many expressed genuine confusion and frustration about what to do. As one woman explained:

> It gets back to the fact — how do you react? Getting on edge every time someone makes a comment? I'm at the point where I can't decide how to react. Should I get up in arms regardless of how innocent this remark is intended to be, just to make a point, or should I just laugh, and take it for what it was intended to be? Supposedly?

Still others admitted that they had simply given up speaking out against perceived discrimination.

> I definitely get the feeling from a lot of men in class, like when we're talking about 'Beer and Skits' or about doctors making offensive jokes, they go 'oh lighten up — what's the big deal? — what's the problem? — there's nothing here, you're creating problems.' They're definitely not willing to see that. Like even if it's not a problem, if I say something that offends someone, I'll make an effort, whether I think it's valid or not, I will make an effort not to say that in front of them again, because you have to have respect for other peoples' feelings and emotions. I just don't feel that they respect what you say, they think it's garbage and fiction.

And, several women expressed that the most painful part was seeing their female colleagues not support each other. However, as one woman explained, using a telling example:

Over and over again, the people that told the smutty jokes were the endocrinologists, the gynecologists, the people that make their money off women — telling jokes about women that were purely offensive, and if you were to change the punch line from being 'woman' to being 'black' or even animal — 'dog' or 'horse' ... people would be up in arms, they would not put up with it. But because the butt of the joke is a woman, everyone, including women laughed. And it breaks my heart to see women laugh like that, but I guess they laugh for the reasons they've laughed for years, because you're nervous about it and you don't want your colleagues to think you're a prude.

Several women commented that a big part of the problem was lack of a visible sense of community or network of support among women in medical school. As one woman explained:

We don't talk about this stuff, that's part of missing the sisterhood. ... [I] felt like I went into [a] kind of situation where is was a man's world and there was nothing to bring women together. And there was no sense of sisterhood or support for each other and a lot of underlying competition.

Women were also interested in their male colleagues' attitudes on the issue of sexism within medical school. Moreover, many women shared their hope for building a support network for students, where all issues of concern could be discussed in an open forum.

Yet, despite the incidents of sexism and discrimination that they related to me, many women also expressed optimism that medical school was becoming a more hospitable environment for women. There was also the sense that while some improvements had taken place, more tangible and lasting change would still occur in the future. Other women were even more optimistic and felt very positive about the changes that they perceived had already taken place. However, there were also many women who clearly did not share such optimism, and their descriptions of their experiences within medical school ranged from disappointment to profound pain, showing clearly just how devastating and debilitating such experiences can be for some women. As one woman explained:

It's been a real lack of loss of idealism. ... I mean, everyday in first year I felt I'd been boxed around a bit. They really try to mold you, and maybe I'm a little melodramatic about that they were trying to break my spirit. I thought they were all fascists, so I think it may be a little bit easier for other women. ... I think men are able to tolerate some of what goes on a little bit better. There's not so much directed at them, it wouldn't be as draining.

Others felt a profound sense of marginalization and isolation within medical school.

I wanted to quit every minute of my first year — every minute I thought 'this is not the place for me.' I never felt so isolated, so different, and made to feel crummy for being different. Qualities that I had thought were good were not appreciated — I was being, in fact, shit on. I wanted to quit all the time. ... I was in such pain, I really was isolated... really had few people here who knew anything about the things I was feeling. ... First year I wouldn't have wished on anybody, I felt it was a nightmare.

Yet others felt a sense of despair and defeat, as well as a perceived helplessness to challenge or change the system. As one woman explained:

I did go home and cry. I didn't want to participate, but I thought I could change it. Well, that's just bullshit. There's no way I can change it. Based on the skits that we saw from other years and our own classmates, based on role models — teachers, profs, medical doctors standing in front of class and telling us jokes that were not funny, that were offensive. Attitudes that I found abhorrent. Jumping up and down in a class many times in a day to try to point out or speak out against this, which is what I thought my mission would be. I'll fail medical school, but I'll make some impact. No, you don't make any impact, except you wear yourself out. ... So many times I would speak out ... I don't know if they groaned or not, it was my impression they groaned. ... And everyday, there wasn't a day that went by that there wasn't something to make me go home and cry.

Furthermore, some women believed that change had to be initiated from within the system. This is exemplified by the following statement:

There needs to be more women in medical school, more women as physicians. ... The only way it'll change is for women to have more control over teaching, over the whole system. If we're not happy with it, we should try and change it, and we should be active in making those changes and the way to do that is to become involved. And the only way you can change the system REALLY is from the inside. It's fine for all kinds of outside people, like medical sociologists, to stand there and say, 'we've done these stats and this is what's wrong,' but the profession will not change from the outside — it's a closed system.

Others, however, questioned the possibility of such a change from within the system:

> In terms of personal experience, it's SO subtle, really subtle — so hard for me to come up with specific examples. But, all the lecturers are men, for one thing. There are some women, but they sort of slide in and out and don't really have any place in the whole running of the school. The people who really make decisions about what happens, the ones you see around a lot, aren't women. That's subtle, but it takes its toll. I think our class is about half and half, but it felt like there's a whole bunch of men and women are kind of dotted — really isolated, separated.

And,

> I don't think things are changing, I don't really think things are changing. Women are there, but we all act like men. We all think like men by the time we're done.

Finally, one woman concluded that she was pessimistic that the system would ever create real change by itself because, in her experience, it worked on so many different, yet interrelated, levels to perpetuate itself, from the selection of students through to the form and context of the dissemination of knowledge, skills and ideology. As she explained:

> I think that it's who the role models are and how we're teaching, not what we're teaching, it's how it's presented. I don't think we need another class on menopause — [there is] an attempt to bring lay people from the community in, to tell their story. Yet, most medical students think of this as 'non-core,' non-significant, not worth listening to. Somehow if this is presented by people medical students think of as powerful — if it's presented as good, then maybe their attitudes will change. I think how it's presented is so important. ... As I came through — I know who I am, I'm stable, [but] it's like being in the Marines the way they train you here. On the one hand, you're the cream of the crop — brilliant, on the other hand, you're shit on, to

build character. I thought this won't work on me because I'm a formed person already, I won't change easily ... but ... you know, in a past life I was a woman, and now I'm a medical student. It really shook me. ... I don't have a wonderful, optimistic attitude.

Discussion and Conclusion

It is apparent from the previous discussion that even though women now constitute almost 40 percent of all students in the Manitoba Medical School, medicine is still a male-oriented profession on many levels and, consequently, women are still discriminated against and/or treated differently throughout their training. All the respondents described experiences and effects of sexism and perceived that gender discrimination still persisted on the campus. Furthermore, these experiences reflected all of the forms of sexism that have been identified by researchers, ranging from subtle sexism, double-binds, and systemic discrimination, through to more overt and blatant examples of sexism and discrimination, many of which fell within the realm of sexual harassment.

It is hoped that the findings of this study would promote meaningful discussion among all those involved in medical training and the medical profession. Such discourse would facilitate fundamental change in the medical school environment. But, for meaningful dialogue to occur, it is critical that discussion move away from 'intentions,' and instead focus on the 'effects' of the latent patriarchal culture within medical school (University of Western Ontario, 1991). It must be recognized that sexism is built into the system at all levels, and consequently, that it is everyone's responsibility to create and carry out permanent and far-reaching systemic change. Furthermore, it is necessary that men, who continue, collectively, to hold the power within the institution of medicine, state publicly that sexism and/or gender discrimination is a problem that needs to be addressed in a serious and immediate manner (University of Western Ontario, 1991). While the institution may be satisfied that they have opened doors to women students which now constitute close to 50 percent of the Canadian medical school population, resistance occurs when women "want to think differently, do different kinds of research, teach differently, say different things, express different interests, challenge the process — that's not as welcome" (University of Western Ontario, 1991). It is hoped that this study provides useful information to initiate institutional changes, including: gender inclusive and specific language within all curriculum materials and learning situations; increase in the number of females teaching in medical school; increase in institutional support of women, such as more daycare spaces, female changing rooms, fair maternity leave policy and flexible residences; and institutional acknowledgment of and negative sanctions against all forms of sexism and gender discrimination. In light of the research findings that students' adaptation to the medical school environment is important as it directly relates to learning and professional performance (Vitaliano et al., 1989:1327), it would be desirable to provide a favourable and friendly learning environment for all students.

In 1892, Harriet Foxton Clarke became the first woman graduate from the Manitoba Medical College (Hacker, 1974:145). Over one hundred years later, the question that must be asked is 'how much has really changed for women in this medical school, and elsewhere?' While fundamental structural changes are not without obstacles, such changes are necessary so that women have the environment and the opportunity to be valued and equal members of the medical profession. Ultimately, this can only be positive for the profession and society, as a whole.

Notes

1. It is reflective of the deeply ingrained hierarchical and counterproductive ordering of health care professionals, which is perpetuated especially by the medical profession, that some medical students would find the label 'nurse' to be derogatory.

References

Altekruse, J. and S. McDermott. 1988. "Contemporary Concerns of Women in Medicine," in *Feminism Within the Science and Health Care Professions: Overcoming Resistance*. Edited by S. V. Rosser. New York: Pergamon Press. Pp. 65–88.

Association of Canadian Medical Colleges. 1991. *Canadian Medical Education Statistics*. Vol. 13.

Becker, H.S., B. Geer, E.C. Hughes and A.L. Strauss. 1961. *Boys in White*. Chicago: University of Chicago Press.

Brown, S. and R. Klein. 1982. "Woman Power in the Medical Hierarchy." *The Journal of the American Medical Women's Association (JAMWA)* 37:155–164.

Dickstein, L. 1990. "Female Physicians in the 1980s: Personal and Family Attitudes and Values." *The Journal of the American Medical Women's Association (JAMWA)* 45:122–126.

Eisenberg, C. 1989. "Medicine is No Longer a Man's Profession." *The New England Journal of Medicine* 321:1542–1544.

Hacker, C. 1974. *The Indomitable Lady Doctors*. Toronto: Clarke Irwin.

Harris, M. and M. Conley-Muth. 1981. "Sex Role Stereotypes and Medical Specialty Choice." *The Journal of the American Medical Women's Association (JAMWA)* 36:245–252.

Harward, D., C. Lyons, C. Porter and R. Hunter. 1981. "A Comparison of the Performance of Male and Female Medical Students and Residents." *Journal of Medical Education* 56:853–855.

Institutional Analysis. 1991. "Statistics." University of Manitoba.

Kettner, A. 1988. "Female Family-Practice Graduates at the University of Manitoba: Career Patterns and Perceptions." *Canadian Family Physician* 34:831–837.

Kirk, J. 1992. *Women in Medical School: An Experiential Account of the Persistence of Sexism and its Consequences.* Master's Thesis: University of Manitoba.

Martin, C., J. Jones and M. Bird. 1988. "Support Systems for Women in Medicine." *The Journal of the American Medical Women's Association (JAMWA)* 43:77–83.

Martin, S., R. Arnold, and R. Parker. 1988. "Gender and Medical Socialization." *Journal of Health and Social Behavior* 29:333–343.

Merton, R.K., P. Kendall and G. Reader (eds.). 1957. *The Student Physician.* Cambridge, Mass.: Harvard University Press.

Osborne, D. 1983. "My Wife, the Doctor." *Mother Jones* 18–44.

Phelan, E. 1991. "A Survey of Maternity Leave Policies in Boston Area Hospitals." *The Journal of the American Medical Women's Association* (JAMWA) 46:55–58.

Shapiro, M. 1978. *Getting Doctored.* Kitchener: Between the Lines.

Simms, G. 1991. "Comments." *The Chilly Climate for Women in Colleges and Universities.* (Video) University of Western Ontario. Executive Producers: Western's Caucus on Women's Issues and the President's Standing Committee for Employment Equity.

University of Western Ontario. 1991. *The Chilly Climate for Women in Colleges and Universities.* (Video) Executive Producers: Western's Caucus on Women's Issues and the President's Standing Committee for Employment Equity.

Vitaliano, P., R. Maiuro, E. Mitchell and J. Russo. 1989. "Perceived Stress in Medical School: Resistors, Persistors, Adaptors and Maladaptors." *Social Science and Medicine* 28:1321–1329.

Wheeler, R., L. Candib and M. Martin. 1990. "Part-time Doctors: Reduced Working Hours for Primary Care Physicians." *The Journal of the American Medical Women's Association* (JAMWA) 45:47–54.

Section Three

HIDDEN FROM VIEW

Chapter Nine

Benevolent Patriarchy: The Foreign Domestic Movement, 1980–1990

Patricia Daenzer

Introduction

The domestic workers' advocacy movement gained momentum in the late 1970s and matured in the 1980s. The maturity of their movement gave them a new legitimacy in Canadian social relations by relocating them from the status of voiceless victims to the position of a special-interest group with the right to advocate for change. While they would still lack significant force, they achieved a level of credibility in the 1980s which would thereafter influence the framework of incremental changes to their condition.

The 1980s, then, were an era of heightened conflict between workers, employers and departmental officials. In September 1980, the new Minister of Employment and Immigration, Lloyd Axworthy, commissioned the Task Force on Immigration Practices and Procedures with the mandate to assess the degree of confluence between the Immigration Act of 1976 and immigration procedures, with emphasis on workers on employment authorizations. In April 1981, the Task Force reported what had been known for a half a century: that domestic workers were disadvantaged in a number of systemic ways. These general and preliminary findings prompted the Minister of Employment and Immigration to initiate an internal review of the domestic workers program. In November 1981, the Minister's advisors provided him with a 97-page report, *Domestic Workers on Employment Authorizations,* which recommended measures which they described as having the force to "assist foreign domestics working in Canada to gain permanent resident status."

The recommendations announced in 1981 proposed measures that were said to be an attempt to balance the needs of Canadian families facing a chronic shortage of servants against the need to protect foreign domestics from exploitation. Two clear policy directions appear in the announcement: first, Canadian families would be assured access to immigrant domestic workers; second, immigrant domestic workers would continue to enter Canada as non-immigrants. However, a limited number of domestic workers were still assured entry into Canada with full immigrant status; analysis of trends would show that these would continue to be mostly British domestics. Many others, however, have the opportunity to "qualify" for landed status only following a period of employment in domestic work. The policy was thereafter known as the Foreign Domestic Movement (FDM).

Internal bureaucratic disagreement over this policy continued for the rest of the decade, as did intensified advocacy. In 1989 the Minister of Employment and Immigration launched another review of the FDM. The 1989 review was hastened by the vociferous criticisms against the policy and by increasing media attention to the plight of domestic workers.

The salient features of the present policy continue to be restricted mobility, the discretion granted to Employment and Immigration personnel in determining the post-contract status of domestic workers, and the unregulated working conditions.

In spite of five decades of deliberations and changes to the policy, many of its worst features remained, and the most redeemable aspect of the policy disappeared. In 1990 the benevolence evident in the policy is patriarchal in nature. Domestics are permitted insignificant rewards and privileges in place of rights, by both the Department of Employment and Immigration and their employers. But they must earn these rewards at pain of dignity.

Five decades have brought domestic workers no further ahead; they still face lost mobility, conditional rights, and marginal and unprotected labour status. In this respect the history of domestic work is unlike that of any other occupation or group (with the exception of the developmentally challenged). While, in general, twentieth-century working conditions in Canada have progressed, albeit incrementally, during the last fifty years, in 1990 domestic workers experienced fewer rights than they held in 1940, and working conditions no different from those experienced in the pre-1940s period. This chapter examines the most comprehensive policy review and subsequent recommendations, and looks forward into the 1990s.

The Task Force on Immigration Practices and Procedures: Domestic Workers on Employment Authorizations

The Minister of Employment and Immigration, Lloyd Axworthy, charged the Task Force of 1980 with a broad mandate for examining the apparent objectives of the Immigration Act of 1976 and the extent to which the objectives of the Act were being met through existing regulations, procedures and practices.[1] Second, the Minister was concerned about the increasing criticisms of the domestic work program, especially charges that his department condoned the exploitation of domestic workers. He was also forced to be responsive to the now evident conflict between domestic workers and employers. Employers continued to experience a shortage of domestic workers and increasingly complained that the Department of Employment and Immigration paid attention to the issues of domestics at their expense. Since they (employers) were the clients of the Department, they expected attention and service. Clearly, the challenge to the new Minister was to balance these competing interests and appear to correct inequities.[2]

The Task Force cut to the heart of the issue swiftly and directly. It acknowledged the most problematic aspects of the working condition of domestic workers:

> [T]here have been sufficient reports of mistreatment to focus public attention on their plight and their particular vulnerability to abuse.[3]

And as had been in each of the last four decades, the Task Force noted the working conditions which contributed to abuse: isolation in private homes, non-immigrant status for some, little opportunity for collective action with others similarly situated, and dependence on the employer for both shelter and wages.[4]

The immigration status of the women received lengthy discussion by the Task Force members. They observed that the increased number of domestic workers arriving in Canada on work authorizations, as non-immigrants, since 1973 found it difficult to obtain subsequent landed status. This difficulty was seen to be related to the varying discretions of immigration officials. They noted that the tenuous immigrant status of the domestic heightened her vulnerability. Since Manpower counsellors had discretion in decisions regarding the suitability of the domestic for life in Canada, and since job stability was used as an indication of economic stability, staying in the job in spite of working conditions was essential for those women aspiring to life in Canada.[5] The Task Force also drew attention to the paternalistic arrangement occasioned by the convergence of the non-immigrant status of the domestic and her dependence on the employer for landed status. Such an arrangement meant that desertion of the abusive employer and working conditions, or being fired, could result in deportation from Canada.[6]

Even with the introduction of minimum wages for domestic workers in some provinces, it was observed that wages continued to be too low. They noted, also, that domestic workers paid approximately $2 million to the Canadian government annually in Unemployment Insurance and Canada Pension Plan premiums. Because many were subject to deportation following completion of their employment contract, very few were eligible to collect these benefits. It was not fair, suggested the Task Force, to have working visitors pay the equivalent of one month's wage to the Canadian government, with no returns. On the other hand, employers too suffered from inequities. They could not include wages paid to domestic workers in tax deductions. Thus the Task Force suggested a compromise: domestics should not contribute to benefits to which they were not entitled, and employers should be induced to pay decent wages by the inclusion of domestic wages in tax-deductible expenses.[7]

On the issue of employment contracts between domestics and employers, the Task Force was inconsistent and unpersuasive. The employment contracts initiated in the 1970s to regulate expectations between employers and domestics were found to be an empty gesture. And the Task Force correctly noted that although this issue had received much policy attention in previous years, the matter of contracts was more problematic than assumed. For example, the report reasoned, there could be legitimate constitutional objections by the provinces to the federal government's role in stipulating and enforcing the terms of employment contracts, an otherwise provincial jurisdiction. Yet they felt that there was a moral imperative to impose guidelines on the working conditions of domestic workers:

> [I]t would be unpalatable simply to allow employers to propose the contract terms without any guidance from federal standards. ... The Federal government has no power to become involved in regulating contracts between landed immigrants and their employers. However, where the employment authorization exists, the opportunity is available to have at least some level of involvement.[8]

So, while negating the 1970s employment contracts, the Task Force sought to retain centrality for the federal government in the daily affairs of servants and their mistresses. It concurrently favoured the provision of non-immigrant status based on the vague argument that working visitors to Canada "could" be eligible for some level of federal protection in employment matters.

Responding to the restrictions of its limited mandate, the Task Force discussed four alternatives which would at best tinker with the existing policy without altering the substantive impact of Canada's immigration policy for procuring offshore labour for low-skilled jobs.

1. Deny entry altogether, either as permanent residents or on employment authorizations
2. Restrict entry to "landed" immigrants only
3. Restrict entry to employment authorization only
4. A continued combination of 2 and 3 but with modifications to present procedures[9]

The first three considerations embody ideological trends. The first is market-driven. By inducing scarcity in the domestic labour pool, employers would be forced to be competitive and (it was hoped) pay appropriate wages. Discontinuating the admission of immigrants into this occupation would then place household service work on equal supply footing with other service occupations in Canada. However, since Canadians had traditionally rejected domestic work, it was felt that this would leave the domestic market open to illegal immigrants; the latter would be subject to even more abuses.[10]

The second alternative was guided by the notion of citizenship entitlement for labour members without regard for length of resident tenure. Admitting all domestics as landed immigrants would have represented a return to rights enjoyed in the pre-1940s era. This would also place household service workers on an equal entry footing with other labour-market immigrants; the system of indenture would be replaced by relative equality of access to the Canadian labour market and its privileges. But, on its own, this alternative lacked the force to change the conditions under which domestics were employed. Other measures would still be necessary to protect this class of workers from the outcomes of the unregulated market system. Lacking these, mobility out of the occupation would continue to operate as the tangential regulator of household service working conditions.

The third alternative, to continue admitting domestics as non-immigrants, adhered to the paternalistic colonization of immigrant women's labour. It also signified a cultural disposition toward artificially prescribing class designation based upon notions of merit derived from race and gender.

The Task Force critiqued at length the practice of undervaluing the occupation of domestic work. The application of the point system of the 1976 Immigration Act was seen to be particularly problematic for domestics wishing to obtain landed immigrant status.

The arbitrarily low value set on domestics' work, particularly with children, is highly questionable ... applicants for landing are given no points in category 4 (occupational demand).[11]

Other immigrants destined for the Canadian labour force received points for occupational demand, skill and training level, and assured employment.

Domestics, it was observed, were assessed differentially; they were not credited for their occupational knowledge and training. Moreover, in the 1960s immigration and employment officials arbitrarily diminished the value of domestic work by lowering its Occupational Demand value.[12] This meant that domestic work was subjected to bureaucratic attitudes and biases which fluctuated.

In addressing the issue of occupational instability, the Task Force attempted a structural compromise to balance conflicts of demand and supply. Wishing to be sensitive to the needs of employers, but wanting to appear morally cognizant of domestics' plight, they only partially rejected the popular alternative of mobility restriction by non-immigrant status. Domestics, they suggested, should be constrained in the occupation for a period of time, but ought to be extended landed status within their first year of service.

> In our view, the most desirable approach is to rely on the market. ... On the other hand, an employer who has made an offer and waited through the landing process may legitimately complain if the person leaves after only a short time.[13]

> We would suggest that officials advise people that generally, the authorizations would not be renewed beyond two or three years. ... It would be ... fair to require landing for a prolonged stay.[14]

This represented a modest change to the existing policy. For new entrants, the proposed change was the "promise" of landed status without having to leave Canada, following a pre-determined period of time served in domestic work. Future arrivals would also have limitations on the number of renewals to their employment visas. They would be required to demonstrate acceptable citizenship characteristics within a two-to-three year period, or be deported from Canada. Thereafter, the risk of creating a pool of *de facto* immigrants without formal status would be greatly minimized. This system of conditional membership in Canadian society most rigidly preserved advantages for Canadian employers of household service workers. Canadian employers were still assured domestics whose occupational mobility would be constrained.

> [I]t cannot be stressed enough that this issue of domestics must be seen in its wider context. Domestic workers are underpaid because domestic work ... is seriously undervalued. Short term solutions must be found. Among them is finding substitutes for our least well-paid domestic worker — those on employment authorizations ... we must

still press for quality substitutes, and ... resist the impetus of mere "market forces" toward plentiful, low quality, day care institutions.[15]

Of the nineteen recommendations made by the Task Force, many are notable for their contradictions. Some, however, reflected attempts to address the marginal status of domestic workers, and to include them as legitimate members of the Canadian labour force. Not surprisingly, however, they proposed unequal privileges to domestics and their employers with employers receiving more beneficial considerations.

Domestics currently in Canada on employment authorizations were to be invited to apply for landed immigrant status. They were to be assessed on the evidence of their present or potential successful establishment in Canada. But the Task Force had critiqued past practices of undervaluing domestic work as an occupation. Yet they too negated the value of domestic work by ignoring it as the dominant criterion during evaluation of the value of the worker to Canadian accumulation.

Similarly, employers were to be required to sign legally enforceable contracts which specified the terms and working conditions. However, the Task Force noted in its deliberation that the federal government was not constitutionally empowered to enforce contracts in provincial jurisdictions. The question of enforcement was left unresolved in their recommendation.

Employers who violated the terms of the employment contract were to be denied future domestic workers through the program. But there would be no measure to prevent employers from sponsoring their own immigrants into abusive conditions. In addition, without an enforcement mechanism, no measure existed to bring to the attention of the Department those frequent offenders.

A Policy of Benevolence:
Misplaced Rights and the 1980s Procedures

In April, September and November 1981, the Minister of Employment and Immigration, Hon. Lloyd Axworthy, and his departmental officials, informed by the statements of the Task Force, announced policy changes in the domestic work program. Thereafter, domestics would depend on the benevolence of their employers, and on the discretions of manpower and employment counsellors of the federal government, for adjustments to their tenuous labour status. Under the new policy, domestics were extended no rights *de jure*.

No changes were instituted in either the 1976 Immigration Act or the Regulations to effect a process whereby all domestics could enter Canada as legitimate labour members. The current process of granting non-immigrant status to most women entering Canada to perform domestic work was strengthened. Of the nineteen recommendations which flowed from the Task Force, the Minister's announcement reflected two of significance. Domestic workers would continue to enter Canada on employment authorizations (as non-immigrants); not for the one-year period suggested by the Task Force, but for a two-year period, with assessments at one-year intervals. Extensions for a third year were only to be granted to those who would ultimately be deported. And domestics were to be differentially awarded increased points for their occupational training.

To facilitate the entry of some domestic workers as landed immigrants, 10 of the maximum 15 assessment points were to be awarded to those with formal training or on-the-job experience in domestic work. The training was to have occurred

> for a period of time sufficient to have provided the applicants with a developmental opportunity which will enable them to earn sufficient income to adequately maintain themselves. ... [16]

The Task Force had taken issue with the arbitrariness of rewarding vocational preparedness of domestic workers. Some domestics were awarded 2 to 3 points for vocational preparation, others were awarded no points.[17] The 10 points to be awarded would be calculated by Immigration officials, and would be based upon an abstract assessment of the complexities of household service work. This system of awarding points for occupational preparedness was based loosely on the existing system of calculating vocational merit in other occupations.

The phrasing of the policy guideline on the assessment of vocational preparation encouraged highly subjective judgments and wide discretions. Not surprisingly, the increase in the vocational preparation value to 10 points was not a widespread benefit to domestic workers; only a small percentage continued to enter Canada as landed immigrants. Within Tables 1a and 1b it can be seen that following implementation of the 1981 announcements, between 1982 and 1985, 8,029 household service workers were admitted as landed immigrants, compared to 54,512 on employment authorizations (non-landed status). And within those numbers, during 1985, for example, 71.5 percent of British domestic workers entered Canada as landed immigrants, while only 53.3 percent of Philippine domestic workers entered as landed immigrants.[18]

Even more contentious than the refusal to grant women full value for knowledge of household service work, and the refusal of the bureaucracy to award the occupation its full value for its persistent demand, was the issue of conditional landing. In spite of the moral arguments put forward by the Task Force against the exploitation of working visitors, no clear statement emerged from the Minister in support of the unconditional rights of domestics to

TABLE 1a
Permanent Residents:
Foreign Domestic Movement (Principal Applicant Only),
1980 - 1985, by Occupation

	1980	1981	1982	1983	1984	1985	Total
Housekeeper	23	104	301	312	629	787	2,156
Companion	3	6	3	15	9	18	54
Servant	31	126	165	276	429	391	1,418
Babysitter	176	201	133	136	196	155	997
Children's Nurse	9	43	119	91	180	172	614
Parent Helper	5	23	70	464	1,239	1,071	2,872
Other	0	0	17	170	326	155	668
Total	**247**	**503**	**808**	**1,464**	**3,008**	**2,749**	**8,779**

Source: Immigration Statistics: Employment and Immigration Canada. Ottawa.
Run Date: 21/04/91.

TABLE 1b
Employment Authorizations:
Foreign Domestic Movement (Principal Applicant Only),
1980 - 1985, by Occupation

	1980	1981	1982	1983	1984	1985	Total
Housekeeper	1,885	2,664	3,034	3,972	4,154	4,006	19,715
Companion	30	83	100	82	87	71	458
Servant	1,031	2,409	2,247	1,775	1,892	1,337	10,691
Babysitter	3,995	2,147	1,150	874	978	804	9,948
Children's Nurse	298	541	1,067	1,058	1,171	1,028	5,163
Parent Helper	1,063	5,030	6,432	5,809	5,451	4,743	28,528
Other	0	1	175	243	326	446	1,191
Total	**8,302**	**12,875**	**14,205**	**13,813**	**14,059**	**12,435**	**75,689**

Source: Immigration Statistics: Employment and Immigration Canada. Ottawa.
Run Date: 22/04/91.

occupational mobility. Landed status was still conditional upon time served as indentured workers.

Related to the resistance to grant domestics unconditional entry into the Canadian labour force was the issue of credit for job demand. The Task Force's recommendation to raise the occupational demand value to 15 was ignored in the Minister's 1981 announcement. Yet the bureaucratically driven fluctuations in the occupational demand value is central to the occupational status ascription process of immigrant domestic workers.

[W]hen the demand for domestics dropped from 15 to 12, and the interview level was raised to 45, we were immediately concerned over the political implications. ... [19]

Recommendation Number Six
In recognition of the high demand for domestic workers in Canada, applicants for permanent residence should be accorded full points under Occupational Demand category of the selection criteria. (Schedule 1, Immigration Regulations)[20]

Instead of a system based on rights, the Minister's initial announcement in 1981 approved a process characterized by token rewards for time served in domestic work. Occupational benefits and privileges extended to domestics were couched in provisional language, prone to subjectivity, and based on unenforceable contracts. In return for being "good" workers, they would be granted considerations from Employment and Immigration officials, and from their employers. This rewarding process was dependent upon four general sets of circumstances:

— the extent to which the benevolence of employers would extend to the granting of time off and support for skills training
— the degree of the compassion of employment counsellors in responding to reported cases of abuse and job loss
— the generosity of immigration counsellors in defining the terms "personal suitability, adaptation, and self-sufficiency"
— the extent to which immigration officials and employment counsellors would subordinate interdepartmental tensions to effective and equitable outcomes during the two-to-three-year process of assessment and processing of domestic workers

New entrants into domestic work were to be granted employment authorizations by overseas visa officers (as had been increasingly the case since the 1970s) if they were assessed as having the personal and vocational suitability to become successful residents of Canada.[21] Ultimately, the potential for successful integration in Canada would be measured by occupational stability in domestic work, and a process of skills upgrading leading to "self-sufficiency." This potential for successful integration was a pre-landed status requisite, and would be monitored during the two-year period of domestic employment.[22] The only concrete measurement factor in the assessment process was the time served in domestic work. All other considerations were based on supposition of potentialities.

Those domestics who were currently employed in Canada as working visitors would also be invited to make application for landed immigrant status. Status would be conferred "internally." They were categorized into two streams: those who had already demonstrated self-sufficiency and those who would require guidance in striving toward "a suitable level of self-sufficiency." Achievers, those who were resident in Canada for more than two years and already proven to be self-reliant, were permitted the opportunity of making application for permanent status, and subject to no further evaluation.[23] Conversely, non-achievers, those having been employed for two or more years and ultimately found to be lacking in initiative and potential for self-sufficiency in Canada, would be returned to their country of origin.[24]

The social condition officials referred to as "self-sufficiency" was central to the revised policy. To facilitate it, a two-part suggestion was offered to employers: First, they were to extend time off for domestics to attend upgrading courses. Second, an appeal was made to them for a financial contribution toward their domestics' self-improvement.

> To ensure that domestics have sufficient time to attend training programs, Canadian employers will be required to allow a certain amount of free time, a minimum of 3 hours ... for their domestic's self-improvement. Also, because their wages are so low, employers will be asked to contribute a certain amount of money towards the cost of training to a maximum of $15.00 monthly. ... [25]

In addition, the inter-class conflict central to this occupation was not minimized by these suggestions. The dependency established by this expectation of employers was significant to the domestic worker's stabilization in Canada. Her chances of becoming a potentially self-sufficient landed immigrant of Canada depended upon the willingness of the employer to extend free time and a pecuniary token. The expectation exaggerated the fundamental antagonism between the domestics and their employers — most notably because one equalizing factor between employer and employee would be the domestic's immigrant status. The non-landed status constrained mobility and occupational freedom in the employer's favour. Yet the federal government set out moral expectations for the employer to assist the domestic in becoming a landed immigrant. In so doing, the employer would facilitate the domestic's mobility out of employer's service, and consequently lose the investment in the form of the occupationally mobilized worker.

Employment counselors and immigration officers were given complementary and key roles in this process of moving domestics through the application stage to the landed immigrant or deportation stage. The former were to give guidance to domestics and negotiate "contracts" with employers; the latter were to assess the outcome of the domestic's preparedness and take appropriate action. Much depended upon the counsellors' persuasiveness in convincing employers to establish and honour contracts, and on the counsellors' interpretation and reconciliation of the tension inherent in their bureaucratic role. They were expected to serve the interests of both employers and domestic workers. Without structural changes to the organization of domestic work, these competing interest were irreconcilable.

It was within this framework of subjective decision making, and mediation which depended upon moral sanction for its legitimacy, that employment and immigration counsellors were charged with the responsibility of implementing the revised policy, the Foreign Domestic Movement. Their interpretations alone directed action in either a denial to employers for access to domestics through the FDM, or a recommendation for the application for landed status, or deportation of domestics.[26] Their administrative outcomes were to be arrived at through their interpretation of the merits of the two claims of the respective clients: the domestic and the employer. There continued to be ample room in this process for personal prejudices and the application of class biases.

Privileges vs. Rights:
Regulating Status Ascription Among Women

That was the tone of policy established following the report of the Task Force, and the internal review requested by the Minister of Employment and Immigration in 1981. Domestics gained procedural rights but no substantive changes to their immigrant and thus occupational status. But the procedural right to "apply" for landed immigrant status from within Canada was overshadowed by the substantive obstacles which continued to characterize domestic work. Entry into Canada as *de facto* citizens was still an illusive privilege.

While the Department of Employment and Immigration encouraged an "employment contract" between employer and domestic, it lacked the authority to enforce such a contract. An unenforceable contract held no suasion with employers toward rationalizing what domestic workers had claimed to be exploitative working conditions. The employers still retained the right to control relations in the "privacy of their own homes."[27]

Research showed that, four years following the Minister's revised policy, domestics in the largest receiving centre, Ontario,[28] were irregularly governed by legislation and CEIC guidelines. Less than half of employers based domestic workers' pay rates on the guidelines established by Employment and

Immigration. Domestics were discriminatorily remunerated for overtime work and vacation. The greatest on-the-job dissatisfaction was due to inadequate wages and overtime pay.[29] The contract between employer and employee, the centrepiece of the 1981 revised policy, had at best an insignificant effect on the Ontario group studied. At least this study showed that servants/ respondents continued to exist in a social location external to the framework of Canadian labour.

The 1981 policy negated the legitimacy and value of housework to Canadian production and the contribution of domestic workers to human and social development. The largest number of domestics performed childcare duties; others were engaged as parent helpers, servants and children's nurses and in other household tasks.[30] Yet implicit in the assessment process during the application to landing stage is the idea that household service work is non-work. Unlike workers in other occupations, the domestic was *not* to be assessed on the years of contribution in domestic work, but on the alternate development of a skill or training in areas other than the range of housework occupations. And self-sufficiency was determined not by the years of self-supporting employment in domestic work — the successful engagement of household management activities — but by criteria external to the occupation.[31]

The policy's implicit categorization of household service work as non-work was at odds with other forms of industrial organization in Canada. Similar occupations existed in the Canadian labour market. Cooks, chambermaids, child-care workers, maintenance workers, hospital aides and attendants, restaurant workers and others performed tasks which were protected by labour legislation and often unionized. Most of these occupations were subject to the normal welfare benefits and relative protections associated with paid employment in Canada. Private household service work was thus categorized into an infrastructure external to the realm of labour and subjected to a non-contributing (to capital accumulation and production) status. Thus household service work lost its rightful place in the market sphere, and domestic workers were reduced to a commodity of convenience. Employers gained privileges through reduction in status and rights endured by domestic workers.

While the federal government implicitly categorized household service work as non-work, the provinces increasingly but cautiously included domestic work in legislations and employment regulations, thus increasingly legitimating its status.[32] And although the policy directions of the federal government negated the value and legitimacy of household service work among Canadian occupations, they ultimately incrementally acknowledged domestic workers on non-immigrant status as members of the Canadian community. But this acknowledgment was philanthropic rather than legislated, and it legitimated domestic workers, not the occupation.

Following Recommendation 9 of the Task Force and recommendations made by INTERCEDE, the domestics' self-advocacy group, the federal government began a system of selective distribution[33] of welfare resources to domestic workers in the FDM program. The Task Force's recommendation that

> [t]he Immigrant Settlement and Adaptation Program (ISAP) should make funds available to community organizations for the delivery of services to people on temporary employment authorizations. Funds should also be made available to assist domestic workers in lodging complaints of violations of the contract ...[34]

was achieved through a 1983 policy statement (implemented in 1986) which directed that community agencies and groups which serve domestic workers be recognized for funding.[35] However, non-statutory funding is a welfare privilege and not a right, and subject to the usual discretions of the rationing process.

In 1983 INTERCEDE, acting as the main advocacy group for domestic workers, rated the policy improvements steming from the 1981 changes as less than satisfactory and made 35 recommendations for moving toward a policy which would institutionalize relative rights for domestic workers on non-immigrant status.[36] And in 1985 the Federal Court of Canada ruled that the "self-sufficiency" criterion of the pre-migration assessment for temporary domestics was illegal. A person seeking a temporary work authorization, suggested the judicial system, could not be assessed on a criterion which related to "the potential for long-term establishment,"[37] Immigration bureaucrats did not have the right to regulate status ascription by interpreting aspirant immigrants' potential. The season of challenges proved trying to Employment and Immigration, and in 1985 the Department announced further policy revisions.

The 1985 revised policy reiterated the benevolent paternalistic tone of the 1981 policy. Highlights show that variations of privileges and degrees of rights of employers over their domestics were still central features:

— Domestics were still required to live in the homes of their employers, but could, with the consent of the employer, opt to live out without penalty.
— Domestics were still to enter Canada without full status as landed immigrants.
— Domestics were restricted to household service work.
— Domestics could not change employment without the permission of Employment and Immigration officials; the previous arrangement by

which employers also had to consent to this change in writing was discontinued in 1986.
— Domestics were required to report job loss.
— Officials would exercise judgment regarding whether domestics had lost their employment "through no fault of their own."
— Officials were empowered to "forgive" minor violations committed by domestics. Living out, or apart from the employer, was such a violation.
— Domestics had to prove that they could manage their finances.
— Domestics were required to report community contacts or activities; these formed the basis of assessment.

In the final analysis, the new policy directive clearly stated:

> [I]t is the individual immigration officer's assessment, based on all the factors and information which is considered relevant, of the domestic's actual or potential successful establishment and self-sufficiency which will determine approval or refusal of landing.[38]

But the employer still exercised privileges in this process. The counsellor's assessment included the report of the employer about the domestic's performance. Therefore, the domestic's admission to landed status was at the discretion of the employment counsellor and the employer.

That the domestic work policy persisted in spite of its legal tenuousness was not surprising.[39] Two 1980s developments are noteworthy. In spite of the ruling of the Federal Court of Canada against the self-sufficiency clause, officials were to continue to consider the criteria for self-sufficiency, but were advised to word refusals with care.

> There may be occasions where domestics who were refused landing by CICs because they had failed to demonstrate sufficient ability to establish in Canada, reapply for new IMM 1102's at visa offices once their three year term is concluded. Officers should ... bear in mind the CICs decision that the domestic has not demonstrated a propensity for successful establishment. In view of this it is unlikely that a visa officer would reach a contrary decision. ... [40]

In addition, throughout the major enterprise of reviews and revised policy decisions, the Regulations to the Immigration Act of 1976 were never changed to legitimate the policy. In effect, the 1981 and 1985 policy directives operated external to the legal framework within which immigration was legislated. The Federal Court's challenge to one aspect of the policy was not only instructive, it angered some officials.

> We do not think that it is the job of the courts to establish the substantive criteria to be employed in the selection of foreign domestics nor do we believe that the courts have any particular competence to do so. As long as the FDM program continues to rest on its current inadequate legal base, and as long as our present selection criteria remain as nebulous as they are, we shall, however, be inviting the courts to continue to establish the selection criteria for us.[41]

In 1988 the Department of Employment and Immigration modified and clarified the issue related to self-sufficiency. Domestics were then encouraged to engage in upgrading not simply toward self-improvement, but "to give them [domestics] the opportunity to become part of the community by making it easier for them to make contacts outside the home environment." Skills upgrading was not mandatory for all household service workers; only domestics who were assessed as requiring this vocational direction would be advised to pursue this activity. In additional, the domestic was then to be assessed on the two years of successful performance in domestic work, among other factors. Finally, it seemed, household service work had gained its rightful place among occupations.[42]

However, the two-phase assessment for landed status was still focussed on "evidence of ability to successfully establish. ... " Officials were instructed to pay attention to the domestic's compliance with advice to engage in skills upgrading.[43] Officers were advised to be "flexible and lenient" at the first stage of the assessment, but "complete and thorough" at the second stage (end of second year) of the assessment.[44] Domestics were to be assessed in the areas of: satisfactory employment experience, with the employer's version included; language proficiency; evidence of financial security and compliance with directions to upgrade; and evidence of skills acquired elsewhere. The domestic's ability to provide for absent dependants was also taken into consideration.[45]

Much of this assessment process was really aimed at differentiating between women who were thought to use the program as a means of entering Canada, and authentic domestic workers. This challenge had been historical and proved the basis of some of the instability of the labour supply in this occupation category. And so the inter-departmental tensions regarding appropriate and fair assessment criteria of domestics continued to the end of the decade. In 1989 one official voiced his frustration and views in an internal memorandum to his superior:

My premise is that the foreign domestic program is really two programs. One is the true temporary worker program involving British nannies and the like. This one should be left alone. The second program involving the Caribbean and the Philippines is, however, a sham. ... [V]ery few people from this latter group come with the intention of remaining in domestic work.. .. And the upgrading courses that we make them take are more show than substance. ... So where does this leave us? ... [I]t leaves us with a program that pumps people, who have gone through a [expression deleted] selection assessment, into the Canadian labour market.[46]

This official also raised questions about the legality of the FDM program. The question of "limits to mobility," he suggested, should be referred to "Justice" for resolution. He recommended a return to the practice of the 1940s and 1950s: that domestics be asked to sign a private contractual obligation.[47] Although by the late 1980s it appeared to the Department of Employment and Immigration that there existed a clear rationale for constraining domestics in their occupation, there continued to be intra-departmental uneasiness with this practice.

By 1989 another departmental review of the FDM was under way. In 1989 also, INTERCEDE, continuing in its role of self-advocacy, conducted a survey into the status and experience of domestics and made recommendations for further policy changes. INTERCEDE showed that at the end of the 1980s domestics were still largely not remunerated for overtime work; sexual harassment of domestics by some employers was linked to the requirement to live in the employer's home; alienation from the larger community was still a problem for domestics; and workers continued to be denied rights such as choice over living conditions and adequate food.[48]

By 1990, males were again accessing the FDM. A survey of the years 1982–1989 shows that 2–3 percent of participants who entered the FDM were males.[49] However, the small percentage of males employed in the program does not alter the primarily female-focussed issues which characterize the FDM. Between 1982 and 1990 more than 67,000 domestics were admitted to Canada under the FDM.[50] Regional shifts in source countries are most evident in the 1980s. In contrast to the 1940s and 1950s, when the majority of domestics were British or European, by 1989, 50 percent of domestics originated in the Philippines (46 percent in 1988 and 49.6 percent in 1989). Only 9.4 percent of domestics originated in the United Kingdom in 1988, and slightly more than 8 percent in 1989.[51] The domestic workers of the 1980s enjoyed fewer substantive rights than those of the 1940s and 1950s.

1990 to the Present: The Live-In Caregiver Program

The largely Philippines-origin domestic work population of the 1990s was subject to further policy changes in April 1992. The policy review initiated in 1989 clarified minor ambiguities in a changed policy entitled the Live-in Caregiver Program (LCP) which in 1992 replaced the FDM. The new policy reiterated that domestics would continue to live in their employers' homes, continue to enter Canada predominantly as non-immigrants, and still require the permission of Employment and Immigration before changing jobs.[52] The Minister announced:

> The new program responds to concerns expressed by employers, domestic workers and their representatives over the course of the extensive review of the former program. I am confident that the new requirements will ensure that those who participate in the Live-in Caregiver Program have the skills and experience to meet labour market demands.[53]

Educational requirements for entry into the program were specified. Domestics had to provide evidence that they had completed the equivalent of a Canadian grade 12 education program, and also completed six months of formal training in household service work. The 1992 announcement also officially removed the requirement that domestic workers obtain letters of release from their employers before changing jobs. This policy continued to supply wealthy Canadian women with alternatives to non-paid housework, and with status in the paid labour force. On the eve of the twenty-first century, immigrant domestic workers were still a disenfranchised state-subsidized convenience for middle-class women.

In 1992 the Province of Ontario made a weak though significant gesture toward granting Ontario domestic workers the right to unionize. Steps were taken to delete the exclusion of domestic workers from access to collective bargaining arrangements.[54] INTERCEDE noted that removal of the exclusion is an insufficient measure to provide domestic workers with protection through collective action. Although this provincial initiative was insignificant in outcome, it is significant in precedence. Domestic workers in Ontario may now look forward to a continuing discussion of legitimating their status in the Ontario labour force.

A Class Above: State Maintenance of Elevated Rank

A stated mission of the Minister of Employment and Immigration for the years 1980–1984 was to mediate the competing interests of employers and domestic workers. He acknowledged that domestics were exploited; the nature of their occupation and their tenuous immigrant status accommodated this exploitation.[55] Class antagonism was understood to be central to the peculiar form of exploitation endured by domestic workers.

Yet, with all of this knowledge, the Minister's charge to the Task Force in relation to domestic workers was to examine the use of employment authorizations. The all-male Task Force[56] consulted the views of women experts and drew selectively on their recommendations and submissions.[57] But however expansive the inquiry might have been, the charge of the Task Force was predicated upon a limited vision. The framing of the review within the existing Immigration Act of 1976 suggested an acceptance of the Act, its intentions and outcome. Yet, in the opinion of domestic workers, the fundamental issues were the apparent inequities and injustices seemingly legitimated by the policy gaps within the existing Immigration Act. To be substantive in its mission, the Task Force should have been charged to examine the spirit of the 1976 Immigration Act and its appropriateness for effecting relative labour-market fairness for new immigrants.

Remarkable inconsistencies are evident between the deliberations of the Task Force and its final recommendations. While its discussions were morally progressive and its concerns for the plight of domestic workers just and persuasive, its ultimate recommendations are pragmatic accommodations.

The proposed compromises which were intended to mediate the competing needs and interests of domestics and their employers personified Canadian welfare accommodations. The moral reluctance to encourage the free reign of the unregulated labour milieu was no less accountable to capital-market ethos. In the capital marketplace, class and capital are synonymous. Protective legislation and the resultant administrative regulations took as their starting point the preeminence of market inequality and freedom, and the rightful power of capital. Ameliorative welfare measures soften rather than eliminate inequalities. In the case of the domestic work policy, job contracts without force of protection, the promise of eventual landed status to domestic workers and the continued assurance of "private" indentured service to employers characterized this tendency to compromise in favour of class interests.

It was customary for Canada to invoke a show of conscience in cases where it was necessary to enact crude market pragmatism. At best the Canadian welfare tradition which developed following the Second World War had settled into an uneasy relationship with the pre-existing legacy of liberalism. Consequently, in recommending the use of employment contracts with the full knowledge that such contracts were unenforceable, the Task Force appeared to be sensitive to the moral imperative to minimize the harsh conditions under which domestics existed. But in reality all they did was to register a moral recognition of inequities and then leave employers to recreate labour conditions known to pre-date the interventionist era. Ultimately, the exploitative conditions of private-household service workers prevailed without state intervention.

Within this state-managed private-market arrangement, there evolved a sanctuary within which woman-driven classism was both revered and reproduced. The discretions continuously granted to Employment and Immigration officials in ascribing and limiting the status of some workers permitted the activation of entrenched biases about some immigrant women and their work while concurrently safeguarding the high status of Canadian women employers who mostly belonged to the dominant classes.

Bureaucratic discussions tended to obscure a significant agenda of the domestic work policy: that of class construction toward class maintenance. The construction and stabilization of a servant class elevated and reinforced the status of the dominant employer class. In the deliberation about whether to deny entry to domestic workers either as immigrants or as working visitors, the Task Force skirted the real issue of regulation of the occupation. The issue was not whether household service workers performed a valuable service in the Canadian labour force, and thus whether they ought to be an admissible class of workers. Indeed, workers were not the issue. The issue was the Canadian state's refusal to locate the occupation of domestic work on the open and competitive market with full rights of collective action and legislated protection. The influence of employers was strengthened by giving them dominance over the unorganized labour of non-immigrants. If domestic work was granted its rightful place among other occupations, the question of non-immigrant entry rank would be nullified.

Only passing reference was made to the relationship between the immigrant domestic work program and the need for adequate childcare in Canada. Yet the issue of the provision of adequate childcare is central to the household service worker policy challenges. Domestics fill gaps in Canadian childcare services, but only for Canada's wealthy. The Task Force hastily abandoned the idea of structural welfare reform, which would have placed many of the household service jobs on the open labour market and created a viable pool of childcare workers. In failing to focus on this issue, the Task Force readily forgave the Canadian state for creating the circumstances which resulted in the resort to offshore workers to supplant childcare facilities.

There was evidence of reluctance to acknowledge the work of women as contributing to accumulation. And in positioning women's work in the labour milieu, the Task Force ultimately situated it outside of the mainstream labour force. Private employers, distanced from household service workers by class and power, were made the custodians and guardians of vulnerable women engaged in their work. Immigrant domestics temporarily lost the freedom to choose occupational direction, employers and domicile. Ultimately, they were to be judged by their aptitude to develop as deserving citizens of Canada.

Notes

1 Canada, Employment and Immigration (1981).
2 Axworthy, Lloyd. Hon. Member of the Opposition. House of Commons; Ottawa. Personal Interview. Ottawa. 15 December 1989.
3 Canada, Employment and Immigration (1981).
4 *Ibid.*
5 *Ibid.,* pp. 13–14.
6 *Ibid.,* p. 12.
7 *Ibid.,* pp. 4, 61–72.
8 *Ibid.,* pp. 81, 95.
9 *Ibid.,* p. 81.
10 *Ibid.,* pp. 81–83.
11 *Ibid.,* p. 21.
12 RG76 Volume 83\84\349 File 5850-6-4-533, Part 2. Memorandum. To: Director, Region "A." From: Director, Foreign Branch. Re: Household Service Workers. Dated 29 November 1968.

   [T]he Regional Economists got together some time ago and simply agreed that the units of occupational demand for housekeepers and domestic service should be seven. I am not aware that they had before them any papers on which their judgment was based. ...

   At the time of the review by the Task Force, the Occupational Demand value had been reduced to zero.
13 Canada, Employment and Immigration (1981), p. 89.
14 *Ibid.,* p. 91.
15 *Ibid.,* p. 96.
16 Department of Employment and Immigration: Policy Files 8600-10. Memorandum from the Office of the Deputy Minister and Chairman. To: The Minister, Hon. Mr. Axworthy. Re: Foreign Domestics. Stamped 24 November 1981. Noted as Seen By the Minister, p. 1 of 13-page document.
17 See Canada, Employment and Immigration (1981), p. 21.
18 Canada, Employment and Immigration. *Data on Participation in the FDM Program.* Memorandum. To: Gene Hersak. From: Claude Langlois. Dated 1 August 1990. Unnumbered tables showing, by year of entry:

	Philippines	
Year	**Number**	**Cumulative**
82	806	3,110
83	479	3,589
84	761	4,350
85	1,543	5,893

	United Kingdom	
Year	**Number**	**Cumulative**
82	1,326	3,142
83	639	3,781
84	572	4,353
85	748	5,101

Also: Permanent Residents by Selected Countries, 1985, Principal Applicant Only. Run Date 12/10/89. BS737 (01), H-I, V-001, P-0002.

| United Kingdom (England, Scotland & Ireland) | 379 + 127 + 29 (535) |
| Philippines | (823) |

19 RG 76 Volume 83\84\349 File 5850-6-4-533, Part 2. Department of Citizenship and Immigration. Memorandum. To: Regional Director "A," Ottawa. From: Officer-in-Charge, Port of Spain. Subject: Household Service Workers. Dated 27 August 1968.

20 Canada, Employment and Immigration (1981), p. x.

21 Department of Employment and Immigration. Policy Files 8600-10. Memorandum. To: Mr. Axworthy. From: Deputy Minister and Chairman. Re: Foreign Domestics, p. 2.

22 *Ibid.,* pp. 1–2.

23 *Ibid.* Addendum. "Domestics currently in Canada." *Step-by-Step Guidelines for Foreign Domestics.* B (4), p. 4.

24 *Ibid.,* B (3)(c), p. 4.

25 Memorandum to Mr. Axworthy, *ibid.,* pp. 2–3.

26 See addendum to Memorandum to Mr. Axworthy, *ibid., CEIC Administrative Procedures — Foreign Domestic Policy.* "Role of Canada Employment Centre Counsellors," A–C; and also "Role of Immigration Officers in Canada," pp. 1–2.

27 Arat-Koc (1989).

28 Employment and Immigration Department. Policy and Program Development Branch. *Foreign Domestic Movement: Statistical Highlight, 1985.* See Table: *Foreign Domestics on Employment Authorizations by Province of Destination, 1984 and 1985.* In 1985, Ontario received 9,185 domestics of the total 15,765.

29 Ontario Ministry of Labour (1985), pp. 23–25.

30 Canada, Employment and Immigration (1981); cited in Table IV A and Table IV B.

31 See the memorandum to Mr. Axworthy, note 21.

32 Department of Employment and Immigration. Policy Files 8600–10. Document *Live-in Household Workers: Minimum Weekly Wage and Working Conditions (excluding value of room and board) Required for Validation of Job Offers to Foreign Workers (as reported by Regions) Table 11.* Revised November 1983.

   The chart shows weekly wages by provinces, a comparison of wage with the legislated minimum wage of the region, and notable fringe benefits offered to domestic workers.

   Most provinces were lagging in equitable remuneration of domestics when compared to other minimum wage workers.

33 Selective distribution means that the benefit was only extended to some workers. Only those who sought the service or were empowered to access the service became recipients. This method of distribution differs from universal or institutional distribution in that the latter assumes need across populations and thus is extended to all.

34 Canada, Employment and Immigration (1981), Recommendation 9.

   See also: Department of Employment and Immigration. Policy Files 8600–10. Memorandum. To: All Regional Executive Directors and Directors General. Signed by H. Johnston, Executive Director, Labour Market Development. Section (A). Dated 30 May 1983.

   The memorandum outlined a number of changes to be included in the policy on foreign domestics.

35 *Ibid.*

36 International Coalition to End Domestic Exploitation (1983).

37 Department of Employment and Immigration. Policy Files 8600–10. Memorandum. To: E. Donagher, Director General, Operations Branch. From: Director General, Policy and Program Development. Re: FDM-Policy Review. Dated 4 June 1985.

   See covering letter explaining rationale for review and revised policy.

38 *Ibid.,* p. 14.

39 Departmental officials were aware of the non-legal status of the FDM. See, for example: Department of External Affairs. Copy in Policy Files 8600–10. Letter. To: Mr. D.G.J. May, A/Chief, Admission Procedures Division, Operations Branch, Employment and Immigration. Signed by: C.M. Shaw, Director Immigration and Refugee Affairs.

   The absence of a firm basis in law for the FDM is an issue which may prove problematic. ...

40 Department of Employment and Immigration. Policy File 8600–10. Memorandum to Donagher, p. 11.

41 *Ibid.* Attachment from: Visa Section, Canadian Embassy, Manilla. Dated 18 February 1987. Paragraph 8; p. 3.

42 Department of Employment and Immigration. Policy Files 8600–10. Operations Memorandum. Number OM IS 330. Title: Selection and Counselling of Foreign Domestics. Re: Admission Procedures (819-994-1678). From: Operations Branch.

The Memorandum cancelled and replaced existing instructions in Chapter IS 4.22 and IS 4.41 on Foreign Domestics. 15 pages with appendices A–E.

43 *Ibid.,* Appendix B, p. 2.

44 *Ibid.,* p. 10.

45 *Ibid.,* Appendix B, pp. 1–3.

46 Department of Employment and Immigration. Policy Files 8600–10. Memorandum. To: Laura Chapman. From: Meyer Burstein. cc. Andre Juneau. Stamped dated 30 January 1989.

47 *Ibid.,* p. 3.

48 Toronto Organization for Domestic Workers' Rights (1989), pp. 3–10.

49 Department of Employment and Immigration. Report from statistical review of FDM program. *Persons Entering the Foreign Domestic Program by Year and Gender, 1982–1989.* 1 page only.

50 Department of Employment and Immigration. Statistical Review. *Table 1. Foreign Domestic Movement Entrants to the Program by Region of Origin, 1982–1990.* (Figures for 1990 were based on first 8 months only.)

51 *Ibid. Estimated Number of Persons Entering the Foreign Domestic Program by Country of Origin, All Countries Ever in Top Ten, 1988.*

Also: *Estimated Number of Persons Entering the Foreign Domestic Program by Country of Origin, All Countries Ever in Top Ten*, 1989.

52 Canada, Employment and Immigration (1992a). 27 April 1992. Package prepared for public distribution.

53 *Ibid.,* p. 1.

54 International Coalition to End Domestic Exploitation (1992).

55 Lloyd Axworthy, Hon. Member of the Opposition. House of Commons. Personal Interview. Ottawa. 15 December 1989.

56 The Task Force comprised the following: W.G. Robinson (Chairman), Barrister, Vancouver; Carter Hope, Barrister, Toronto; David Matas, Barrister, Winnipeg; Ed Ratushny, Law Professor, Ottawa; Manon Venna, Barrister, Montreal.

57 For example, the Task Force lists in its appendices the recommendations of the following persons and reports:

    1 Royal Commission on the Status of Women.

    2 A Brief from INTERCEDE (domestic advocacy group).

    3 Resolutions from the Ethnic Women's Conference, Winnipeg.

    4 Recommendations of the Association of Immigration Lawyers.

    5 Sheila M. Arnopoulos, on Immigrant Women.

    6 Resolutions from the National Action Committee on the Status of Women.

    7 Susan Ballantyne, Law Student, University of Toronto.

    8 Montreal Household Workers Association.

    9 Nancy C. Hook, Final Report on Domestic Service Occupation Study.

References

Arat-Koc, S. 1989. Spring. "In the Privacy of Our Own Home: Foreign Domestic Workers as Solution to the Crisis in the Domestic Sphere in Canada." *Studies in Political Economy* 28: 33–28.

Canada, Employment and Immigration. 1981. *Domestic Workers on Employment Authorizations: A Report on the Task Force on Immigration Practices and Procedures.* Ottawa: Minister of Supply and Services.

———. 1991a. April 21. *Immigration Statistics.* Ottawa.

———. 1991b. April 22. *Immigration Statistics.* Ottawa.

———. 1992a. 27 April. *For Release: Valcourt Announces New Live-in Caregiver Program.* Ottawa: Supply and Services Canada.

International Coalition to End Domestic Exploitation (INTERCEDE). 1983. *Implementation of the Special Policy on Foreign Domestic Workers. Findings and Recommendations for Change. A Brief to the Minister of Employment and Immigration.* Toronto: INTERCEDE.

———. 1992. "Response to the Proposed Reform of the Ontario Labour Relations Act." Toronto: INTERCEDE.

Ontario, Ministry of Labour. 1985. *Study of Wages and Employment Conditions of Domestics and their Employers.* Study conducted by Currie, Coopers and Lybrand, Management Consultants. Toronto: Province of Ontario.

Toronto Organization for Domestic Workers' Rights. 1989. December. *Report and Recommendations for the Review of the Foreign Domestic Works Movement Program.* Toronto: Toronto Organization for Domestic Workers' Rights.

Chapter Ten

The New Wageless Worker: Volunteering and Market-Guided Health Care Reform

Elizabeth Esteves

Introduction

The recent process of health care reform in Canada has received increasing scholarly attention. Within a hospital context, studies have focused on the impact of these reforms on the paid providers of health care services and/or their recipients and families (Armstrong et al. 1993, Armstrong et al. 1997). Similar attention has not been given to the impact of reform on hospital volunteers whose unpaid health care services historically have been provided predominantly by women.

This chapter considers the impact of health care reform on the caring work of such volunteers. I argue that hospital volunteer work is fundamentally linked to market guided health care reform and that this changes the social relations constituting volunteer work. Volunteers, many of whom are women, are being transformed into wageless workers with less control over their caring work. I demonstrate that market-driven health care reform has transformed all work, paid and volunteer, in a process which limits caring and instead emphasizes task-based work. Also, it appears that younger volunteers are beginning to dominate volunteer membership, as they are perceived to be able to perform more task-based, unpaid labour. Older women, those with the greatest volunteer experience, once brought to hospitals the caring component traditionally centred in volunteer activity. But today they are less valued for this contribution and as a consequence, many have resigned.

This examination of organized hospital volunteer activity in the existing context of health care reform is based on my research in progress at a major metropolitan hospital in Ontario. Given the lack of research on hospital volunteer work and the incomplete nature of research at the time of writing, the intent here is not to present conclusions but rather to illuminate key issues and illustrate them with data gathered from participant observation during one year's anthropological fieldwork. This examination presents realities encountered in fieldwork. By situating such realities in the historical and contemporary contexts in which they are embedded, I begin to explore some of the social relations which serve to govern volunteer work.

At the time my fieldwork began, January 1998, people who volunteered at City Hospital[1] did so within a structured volunteer department and/or auxiliary organization, which were products of a particular social and historical process that originated at the turn of the century. This process was tied to the history of the hospital and ultimately to the historical development of health care in Canada. The activities performed by these volunteers are part of an historical tradition of allocating certain work to individuals specifically organized for its performance. They provide an example of the historically gendered allocation of volunteer work, of certain types of caring labour, to women. This delegation of responsibility to volunteers accords with a wider social valorization of voluntary participation. Unfortunately, the social and cultural construction of volunteering in Canada, in national and regional contexts, has received very minimal scholarly attention.

Scholarly study of the voluntary sector has tended to focus on volunteering on a macro level. Increasingly sophisticated statistical surveys have measured the magnitude of the nation's voluntary sector, of which *The National Survey of Giving, Volunteering and Participation* (NSGVP), a large-scale survey even by international standards, is the most recent example. According to the NSGVP, 31.4 percent of the population aged fifteen and over volunteered for a non-profit organization in the period November 1, 1996 to October 31, 1997 (Statistics Canada 1997a). This figure, representing 7.5 million Canadians, is indicative of the widespread participation of Canadians in voluntary organizations. These statistical surveys are useful in the data they yield regarding the scope and scale of voluntary participation, but they are limited in their examination of transformations within the voluntary sector.

Some theoretically oriented literature examines the historical and contemporary relationship between voluntary and state sectors. Of particular relevance to this discussion are the works of Mishra, Laws and Harding (1988), Rekart (1993) and Valverde (1995). Their investigations, which consider specific contexts of voluntary participation within the voluntary sector, yield data which large-scale surveys are unable to provide. Each examines the complex relationship between the voluntary non-profit sector and the state in the provision of social services.

Mishra et al. (1988) investigated privatization as part of Ontario's social policy under a Conservative government in power until 1985. These scholars argued that conservative ideology played a significant role in the complex process of the privatization of social services. The Ontario Progressive Conservative party (re-elected to power at the time of this writing) continues to assert an ideological commitment to privatization. The contemporary effects of privatization were also the focus of Rekart's (1993) work. Her examination of the privatization of social service delivery in British Columbia demonstrated the increased dependency of voluntary organizations on the state and illuminated the relationship between the voluntary sector and the state in a contemporary context. Valverde's historical examination of a mixed economy of social service delivery challenged the opposition of state and civil realms and pointed instead to a "complex web of relationships linking the two supposedly separate realms" (1995:34).

Collectively, these works provide the theoretical framework for my examination of volunteering at City General Hospital. This chapter demonstrates the inter-connectivity of the voluntary sector and the state sector, and the ways that volunteer services in one hospital context are being transformed by health care restructuring.

My exploration of the work of hospital volunteers in one Canadian hospital proceeds in three sections. The first section presents the historical development of volunteer work at City General Hospital. This serves to introduce volunteering in this location and to stress that contemporary volunteering is a product of a specific historical process. The second section explores the transformation of volunteering in light of current health care reform. It details changes in volunteering at both organizational and performance levels. In the third section, I argue that market-driven reform initiatives are transforming volunteering and constructing volunteers as wageless workers. I begin with a brief description of the methodology.

Methodology

The data presented here are the result of ethnographic research in a major metropolitan hospital in Ontario initiated in January 1998. Primary data were gathered both from participant observation and archival research. In addition to observing volunteers as they carried out their volunteering and engaging in informal discussion with volunteers, I conducted interviews and attended meetings relating to volunteering both inside and outside the hospital. Forty semi-structured interviews with volunteers were completed at the time of writing. Non-volunteer hospital staff were also interviewed.

In order to discover the history of organized volunteering, I researched, with the permissions of the Auxiliary, the loosely organized material contained in the archives of the Auxiliary of City General Hospital. These archives consisted mainly of the minutes of the committee meetings of the hospital's volunteer organization, dating from 1911. Early records consisted of minute books while later material was organized yearly into binders. Each binder also included reports of other official meetings, such as annual meetings. During the time I began researching the archives until the time of this writing, the archives, which had been the private domain of the Auxiliary, became the property of City Hospital and are now being processed by the hospital.

The historical examination in the first section of this chapter draws extensively on archival data and every effort is made to fully cite the sources. These data, while providing some information on the organization's structure and activity, focus on the activities of the organization's executive body. The greater visibility of the leadership body in archival material and the difficulties this generates is acknowledged by historians of women's organizations (Prentice 1985). In order to address the limitations of archival material, I also draw on the experiences of volunteers. During the course of research, I interviewed women with a considerable history of volunteer work at City General Hospital. Through these various practices undertaken in ethnographic research, I was able to conduct in-depth analysis of volunteering in this local context. Drawing on these various resources, I examine the transformations in volunteering at City General Hospital.

The Historical Development of Organized Volunteer Participation

Organized volunteering at City General Hospital began as a semi-autonomous association of white, middle-class, Protestant women founded in 1911 and developed over time into the contemporary context of volunteer participation directly and exclusively controlled by the hospital's Volunteer Department. In this section I show how volunteering at City General Hospital not only responded to, but was part of, connected processes that involved the transformation of gender relations and the rise of the welfare state.

Gender and Volunteering

Volunteering is largely the work of women, both in terms of its symbolic construction and material performance; therefore an analysis of gender relations in the development of volunteering at City General Hospital is of key importance. City General Hospital's volunteer organization began in 1911 with fourteen volunteers and for over fifty years was exclusively composed of women. While membership expanded to include men in the mid-1960s, volunteer activity continues to be predominantly performed by women. While white, middle-class women founded and dominated most of the history of organized volunteer work at City General Hospital, this, too, has changed in recent years.

The formation of the Ladies Committee in 1911 was typical of urban[2] pre-welfare-state responses to poverty in Ontario. In one of the few examinations of the history of Canadian women's association activity, Brandt (1985) notes the formation in the 1880s and 1890s of organizations devoted to addressing Canadian social problems resulting from industrialization and urbanization. Typically, these associations were formed by a membership of English Protestant middle-class women. Although Auxiliary archives do not provide explicit data on the membership of the Ladies' Committee, it is, however, possible to infer that the founding members of the Committee were white, Protestant and drawn from the upper and middle classes. This homogeneous group of women raised funds through garden parties and teas and were able to secure the presence of prominent political figures such as the lieutenant governor at their annual meetings. Thus, the work of social reform performed by the volunteer association at City General Hospital was linked with women of a particular class, age and race.

The work of social reform undertaken by the Ladies' Committee was also linked with changing female gender roles and grounded in the essentialist notions of femininity of the first wave of feminism in Canada. By engaging in the public work of social welfare these women confronted the state. As advocates of health care reform, for example, they wrote letters to municipal officials, usually petitioning the mayor directly (Minutes of the Regular Monthly Meeting, March 6, 1913, City Hospital Auxiliary Archives). Additional historical sources point to the participation of members of the Committee in the women's movement. Roberts notes that they were central figures in "the first self-conscious generation of women activists in Canadian history" (1979:45). The committee's approach to social welfare was consistent with the ideology, namely maternal feminism, that governed the activities of many women reformers at the time. Kealey defines maternal feminism as,

> The conviction that women's special role as mother gives her the duty and the right to participate in the public sphere. It is not her position as wife that qualifies her for the task of reform, but the special nurturing qualities which are common to all women. (1979:7–8)

In 1917, the hospital's superintendent thanked the "ladies who, through their nurturing efforts, support" social service endeavours (Annual Meeting, Social Service Department, City General Hospital, January 9, 1917, City Hospital Auxiliary Archives). The social reform work of women challenged traditional notions of the proper sphere of engagement for the upper- and middle-class woman (Roberts 1979:19) while retaining and building upon the essentialist notions of women's activities as caring and nurturing. The gender link between women and volunteer work continued throughout the history of organized volunteering at City General Hospital, yet in a process that responded to women's changing roles.

The most significant transformation in gender relations to affect voluntary participation occurred following the second wave of feminism with the entry of increasing numbers of middle-class women into the workforce. Jill, eighty year old at the time I interviewed her, had volunteered at City General Hospital for forty-eight years. She quit her work as a hospital lab technician and began volunteering after her marriage to a City General Hospital doctor. Jill explained her decision saying, "Socially it was the thing to do. Women didn't work in those days, they were expected to volunteer, to do something." Jill's decision to cease paid employment upon marriage and begin volunteering was typical of women who began their volunteering at City General Hospital between 1950 and 1970.

Increases in women's labour force participation transformed the nature of women's volunteering and volunteer membership at City General Hospital. Student volunteers began to account for an increasing portion of volunteers with the inception of a female youth volunteer program in the 1960s. Falling membership became a significant concern, as evidenced by the many Auxiliary membership drives during the 1970s and 1980s. Men were recruited in the 1970s and male membership was recognized by the renaming of the volunteer organization in 1977. This change is marked in this discussion by the fictitious title Auxiliary of City General Hospital, which replaces Women's Auxiliary of City General Hospital. Older individuals also began to account for an increasing number of volunteers, specifically in the Auxiliary. Membership diversified in terms of race, religion and class as well. The reasons for these various aspects of diversification are complex, elusive and worthy of further exploration. I limit the discussion here to the gender-related transformations.

Phillips and Phillips point to a revolution in married women's labour force participation, especially with respect to women in their mid-twenties (1983:37). Armstrong and Armstrong (1984:Table 20) note that in 1941 less than 5 percent of married women participated in the labour market while in 1981 this figure had risen to more than 50 percent. The career volunteer also vanished. When women married, they were not leaving the paid sector to join the voluntary sector. My fieldwork reveals that by the 1990s women were becoming volunteers in response to retirement, joining the organization after their labour force participation. In addition to these gender-related transformations, volunteering at City General Hospital was also influenced by the development of the welfare state.

Volunteering and the State

When the Ladies' Committee formed, the Advisory Board of the City General Hospital appointed the committee as "voluntary helpers" for a social service nurse (City General Hospital Minutes Medical Advisory Board 1910–1911, Cases from Social Service Department, October 11, 1911, City Hospital Auxiliary Archives). In addition to raising money for the salary of a social service nurse, the committee members also organized and provided relief to the needy by visiting patients in the hospital wards and in patients' homes. At its origin, the work of this committee had two dimensions: financial responsibility for a social service nurse and the practical work of patient care. Through the course of its history its contribution, both financial and practical, in the form of voluntary patient care work, increased and diversified in scope.

This organization of fourteen women volunteers played a key role in funding and administering what would gradually become a hospital department devoted to social services. The Social Service Department was composed of the superintendent of the hospital, nurses and volunteers. In 1921, the Social Service Department reorganized and the volunteer association was renamed. The Ladies' Committee became the Social Service Association. It was composed of "active" members, who assisted with the work of the Department, and "sustaining" members, who supported the Association financially. This separation of membership into active and sustaining members continued throughout history. The objectives of the Social Services Department and its Association were outlined in the department constitution:

> To assist the medical profession in all branches of preventive medicine by cooperation in the Hospital, the Out-Patients Department and in the homes of the patients. To endeavour to effect family rehabilitation and to cooperate with all charitable organizations engaged in similar work by interpreting the medical viewpoint, physical, mental and moral that will enable them to deal intelligently with the social problems of the families. (Constitution of the Social Service Department of the City General Hospital, City Hospital Auxiliary Archives)

City General Hospital's voluntary social service organization was a characteristic outgrowth of a particular type of pre-welfare-state initiative to address the needs of the poor in Canada. Approaches to poverty varied regionally across Canada. In their historical examination of the beginnings of the welfare state in Canada, Moscovitch and Dover (1987) outlined three organized practices toward social welfare in pre-confederation Canada. In the Maritimes, relief was guided by English poor laws. In Quebec, welfare organizations were primarily church run. Ontario, which did not adopt so-called "poor laws," evolved a system of poor relief, which linked private and public sectors. In this mixed economy of social services, voluntary charitable organizations played a key role.

The evolution of Ontario's mixed economy of social service delivery can be traced to the ideal of an independent civil society. Valverde's (1995) analysis of the development of government funding and the inspection of charities in Ontario illustrates that the emergence of a mixed economy system is related to a prominent ideal in the development of Ontario. Valverde explains how the mythical "image of a self-sufficient civil society of hardy pioneers and charitable philanthropists" (1995:43) existed alongside a system of private and public cooperation in social welfare. This construction continues throughout Ontario's history. City General Hospital's voluntary organization reflected the partnership between public and private sectors in addressing social welfare in Ontario.

The development of organized volunteering at City General Hospital was also related to the state's evolving approach to social welfare. Originating as a self-financed association directing and funding social service programs, this association gradually began to expand its activities and to receive public funding, channelled through the hospital. In the 1930s and 1940s, it held a prominent role in managing social programs and developing social services. By the 1950s, its social service role had diminished and City General Hospital's organization of volunteers decided to expand the scope of their activities to address the needs of patients in other hospital departments.

Moscovitch and Dover (1987) trace the development of the welfare state and identify three periods: "Reluctant Welfarism 1891–1940"; "The Establishment of a Welfare State 1941–1974"; and "The Appearance of Fiscal Crisis 1974–78." The transformation in volunteering at City General Hospital may be understood using these periods while attentive to the mixed economy nature of social delivery in Ontario.

The formation of Canada marked increased state involvement in social welfare, but the period of 1891–1940 was one of reluctant government spending on social welfare. In the early years of this period, Moscovitch and Dover note that the establishment of wide range of political and social movements characterized by social ferment resulted in only minor changes in state social expenditure (1987:20). They insist that relief was largely a private undertaking achieved through "so-called scientific philanthropy and the more systematic organization of charity" (20). Volunteer organizations dedicated to social relief, such as the self-financed Ladies' Committee of 1911, played a key role during this period of limited state spending in social welfare. By the 1920s the Social Service Association had joined with local charity organizations, depending on them, not the state, to finance their increasing social service efforts. Moscovitch and Dover argue that even though state involvement in social welfare expanded during the period, the state was devoted to strengthening Canadian capitalism (25) and social expenditure remained relatively insignificant until the 1930s. The depression of the 1930s forced the expansion of social expenditures, establishing the principle of major state involvement in welfare (38).

The period referred to by Moscovitch and Dover (1987) as the "Establishment of a Welfare State 1941–1974" was characterized by a marked change in the state's response to social welfare. The expansion in state expenditure led gradually to a substantial number of social reform programs. Social expenditures, for example, on social welfare, health and education, grew from 4 percent of the Gross National Product in 1946 to 15 percent by the mid-1970s. The state's new approach to social welfare is evident in the area of health. The *Hospital Insurance and Diagnostic Services Act* in 1958 put in place national legislation to cover the cost of hospital care for all Canadians. Hospital insurance was followed by comprehensive and universal health insurance with the establishment in 1966 of the federal and provincial *Medical Care Insurance Act.* These developments transformed Canadian health care. They reshaped the role of hospitals as major components in the delivery of health care and in so doing affected related volunteer organizations.

During this period, City General Hospital's volunteer organization assumed a new role in social welfare provision as it entered into a partnership with the hospital and the Welfare Council. This new status involved establishing and improving social service provision and developing student training in social services (Report to the Finance Committee, The Social Service Association of the City General Hospital, January 19, 1953, City Hospital Auxiliary Archives). Gradually, the hospital assumed some of the financial burdens of the Association. In the 1940s, it began to pay the salaries of some of the Social Service Department workers. In 1949, the hospital took advantage of increased state funding to apply for federal health funds for the Social Service Department. Demands for provisioning social service work soon outstripped the Association's possibilities. In 1953, the hospital assumed complete responsibility both administratively and financially for its social services endeavours (Annual Meeting, The Social Service Association of the City General Hospital, January 26, 1954, Report of the President, p. 3, City Hospital Auxiliary Archives).

This organization of volunteers entered into another phase in its existence. Relieved of its social service responsibilities, the Association directed its fundraising efforts and patient care work to a variety of hospital departments and patient needs. This shift was marked by a name change in 1955 as the

Social Service Association became the more expansive Women's Auxiliary of City General Hospital. In 1956, 323 of the Auxiliary's 416 members actively volunteered their time in the hospital, with the remaining inactive members supporting the work of the Auxiliary financially (Annual Meeting, The Woman's Auxiliary of the City General Hospital, January 31, 1956, City Hospital Auxiliary Archives). These auxillians visited patients and served as clinical aids, interpreters, receptionists, hairdressers and librarians. They also organized sewing committees and seasonal festivities, such as Christmas parties. Volunteers also administered gift shops which served as key sources of funding. Within a decade, the scope of voluntary effort in the hospital increased substantially. Just as the hospital assumed the responsibilities of the Association's social service work, in time, it would assume the increasing volunteer work organized and performed by auxillians.

In 1967, City General Hospital administrators created the Department of Volunteers, which together with the Auxiliary, administered the activities of volunteers. The hospital-appointed Director of Volunteers worked with the Auxiliary to provide, facilitate and extend patient care delivered in the hospital by volunteers. The partnership into which the hospital and the Auxiliary entered was ill-defined. The distribution of powers and responsibilities was unclear; yet this partnership in volunteering was successful for twenty years. In the intervening years the Auxiliary expanded its activities in response to the challenges posed by the next stage of the development of the welfare state.

Moscovitch and Dover (1987) identify the years 1974–1978 as a period of fiscal crisis marked by cuts in state funding of social services. These cuts affected the hospital's delivery of health care. The Auxiliary responded by strengthening its volunteer services and fundraising efforts. First mention of the effects of hospital budget cuts was made in documents of the Auxiliary's January 14, 1975, Executive Committee Meeting. The minutes of this meeting note the hospital's request to the Auxiliary for volunteers to fill positions left vacant by staff cuts. In the March 9, 1976, Executive Committee Meeting, Auxiliary leadership considered supplying facial tissue in patient rooms because it was no longer provided by the hospital due to budget cuts.

The Auxiliary's fundraising efforts expanded throughout the 1980s in an attempt to address the hospital's increased requests for funding. These requests amounted to hundreds of thousands of dollars in one fiscal year (Minutes of the Executive Committee Meeting, Auxiliary of the City General Hospital, May 31, 1983, City Hospital Auxiliary Archives). The Auxiliary was not able to undertake such major fundraising efforts. Its Long Range Planning Committee recommended on April 20, 1985, that large-scale funding projects should be left to the hospital's Foundation (an association dedicated exclusively to hospital fundraising). While the Auxiliary continued to raise modest amounts of funds for the hospital, it decided to focus its efforts on the practical work of patient care.

The history of organized volunteer participation reveals various transformations in volunteering with respect to gender and the state. Originally the exclusive preserve of White English, upper- and middle-class women, volunteer membership responded to wider developments in gender relations. Material changes in the volunteer work accompanied the diversification in membership composition. Volunteer activity also responded to the changing role of the hospital in the development of Canadian health care. Organized volunteer participation continues to undergo transformations in response to contemporary health care reform.

Contemporary Changes in Organized Volunteer Participation

The most fundamental changes in the organization of volunteering in the hospital occurred in the 1990s, especially in 1998. During the course of my research, the City General Hospital Auxiliary experienced a merger and then a dissolution. The hospital's Volunteer Department became the only structure organizing and controlling all aspects of volunteering within the hospital. This subsection describes the contemporary organization of volunteering.

At the onset of my research, City General Hospital volunteers included both Volunteer Department volunteers and Auxiliary volunteers. As of January 1998, total membership of the Auxiliary of City General Hospital was 529 (City Hospital Auxiliary 1998a:22). Based on my observations, women continued to dominate as volunteers. The composition of volunteer membership was also significantly marked by age. The majority of volunteers were largely either student volunteers in their late teens and twenties or retired volunteers aged fifty-five years and over, with older volunteers dominating the Auxiliary membership.

At the onset of 1998, two auxiliary organizations existed at two of the three hospital sites and were in the process of merging. City General and City Western Hospitals, two of the three hospital sites composing City Hospital, each contained auxiliaries which were very similar. They shared a comparable process of historical development and were alike in their organization, composition and functioning. Efforts to merge the auxiliaries began with the merging of the two hospital sites but these efforts were resisted by Auxiliary members. Interviews with Auxiliary leaders in both of the organizations revealed that the merger was resisted because a newly merged organization would put an end to the distinctiveness that each auxiliary organization was felt to have held. Ultimately, Auxiliary leadership decided to accept the hospital's requested merger plans, and the hospital agreed to delay the merger until the auxiliary of the Western Hospital site celebrated its one hundredth anniversary. By the spring of 1998 the unified City Hospital Auxiliary came into being. In general, auxillians that I interviewed were satisfied with the process of the merger and they held a positive outlook on the organization's future. Both the existence of the unified auxiliary and the positive outlook were, however, short lived.

By the fall of 1998, the City Hospital Auxiliary had ceased to exist. Within months of its unification the Auxiliary began a process of dissolution. Its president resigned in response to changes in the reporting structure of the Auxiliary and as a result of increased difficulties in dealings with hospital administration. The Volunteer Department assumed an increasingly active role in Auxiliary affairs, unprecedented in the history of its relationship with the Auxiliary. As conditions deteriorated both parties came into increasing conflict. Speaking on behalf of the Auxiliary, a leader within the organization explained after the dissolution, "We didn't like the interference in Auxiliary affairs, but we hoped that we could work something out."

As mentioned earlier, the archival material indicated that the distribution of powers between the Auxiliary and the Volunteer Department was not well defined. The Auxiliary had always enjoyed autonomy even though it was ultimately subject to the authority of the hospital's executive leadership. In the course of the history of organized volunteering at this hospital, the reporting structure of this semi-autonomous association had changed very minimally. In 1988, the Auxiliary reported to the hospital's president through his vice-president or the vice-president of nursing (City Hospital Auxiliary, Administrative Organizational Chart, revised March 1988, City Hospital Auxiliary Archives). In City General Hospital's Organizational Chart (1998a), the Auxiliary had become a division of Human Resources. While the Volunteer Department was listed as a separate division, also within Human Resources, the Auxiliary's activities became increasingly controlled by the Volunteer Department's administrator.

With the dissolution of the Auxiliary, the Volunteer Department became the only body controlling and developing volunteer programs in the hospital. The dissolution resulted in the departure of many auxillians. The Volunteer Department assumed some Auxiliary administered and staffed programs, such as the patient library. Auxiliary fundraising projects were discontinued with the exception of the lottery program. Between 1997 and 1999 the hospital's Volunteer Department grew considerably. At the time of this writing the Volunteer Department at City Hospital, a branch of Human Resources, is administered by a volunteer director aided by a senior secretary. Three site managers, each assisted by a secretary, report to the volunteer director. Two years prior, when City Hospital was composed of two, not three hospital sites, combined administrative staff totaled three individuals. The organization of volunteering has changed considerably at City General Hospital since the inception of the Ladies' Committee. The contemporary changes I outlined occurred within particular climate characterized by health care reform, which is the focus of the next section.

Volunteering and Health Care Reform

This section focuses on the way in which market-driven health care reform is transforming volunteering alongside and in connection to the way in which it reshapes the work of paid hospital health care staff. Drawing on the work of scholars who have explored the impact of health care reform on paid health care work, this section begins with an outline of the context of health care reform. The reforms identified by these scholars are then considered in relation to the organization and performance of volunteering at City General Hospital at the time of my research.

A neoconservative agenda has resulted in market-driven health care reform. Armstrong and Armstrong argue that "the North American Free Trade Agreement has further consolidated the conservative agenda, based as it is on the understanding that free market principles will apply in all aspects of society" (1994a:31). The running of health care like a business has become increasingly dominant within the health care sector.[3] The result is a significant impact on volunteering, given the relationship identified by Mishra et al. (1998), Rekart (1993) and Valverde (1995) between the volunteer sector and the state in providing social services.

Hospitals, as key components in the delivery of health care, have experienced the impact of the market on a variety of levels. Armstrong and Armstrong argue, "The pressure to cut costs, combined with the pervasive business philosophy, has been a major factor in the transformation of health care delivery" (1994a:36). A privileging of market management within hospitals has occurred with a resulting increase in the power of management.

> The threat of transfer to private management firms, combined with significantly reduced budgets and a new ideology of efficiency defined in money terms, encouraged public sector managers to follow the practices developed for profit-making systems. Private and public, these managers have sought to rationalized the system, intensify labour, and increase control over workers. (36)

In Ontario, hospital mergers and closures have been a significant dimension of health care restructuring. Armstrong and Armstrong note that "like big business, hospital's and other health care services have been merging as a means of reducing costs and increasing control" (1994a:36). City Hospital is a prime example of hospital merging practices. City Hospital is a composite of three geographically separate hospital sites. In addition, it has incorporated some of the services of a hospital forced to close under provincial directives. This mega hospital provides the new context in which volunteering occurs, a context characterized by a tightening of administrative control. These mergers have facilitated the application of corporate sector techniques aimed at rationalizing production and intensifying labour (38).

In their examination of the impact of reforms on nursing work, Armstrong et al. write, "Cutbacks have meant an intensification of labour, a reduction in jobs and a disciplining of workers" (1993:40). The development of management techniques such as task-based formulas are also noted as part of an attempt by administrators of large urban hospital's to control workers (43). Cutbacks have increased the demands placed on nursing work, resulting in work which is more carefully monitored, with an emphasis on measurable tasks (45). Market management and the resulting mergers and reorganizations in paid health care labour have also had an effect on the organization and practice of volunteering. For instance, health care reforms have allowed City Hospital to increase its control over volunteering.

Mergers have been a technique used by hospital administrators to increase control over sectors within the hospital. Armstrong and Armstrong write, "In addition to negotiating mergers and combinations outside their institutions, health care managers have also been rationalizing and merging sectors within their institution" (1994a:38). The merger of the auxiliaries in 1998 was connected to the hospital's response to legislated hospital reform initiatives which related to the tightening of control, financing, cost reduction and revenue generation. The merger represented the first step of the hospital's attempt to gain full control of volunteering and resulted in the loss of one of the two auxiliary seats on the hospital's Board of Trustees. While the seat continues to be associated with volunteering, it is now held through the hospital's Department of Volunteers, and is thus under hospital control.

In the creation of one auxiliary organization, the hospital was able to focus its attempt to control auxiliary activities by dealing with one single auxiliary governing body. Increased interference by hospital administrators in Auxiliary affairs and changes in the Auxiliary's reporting structure resulted in its dissolution. A senior member of the Auxiliary's leadership body recounted the repeated attempts by the Auxiliary to reach a compromise with the hospital and stated, "We could never get through. It had to be [name of the volunteer director's] way or [name of the hospital president's] way or the highway."

The demise of the Auxiliary also allowed the hospital to control the Auxiliary's principle revenue generating source, the gift shop. Two of the three hospital sites contained gift shops that sold a variety of merchandise, such as flowers, greeting cards and personal care products, to patients, visitors and hospital staff. Since their inception, the Auxiliary had maintained complete responsibility for administering and operating the shops, although revenues raised in the shops were turned over to the hospital. In 1998, the City General Hospital gift shop reported a profit of $135,000, more than half of the Auxiliary's $233,059 contribution to the hospital for that year (City Hospital 1998a:14). Despite these profits, hospital administrators felt that the shops were not run efficiently and attempted to increase their control over the running of the shops. Even prior to the official dissolution of the Auxiliary, the administration hired consultants to increase the gift shops' profitability. The new gift shops will take their place alongside the many profit ventures, such as the coffee shop and pharmacies, dominating the entrances at the three hospital sites. These provide a physical document of the impact of the market in the hospital.

The assumption by the Volunteer Department of complete responsibility for volunteering within the hospital resulted in a concentration of power in the hands of hospital administrators. Prior to its demise the Auxiliary's organizational structure allowed for a distribution of power among volunteers. Auxiliary-elected volunteers led the organization and its development of programs and services. In accordance with the City Hospital Auxiliary Constitution, the Auxiliary was governed by an executive committee composed of officers, the immediate past president, the elected coordinators of services and four members-at-large (1998b:article III, section 2). Executive officers and members-at-large were elected annually by Auxiliary members (article III, section 3), providing them a degree of power in the administration of volunteering. The Volunteer Department, in contrast, is part of the rigid bureaucratic structure characteristic of mega hospitals.

With volunteering organized exclusively within the hospital's Volunteer Department, administrators have increased their control over volunteer membership. As Armstrong and Armstrong (1994a) show, health care reform resulted in a corporate sector approach to delivering care in hospitals. This is evident in the recruitment of new volunteers. A prospective volunteer is given a seven-page application package, consisting of two reference check forms, in which applicants are asked to be evaluated on their reliability, flexibility and communicative, interpersonal and time management skills. Volunteers are also provided with an eighteen-page handbook outlining the guiding principles of the hospital and of the Volunteer Department (City Hospital, n.d.). This material informs volunteers of what is expected of them. It also provides an indication of the extent of control the hospital exerts over them. For example, the "Volunteer Code of Ethics" specifically forbids a volunteer to "speak on behalf of the organization or mention any affiliation with the hospital to the press or other public groups (unless written approval has been given by the Department of Public Affairs)" (5).

In addition to the transformation of the organizational structure and membership composition of volunteering in the hospital, the activities performed by volunteers also have been affected by health care reform. As Armstrong et al. (1993) found with nursing work, volunteers are experiencing in health care reform an intensification of certain aspects of their contribution and a minimization of others. Concerns have been raised by volunteers about their ability to provide care in a context in which they are called upon to perform an ever increasing number of task-based activities. A volunteer in one of the surgical waiting rooms noted how her volunteering had changed over time. "We used to be able to sit with distressed families, to get them coffee and to talk. We don't have time for that anymore. It's rush, rush, rush." She went on to outline the various tasks that were expected of her, tasks whose completion resulted in very little time for her to provide care. These findings are similar to those reported among paid heath care workers. Armstrong et al. said of nursing work, "with the emphasis on measurable and visible tasks, there is little room for the caring work" (1993:45).

Such an intensification of certain components of volunteers' activities is related in part to the relationship between paid and unpaid work in the hospital. Volunteers are assuming more work as a result of reductions in paid hospital staff and the loss of volunteers following the demise of the Auxiliary. In response to cuts in paid hospital staff, volunteers are assuming activities not previously undertaken. For example, volunteers comment on having to clean their work areas, previously maintained by paid housekeeping staff. Volunteers are also providing support services in various hospital departments. In the hospital's endoscopy unit, volunteer assistance is provided by three individuals, and many of their activities are essential to the unit's functioning. Rita, one of the endoscopy unit's paid hospital staff, explained how these volunteers assisted her by preparing patients for their medical procedures and by compiling the unit's statistical information.

Volunteers are aiding the work of paid hospital staff, yet their role is not exclusively one of support to paid labour. In some instances volunteers are completely assuming work previously undertaken by paid hospital staff. At City Hospital, General Division, the entire department of information desk workers was laid off, and volunteers were called upon to provide information services. Within the hospital, volunteers are prohibited from replacing unionized staff, but the jobs of non-unionized staff are not similarly protected.

The issue of labour replacement has been problematic for volunteers, not to mention to paid staff they replace. While all volunteers stressed the value of their contribution in providing essential services, opinion varies among volunteers about assuming previously paid jobs. Some volunteers shared the hospital management's labour cutting goals. They viewed their activities as free labour and thus cost saving for the hospital. Anne, who had volunteered at City Hospital for one year, constructed her volunteer activity as free labour for the hospital.

> The job that I'm doing now is the office work of the hospital. It is not extras. It is something that has to be done. But I see nothing wrong with it. If the cutbacks can improve other areas in the hospital that's fine.

Many volunteers, in contrast, expressed considerable distress at the prospect of serving as labour replacement. Janet, a volunteer at City General Hospital for fifteen years, said that she had often felt that she was "taking away someone's job." Later, she added, "but who would do the job, it would just go undone." Viewing volunteering as labour replacement has significant implications that are the focus of the next section.

The Volunteer as a Wageless Worker

Volunteering is in a certain manner undergoing a process of commodification. It is not a process in which the activities of volunteers are gradually coming to be remunerated monetarily and thus commodified, but one in which volunteer activity is constructed as if it were commodified labour, governed by the market sphere of exchange. Volunteering as the giving of time captures relations which are located within the sphere of gift exchange. Mauss[4] (1925/ 1990) delineated the opposition between gift and market spheres, pointing to a dichotomy between free gift and economic self-interest as a particular creation of western society. Parry (1986:458) further stresses Mauss's contention that relations occurring within the market sphere are opposed to those in the gift sphere, as each are governed by contrasting ideologies. The result is market exchanges which are defined as obligated and based on self-interest, and gift exchanges premised on notions of freedom and disinterest. The existence of two opposed and separate spheres of exchange is a key Western construction which illuminates the relations which compose volunteering. With the increased market influence on volunteering, the opposition between gift and market spheres has been blurred, challenging key conceptual boundaries. In this final section I will demonstrate the breakdown of this dichotomy by detailing how market principles have increasingly dominated the practice, evaluation and valuation of volunteer activity in a process in which the volunteer is becoming the hospital's wageless worker.

The administrative relocation of the Volunteer Department under Human Resources rendered volunteers *de facto* workers. Volunteer activity is treated as if it were interchangeable with wage labour. It is this perspective that has allowed administrators to find solutions to budget cuts by replacing paid hospital staff with volunteers. Volunteer labour has been use to assist, and in some instances, completely replace the work of paid hospital staff.

Market principles are evident in the construction of volunteer labour as paid labour. The handbook, which is given to new volunteers by the hospital's Volunteer Department is a good example (City Hospital, n.d.). In the handbook, volunteers are referred to as if they were paid workers. The language used to discuss volunteering is the same as that which is used in commodified work. Additionally, it reflects the material changes underway in volunteer activity. It has become mandatory for all volunteers to sign in and out at the "completion of their shifts" (15). Volunteers intending to take a "vacation" or "leave of absence" are required to provide a two-week notice in writing to the Volunteer Department (15). Shaping volunteering as work has been a mechanism by which hospital administrators have been able to increase their control over volunteers and their activities.

Market principles like productivity and efficiency guided hospital administration in their evaluation of volunteer participation. The ideal volunteer was a younger and more efficient individual, active in, or seeking entry into, the workforce. Older individual who were no longer in the paid workforce were less welcomed by the Volunteer Department. Many elderly volunteers sensed the hospital's unwelcoming stance toward them as tensions escalated between the hospital administration and the Auxiliary. Through official and information meetings, volunteers learned that age would become an important factor in the evaluation of their performance. During an Auxiliary Executive Committee Meeting, the Volunteer Director informed the Committee members that "experienced" volunteers would be matched up with "less experienced" volunteers, namely students, in an effort to facilitate their work. Volunteers understood that the value of their contribution was been questioned because their age rendered them less efficient. Not surprisingly, when the Auxiliary, composed largely of older members, later dissolved, many auxillians ceased volunteering.

With the escalation of tensions between the hospital and the Auxiliary, the hospital's attitude toward the older volunteer was more directly stated. I was told on various occasions by auxillians that a senior member of the Volunteer Department referred to older auxiliary volunteers as "geriatric retreads." One Auxiliary member commented on the change in attitude of hospital management towards volunteers,

> The trend now with volunteers as far as I can see — what they want is they want capable staff that aren't paid. ... You are supposed to come in and do a job for four hours. And this job matters and is enough for you. And the fact that you can't perhaps run up and down the passages as many times as the teenager means that you can't do the job, so go away.

Although precise statistics on the age of volunteers were not available to me, it appeared to me that younger volunteers have begun to dominate volunteer membership, and they represent an overwhelming majority of new applicants.

The construction of the volunteer as a wageless worker is further evident in the hospital's valuation of volunteering. Volunteers as not valued because their work brings to the hospital a caring dimension, rather they are valued because they provide unpaid labour. The contribution of volunteers is quantified and it is measured monetarily. The City Hospital *Staff Newsletter* (1998b) profiled a seventy-year-old retired orderly who volunteered at City Hospital, providing volunteer labour four days a week, seven hours a day, in the hospital's hemodialysis unit. The efforts of this volunteer were praised because they "save the hospital more than $100,000 a year" (2). Hospital administrators are primarily concerned with the hours of labour delivered by volunteers. The Volunteer Department was unable to provide precise information on the total numbers of individuals volunteering in the hospital. Monthly totals of the number of hours volunteered at the hospital were, however, available. The Volunteer Department's market-driven concern with an abstracted labour contribution of volunteers, measured in time, results in a depersonalization of volunteer effort. It contributes to reshaping volunteers as wageless workers.

Care by volunteers has suffered with the loss of the Auxiliary and it also continues to be weakened within the hospital's Volunteer Department. The approach to volunteers as wageless workers minimizes the caring component traditionally central in volunteer activity. It is not that commodified labour is, in and of itself, an anathema to care. Care is a component in both paid and unpaid hospital work. The danger of health care reform is that it is transforming all work in the hospital, both paid and unpaid, in a process which limits care. The reduced delivery of care is a product of the intensification of volunteer activity and its refashioning as task-based work. The impact of minimizing the care in volunteer work is greatly significant.

Care serves not only to describe the type of activities that volunteers, like paid hospital workers, deliver; it is also fundamental in the non-market relations governing volunteering. Volunteer work is being transformed on many levels of which its material practice is but one.[5]

Volunteering is not work in the sense of commodified labour. However, the activities of volunteers do constitute a non-wage form of labour, which is valuable in the hospital setting. Within anthropology, arguments have been made for broadening definitions of work to include non-wage forms of work, in order to more fully comprehend work which contributes to the maintenance of major social institutions (Wadel 1979:368). Within sociology, feminists who have specifically examined caring work have also stressed the need to view such work as involving not only psychological elements but also as constituting labour (Graham 1983). Volunteering, while not commodified labour, is a form of labour. The transformation of volunteering underway has resulted in a contradictory relationship between volunteer activity and commodified labour, between giving and market exchanges. Health care reform has resulted in a fashioning of volunteer activity as wage work. This examination has attempted to uncover this change in volunteering which has the potential to remain obscured by the very opposition of volunteer work and market work.

Transformations in volunteering have had an impact on those individuals who deliver care and on the delivery of care. Volunteers have increasingly assumed work that was previously undertaken by paid staff. Changes in paid health care work have lead to an intensification of the work performed by volunteers. Volunteers are assuming more work in an organizational structure which limits their ability to determine the performance of work dominated by market principles in its practice, evaluation and valuation. Their work is increasingly task-based and under the control of the hospital's bureaucratic structure. Market-driven health care reform has resulted in the decreased ability of volunteers to deliver care. Many auxillians, women with the greatest volunteering experience, have resigned. Their resignation has resulted in a loss of the skills they have acquired over time. A member of the Auxiliary who had been volunteering for seven years noted in the beginning of 1998 the contribution of the older volunteer,

> These women are amazing. They come in, sometimes it takes them the whole day. They live a way out. They take buses. They come in the cold and they do their four hours. ... They don't take off for being sick, and if it is very bad weather they are bound to come in. They are amazing. But they are old. So they are slow. I'm not sure the hospital wants this. They want people who are younger and

smarter and faster and you can see why, because their focus is that this is a job.

Implications for Future Research

With its focus on hospital volunteers, this chapter addresses a neglected dimension of health care reform scholarship. I argue that market-guided health care reform is transforming the volunteer into a wageless worker and reorganizing volunteer participation. Volunteering currently unfolds within a context of reform characterized by market-driven management practices designed to cut costs through mergers and the reorganization of labour. These reforms have resulted in volunteer work which is performed under greater hospital administrative control. In order to put these contemporary changes into context, I took an historical look at this localized practice of volunteering, outlining the development of organized volunteer participation at City General Hospital with respect to gender and the state. The unpaid health care services provided predominantly by women have undergone transformations in relation to the state's evolving approach to health care. Further research is required to explore this historical process of change in its social, political and economic contexts.

While the structure and composition of organized volunteer effort at City General Hospital has changed over time, individuals have always contributed their time to the hospital. The contribution of these individuals and the way their work is constructed must be examined within the wider social context in which it is embedded. In a mixed economy of social service delivery, exploring the part played by volunteers in Canadian health care is vital. Various avenues of research are open given the relatively unexamined role of volunteers in Canadian society.

The long-term impact of contemporary transformations in the social relations that govern volunteering still needs to be explored. How will a market approach to volunteering alter not only the practices of volunteers but also the meaning structures which govern the symbolic construction of volunteering? What are the consequences of the dominance of the market in giving with respect to our key cultural dichotomy of gift and market exchange? In addition, future research needs to examine the implications of the changes identified in this discussion, not only on the construction of volunteering but also on the delivery of care. For example, who will provide services previously performed by women volunteers with a long history of volunteer participation? My investigation, together with the analysis of these and other questions, will contribute to a greater understanding of this female dominated domain of unpaid work and in so doing will unravel the complexity of one aspect of voluntary participation in Canadian society.

Notes

1   The name of hospitals, organizations and people used in this discussion are pseudonyms. City Hospital refers to the corporation formed of the merger of City General Hospital with two other area hospitals. This chapter focuses on the history of volunteering at one location, that is, City General Hospital.

2   These organizations were more common in urban contexts than in smaller communities where "women played little or no role in poor relief" (Marks 1995:80).

3   Doris Grinspun (2000) critically examines the shift in Canadian hospital management from the carative-curative paradigm to the business paradigm.

4   Mauss is most remembered, not for his delineation of the dichotomy of gift and market spheres in the West, but rather for his elaboration of obligated and interested giving in non-market societies where a system of reciprocity played a key role in the maintenance of social relationships. Parry (1986) contends that the implications of Mauss's theoretical perspective on exchange has largely been overlooked in the West.

5   For the purpose of this examination, the intersection of caring and volunteering is discussed on the level of care as a material activity performed by volunteers, as the actual delivery of care through voluntary participation. This narrowing of focus does not imply that the material work of volunteers can be separated from other aspects which combined constitute volunteering as a whole. By virtue of giving their time freely, volunteering is performed in non-market relationships structured by care. Researchers have argued that the commercial relationships prevailing in the market are contradictory to the relations governing the health care system, relations which are based on care (Armstrong et al. 1997). White (1997) also identified the problems with treating paid health care work as a commodity.

References

Armstrong, P. and H. Armstrong. 1984. *The Double Ghetto: Canadian Women and their Segregated Work*. Revised edition. Toronto, ON: McClelland and Stewart.

——. 1994a. "Health Care as a Business: The Legacy of Free Trade." In P. Armstrong, H. Armstrong, J. Choiniere, G. Feldberg and J. White (eds.).

Armstrong, P., J. Choiniere, and E. Day (eds.). 1993. *Vital Signs: Nursing in Transition*. Toronto, ON: Garamond Press.

Armstrong, P., J. Choiniere, E. Mykhalovskiy and J. White (eds.). 1997. *Medical Alert: New Work Organization in Health Care*. Toronto, ON: Garamond Press.

Brandt, G.B. 1985. "Organizations in Canada: The English Protestant Tradition." In P. Bourne (ed.), *Women's Paid and Unpaid Work: Historical and Contemporary Perspectives*. Toronto, ON: New Hogtown Press.

Graham, H. 1983. "Caring: A Labour of Love." In J. Finch and D. Groves (eds.), *A Politics of Women's Spirituality*. Garden City, NY: Anchor Books.

Grinspun, D. 2000. "Taking Care of the Bottom Line: Shifting Paradigms in Hospital Management." In D.L. Gustafson (ed.), *Care and Consequences: The Impact of Health Care Reform*. Halifax: Fernwood Publishing.

Kealey, L. (ed.). 1979. *A Not Unreasonable Claim: Women and Reform in Canada, 1880–1920s*. Toronto, ON: Women's Press.

Marks, L. 1995. "Indigent Communities and Ladies Benevolent Societies: Intersections of Public and Private Poor Relief in Late Nineteenth Century Small Town Ontario." *Studies in Political Economy* 47.

Mauss, M. 1990. *The Gift: The Forms and Reason for Exchange in Archaic Society*. (W.D. Halls, Trans.). London: Routledge. (Original work published in 1925).

Mishra, R., G. Laws and P. Harding. 1988. "Ontario." In J.S. Ismael and Y. Vaillancourt (eds.), *Privatization and Provincial Social Services in Canada: Policy, Administration and Service Delivery*. Edmonton, AB: University of Alberta Press.

Moscovitch, A., and G. Dover. 1987. "Social Expenditures and the Welfare State: The Canadian Experience in Historical Persepctive." In A. Moscovitch and J. Albert (eds.), *The Benevolent State: The Growth of Welfare in Canada*. Toronto, ON: Garamond Press.

Parry, J. 1986. "The Gift, the Indian Gift and the 'Indian Gift'." *Journal of the Royal Anthropological Institute* 21.

Phillips, P. and E. Phillips. 1983. *Inequality in the Labour Market*. Toronto, ON: James Lorimer and Company.

Prentice, A. 1985. "Themes in the Early History of the Women's Teacher's Association of Toronto." In P. Bourne (ed.), *Women's Paid and Unpaid Work: Historical and Contemporary Perspectives*. Toronto, ON: New Hogtown Press.

Rekart, J. 1993. *Public Funds, Private Provision: The Role of the Voluntary Sector*. Vancouver, BC: University of British Columbia Press.

Roberts, W. 1979. "Rocking the Cradle for the World: The New Woman and Maternal Feminism, Toronto 1877–1914." In L. Kealey (ed.), *A Not Unreasonable Claim: Women and Reform in Canada, 1880–1920s*. Toronto, ON: Women's Press.

Statistics Canada. 1997a. *Caring Canadians, Involved Canadians: Highlights from the 1997 National Survey of Giving, Volunteering and Participation*. [Catalogue No. 71-542-XPE]. Ottawa, ON.

Valverde, M. 1995. "The Mixed Social Economy as a Canadian Tradition." *Studies in Political Economy* 47.

Wadel, C. 1979. "The Hidden Work of Everyday Life." In S. Wallman (ed.), *Social Anthropology of Work*. Toronto, ON: Academic Press.

White, J.P. 1997. "After Total Quality Management, What?: Re-engineering Bedside Care." In P. Armstrong, H. Armstrong, J. Choiniere, E. Mykhalovskiy and J. White (eds.).

Chapter Eleven

"Who Else Would Do It?": Female Caregivers in Canada

Kristin Blakely

I became interested in the subject of family caregiving after the diagnosis of my mother's cancer in the fall of 2000. Although my experiences pale in comparison to those of others — women with childcare responsibilities, fewer resources of support, greater workplace demands, and a host of other factors — I do have some understanding of what it means and entails to provide care to a loved one. That being said, I have written this paper with the utmost respect and admiration for the women who do the "caring work" for their chronically ill and elderly loved ones and also for my mother, who has now recovered almost completely from cancer.

The Canadian health care system is in crisis: rising health care costs, a huge federal debt, cut-backs in funding, downsizing in health services, and a population that is growing older and sicker each day.[1] What we have are the essential ingredients of a recipe for disaster.

Like most disasters, this one is not victimless. Nearly all Canadians have been or will be affected in some way by the health care crisis. All of us hear about (some of us have directly experienced) seemingly endless line-ups in hospital emergency rooms; the sometimes fatal, often serious result of ambulances re-routed from one closed emergency room to another; new doctor fees; increasingly long waiting lists for surgery; nurses going on strike; massive firings of health care workers; depleting coverage of physiotherapy; and much, much more.

The most widespread impact of the health care crisis, as Neufield and Harrison (2000) argue, is the dramatic escalation in the expectation that families will provide care to the sick and the elderly. Government cuts to health care — including shortened hospital stays; more day surgeries; fewer hospital beds and health care professionals available to elderly patients; and reductions in services such as meals-on-wheels, home-visiting nurses, publicly funded homes for the aged, nursing homes, and chronic care facilities — have contributed to the shifting of caring work from within the public sector to the private domain (Armstrong et al., 1996:88; Aronson, 1998:116). For families who cannot afford to pay an external caregiver (which is the case for most) but must rely instead on their own resources, the responsibility of caring for the chronically ill elderly falls upon the home, where it is invariably assumed by women. These family caregivers are the less visible, indirect victims of the health care crisis, as they end up filling in for the system when it fails to provide the care needed.

Like other unpaid labour in the home, family caregiving is viewed as women's work. It is taken for granted, overlooked, and not recognized as "real work" with "real value" in Canadian capitalist society. Ironically however, the social value of this labour is tremendous, with an estimated 90% of the care of the elderly population being provided informally, outside of the health care system (Aronson, 1998:114). In light of a rapidly aging population, increasing life expectancy rates, rising number of incidences of chronic illness among the elderly,[2] and a system that is retreating further and further from patient care and responsibility, the need for family caregivers is at an all-time high. The 2.8 million Canadians currently providing unpaid care to persons with chronic health conditions (Statistics Canada, 1996) are an indispensable pool of free, exploitable, and reliable labour to the provincial and federal governments. Not to mention, they are an invaluable resource to the elderly who are dependent upon them.

Regardless of their social need and value, family caregivers continue to be undervalued, overworked, and often forgotten in the health care crisis. They are casualties — only less visible — of the same disaster as the elderly for whom they care.

My intention in this chapter is to provide a balanced overview of family caregiving in Canada that addresses some central questions about the labour itself, the providers of care, and the impact upon them. By "balanced," I mean without romanticizing the work or denying its exploitative nature. I will present a theoretical analysis of the gendered nature of caring work, its devaluation, and the possibilities for the future.[3] In places, I reflect on some of my personal experiences of caregiving for my mother. Even though we are both younger than the caregivers and care-recipients who are discussed in this analysis, I share some of my own thoughts and feelings in an effort to provide some insight into caregiving experiences.

I should clarify that I will focus specifically on the provision of care to elderly family members with chronic illnesses.[4] I am troubled by such terms as "eldercare," which seem to imply that the sole reason for the care is the receiver's age; therefore, I feel it is important to indicate that the elderly person has a chronic health condition and is in need of care. Distinguishing family caregiving from eldercare in this way helps to avoid perpetuating myths around illness, dependency, and the aged.

What Does it Mean to "Care"?

"Caring" and "caregiving" are ubiquitous terms, their meanings often taken for granted. Most of us perform activities in our day-to-day lives that we consider to be "caring" work. However, the definitions and boundaries of what is included in "caring" and "caregiving" are not always clear.

It seems reasonable to use a dictionary definition as a starting point for this discussion. Broadly defined, caring is "to be concerned; to have regard or consideration; to provide physical needs, help, or comfort" (Collins Dictionary). From this definition, we see that caring comprises both "doing" and "feeling." The physical dimension of caring can be thought of as "caring for" or "taking care of" a loved one, while the emotional side can be thought of as "caring about" or having feelings of concern for someone (see Waerness, 1996, and Schofield, 1998).

Other theorists make the distinction between "caring about" and "caring for," labelling the former as "love" and the latter as "labour" (see Luxton, 1980; Lewis & Meredith, 1988; Waerness, 1996; Gordon, 1996; Kittay, 1999). Viewing "caring" as a "labour of love," especially in the context of the family, emphasizes the difficulty in divorcing the labour of caring work from the feelings of love and the ties of obligation.

I recall thinking that caring for my mother was not work but something more like help or just part of being a daughter. After all, she raised me, gave up so much of herself and her time for me. She is my mother. I love her and would do anything for her. But beneath these "labour-of-love-type" thoughts was the fear that to admit that caring for my mother was laborious and required sacrifices of myself and of my time somehow meant that I was being selfish, aloof, apathetic, even a bad daughter. How could I be thinking about all the work that I had to catch up on while she was lying there after cancer surgery? I became overwhelmed by feelings of guilt.

Caring can be broken down into normal care and caregiving. We can say that a woman who makes dinner for her husband is providing "normal care" because this is a regular occurrence, a normative and pervasive activity within the household or family. However, if her husband was recovering from a stroke and had severe physical limitations, this act of food preparation would be deemed "caregiving," for she is now providing care to a dependent loved one who by normal standards is unable to take care of himself. Thus, caregiving represents the additional increment of extraordinary care or that which goes beyond the bounds of normal or usual care (Biegel et al., 1991: 16–17; Waerness, 1996:235).

Who Is Doing the Caring?

The research on caregiving indicates that when an elderly family member is chronically ill, daughters, daughters-in-law, wives, and mothers, regardless of their employment status, are the most likely to provide the care needed (Morris et al., 1999:18; Neufeld and Harrison, 2000:249). Two-thirds (66%) of informal, unpaid caregivers in Canada are women, and, of those caring for persons with dementia, 72% are women (Statistics Canada, 1996).

Caregivers for a chronically ill, elderly family member are typically middle-aged women from all racial, cultural, and ethnic backgrounds. Statistics Canada (1998) found that the highest proportion of any age group providing more than 10 hours per week of care to seniors are women in the 45 to 64 age cohort. Cranswick (1997) reported that two-thirds of all unpaid caregivers work outside the home, and the majority are married and have children.

The Work of Caring

Caregiving for a chronically ill, elderly family member involves a range of activities that can be divided into three categories: physical labour, managerial or organizational labour, and emotional labour (Arber and Ginn 1995 in Nolan et al., 1996:30). The former two are part of the "caring for" or "doing" aspect of caring, while the latter is considered "caring about."

Physical

The physical work is the most obvious and visible form of caregiving. It can include such chores as housekeeping, cooking, shopping, and doing the laundry, as well as such tasks as administering medicine, preparing special diets, and helping the care-recipient with exercising, bathing, eating, dressing, moving about, and going to the bathroom (Schofield et al., 1998:29-33).

Before my mother began radiation, she was placed on a highly restrictive diet. She was so limited to what she could eat that grocery shopping became more like an exercise in investigative research and the honing of my detective skills. Breakfast, lunch, and dinner became much more than meals — they were well-imagined, carefully thought-out, and time-intensive culinary events.

Organizational

Organizational labour is the work involving the management of such tasks as home maintenance and repairs, paying bills and taxes, and looking after other finances for the care-recipient. A caregiver becomes a "medical manager" insofar as she or he monitors the elderly person's illness(es), including the arranging of and transporting to medical appointments; managing medication regimens; and learning about the illness(es) in question in order to recognize important signs and symptoms and to know what to ask doctors and other health professionals (Bruhm et al., 1998; Schofield et al., 1998: 29–33).

After the initial diagnosis, I felt that I had to learn about what was happening to my mother and, perhaps more importantly, what was going to happen. What was this pill for? Why is this recommended and that discouraged? How long until her next surgery? Why does she look this way and feel like that? Finding the answers to these questions was surprisingly comforting and continued to be so throughout the whole process. It felt productive.

Emotional

The least visible of the three types of family caregiving is the most intangible aspect of caring, primarily consisting of the provision of love and emotional support to the chronically ill, elderly loved one. It is difficult to define "emotional work," since the activities that constitute it are not easy to pinpoint or separate from physical and managerial labour. For example, is taking the care-recipient to a medical appointment considered emotional work? It does involve physically driving to the hospital and the organizational task of scheduling the appointment, but does it also involve feelings of love and concern? Most likely.

I can honestly say that caring for my mother while she was ill, from the most menial of tasks to the most difficult felt like emotional work. Even by just passing her a tissue, I was loving her and providing support. There were times when I sat beside her with our fingers interlocked, reassuring her, hoping to allay some of her anxieties and pain. Whispering comforting words and simply spending time with her — often in silence — was indeed emotional work.

It is emotions that define family caregiving and distinguishes the work from professional or paid care provided in an institutional setting. Having said that, it should be mentioned that many situations of family caregiving are absent of love, and, conversely, many paid caregivers do give emotional support to care-recipients. However, it is presumed (at least in theory) that the level of concern and emotion will be higher in a family than in a professional setting (Nolan et al., 1996:33).

While my mother was in the hospital, I felt that I had to be with her as much as possible. This was not because the doctors and nurses were not providing her with the care that she needed, but because they could never give her the same kind of care that I or my sisters could: care with love, tenderness, and affection; the care of a family member; the love from her own child.

When the work of caring is broken down along gender lines, women are shown to provide more of all the caregiving activities (physical, organizational, and emotional). Kaden and McDaniel (1990) found that, between spouses, wives did 77% of the work. With children, the breakdown was 87% for daughters and 13% for sons. The gender discrepancy evident in their findings led Kaden and McDaniel to propose that family caregiving is really a euphemism for wives and daughters.

The Impact of Caring

In the previous section, we saw that being a family caregiver means that one has multiple roles, varying from housekeeper to cook to financial planner and medical expert. Women providing unpaid care to a chronically ill, elderly family member may also be a wife, girlfriend, mother, daughter, daughter-in-law, employee, friend, volunteer, and so forth. It is important to keep this in mind during the following discussion on the physical, economic, and emotional impact of caregiving, since the effects of providing care are really additional burdens to those already experienced by women in their daily lives.

Physical

The physical consequences of providing care to a chronically ill, elderly family member can include exhaustion and muscle tension (from the more laborious aspects of the work) to such stress-related health conditions as headaches, stomach aches, weight loss or gain, insomnia, hypertension, heart attacks, ulcers, alcoholism, and other substance abuse problems. As a group, family caregivers report poorer physical health, lower physical stamina, and greater use of prescription drugs (Hooyman and Gonyea, 1995:142). Statistics Canada (1996) found that 20% of caregivers do suffer a decline in their health and that 25% experience sleep disturbances.

Women caregivers are especially prone to having physical health problems. Cranswick (1997) discovered that 27% of female respondents reported a deterioration in their physical health, whereas only 12% of the men did. Another report estimates that daughters who are primary caregivers have a 75% chance of suffering from poor physical health; this is an alarming number of potential new patients and users of an already strained health care system (Rhodes, 1997).

Economic

In Canada, family caregiving is essentially "free" labour, since it is unpaid and has no economic benefits such as tax advantages or pensions. The hours dedicated to providing care are hours not spent working at a paid job, and the money put toward the care of the elderly family member is money not reimbursed to the caregiver. There are often financial strains from the purchase of health care equipment for the home, medication, and food, to name a few. Cranswick (1997) found that 40% of informal family caregivers in Canada incur expenses from their own pocket.

Employment can be affected through a loss of income from a decline in paid hours worked, a loss of advancement opportunities, a reduction in pension accumulation, or the termination of one's job altogether. This could occur either unwillingly or voluntarily, in order to keep up with caregiving demands (Hooyman and Gonyea, 1995:144-46). In a job loss situation, the female caregiver is put at a further disadvantage, for without her own income, she is forced to rely on an alternative source, possibly her family, partner, or the state. This increases her susceptibility to poverty.

The Statistics Canada survey entitled "Who Cares? Caregiving in the 1990s," found that half of all participants interviewed reported repercussions at work because of their family caregiving duties. When divided along gender lines, Cranswick (1997) found that 55% of women and 45% of men said that their work was affected by caregiving. Another project, focused solely on female caregivers, reported that three-quarters of respondents had given up employment in order to provide care, and 15% said that they did not even have enough money to feed all of the members of the household (Bruhm et al., 1998:20).

Emotional

In addition to the physical and economic consequences, there is considerable evidence to support the claim that family caregivers for the chronically ill suffer psychological stresses. Indeed, the subjective experience of providing care can often include anxiety, anger, loneliness or isolation, helplessness, guilt, loss of identity, frustration, fear, and depression.

Failure to cope with these emotional strains in addition to the physical and economic stresses is referred to as the "caregiving trap." It renders the caregiver unable to function effectively as the primary caregiver (Bruhm et al., 1998:21). In other words, she is burnt-out!

Researchers have found that women providing care to their elderly family members are more likely than men to experience greater stress and are at a higher risk of depression. This is often related to data showing that female caregivers consistently report more role strain and demand as wives, mothers, employees, and so forth, than do men (see Neufeld & Harrison, 2000; Hooyman & Gonyea, 1995; Nolan et al., 1996).

The emotional impact of caregiving can also bleed into the other areas of a woman's life, affecting her job performance, mothering abilities, personal relationships, and day-to-day functioning.

I distinctly remember driving to the mall about a week before Christmas when my mother was home from the hospital but still quite sick. I was preoccupied, consumed with anxiety, and unfocused — I should not have been driving. Luckily, I only hit a concrete median in the mall parking lot and not a person or another car. When I got out to check the damage, I was numb, unshaken, and not even bothered by all the scratches on the front of my car. I barely even felt the cold of that winter day. My mind was on my Mom. I don't even think the event mentally registered until that evening or maybe it was the next morning.

Women are paying a high price for caregiving, but the impact is greater for some women than it is for others. The economic and employment-related consequences of caregiving are particularly burdensome for low-income women who rely on the income of paid work to survive. The burdens are increased for families with children and with no second income to supplement that of the caregivers. This can add to the emotional impact of providing care, for financial worries have been shown to contribute to stress and lead to depression (Hooyman & Gonyea, 1995:144). Low-income women, especially those who are single with children, are thus adversely impacted by the caregiver burden and extremely vulnerable to poverty.

I must also call attention to the particularity of the cultural conditions of unpaid caring in women's lives. The intersecting dynamics of gender, race, ethnicity, and class have a significant impact on women's experiences as family caregivers. Immigrant women, women of colour, and visible minority women in Canada are adversely affected by the caregiver burden because of the widespread forms of racial and ethnic discrimination embedded within Canadian society. Aboriginal and visible minority women, for instance, who earn less than the average for all Canadian women, are more susceptible to poverty and other economic repercussions as caregivers than white women (Morris et al., 1999:4).

The unpaid, caregiving work of immigrant women, women of colour, and visible minority women is a hugely under-researched area. There is much work needed to fill this void in order to further our understanding of the diversity of women's caregiving experiences (George, 1998).

Why Do Women Care?

Explanations for the prominence of women as unpaid family caregivers have come mainly from feminists. In Western feminist circles of the late 1960s and 1970s, caregiving was attacked for its oppressive effects upon women. The focus was primarily on childcare and the institution of motherhood, ignoring women's caregiving responsibilities to their chronically ill, elderly family members. It was not until the 1980s, with the dramatic growth in seniors requiring care and the onslaught of evidence indicating that this phenomenon was going to continue, that these latter issues were recognized as critical and put on the feminist agenda (Hooyman & Gonyea, 1995:18-19).

Relational feminism and the work of Carol Gilligan, popular within the Western feminist movement of the late 1970s and early 1980s, became widely used to explain "why women care." Gilligan (1982) argued that caring is natural and that women have "an ethic of care that reflects both their sensitivity to others and their responsibility for caregiving." She stressed women's nurturing and expressive qualities as sharply contrasted to men's underdeveloped emotional capacities. Other feminists (see Chodorow, 1978; Graham, 1983; Noddings, 1984) have put similar explanations forward, arguing that "women's caregiving is motivated by their emotional attachment to care receivers; by the fact that caring is central to their identity, and by their capacity for self-sacrifice and sense of altruism" (Hooyman & Gonyea, 1995:21-22).

These arguments are problematic on many levels, but, within this context, they are inadequate in providing an explanation of "why women care." Gilligan and relational feminists postulate a uniform feminine personality that is, first of all, inaccurate, since women are not invariably nurturing and, second of all, reductionistic, as it ignores the differences among individual women. They do not take into account the underlying power dynamics in society, particularly the interrelationship between patriarchy and capitalism in both the home and the marketplace. Emphasizing a biological basis for women's caregiving responsibilities also overlooks the role of socialization and the social construction of gender and gender roles. In fact, relational feminists contribute to traditional sexism and the patriarchal social structure by emphasizing women's natural embodiment of "feminine" traits traditionally used to justify the relegation of women to the private sphere (Hooyman & Gonyea, 1995:22–23, 25). They have romanticized the role of the family caregiver and in an indirect way have told women to go home, provide care, and, thus, fulfill their "natural" responsibility.

Then why do women care? Socialist feminist theory is a useful critical framework from which to understand the relationships between women and work. This tradition has a strong history of challenging traditional assumptions of the family and for addressing issues around domestic labour and women's experiences of providing care.

Socialist feminism, in brief, combines the insights of Radical and Marxist feminism by holding that women's oppression is rooted in both patriarchy (men's control of sexuality and reproduction) and capitalism. It is a kind of hybrid. Sexism, therefore, cannot be understood without placing it in the context of capitalist society. Socialist feminists view capitalism as a political/ economic/cultural/social totality, enabling them to extend their Marxist framework to address feminist issues related to the private life (such as the family), which have nothing superficially to do with production or politics. They stress the integral connections between ideology and the relations of production. Moreover, the separation between public and private life (or the ideology of separate spheres), the ideology of familism, which delegates to women the principal responsibility of the home, and the gendered division of labour are viewed as central to the exploitation and subordination of women in capitalist societies (Barrett, 1997:94; Ehrenreich, 1997:66–70; Luxton, 1990:39).

According to socialist feminists, women do not perform domestic labour and unpaid caring work because it is intrinsically natural and inevitable or out of their own free will, but because the patriarchal and capitalist social structure has predefined and allocated their location in the social world. The dominant societal ideologies of separate spheres and familism embedded in capitalism set out the appropriate meanings of labour for men and women, enforcing male domination in both the marketplace and the family. A vicious circle exists in which gender inequality in the home reinforces women's disadvantaged position in the marketplace and, in turn, her restrictive job opportunities and income-earning potential, which fuel her vulnerability and dependent status in the family (Hooyman & Gonyea, 1995:29–31).

In terms of women's willingness to give care, socialist feminists recognize the presence of compulsory altruism and the reality of women's restricted choices on such issues as the provision of care to an elderly family member. Although they do not deny the existence of love in family caregiving relationships, socialist feminists argue that it is difficult to know how much of the work is done out of love and how much is done out of social expectation and the internalization of cultural norms.

On this latter point, the prevailing traditional cultural definitions of masculinity and femininity construct women as "domestic guardians of the home front" and men as "breadwinners" and serve to relegate "women's work and responsibilities" to the private arenas of the home and family (Wilson, 1996:49). These gender constructs are transmitted through socialization processes, so women internalize the role of caregiver because compassion and caring are entrenched in the cultural ideals of womanhood and femininity (Neufeld & Harrison, 2000:255). Reitsma-Street (1998) has found from her work on girls and caring that young and adolescent girls learn that to be good and feminine means to be caring and selfless.

Research on family caregiving reveals that women typically take on the caring work not necessarily out of choice, but because there is no other choice. They assume it to be their responsibility; otherwise, who else will do it? Therefore, the question — why do women care? — should really be replaced with this rhetorical one: "who else would provide the care?"

An interesting, non-theoretical reason for why women care is based on research that has found the care of chronically ill, elderly family members to occur frequently along same-sex lines. Since elderly women substantially outnumber elderly men, there are more female than male caregivers. According to Statistics Canada (1997), women comprise 58% of those aged 65+ and 70% of those aged 85+. Although this finding fails to account for issues of power discussed earlier, this idea of caring along gender lines is worth exploring.

Rose Dobrof, a professor of gerontology, writes, "because women know in their guts that they are going to be recipients of care, they become caregivers as a way of shoring up brownie points" (Bader, 2000). It is quite possible that some women do feel this unconsciously while grappling with their present day-to-day realities as a caregiver, mother, worker, and so forth.

Montgomery and Kosloski (1994) found that sons are also more likely than daughters to institutionalize their ill, elderly parents, and, as a result, women outnumber men as caregivers. Perhaps then, a motivation for women to provide informal family care and collect these "brownie points" is to lessen their chances of institutionalization. However, I am inclined to think that men institutionalize their chronically ill, elderly family members (especially in situations where there are no available women caregivers) because they do not view the provision of care as their responsibility.

I am reminded of my mother smiling at us in her bed, just listening to my sisters and I gab about this and that. "How lucky am I," she said, "to have daughters that I know I can count on to take care of me ... thank goodness that I had girls." We laughed and kept talking. It's funny how we all knew what she meant and what was implied. We were a room of four women with no men in sight.

The average family size in Canada has decreased since the baby-boom years, in large part due to women's greater participation in the paid labour force, meaning that elderly people have fewer available relatives on whom they can depend for care. For those providing the care (mainly women), diminished household numbers mean that the potential for sharing the caregiving work is lower (Grunfeld et al., 1997:1102). Thus, women are now often working both outside and inside the home as well as caregiving by themselves, with less help from children and other relatives. This echoes the socialist feminist thought: women provide care, for who else will?

Why Is Caregiving Devalued?

Family caregiving has historically been considered women's work, linked to cultural assumptions about "femininity," relegated to the private sphere, and lumped in with other domestic tasks. In Canada, work is primarily defined in terms of measurable output and wages. Since "real" work occurs in the public sphere, women's unpaid work in the home is viewed as peripheral to the marketplace and as being non-work, unproductive, and as having no "real" value. Thus, family caregivers are devalued and branded as not doing "work" but rather "domestic labour," defined as drudge-work, involving tedious, undesirable activities.

Family caregiving conflicts with the Western capitalist social values of individual autonomy, independence, and youthfulness. It denotes illness, old age, frailty, and a relation of dependency — all of which are undesirable signs of human weakness and defectiveness. Keeping caring work invisible, hidden by the walls of the private sphere, serves to shelter us from reminders of these human "deficiencies," our own mortality, and of our needs and dependencies upon other people.

As a result of its devaluation, family caregiving has suffered immensely from negative misconceptions and stereotypes that have impeded the social understanding of this human activity. It is time for change.

Future Possibilities

The crisis in the Canadian health care system, along with the alarming demographic projections for the population, have made the issue of family caregiving a pressing one — one that must take a front seat in the public policy arena. As unpaid labour in the home, with no economic benefits, little to no social recognition, and a host of physical, financial, and psychological consequences, family caregivers must be recognized and valued for their work. Without romanticizing the labour or denying its exploitative nature to women, it must be said that family caregiving is truly admirable and commendable work, requiring time, patience, and effort and involving skill, practical knowledge, relational intelligence, and, in a number of areas, expertise. Although family caregiving can be a gratifying and rewarding experience for some women (particularly for those on whom the work does not have as great an impact), providing care to a chronically ill, elderly family member is, for the most part, intensive and burdensome. This situation needs to be addressed in order to ensure a better future for the caregivers of today, for those of tomorrow, and for all of the potential and current care-recipients.

Researchers have articulated numerous solutions for family caregivers. The main proposals in the Canadian context include increased help and support on an informal level from family and friends; the implementation or expansion of home and community services, such as respite care (or government-funded temporary relief for caregivers); and counseling, education programs, and support groups for care providers (Schofield et al., 1998:123–64; Neufeld & Harrison, 2000:261–66).

The central problem with these solutions is that they are not alternative answers to the problem but rather supplements to the existing informal structures for providing care. They offer help and, in many cases, reduce the impact of the work of caregivers, but they naturally assume that women will continue to act as the primary caregivers for the chronically ill (Waerness, 1996:233). They do not address the fact that women continue to provide the majority of care and are adversely affected by its physical, financial, and emotional consequences. It also does not recognize the underlying reality that family caregiving is largely invisible, devalued work, hidden in the home and with few benefits to the providers (see Armstrong, 1996; Hooyman & Gonyea, 1995; and Morris et al., 1999).

From a socialist feminist perspective, these supplemental solutions embody the socially structured assumption that women will automatically and willingly care. This is reflective of the "bigger picture" or the strength and pervasiveness of the ideologies of separate spheres and familism, as well as the socially constructed notions of "femininity" embedded in patriarchal capitalist society. What, then, can be done to prevent the further exploitation of women for their capacity to caregive?

Four Canadian studies — see the Caregivers' Research Project (Bruhm et al., 1998); Keefe & Fancey (1997); Who Cares? (Statistics Canada, 1996);

and CRIAW (1999) — found that unpaid caregivers overwhelmingly desire to have their worked valued, as the devaluation contributes to their burden. Caregivers want their work to be recognized as a significant contribution to the economy and as a substitute for costly formal care.

However, prevailing social attitudes, which regard caregiving as "women's work" and position it outside of the marketplace, have served to maintain the devaluation of this labour. As shown earlier, the unpaid provision of care to a chronically ill, elderly family member, is not considered to be "real" work with value in capitalist society. In order to establish caregiving as legitimate work, we need to recognize the caregiver role as an occupation involving skills and relational intelligence.

I am arguing for a reconceptualization of the work of caring, beginning with the acknowledgment that the capacity to care resides in all human beings. There is no caregiving gene, hormone, or more suitable gender. Furthermore, the caregiving role needs to be recognized as work that is labour-intensive and burdensome. The wider community has to accept social responsibility for the care of dependents and support for their caregivers, particularly the women.

One solution, although not a cure-all, is to compensate caregivers for their work in the form of a nation-wide payment system. Keefe and Fancey (1997) point out that even minimal compensation refutes the invisibility of caregivers' labour. By making the invisible visible, women's caring work inside the home and for the family is shown to be just "as demanding and important as any that men have done, and that it also furnishes lessons, attitudes, and skills that are as critical as those learned in the male marketplace" (Gordon, 1996:274).

For more than a century, socialist feminists like Marilyn Waring (1988) have challenged "the physical separation of household space from public space, and the economic separation of the domestic economy from the political economy." They have objected to the patriarchal and capitalist denial of women's labour in the home as "work" and argued that women, like any other service workers, should be paid (Wilson, 1996:49, 58–59). Applying these ideas to family caregivers would be a concrete recognition of the social value of the work. It would refute the invisibility of the labour by combining the domestic and political economies, and it would help to reduce some of the financial and emotional strains, especially for low-income women.

Currently, economic compensation for caregivers exists in Sweden, Norway, and Australia.[5] Persons who are primary caregivers or work between 20 and 40 hours a week at caregiving activities and are within the legal working ages are reimbursed actual market wages from the state and receive regular employment benefits such as vacation and pensions. Assessments of these programs have been positive overall, and family members who participate in them report having less caregiver burden (Hooyman & Gonyea, 1995:250; Bruhm et al., 1998:20; Johansson, 2000).

Public criticisms of such payment programs have focused on the "supposed" damages to the quality of care through the introduction of market values into family caregiving. (This however, has not been found to be the case in either Norway or Sweden). Out of their own contempt for housewives and dependency workers, neo-conservatives have attacked feminists for threatening family life and for wanting women to work for wages in the private sphere. "This is a cruel joke," writes Meg Luxton, "against women who are struggling with economic insecurity and impossible caregiving choices" (Luxton, 1990:23).

Although the Canadian government has typically only paid lip service to such suggestions, this solution should be taken seriously because of the critical nature of the caregiving situation. With respect to funding such a compensation program, the Canadian government saves approximately $5.7 billion each year from family caregivers' contributions in unpaid labour and services. In 1996 alone, the sum amount of labour performed by unpaid caregivers is equivalent to the work of 275,509 paid caregivers (Fast & Frederick, 1999:4).

It remains to be seen if family caregiving will receive compensation from the government, but I can say that, at least for the near future, I am not optimistic, as such suggestions have generally been ignored in policy debates around health and continuing care policy reform.

Notes

1   Until 1977, the federal and provincial governments shared the responsibility for health care on a 50-50 basis. Throughout the 1980s and 1990s, the federal government steadily withdrew more and more funding in an effort to reduce huge annual deficits and mounting debt, so that health care is now almost entirely a provincial burden (Northcott, 1994:76–77). The provinces have been unable to keep up with rising health care costs and the increasing health needs of the population (i.e., higher rates of life expectancy, incidences of illness, and number of ill elderly persons) and have thus responded to the situation with cut-backs and downsizing. Consequently, there exists a large gap between the health demands of Canadians and the capacity of the existing health care system to satisfy them (Dickinson, 1994:106).

2   There are currently 3.86 million Canadians aged 65 years and over, and by 2016, it is predicted that this number will rise to 5.70 million (Statistics Canada, 2000). The predominant reasons given for this expected increase are that the "baby boomers" (or those born in the 20 years after World War II) are aging and approaching retirement age, life expectancy rates for this

cohort are higher, and fertility rates for the general population are lower. By 2031, it is predicted that one in four Canadians (or 22% of the population) will be a "senior citizen" as opposed to one in every eight persons in 2000 (Statistics Canada, 2000). Since elderly persons are the highest users per age group of the health care system (Frankel et al., 1996:172-74, 178), a rise in this cohorts' population translates into more demands on a health system already unable to cope with the current health needs of Canadians.

The life expectancy rates have risen substantially in Canada. From 1976 to 1994, the average age for men climbed from 70.5 years to 75.1 and for women from 77.8 to 81.2 (Grunfield et al., 1997:1103). In 1960 for instance, only 16% of Canadian women over the age of 50 had a surviving parent, but by 2010, this proportion is expected to reach 60% (MCEWH, 1998).

The National Population Health Survey revealed that one-third of Canadian senior citizens had at least one chronic condition and it is predicted that about one million elderly people will have a chronic condition by 2011 (Stewart et al., 2000:4). Additionally, both the rate and number of such illnesses increase with age (Frankel et al., 1996:177), so that the older one gets, the more likely one is to have multiple chronic conditions.

3   This paper focuses specifically on family caregiving in Canada. For a wide range of international perspectives, see Kosberg (1992); this reader contains works on 16 world countries.

4   "Chronic illness" is used to refer to physical and mental long-term conditions, disabilities, and health problems resulting in moderate to severe restrictions in physical functioning and the inability to perform the daily activities involved in looking after oneself. For example, cancer, heart disease, stroke, multiple sclerosis, Parkinson's disease, emphysema, head and spinal injuries, and Alzheimer's disease (Lyons et al., 1995:5-7).

5   See Lingsom, 2000.

References

Armstrong, P. & Armstrong, H. (1996). *Wasting away: The undermining of Canadian health care*. Toronto: Oxford University Press.

Aronson, J. (1998). Dutiful daughters and undemanding mothers: Constraining images of giving and receiving care in middle and later life." In C.T. Baines, P.M. Evans, & S.M. Neysmith (Eds.), *Women's caring: Feminist perspectives on social welfare*. Toronto: Oxford University Press.

Bader, E. (2000). Elder care special: Women's issues in caregiving for the elderly, the personal becomes political. *Lilith: The Independent Jewish Women's Magazine*. Spring.

Barrett, M. (1997). Ideology and the cultural production of gender. In R. Hennessy & C. Ingraham (Eds.), *Materialist feminism*. New York: Routledge.

Biegel, D.E., Sales, E., & Schulz, R. (1991). *Family caregiving in chronic illness.* Newbury Park, CA: Sage Publications.

Bruhm, G., Campbell, J., & Lilley, S. (1998). Caregivers' support needs: Insights from the experiences of women providing care in rural Nova Scotia. *The caregivers research project.* Halifax: Maritime Centre of Excellence for Women's Health Research. November.

Chodorow, N. (1978). *The reproduction of mothering: Psychoanalysis and the sociology of gender.* Berkeley, CA: The University of California Press.

Cranswick, K. (1997). Canada's caregivers. *Canadian social trends.* Ottawa: Statistics Canada. Winter.

Dickinson, H. D. (1994). The changing health-care system: Controlling costs and promoting health. In B.S. Bolaria & H.D. Dickinson (Eds.), *Health, illness, and health care in Canada.* 2nd ed. Toronto: Harcourt Brace.

Ehrenreich, B. (1997). What is socialist feminism? In R. Hennessy & C. Ingraham (Eds.), *Materialist feminism.* New York: Routledge.

Fast, J. & Frederick, J. (1999). Informal caregiving: Is it really cheaper? International Association of Time Use Researchers Conference. Colchester, England.

Frankel, B.G., Speechley, M., & Wade, T.J. (1996). *The sociology of health and health care: A Canadian perspective.* Toronto: Copp Clark.

George, U. (1998). Caring and women of colour: Living the intersecting oppressions of race, class, and gender. In C.T. Baines, P.M. Evans, & S.M. Neysmith (Eds.), *Women's caring: Feminist perspectives on social welfare.* Toronto: Oxford University Press.

Gilligan, C. (1982). *In a different voice.* Cambridge, MA: Harvard University Press.

Gordon, S. (1996). Feminism and caring. In S. Gordon, P. Benner, & N. Noddings (Eds.), *Caregiving: Readings in knowledge, practice, ethics, and politics.* Philadelphia, PA: University of Pennsylvania Press.

Graham, H. (1983). Caring: A labour of love. In J. Finch & D. Goves (Eds.), *A labour of love: Women, work, and caring.* London: Routledge and Kegan Paul.

Grunfield, E., Glossop, R., McDowell, I., & Danbrook, C. (1997). Caring for elderly people at home: The consequences to caregivers. *Canadian Medical Association Journal* 157(8): 1101–1105.

Hooyman, N. & Gonyea, J. (1995). *Feminist perspectives on family care: Policies for gender justice.* Thousand Oaks, CA: Sage Publications.

Johansson, L. (2000). *From policy to practice: The Swedish model.* 2nd International Conference on Caring: "Share the Care." Brisbane, Australia. March.

Kaden, J. & McDaniel, S. (1990). Care giving and care-receiving: A double bind for women in Canada's aging society. *Journal of Women and Aging* 2(3): 3–26.

Keefe, J. & Fancey, P. (1997). Financial compensation of home help services: Examining differences among program recipients. *Canadian Journal on Aging* 16(2): 254–78.

Kittay, E.F. (1999). *Love's labour: Essays on women, equality, and dependency.* New York: Routledge.

Kosberg, J.I. (Ed.) (1992). *Family care of the elderly: Social and cultural changes.* Newbury Park, CA: Sage Publications.

Lewis, J. & Meredith, B. (1988). *Daughters who care: Daughters caring for mothers at home.* New York: Routledge.

Lingsom, S. (1994). Payments for care: The case of Norway. In A. Evers, M. Pijl, & C. Ungerson (Eds.), *Payments for care: A comparative overview.* Aldershot: Avebury, 1994.

Luxton, M. (1980). *More than a labour of love: Three generations of women's work in the home.* Toronto: Women's Press.

——. (1990). Two hands for the clock: Changing patterns in the gendered division of labour in the home. In M. Luxton, H. Rosenberg & S. Arat-Koc (Eds.), *Through the kitchen window: The politics of home and family.* Toronto: Garamond Press.

——. (1997). Feminism and families: The challenge of neo-conservatism. In M. Luxton (Ed.), *Feminism and families: Critical policies and changing practices.* Halifax: Fernwood Publishing.

Lyons, R., Sullivan, M.J.L., Rivoto, P.G., & Coyne, J.C. (1995). *Relationships in chronic illness and disability.* Thousand Oaks, California: Sage.

Maritime Centre of Excellence for Women's Health (MCEWH). (1998). Home care and policy: Bringing gender into focus. *Gender and Health Policy Discussion Series* 1. Halifax. March.

Montgomery, R. & Kosloski, K. (1994). A longitudinal analysis of nursing home placement for dependent elders cared for by spouses vs. adult children. *Journal of Gerontology* 49(2): s62–s74.

Morris, M., Robinson, J., & Simpson, J., with Galey, S., Kirby, S., Martin, L. & Muzychka, M. (1999). *The changing nature of home care and its impact on women's vulnerability to poverty.* Canadian Research Institute for the Advancement of Women (CRIAW). Ottawa: Status of Women Canada. November.

Neufeld, A. & Harrison, M. (2000). Family caregiving: Issues in gaining access to support. In M. Stewart (Ed.), *Chronic conditions and caregiving in Canada: Social support strategies.* Toronto: University of Toronto Press.

Noddings, N. (1984). *Caring, a feminine approach to ethics and moral education.* Berkeley, CA: University of California Press.

Nolan, M., Grant, G., & Keady, J. (1996). *Understanding family care: A multidimensional model of caring and coping.* Philadelphia, PA: Open University Press.

Northcott, Herbert C. (1994). Threats to Medicare: The financing, allocation, and utilization of health care in Canada. In B.S. Bolaria & H.D. Dickinson

(Eds.), *Health, illness, and health care in Canada.* 2nd ed. Toronto: Harcourt Brace.

Reitsma-Street, M. (1998). Still girls learn to care: Girls policed to care. In C.T. Baines, P. M. Evans, & S.M. Neysmith (Eds.), *Women's caring: Feminist perspectives on social welfare.* Toronto: Oxford University Press.

Rhodes, A. (1997). *Take care: A practical guide for helping elders.* Toronto: HarperCollins.

Schofield, H. (Ed.). (1998). *Family caregivers: Disability, illness, and ageing.* Sydney: Allen and Unwin.

Statistics Canada. (1998). 1996 census: Labour force activity, occupation and industry, place of work, mode of transportation to work, unpaid work. *The Daily.* 17 March.

Statistics Canada. (1997). *A portrait of seniors in Canada.* Ottawa: Minister of Industry.

Statistics Canada. (1996). Who cares? Caregiving in the 1990s. *The Daily.* 19 August.

Stewart, M. & Langille, L. (2000). A framework for social support assessment and intervention in the context of chronic conditions and caregiving. In M. Stewart ed., *Chronic conditions and caregiving in Canada: Social support strategies.* Toronto: University of Toronto Press.

Waerness, K. (1996). The rationality of caring. In S. Gordon, P. Benner, & N. Noddings (Eds.), *Caregiving: Readings in knowledge, practice, ethics, and politics.* Philadelphia, PA: University of Pennsylvania Press.

Waring, M. (1988). *If women counted: A new feminist economics.* San Francisco, CA: Harper and Row.

Wilson, S.J. (1996). *Women, families, and work.* Toronto: McGraw-Hill.

Chapter Twelve

Marginal Women: Examining the Barriers of Age, Race and Ethnicity[1]

Robynne Neugebauer

Introduction: Exploring Intersections of Exclusions

The study of aging is an examination of processes of being, becoming and experiencing differences. Typically, cultural constructions of differences such as gender, race and ethnicity are used to justify inequality. Consequently, these values serve to maintain the "marginalized" locations of older women by conditioning the aging process. This paper examines the societal barriers to equality experienced by senior ethnocultural and racial minority women. Specifically, senior ethnocultural and racial minority women face societal barriers on many fronts. They are victims of multiple jeopardy due to the combined discrimination based on age, gender, race and ethnocultural minority status. The multiple jeopardy hypothesis of aging has been previously investigated by several authors — Penning (1983), Abu-Laban and Abu-Laban (1977), Bengston (1979), Chappell and Havens (1980) and Havens and Chappell (1983).

Age, gender, race and ethnicity are representations that challenge particular socially reproduced and historically rooted social orders. The study of aging, especially in terms of these fundamental features, therefore, is about the privilege of power and the contexts of exclusion. The repercussions of inequality range from compulsory retirement to the violent victimization evident in cases of elder abuse, neglect, poverty, etc. Thus, inequality, expressed as felt or lived experiences, punishes differences. Expressions of inequality are also wide ranging, from extremely coercive forms of institutional confinement to seemingly more innocuous dependency relations such as subsidized social services and health care. Within the more economically developed societies, older citizens[2] are disciplined; they are transformed as "docile bodies" (Foucault, 1977) to be forever controlled and stripped of their individuality. They are, therefore, homogenized whereby issues of gender, age, race and ethnicity are discarded in favour of new and improved commodities in order to enhance conformity to roles and rules. The origin, construction and subsequent definitions of ageism are linked to the social organization of conformity — control.

In general, the study of inequality is about domination and devaluation. Inequality constitutes the "social" dimension of age-based, gender-based, race and ethno-based patterns of discrimination. Aging is constructed in reference to well-established, but poorly understood, impressions that are maintained by symbols, stereotypes and series of over-categorizations that code images, which in turn become convenient mechanisms for understanding the aging process. Although senior adults (persons 65 years and older) are among the fastest growing segments of society, the aging process affects many people in different ways and at various stages of their lives. Clearly, a sensitivity towards the needs of seniors is long overdue if only for obvious demographic data that show that Canada's older population continues to grow. More precisely, this paper generates generic social justice concerns experienced by ethnocultural and racial minority senior women by analyzing the social justice concerns experienced by ethnocultural and racial minority senior women by analyzing the social organization of interpersonal, institutional and structural barriers. In so doing, we learn to question fundamental assumptions about the causes and consequences of exclusion.

From a general interpretive perspective, aging is viewed as a social accomplishment, constructed and negotiated in ongoing interactions with various social agents. Definitions of aging are problematic because of their emergent character. An interpretive paradigm challenges the normative characterization of aging as a given and static phenomenon. In brief, normative approaches consistently have argued that aging as a social reality is constructed by external forces that propel forms of adaptation. Fixed sets of norms and values set the boundary by which aging is defined. Within the interpretive model, on the other hand, seniors are presented as creators of their environments. In this context, actors engage in a continual process of meaning construction in relation to their social realities. As agents, they reflectively shape their experiences and the experiences of those with whom they routinely interact. Through interaction, individuals collectively define situations. Participants, therefore, negotiate and reconstitute meanings. This paradigm calls for a sociology characterized by what Max Weber (1969) called "verstehen" — an empathic and interpretive understanding of the subjective meanings that actors attach to social action. The only way to contextualize social action is to know the subjective meanings of actors. Actors take into account the actions of others and are guided by these subjective meanings. Action incorporates all human behaviour to which the acting individuals attach subjective meanings. The individual actor, therefore, becomes the basic unit of analysis, and the process by which meanings as assigned becomes a focal point of enquiry.

Consistent with this theoretical framework, a methodology was adopted that appreciates participants as acting subjects and subjected actors. Triangulation (Denzin, 1978), the examination of single empirical events from the vantage of different methods and viewpoints, is highly congruent with this task. The accuracy of individual responses is checked by comparing accounts of all subjects, especially those that differ widely in the levels of participation in specific activities and identity constructions.

This paper is part of a larger study on ethno-racial senior women conducted from 1993 to 1995. Interviews were held with 200 female respondents of a purposive sample stratified according to racial and ethnic factors. A survey instrument accompanied "face to face" interviews and on-site observations in their homes and recreational facilities. A large number of questions, formulated on the basis of a literature review, delved into the perceptions of older women regarding the following barriers to access: information and awareness, physical/geographic, cultural, administrative (institutional) and economic. In addition, we examined specific measures or strategies that organizations had taken to improve access, and the ones that respondents felt should be taken in the overall system of services regarding "multicultural" policies and measures, composition of staffing and personnel patterns, linguistic and planning data. Interviews were conducted in the native language of non-English-speaking respondents. With the assistance of local community associations, several focussed group discussions were conducted. Representatives also reviewed initial findings. The study used a community development approach, involving participants in a variety of ways throughout the process of the research. In this action research, participants were involved in diagnosing problems, collecting information to make necessary changes and evaluating the effectiveness of changes recommended.

The sample consisted of the following group representations, as identified by the individuals (self identified): 50 Europeans (Italians, Portuguese, Greeks, Poles, Russians); 50 African Canadians (Somalis, Afro-Guyanese, Jamaicans, black Canadians — who enjoyed several generations of Canadian ancestry, Trinidadians); and 100 Asians (Indians, Chinese, Koreans, Vietnamese, Filipino).

Interpersonal Relations: The Sociology of Emotions

Aging, as a cultural phenomenon, varies significantly according to class, gender, race and ethnicity. But researchers have only begun to touch the surface of

Table 1: Demographic Profile

National Origin (self-identified)	English Speaking	Non-English Speaking
Somalis	5	5
Afro-Guyanese	5	5
Jamaican	10	0
African Canadian	5	5
Trinidadians	10	0
Italians	5	5
Portuguese	5	5
Greeks	5	5
Poles	5	5
Russians	5	5
Indians	10	10
Chinese	10	10
Koreans	10	10
Vietnamese	10	10
Filipinos	10	10
TOTAL	**110**	**90**

inter- and intra-group variations. Typical gerontological data tend to group minorities in terms of banal (over-generalized) observations. There is little knowledge of the unique social, political, economic and cultural contexts within which minority seniors live. Old age is equated with the three Ds: the dreadful designations of disability, disease and death. As a woman grows older there is a tendency to trivialize her social, physical and emotional well-being.

This project explores the relationship(s) of the self, community and institutions by juxtaposing the agency of the older person and ageist structures. Generic processes of the situation in reference to contexts, consequences and contests of meanings are studied in order to develop analytically the challenges and prospects of linking the actor and community. Specifically, this paper challenges the boundaries of aging research in order to understand aging in reference to processes of negation and marginalization.

Living in Fear: The Liabilities of Aging

The social psychology of vulnerability has generated anxieties and exaggerated fears. A constant worry about being victimized among seniors has in itself become a social problem especially when it excites counterproductive responses such as alarmingly high levels of trepidation leading to a fortress mentality, a "cocooning" orientation — staying at home, arming oneself and

Table 2: Sample Characteristics

a) Nature of Accommodation

Non-institutional	180
Institutional	20
Total	**200**

b) Living Arrangements

Alone	54
With spouse/partner	74
With relative/family	55
With a female friend	17
Total	**200**

avoiding "the strange others out there". According to our survey (N=200), 84 per cent of respondents indicated that they feared violence. When asked about which types of crimes they were most concerned, 88 per cent of the respondents selected assault. Three-quarters of the women surveyed reported that they were "very fearful" that they would become victims of violent crime; 70 per cent of non-English-speaking women and 90 per cent of English-speaking women of colour felt that violence is worse now than ever before. Interestingly, violence attribution varied; 80 per cent of black women felt that they would be targetted because of their colour while 80 per cent of white women noted gender and age respectively. Contrast the above alarming data with general statistics: in a poll conducted by *Maclean's*/Decima, 44 per cent of women expressed concerns about walking home alone at night; 80 per cent of the respondents in Toronto said that they would always keep their doors locked, even if they were home (*Maclean's*, 7/01/1991:31). Nationally, 49 per cent of men and 54 per cent of women said they kept their doors locked at all times when they were at home according to the results of a *Maclean's*/CTV national poll released in 1993 (Chisholm, 1993:24–25). A 1992 Gallup Poll noted that 54 per cent of women in Canada noted that there are areas within one mile of their homes where they were afraid to walk, compared to 17 per cent of men who expressed this fear (*Toronto Star*, 28/11/1992:A1). Thirty-three per cent of Canadians, half of whom are women reported that they are afraid to walk alone outside at night (Chisholm, 1993:24). According to the largest national survey on violence against women, conducted by Statistics Canada in late 1993 involving 12,300 respondents, more than 80 per cent of women fear entering parking garages, 76 per cent worry about using public transportation after dark and 60 per cent fear walking in their neighborhoods after dark (*Toronto Star*, 19/11/1993:A29).

An individual's perception of the level of risk is related to the fear of being tyrannized, especially by strangers. Fear of victimization are expressed more deeply by more vulnerable individuals or groups in our communities, notably, women, the elderly, newcomers/immigrants, the poor, gays and lesbians, and non whites. For instance, blacks expressed more fear of crime than whites, the poor more than the wealthy, and inner-city dwellers more than suburbanites (Moore and Trojanowicz, 1988:2). Seniors experience greater rates of victimization by assaults, robberies, muggings and extortions. Seniors, particularly women, who are most likely to live alone, feel more socially vulnerable and fear to be out alone at night. Fear of violence is determined by perceptions of vulnerability to crime based on individual demographic factors such as age, gender, race, ethnicity and experiences with victimization. The greater the perceived vulnerability, the greater one's fear. Vulnerability includes both physical and social elements. Perceived isolation or attenuation of sentimental bonds makes the senior feel more vulnerable and therefore more afraid. Fear of violence is generalized as a result of the perceived personal, neighbourhood and community disintegration. Fear is also attributable to living close to others whose cultural backgrounds are different from one's own. More recently, investigators have analyzed the influence of cultural settings on fear.

Fear is also associated with lack of economic opportunities. For example, the wealthier women expressed less fear as a result of their relatively safe living circumstances. Fear was frequently articulated by poorer women who talked about the lack of privacy and protection. Poorer women as well as non-English-speaking women noted that their worries were seldom taken seriously by authorities. For instance, when they report their contacts with authorities (police, landlords, directors of nursing homes, caregivers) as well as relatives, they stated that their suspicions and fears were readily dismissed. Thus, societal reactions are the processes that create, maintain and intensify fear. Cultural constructions of crime "dramatize evil" and traumatize the more vulnerable.

The Shame of Incompetence: Gender as Stigma

The failure to experience, establish and negotiate the situated "social" self within structured contexts has resulted in the amplification of defect or "stigma". Stigmatization, or the collective designation of disgrace, has extensive consequences for the self-concept of older women. Identities are increasingly crystallized; labels generate new definitions of self for the particular person, for her reference group and for the larger societal audiences. Furthermore, when older women fail to shed this designation they are often impelled to personalize and conscientize labels by organizing their lifestyles around distorted assumptions associated with painful labels. A "master status" emerges and overshadows all other aspects of identity. In response, older women are expected to disconnect from familiar and familial faces by retiring quietly and transforming themselves into passive dependents. This conversion is evident especially in reference to sexual activity. The sexuality of senior women continues to be depicted pejoratively in all major institutions from the family and religion to the media. The preponderance of sterile images causes older women adults to conceal their normal sexual feelings and sexual relations. As one 76-year-old Italian woman, Maria, expressed in our study:

> Everybody, everybody including the people who say they love you want you to act your age. What does that mean? Act my age! It's not right for me to think like a woman with some feelings here and there. I got to hide it. Pretend that I'm a virgin. Pretend that I'm the Virgin's mother. That's not right.

In general, negative stereotypes about older sexually active people create feelings of shame, which in turn evoke images of incompetence (Neugebauer-Visano, 1995). In other works, older sexually active women are expected to feel incompetent as genuine people. They are obviously disturbed, according to this logic, for not "acting their age". They are encouraged to refrain from sexual behaviour. Rather than suffer the condemnation, it is safer to hide or deny one's sexual activities. The sexual behaviour of women is culturally perceived as defiance and as deviance, controlled by a pathologizing script. Cultural stereotypes contribute to compliance and decreased involvements.

Dependence and Dignity: Roles and Rules of Gendered Texts

A major problem facing most older people concerns the loss of independence. Older women feel guilty about being a burden to their family and friends even though in a patriarchal society women, especially older women, are expected to be dependent economically, emotionally, psychologically and socially. Regrettably the family as an institution fosters dependence and transfers this dependence to other agencies. Despite the efforts of the family, peer socialization has become one of several ways in which older women seek a modicum of independence.

Older women respond, reproduce and reshape their identities by accommodating, neutralizing and managing dependency relations by denying the concomitant discomforts of dependency. Sixty per cent of non-English-speaking women who lived with their families were inclined to accept more traditionally defined submissive roles while 80 per cent of English-speaking respondents who live alone resorted to an interpretive framework that consisted of protest, resistance and challenge to stereotypes. Our respondents suggest that they learn to develop a theory of sociality within a broad sociology of emotions. Accordingly, techniques of neutralizations, excuses and generalized appeals, a vocabulary of motives, etc., are routinely used to deal with troublesome situations whereby the cool out the situation, grapple with shame, fear, remorse, etc. In doing so, they become survivors committed to stability rather than drifting from occasion to occasion. In terms of identity management, older women are extremely adept, refusing to simply accommodate and move towards more enabling activities. Research on aging has typically stressed the former — forms of static accommodation. In this project it was quite apparent that old women were engaged in the active social construction of identities, self-acceptance, recoveries of self, fostering and reshaping identities, managing information, drawing comparisons, seeking to control and reshape their identities, managing respectability, etc. Unlike popular media accounts or Hollywood stereotypes, seniors are less concerned with memorializing and immortalizing images of themselves; rather they are more determined to express themselves as individuals struggling with some difficulty to remove the blinders of bigotry.

The Promises and Paradoxes of the "Functional" Family

The family as a dynamic institution plays a key role in the development of identity, character and competence. For decades researchers have established the salience of the family during the formative years of child development. Typically within a normative child development paradigm, the child was nurtured, guided and protected. Later in life, other influences emerge outside the family: peers at school during the teenage years and eventually paid work or unpaid housework become central.

Clearly, sociology enjoys a rich tradition that documents the various functions of the family as a critical agency especially for its older members. Ideally, the family provides opportunities that enable all of its members to care and support each other in a familiar environment. In this site of mutual respect and unconditional trust families project general orientations and provide an interpretive framework that guides the reinforcement of positive self-images as well as the independence of all of its members regardless of age. The role of the family is also anchored in the world of rules. Roles are adopted that assist in sustaining helpful relationships (Neugebauer, 1989). Our data suggest that older women want to be integrated "in" and "of" the family. All of the respondents expressed a desire to share activities with their children. Their expressed interests did not diminish with age. Older mothers who have surviving children look forward to whatever quality time is available. More than any other familial constituency, the older members promote a sense of belongingness with the family. According to 60 women, they saw themselves sustaining relationships. They continue to link their children and grandchildren with each other in order to keep the family intact. They perceived themselves as actively engaging in family building, that is in responding, reproducing and reshaping identities. In this regard family traditions were useful in ensuring a commitment to "the" family. Our respondents (77 per cent) noted that they helped in stabilizing relations in the changed family.

But the family is also a site of struggle. The family as an institution reproduces conflict. In reality, the family is derivative of wider ageist social orders. Aging in North America transforms authority relations in the family as well. Beyond a certain age, according to our data, deference to the authority of more senior family members discontinues. Thus, in terms of independence and its concomitant privacy, seniors are not encouraged to pursue separate interests without the consent of others — younger family members. In moving from disablement to enablement, respondents met considerable resistance. Women interested in seeking a measure of independence were treated with suspicion and distrust. Of the 180 non-institutionalized respondents, 85 per cent described the reactions of their children as hostile, ranging from civil inattention ("being ignored") to open conflict ("being insulted verbally", "being punished") in everyday encounters. Consequently these occasions resulted in more tenuous relationships and limited communication.

During these episodes of disagreement, respondents noted that they were refused the right to negotiate compromises. As Paulette, a 69-year-old Jamaican-Canadian elaborates:

> When you get old the tables turn on you. Yes, the kids love you but they love what they want to see. You see it's like politics. It's like war. It's like love. It's like everythin', if you need them, the balance changes. They want to show that they are right and your traditions are out of place and maybe you don't belong. If this was Jamaica I know it be different. And you know after a short time, you become too tired to fight over things that they really don't know about.

The above excerpt highlights a number of dilemmas attendant with resistance. For instance, there is always a fear that a misunderstanding can be easily manipulated into a major confrontation or panic. According to our respondents, the ability to listen, share interests and take time to communicate is frequently exacerbated by a failure to cope with perceived and actual changing leadership patterns in the family structure. Hence, a communal orientation is easily lost. Another area of concern to women pertained to barriers in relationships with grandchildren. Since many grandchildren were third-generation Canadians who were unfamiliar with their ancestral language, women reported a very serious language and, therefore, communication gap between ethnocultural women and their grandchildren. Women lamented over the fact that this communication gap not only weakened the bonds between themselves and their grandchildren but also rendered them isolated at family gatherings. A source of deep regret for many women, this experience of isolation, relegated them to an inferior position in the family.

The independence of older women is also tied to others in the community, namely friends and neighbours who also provide support. The strength of this independence depends on the multiple connections of older women to religious organizations, community groups, as well as other independently oriented women who promote their wellness. Weak ties play a critical role in developing self-reliance. Women who enjoy a multiplicity of ties in their interactions are able to access a greater degree of well-balanced set of resources. Lamentably, 70 per cent of women simply do not have accessible outside resources. They feel that they had expended much energy throughout their lives in sustaining their respective families without developing links outside the family. Their few contacts were limited to ethnocultural activities that were fleeting and segmented. This isolation was especially evident in our sample of non-English-speaking women who live alone. Non-English-speaking women were more resigned to the institutional care giving offered in nursing homes. Moreover, non-English-speaking women note that they remained in abusive family relationships because they perceived limited options. Rather than live with their abusive adult children, English-speaking respondents prefer to be on their own, with their marital partner or a female friend. All respondents, however, articulated a preference for healthy family relationships. In the absence of caring families they defaulted to other forms of support, care and assistance.

The Tyranny of Elder Abuse: In the Name of the Family
Elder abuse is ubiquitous; it is not class-based nor ethnoculturally oriented. Both qualitatively and quantitatively there are striking variations in the response to this tragic phenomenon. More impoverished and recently arrived respondents tolerate greater levels of abuse. Before they apprise let alone summon authorities or friends, they suffer a great deal of pain. Notwithstanding the different types of abuse, all respondents discussed at great length the issue of abusive family relationships. The older members of our study, 40 respondents who were over the age of 75, were prepared to comment freely about neglect. They were not particularly reluctant to offer detailed information about their own personal experiences. Accounts of abuse were framed as neutralizations of excuses. For example, the following were proffered that dealt with the issue of unwillingness to report violence or neglect: fear of reprisals, denial of injury, ignorance regarding remedies and

services, and appeals to family loyalty. Other reasons noted for the lack of reporting were internalized feelings of disgrace, embarrassment, fear of uncertainty, anticipated loss of self-determination, complicity in their victimization, fear of placement in a nursing home, loss of their dependency, the absence of appropriate remedies, etc. Elder abuse consists of physical abuse (the deliberate physical injury), material abuse (the misuse of property and/or fiduciary rights as a result of fraud), neglect (the failure to provide basic services and goods) and self-neglect. In this regard most English-speaking and all non-English-speaking older women talked about tolerating the abuse as less harmful than proceeding against their caregiving children. There was a willingness to redirect the discussion to the abuse inflicted by strangers. Abuse is often attributed to the situational stresses of the abuser. The abuser is frequently someone who needs the older person especially for financial assistance. The perceived power imbalance or the privilege of the older family member is punished by a younger relative who depends on the senior for assistance. Second, respondents equally reported that abuse is a function of the powerlessness of the elderly; they are considered easy targets of exploitation. Respondents indicated that 75 per cent of abuse cases consist overwhelmingly of verbal insults and threats of neglect. With greater candor, however, respondents talked more about spousal violence. Non-English-speaking respondents also spoke of institutional caregivers, public agencies and service providers as more abusive than their families. English-speaking respondents were more frequently abuse by poorer family members. Respondents did not wish to see their children or relatives prosecuted. Instead, they cited the following preventive measures that could deter abuse: public services that facilitate financial or legal assistance, emergency accommodation (safe shelters), immediate medical responses, counselling for the abuser, supportive networks, etc.

Beyond The Local: Self-Community Linkages

Sociology enjoys an impressively rich tradition that documents the transformation of social relations between the self and community. Urban sociology has singled out the three themes that characterized these changing social links: the community as lost, the community as saved and the community as liberated. The literature in network analysis clearly notes that older citizens enjoy dynamic links with others. Our respondents do not "lock" themselves in nor do they appreciate being "shutouts". A public perception exists that "speaks" on behalf of safety issues for seniors. Our respondents unanimously note that although the city is presented to them by the media, the police, service providers, etc. as a strange and dangerous place, they consider themselves to be "part" of and not apart from the community.

Institutional Barriers: Access to Services

Services for seniors have increased dramatically within the last few decades. And yet there is an overwhelming level of ignorance concerning the cultural and socio-economic viewpoints of seniors, particularly from diverse ethnic, cultural and racial backgrounds.

Layered with ageism and misogyny, ethnic bigotry and racism serve to marginalize, exclude and finally negate identity. Of central concern to our discussion of fundamental institutional barriers are the following: the culture of intolerance; anti-racist ideologies; the hegemony of paternalistic mythologies; aging as a complex of social meanings constantly transformed by politics, medicine and culture; and ageism as an integral feature of current cultural ideologies.

Canada's seniors are entitled legally to social services but often do not receive them in an equitable manner. In his seminal study, Kahn (1973:31) noted that the following obstacles exacerbate access to services: discrimination; cultural distance; the complexity and bureaucratic nature of the service system; variations among consumers in knowledge and understanding of their rights, resources, benefits and entitlements; costs; and geographic distance between people and services. Typically, older consumers of human services are bewildered by the complex array of agencies. Confusing eligibility rules and criteria ensure that only a few consumers have the capacity and opportunity to fully acknowledge their entitlements to services and the ways that they can use to access those services. It is very surprising that only a few service organizations have sufficiently changed their structures and operations to make their programmes and services more accessible to the changing needs and demands of consumers. The interest and the needs of elderly consumers are not always similar — consumers have different orientations. These differences are seldom appreciated by service providers. The latter appear limited as a result of shrinking organizational resources, cutbacks in programmes, lack of accountability, etc. The interests and mandates of service delivery systems appear to be different from the needs of seniors. For seniors, issues of access and social change are central whereas institutions are concerned with containing the problem of increased demands and costs. Underfinanced and inadequate services are failing our older consumers, symptoms of our social crisis. Our respondents (98 per cent) know all too well how poorly they are treated. Unacceptable standards of conduct limit access.

Access is located within the structure of inequality in the human services delivery systems. In Canada, the U.S.A. and the U.K. services are offered by both mainstream and ethnospecific agencies; the former refers to organizations that serve anyone in the community who meets general eligibility criteria.

This general provision of service is not based on membership within any particular cultural or racial group. On the other hand, ethnospecific organizations deliver services on the basis of general criteria that emphasize membership in a particular cultural or racial group.

In the world of multiracial and multicultural service delivery systems, it is important to differentiate between availability and access. Availability simply refers to the presence of provision of a specific service. Access relates to the actual delivery of a service to the consumer. What is often presented as available may in fact be inaccessible. Access consists of two components: (a) client access — the extent to which consumers are able to secure much-needed services; and (b) organizational access — the extent to which consumers (members of diverse cultural and racial groups) are represented and also participate in the planning, development, delivery and administration of those services. Organizational access is important since it relates very closely to the purposes and effectiveness of service organizations; reflecting the diversity of communities they serve while remaining culturally sensitive to consumers who seek their assistance. Doyle and Visano (1987) in *A Programme for Action* analyzed the issue of access for members of cultural and racial groups to health and social services. Five types of barriers were identified: information and awareness, physical/geographic, cultural, administrative and cost. It was found that only a few mainstream organizations devote much energy to effect change beyond the identification of barriers. While service providers express a sensitive appreciation of the problems inherent in securing access, the results are disturbing in terms of actual adoption of specific measures to reduce barriers. Serious gaps were revealed in the information base of agencies regarding the cultural and racial characteristics of the clientele and workforce, including board and volunteer representation. The following general conclusions were drawn from their findings:

- agencies are unwilling to share information or organizational data regarding the cultural and racial characteristics of their clientele, staff and volunteers;
- agencies fail to respond to barriers and are unable to devise strategies and programmes to effectively address these barriers;
- cost is a factor constantly articulated, but it must be noted that changes to improve access require few additional costs for agencies;
- change efforts within individual agencies are not sufficient to assure the necessary system improvements;
- "collective" responses by service agencies, rather than ad hoc, isolated remedies, are required to achieve more equitable access for minority groups.

It was discovered that mainstream agencies do not respond effectively to their new multiracial/multicultural realities. The onus for ensuring access falls on smaller, poorer funded and understaffed ethnospecific agencies. Mainstream and ethnospecific organizations seem to operate as two solitudes in separate systems, rarely taking into account their respective efforts to plan and deliver services without competing for scarce resources.

Interviews confirmed that our respondents experienced difficulties in securing access. These older consumers attribute obstacles to factors such as lack of information, styles and techniques of interaction, and lack of knowledge and understanding of cultural linguistic factors that complicate delivery patterns. Consumers expressed feelings of uncertainty, powerlessness and distance from agencies set up to serve them. It was found that cultural factors inhibit consumers from approaching agencies. There is also widespread discontent among consumers about agency staff and the services obtained. The most frequent criticism directed at staff concerns their failure to appreciate the predicament experienced by people of different cultures. Consumers from racial and cultural groups encounter acute problems: limited knowledge of rights and entitlements, limited language ability that renders it more difficult to secure services, and cultural differences that make them more susceptible to misconceptions and negative judgements. They risk double exclusion, making it difficult for them to be considered as full and equal members of society. As for information barriers identified in this access study, 92 per cent of non-English-speaking women were ill-informed about available services. And yet, only a minority of English-speaking respondents (10 per cent) felt disadvantaged in this regard. Concerning cultural barriers, 98 per cent of respondents do not understand the role of helping professionals. Only 20 per cent of respondents indicated that their agencies for seniors provided specific programmes/services directed to ethnocultural groups. Also, 90 per cent of respondents agreed that service delivery is frustrating and confusing; 80 percent of respondents noted that as clients they always have to wait a long time for appointments; 92 per cent of respondents reported that office hours are inconvenient. Despite their complaints they noted that agencies were ill-prepared to confront barriers. Agencies fail to respond sensitively to consumers and fail to assume their helping roles in a responsible manner. Agencies, respondents argued, are only comfortable with isolated solutions. Like the consumer survey findings of Doyle and Visano (1987), it was discovered that most consumers from ethnocultural populations find out about services from their families and friends rather than from agencies. Indeed, 88 per cent of our respondents generally do not know what services are available to them.

As a result of age-related changes in the physical body, common symptoms and signs often go unreported. Doctors also "expect" older adults to have aches and pains, which may result in their glossing over symptoms that should be noted. Doctors' attitudes reflect these expectations. Commenting on multiple conditions, respondents suggested that physicians are often impatient with older adults who recite a long list of complaints. Chronic conditions in older adults present perplexing problems for a physician who is trained to "cure" patients. Older adults are keenly aware of the physician's frustration in dealing with them. Respondents observed that open communication with a physician is vital to ensuring quality medical care. In communicating with a doctor, older adults are consumers of service. They have the right to know more about their condition, prescriptions and the right to a second opinion.

Cultural factors are important for understanding the general dissatisfaction. They identified numerous factors: a lack of information, staff in mainstream organizations who do not understand them or appreciate their cultural differences, problems in communicating with service providers, and the unavailability of services specifically geared to serve them. Health service organization (hospitals, chronic care facilities, health centres) need to provide a more community-based approach to serving the health care needs of a diverse multicultural population, involving consumers in health service organization and delivery. The following conclusions were drawn:

- There is a need for increased public consciousness, tolerance and respect of a new multicultural reality; currently, there is no shared vision to reflect equal and responsible entitlements.
- There is a need for ethnocultural communities to be organized so that they can articulate their own needs and resources for health.
- An agenda for antiracism that is clear, consistent and reflective of the input from various constituencies is absent.
- There are few legislative commitments to support policy initiatives.
- There is a lack of effective structures to organize and maintain efforts to enhance accessibility.
- There are no coherent and multitiered strategies to achieve access.
- There is an abundance of rhetoric suggesting entitlements of all citizens to public services and resource such as health.
- There is a lack of commitment by service providers/funders to confront the realities of exclusions.
- There is a need to change the organizations that provide (health) services to make them reflective of the multicultural reality.
- There is a need to develop an ethnocultural database in all sectors including health.
- There is a need to address specific barriers to equity and access in existing organizations and in the society.

According to the comments of respondents, service delivery systems need to be restructured to "fit" the demands of older minority women. Several models are instructive such as the Anishnawbe Health Centre in Toronto. In 1986 the Aboriginal Health Professions Programme (AHPP) was established at the University of Toronto. Its mandate is to increase the number of Aboriginal health care professionals having a knowledge of both traditional and modern medical practices so that they can better serve First Nations people whether in urban centres or First Nations communities.

Even though services have proliferated, our data indicate that 78 per cent of all care services provided to older people come from their respective family members — their spouses or married daughters or daughters-in-law. Minority women are denied access to institutions of care giving. Health and social services are primarily family-based. This focus is highly problematic whenever families are engaged in abusive relationships as noted earlier. Likewise, whenever families are dispersed over geographic distances transportation is a major concern for seniors. In either case seniors are required to resort to bureaucratic regulations that silence the participation of older women who are perceived to be more marginal to the "Canadian" social landscape. Institutional responses tend to rely on an authoritarian deference to alien rules. But institutions alone cannot compensate for the disadvantages created. The family, the community and institutions of welfare, social and health services momentarily mitigate a crisis but cannot hold too many promises without some appreciation of larger derivative orders. Historically, legal structures and trends in the political economy have equally contributed to the general impoverishment of the older minority women.

Structuring Inequality: From Law to Political Economy

Human rights legislation has failed to alleviate feelings of frustration, alienation and powerlessness. Legal gains have been extremely limited. Although older women have avoided legal options for a large number of legitimate reasons, Baer (1991:136) argues that the law should still be used to achieve much more. The relations of patriarchy to race and class oppressions are comprehensive. The layering of colour, age, class and gender cannot be ignored. Race and gender cannot be treated separately. Nitya Duclos (1993) studied race and sex discrimination cases reported in the *Canadian Human Rights Reporter* from 1980–1989. In assessing the responses of these tribunals, Duclos argued that the concept of discrimination that informs current human rights law is unduly simplistic and reflective of the privileged perspective of the dominant group. There is an erasure of racial minority women throughout Canadian law. Although racial minority women have distinctive subjective experiences of racism and sexism, their race and gender characteristics are taken for granted. Human rights laws are incomplete remedies. The lack of appreciation of the existence of racial minority women is so complete that one frequently cannot even discover whether a complainant was a racial minority woman (Duclos, 1993:30). They are absent from reported decisions on race and sex discrimination. Of the 416 cases where race or sex discrimination (or both) was alleged in a ten-year period 1980–1989, 299 cases were replete with inadequacies of information (Duclos, 1993:32). Race is not mentioned in sex discrimination cases just as sex is not mentioned in race discrimination cases. In addition to the invisibility of these women, the following factors explain why advantaged women do not make claims (Duclos, 1993:37–39):

1. a lack of awareness that they have legal rights;
2. a general and well-founded distrust of the legal system;
3. the complaints procedures do not correspond to the reality of their lives.

Both the concepts of race and gender in law are so impoverished that it has become convenient to ignore differences. Unconscious assumptions about gender and race, however, inform the normative contours of legal understanding. A relational view of inequality in which components of coercion consist of the institutional configurations of political economy, the ideology of patriarchy and law is long overdue. Culture constitutes law and legal relations relegate minority women to the margins.

The Canadian political economy privileges some and punishes "others" in terms of pervasive class inequality. Within the wider political economy the linkages of power are generally unaccountable. From the discretionary practices of corporate capital interests to the materialist conditions of culture poverty is socially organized. Poverty is contextual — a condition and a consequence of the ravages of profit. As a cultural characteristic of capital, poverty is socially constructed by a political economy that is unresponsive to a just allocation and distribution of resources. The profit motives of corporate capitalism inferiorize, isolate and painfully impoverish millions of Canadians.

Poverty, as a condition of relative deprivation, exists as long as fundamental differences in income and wealth are maintained structurally. There are numerous measures of poverty; however, such indicators of inequality as hunger, housing and unemployment are instrumental in developing a critical appreciation of the social injuries that contribute to poverty. Poverty is a condition of dependency that negates meaningful participation in the social order by relegating millions of people and their communities to positions of marginality, vulnerability and control.

Resources are inadequate for elder minority women. In addition to the "feminization of poverty", Aboriginals, the elderly, people of colour, youth, the casually employed, refugees and the differentially abled continue to suffer form ravages of poverty.

An underclass of single and battered women, youth, mentally and physically challenged and the elderly has flourished. Current intervention is usually punitive — ranging from surveillance to the mental/public health acts (involuntary committal) and criminal code provisions. These interventive designs keep the homeless colonized and less threatening. Older Canadians who are physically challenged or differentially abled will continue to suffer the injuries of class.

The concept of individualism per se contributes to the impoverishment of many older Canadians. Individual worth, individual claim and individual effort are criteria often invoked to assess social welfare needs. The emphasis on the reified individual facilitates a total disregard of historical trends, culture and political economy.

Conclusions

Processes of marginalization consist of the systematic reproduction of inequality within structures ostensibly designed to promote equality. Normative roles and rules, ideologies and their everyday applications operate to oppress and devalue the so-called "othered", that is, older women of diverse ethnoracial backgrounds. Admittedly, the aging process is very natural and normal, but the implications of aging as a social process of inequality are appalling. Unfortunately, professionals, policy makers and families are often unprepared or ignorant about the relationships among misogyny, racism and ageism. There is a need to provide both minority and nonminority practitioners with an understanding of and sensitivity to the needs of seniors and with an understanding of their culture and the structure of their environment in order to communicate fully with disadvantaged seniors.

The unprecedented increase in life expectancy has resulted in a large number of older people in the population, many of whom are vulnerable to abuse. Inequality as a form of abuse occurs in many institutional sites: health, social services, law, media, work, family, recreation, etc. While past longitudinal studies of aging have provided some invaluable insights into the increased vulnerability of seniors, it is quickly apparent that more compelling multidisciplinary strategies are warranted that implicate critical analyses. New research frontiers will provide measures of ageist, ableist, heterosexist, misogynist, elitist and racist trends in populations, institutions and structures. This paper brings together issues that are seldom weaved coterminously in an effort to stimulate theoretical developments and insights into determinants of ageism. This discussion details themes that are pivotal in cross-sectional and longitudinal studies of aging. This action-based research is designed to prompt meaningful action in a number of social policy initiatives that link power, equity and commitment. The key to social reform work is the collaboration of various constituencies — seniors, family, education, human service agencies, community-based organizations. Complex problems call for a comprehensive inventory of strategies to overcome inequalities. It is, however, crucial to move beyond the myopic gaze of institutional convenience or bureaucratic benevolence towards an imagination that inspires more holistic analyses. Within this context it is imperative to consider seniors not as "junk" to be fossilized in warehouses euphemistically described as caregiving institutions. Sadly, there are discernible trends towards privatization (for profit) in social welfare. In the U.S., for example, caregiving and the corresponding wellness of seniors are contingent upon the mercantile impulses of corporate profit. Animated solely by the bottom line on the ledger sheet, health and social service agencies are cutting corner at the expense of those who have been silenced and disabled — seniors. In addition to the above ravages of ageism, our respondents articulated experiences of exclusion as a result of their race, ethnicity and gender. These integral members of our society continue to their race, ethnicity and gender. These integral members of our society continue to remain as separated categories. Complementarity in action on many different fronts will move towards the elimination of exclusionary practices concomitant with dependency.

Gendered orders and racialized or ethnicized differences reinforce notions of the patronized, pathetic and pathologized other. In addition to the findings presented above, the following partial list of observations are also offered at the interpersonal (interactional), institutional (organizational) and structural (systemic) levels of analysis. At the interactional level, our interpretation of the data indicates that:

- Isolation shapes and is shaped by the nature of one's self-concept.
- Delayed reciprocity is differentially evaluated in modified families.
- Benefits are based on functional exchanges of resources. The negotiative ability of a senior declines as benefits are reduced.
- Intergenerational encounters are framed within imbalances that discredit seniors who are compelled to comply.
- The newly arrived (immigrant) seniors experience greatest fears of distance, isolation abandonment, instutionalization.

At the institutional level we note the following:

- Institutions shape the well-being of Canada's elderly.

- In terms of the family, immigrant non-English-speaking women expect greater support from relatives.
- Delayed reciprocity is more apparent with immigrant non-English-speaking women.
- English-speaking women who have become somewhat assimilated maintain a variety of contacts in the wider community even though they tend to feel more abandoned by their families. The more established English-speaking enjoy a greater degree of independence and understanding of community supports.
- Privileges are enjoyed by coupled, assimilated, noninstitutionalized and family-oriented healthy connections.

The following enclosed overview summarizes structural conditions that maintain inequality:

Techniques of Exclusion:[3]
Denial: The refusal to recognize the cultural an institutional bases of ageism.
Omission: The ageist, racist and misogynist dimensions of social interaction are ignored.
Decontextualization: The recognition of ageism in only distant or "other" contexts.
Colour-blind approach: Racial and ethnic minorities are treated as if they are the same as whites.
Dumping approach: The responsibility for antiracism rests with racial minorities.
Patronising approach: Whiteness and maleness are deemed superior but tolerant of others.
Avoidance: Opportunities for confronting exclusion are avoided (law, culture, economy).

Notes

1   My deepest gratitude is extended to all of the people who participated in this project.
2   Terms used in this paper reflect the choices of the respondents. The paper was edited and reviewed by the seniors on the project and respondents. This practice is consistent with our collective notions of "collaborative" research. Also this protocol enhanced the validity of the findings.
3   Techniques of exclusion is based on categories adapted by L. Dominelli in *Anti-Racist Social Work*, London: The Macmillan Press Ltd, 1997.

References

Abu-Laban, S. and Abu-Laban, B. (1977). Women and aged as minority groups: A critique. *Canadian Review of Sociology and Anthropology* 14(1): 103–116.

Baer, J. (1991). *Women in American Law.* NY: Holmes and Meier, 1991.

Bengston, V.L. (1979). Ethnicity and aging: Problems and issues in current social science inquiry. In D.E. Gelfand and A.J. Kutzik (eds.), *Ethnicity and Aging: Theory, Research and Policy.* New York: Springer.

Chappell, N.L. and Havens, B. (1980). Old and female: Testing the double jeopardy hypothesis. *The Sociological Quarterly* 21 (spring): 157–171.

Chisholm, P. (1993). The fear index. *Maclean's* (January 4): 24–25.

Denzin, N. (1978). *Sociological Methods: A Sourcebook*: New York: McGraw-Hill.

Doyle, R. and Visano, L. (1987). Access to health and social services for members of diverse cultural and racial groups in metropolitan Toronto. Report I *A Time for Action* and Report II *A Programme for Action.* Toronto: Social Planning Council.

Duclos, N. (1993). Disappearing women: Racial minority women in human rights cases. *Canadian Journal of Women and the Law* 6: 25–51.

Foucault. M. (1977). *Discipline and Power* N.Y.: Pantheon.

Havens, B. and Chappell, N. (1983). Triple jeopardy: age, sex and ethnic variations. *Canadian Ethnic Studies* 15(3).

Kahn, A. (1973). *Social Policy and Social Services* New York: Random House.

Moore, M. and Trojanowicz, R. (1988). Policing and the fear of crime. *Perspectives on Policing* 3 (June).

Neugebauer, R. (1989). Divorce, custody and visitation: The child's point of view. *Journal of Divorce* 12(2/3): 153–170.

Neugebauer-Visano, R. (1995). Seniors and sexuality? Confronting cultural contradictions. In R. Neugebauer-Visano (ed.) *Seniors and Sexuality: Experiencing Intimacy in Later Life.* Toronto: Canadian Scholars' Press.

Penning, M.J. (1983) Multiple Jeopardy: Age, sex, and ethnic variations. *Canadian Ethnic Studies* 15(3).

Weber, M. [1947]. (1069). *The Theory of Social and Economic Organization* Translated and edited by A.M. Henderson and T. Parsons. New York: Free Press.

Newspaper and Magazines

Maclean's, 7/01/1991:31

Toronto Star, 28/11/1992:A1

Toronto Star, 19/11/1993:A29

Section Four

PROMOTING SOCIAL CHANGE

Chapter Thirteen

Creating Understanding from Research: Staff Nurses' Views on Collegiality

Merle Jacobs

Much has been written about gender and power. Usually this discussion has focused on men's dominance of women in the workplace. Nursing, a female-dominated profession, should be very different from male-dominated workplaces in terms of how behaviour is constructed and how interaction occurs. After all, women have struggled for the right to vote and the right for equal pay for equal work and would therefore understand the importance of equality and rights within a profession. When dealing with changes within the profession, a consensus-building model rather than a hierarchical one should be highly valued by female leaders. However, nursing is not an egalitarian profession but a hierarchical one with layers and levels of professional governance.

Research can provide a platform for presenting the views of those who are usually marginalized because of their rank in the hierarchy. Often elites within the nursing profession have objectives and strategies to improve "nursing work life" and "patient safety." Staff nurses are usually not in a position of creating nursing theories or constructing concepts because this activity is done by nursing educators, nursing researchers, and nursing management types within the profession. Perhaps, as the researcher in this work, I am part of the elite. However, I still work as a staff nurse, so I remain very much a part of this group. In this chapter, I will attempt to address how concept construction is accomplished when staff nurses express themselves.

The concept of collegiality is used within many professions to describe positive behaviours. The more frequently the concept is used within professional discourse, the more it is taken into account and described as a professional characteristic. Often nurses who discuss conditions of nurses' work are in positions of power, so that such a concept as collegiality is constructed from the top down. At times, those constructing the concept do not pay attention to the experiences of front-line participants and start to look for behaviours that will enhance interactions among members in order to promote another characteristic, the concept of professionalism. When theorizing about nursing work, the aim is to move the profession in a new direction rather than bring about changes by trying to understand the role and needs of staff nurses. Of central concern to this discussion is the link between the theoretical constructs of nursing collegiality that are prescribed by nurse leaders, and the everyday behaviours that the staff nurse encounters. Professional organizations or associations have a codified formal culture and individuals therein must follow a code of interaction. Sanctions take place when deviations from the code occur. Staff nurses traditionally do not have the time or the energy to challenge the assumptions made, or reflect on how these concepts came to be accepted by the profession. These concepts, such as collegiality, are used as tools by those in positions of power to manage those within their sphere of control.

Staff nurses, although they constitute the majority in the nursing profession, are similar to those in the lower classes of society. They lack voice in the construction of professional standards. Kirby and McKenna (1989) found that research from the margins is about research subjects taking control of the information that is presented to the researcher, who then presents it on behalf of those who are at the margins.

I focused my research on staff nurses and their interactions with each other. Before starting this research, I knew a lot about the topic experientially. I had many staff nurses as friends, and had my own experiences as a staff nurse as well. During this research, my position was that of a nurse manager. In order to be part of the staff nurse group, I spent time with staff nurses who worked in different hospitals and spoke with them about topics related to work and the health care industry. At these times their friends, who were also staff nurses, would drop in and join the discussion. To research the relations between staff nurses, it is essential to present the experiences of the individuals in their natural environment. The research subjects' subjective interpretations create meaning for the observations of the researcher. When sharing the idea of collegiality with several staff nurses and discussing with them issues regarding interaction, it became clear that there were insights to be gained by looking at collegiality from their perspective.

Other concepts used within the nursing profession are such action words as "team building," "communication," and "caring." Many of these notions have relevance as they are behaviours required by those discussing the constructs as to what is expected from others within the profession. Many concept builders approach these terms from their own reality. While they may seem objective, these concepts cannot be understood in isolation or be viewed as neutral. My understanding regarding the construction of meaning is that the concept must not only be understood by the majority as relevant, but must also be accepted by the majority within the profession. Otherwise, most of these concepts will be irrelevant to the mainstream within the profession in their day-to-day interactions and will be dismissed as only elite theorizing. In order to discuss the construction of the concept of collegiality, it is important to review some previous deliberations regarding this term, especially within the profession of nursing.

Collegiality is not only about getting along with others, but includes such themes as job stress, nursing roles, autonomy, professionalism, and education, which will be discussed later.

Collegiality Reviewed

Studies (Beyer and Marshall, 1981; Evans, 1978; Gagnon, 1991; Levine, 1974; McMahon, 1990; Nolan, 1976; and Styles, 1982) have focused on collegiality in nursing as an important behaviour for nurses. These writers discuss collegiality as desirable behaviours that nurses should use as a standard in their interactions. Class, gender, and race are not part of the discussion within this discourse. Collegial relations, when considered by Styles (1982), includes components such as culture, decision-making, structure, and a system of behaviour that she regards as the required characteristics of collegial relations of everyday nursing behaviour. Briefly, collegiality within nursing is a construct that refers to behaviours that foster rules for how nurses treat one another and how nurses should behave.

Most of the research is descriptive rather than stemming from studies based on circumstances and communication patterns (Mackay, 1989; Ross, 1961). "Wanted: Colleagueship in Nursing" by Nolan (1976) presents colleagueship as a common intellectual interest and suggests that "nurses approach each other as peers." Beyer and Marshall (1981) describe collegiality as interpersonal dimensions within peer relations. Their eight components, which include behaviours such as confidence and trust, mutual support, and friendliness, are much like Styles (1982), who provides a wish list of behaviours rather than discussing collegiality in nursing. Hardy (1996) argues that institutional collegiality is an important mechanism in managing competing pressures.

The need for collegial relations in nursing has been identified by several writers, such as Nolan (1976), Levine (1974), and Evans (1978). Most of the writers focused on characteristics of collaborative collegial relations and used these characteristics to examine what collegial relations should be. For these researchers, collaborative behaviours promote collegial relations. In order to develop collegial relationships, it is necessary, in nursing research, to focus on collaboration (Fitzpatrick et al., 1990). Deutsch (1969) comments on the tenuous link between what people say they do and their actual behaviour, in an attempt to overcome some problems associated with the discrepancy between words and deeds. McMahon (1990), in his study of collegiality, recorded impressions of both the investigator and the subjects of the research.

According to Gagnon (1991), colleagues and collegiality is about learning from each other, sharing issues of the nurse's experience, sharing educational resources, and strengthening relationships. She sees building on the shared experiences of colleagues as the way to begin. However, Roth (1995) compares collegiality in nursing to an all-pro football game, as status and role conflicts involve tensions generated by structural controls within the institution. The specialties of nursing practice are analogous to the individual football teams. To successfully resolve these problems, Roth wrote, nursing must clear up individuals' differences and foster unity. The responsibility for creating an environment (Nolan, 1976:43) that promotes collegial relationships lies with nurses in management. This type of argument again looks at collegiality from the top down.

A major contributor to the understanding of collegiality is Bess (1988), who studied collegial behaviour in universities and provided a model for understanding collegial behaviours. He dealt with three components: culture, structure, and the process of behaving. He describes them as follows:

> Three distinct components, two of which are relatively static, the other dynamic ... This first is culture (or normative framework); ... the second, decision-making structure; ... and the third the process of behaving, which is constrained by the first two." (Bess, 1988:92–97)

For Bess, culture, structure, and behaviour are the major components of collegiality, which can be viewed as a dynamic definition of the self, the reflection process, and the reference group interacting in a world that is interactively defined. By linking the understanding of "micro" social actions with a "macro" understanding of organizations, we can account for social life without neglecting the structural settings in which these actions occur. Rather than describing what should be collegial behaviours and constructing collegiality, Bess provides a framework that allows us to construct collegiality. Perhaps it is by using Bess's work that we can develop the concept of collegiality within nursing from the viewpoint of the majority, the front-line nurses.

The social meaning of collegiality, when constructed through everyday interactions using the components that Bess provided, could explain behaviours experienced in encounters. In order to construct a concept of collegiality in nursing that has meaning for the majority of those working in the profession, it is necessary to understand what would constitute important behaviours for them as reported from their perspective. In nursing, it means that unit nurses' interactions with each other become important reflections. Staff nurses also assess each other's actions and label the interactions as collegial or conflictual: supportive or non-supportive. This is an alternative way to construct collegiality.

Taunton and Otteman (1986) demonstrate that staff nurses' concept of their role is based on the expectation they have for their own behaviour and the behaviour of other staff nurses in providing services to clients. Like role expectations, staff nurse collegiality comes from several different levels. This is another understanding of role behaviour within a profession. To deal with this concept from the perspective of those who experience collegial behaviours, I will present staff nurse collegiality as they discuss it.

Constructing Staff Nurse Collegiality

Within a hospital, staff from other professions interact with nurses. In the past when observing the behaviour of nurses (Bingham, 1979), it was clear that they were instructed to obey doctors and be willing and ready helpers. This is an example of how those in power constructed how others should behave in a way that was submissive to those in authority. This type of construction is similar to how current constructs of professionalism and collegiality are defined within the profession of nursing. The question we need to ask is whether nurse leaders have replaced physicians as the ones in power who determine how staff nurses should behave.

Behaviours important to front-line nurses as they manage relationships with each other are important in the construction of the concept of collegiality in nursing. Therefore, we must use their experience as the foundation for the concept of collegiality rather than teach them what is expected of them. If we find non-supportive behaviours, it is important to look at the root causes of these behaviours rather than just the behaviours themselves. The root causes can lead us to examine nursing workloads, overtime hours worked, management interventions, and the structures of the health care system, as well as the culture of the nursing profession.

Most nurses work in hospitals within individual units. The patient care unit can be seen as several dyads (pairs) of staff nurses who together form one level of interaction within the hospital. They work together as a team and with other health care professionals. All these patient care units, along with other departments, make up the hospital. From the perspective of the dyad, we can view collegiality as it works its way outwards and what it means for staff nurses' supportive or non-supportive behaviours. This would be a bottom-up rather than a top-down construct of collegiality.

Figure 1: Nursing Collegiality and the Staff Nurse

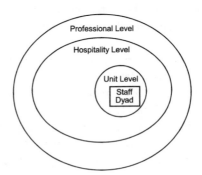

Rather than defining collegiality for staff nurses at the professional association level, which is the usual method, the context for the staff nurses' collegiality will start with the dyad. With an understanding of their own role at the unit level and their relationship to the nursing profession, staff nurses use codes of behaviour and reactions to review peer behaviour at work. It is my contention that those within this group can relate and create what they view as collegial behaviours, thereby creating a culture of collegiality and concepts regarding collegiality.

The diagram in Figure 1 depicts the four levels where staff nurses can experience collegial behaviour. At all these levels, staff nurses who are registered nurses (RN) interact both with each other and with nurses who are registered practical nurses (RPN). Rules of conduct for RNs originate from the outside circles and are directed toward the unit and the dyad. However, rules of conduct at the unit level directly involve those individuals at this level. Unit rules of conduct rarely become the nursing professional association's rules of conduct. In the following sections, I will put together a concept of collegiality from the data provided by staff nurses in surveys and focus groups.

Collegiality Between Staff Nurses

Understanding collegial behaviour among staff nurses starts at the individual staff nurse's face-to-face interaction with a peer when they are in contact with each other for various reasons. Some of the contact is over tasks, while other interactions have to do with social relationships. Within task-related interaction, collegiality can be prescribed through rules of conduct, while in social relationships, collegiality is recognized through positive communicated meanings that the individual reflects and interprets. The latter is far more subjective and includes what the nurses know of each other through past experiences.

An examination of collegiality as a process starts from the first level, that of the individual staff nurses and the behaviours that are important to them. Helping behaviours are regarded as desirable among staff nurses in this research. The norm of helping is part of the socialization process when students work together on patient care projects and in clinical areas. In their interactions during this period, nurses are socialized into understanding this behaviour. They realize that the rules for nursing interaction require them to work together as a team and provide good patient care. This rule of interaction leads to prescribed behaviours pertaining to patient care tasks.

At the dyad level, collegiality is conducted in an informal manner. Observations of staff nurses show that they turn to each other in time of need and work stress. For example, if a patient's family member insists on staying past visiting hours, a nurse can request a peer for backup to remind the family that visiting hours are over. Making a cup of coffee or tea for a co-worker who has not gone on a break, for example, also shows concern and acknowledgement of the other's situation.

Interactions also promote social relationships that provide friendships in and out of the unit. Friendships can help foster collegial behaviour and provide support, which may not be there for those staff nurses who do not get along with each other. It seems then that friendship plays a role in collegial behaviour, but not when it comes to patient emergencies. In patient emergencies, nurses help each other and provide support regardless of personality conflicts in order to give the patient good nursing care. Collegial behaviour at this level is demonstrated when nurses:

- help one another with heavy workloads when their own work is done
- help out each other when the patient needs two nurses in an area of care
- facilitate each other's understanding of signs and symptoms of illness, and provide information on how to deal with patient problems
- assist in patient care emergencies that occur in the unit
- give each other feedback, share information about the work environment, and support each other when problems arise with physicians
- respect another's view or ideas even when there is disagreement

These were examples of supportive behaviours that staff nurses said they performed or did not receive from a peer. For example, one nurse said that "she did not help me turn Mr. X." Staff nurses look to each other, ask for assistance when they cannot turn over a heavy patient, and view this behaviour as supportive. This is very important for them because of the risk of back injuries. Therefore, assisting a peer in patient care is viewed as collegial behaviour. Staff nurses also spoke of behaviours when peers provided information, guidance, assistance, and support from other staff nurses who helped them provide good patient care and avoid making errors. When an emergency occurs, a nurse needs a peer to assist in providing the required patient care. In a dyad, the other nurse is important in summoning others to the scene if there is an emergency.

Helping is a lot more than just "doing something" as it also implies the ability to judge a peer's workload, to provide backup, and to assist a co-worker with treatments or care needed by patients. For example, when a nurse sitting at the desk does not answer the call of another nurse's patient while the other nurse is busy with treatments, the former is seen as not helping a peer who was not available, nor was she helping a patient who needed care. Help in answering a call bell is regarded as both professional and collegial behaviour. A collegial staff nurse would help a peer answer a call bell regardless of whether the patient was one of his or hers. Nurses who help each other in this type of need are regarded as "good" nurses and colleagues. A staff nurse in Survey #41 stated that:

> Some of us work well together, always assisting each other with bathing, turning, lifting, repositioning our patients. Other nurses you can never find to assist you when you need help. Some of us enjoy going out together, meeting on social occasions, [going] out to dinner or a ball game; we even hold baby and bridal showers and going-away parties here in the unit.

Turning a patient is one of the most common needs that nurses have and therefore it comes up repeatedly when staff nurses describe helping behaviours. It is also expected behaviour, as #41 made clear in her response. There was anger expressed toward those nurses who avoided meeting this need. The only exceptions were nurses who had already injured their backs. For many nurses, assisting each other led to outside social activities where collegiality existed.

At the dyad level, collegiality is based on exchange. Staff nurses who help others with patient care and support are also the ones who are most often helped in return. Those nurses who do not help colleagues are not given assistance by their peers. Staff nurses keep scorecards regarding those who help and those who do not help. I have observed this behaviour and have been informed by staff nurses that they remember who helps and who avoids helping them. Staff nurses will use embarrassment to force others into helping by pointing out to the individual that help is needed.

The consequence for not being helpful is becoming the target of gossip and blaming. Staff nurses in a unit talk to each other about a co-worker's non-supportive behaviours, and the word "lazy" is at times used to describe nurses who fail to help their peers. Staff nurses who are regarded as "ideal nurses" by their peers are willing to assist, provide feedback, and be there for them. The term "lazy" is applied to a nurse who does not attend her or his patients; or who avoids another nurse's patients; or who likes to sit at the desk and read charts or newspapers, or talk on the phone to friends and family while others are busy working. The term "lazy" as described by staff nurses has not been part of the literature on collegiality.

Appearing busy is another way to avoid helping a co-worker. In order not to help a peer, the staff nurse who has finished her or his work must be seen to be doing something other than just sitting around. Sitting around is not acceptable behaviour when others are busy or overworked. Asking for help constantly can also be viewed as not being helpful. When done frequently and when other staff nurses are "run off their feet," this is viewed as non-supportive and non-collegial behaviour. Workload is part of the problem and has less to do with staff nurses and more to do with management behaviours. However, this influences how nurses interact and view each other as colleagues.

Helping behaviour has rules and nuances. It includes historical information that one staff nurse must know about the other staff nurse within the dyad of interaction, or within several dyads of interaction. As interactions occur over time, this knowledge expands. Nurses usually expect a peer to help them, such as in emergencies and when they ask for help in patient care. In general, the knowledge about who helps and who does not comes from first-hand information, as well as through second-hand gossip.

The exchange of clinical ideas and the support that nurses give each other are part of collegial behaviour as described by Styles (1982). At the staff nurse level, the exchange of clinical ideas is based on providing verbal information to a peer in relation to active patient care. Staff nurses with more experience share knowledge about signs and symptoms regarding patient care with other nurses. They also consult each other about providing care for patients and when other difficulties arise. This is another way of helping as well as exchanging ideas and interacting directly.

Respect is another component of collegiality at the individual level. Signs of respect are the tone of voice used when communicating and allowing others to express ideas. Nurses who feel that another staff nurse is not using the right tone or words will label that nurse as "rude." For example, staff nurse Survey #57 described the following:

> Nurses treat each other on a daily basis with respect in their job setting even though there are some who have dinosaur brains, who think of the old days of nursing. There are new ideas, new techniques as well as new blood who can be great assets to them. Nurses can be professional at their job even though there may be a personal disagreement between them.

In an interview, E.D. (1997), a staff nurse, informed me that the "dinosaurs" were the problem. Those who cling to old ways of doing things seemed to this nurse to not understand what younger nursing staff want in the unit. Calling a colleague a "dinosaur" within earshot of the other nurse would have been viewed as rude and non-supportive. I found that the lack of discussion about what behaviours and attitudes mean at this level leads to a lack of respect for others' views. Collegiality at this level would be listening to each other and taking in new ideas while providing mentoring. Both new graduates and experienced nurses have much to offer each other. Name-calling hinders this.

For the staff nurse, respect for a peer's work in caring for patients is another component of collegiality. "In most cases, nurses respect a peer during work regarding assessments, interventions, rationale, etc." (Survey #52). It is this respect that brings nurses together as colleagues when they report on patients' conditions to the oncoming nurses. Nurses need to know that the information they are receiving is accurate and that they can continue the care required by the patient. The ritual of reporting is an opportunity for collegiality to occur. Within this ritual, there is respect for the individual providing the information. While a staff nurse is giving a report, the one receiving the report listens or asks questions pertaining to the patient's condition. Non-supportive behaviours would be not listening, reading a newspaper while the other nurse is giving the report, or telling the information-giver that she or he was taking too long with the report. This kind of behaviour would be regarded as disrespectful and non-collegial. Respect in formal actions such as giving a report is maintained even when there are personality disagreements, as there are rules and rituals in the action of giving and receiving reports about patient care. This is different from spontaneous interactions, which may result in conflict that can prompt one nurse to call another "dinosaur brain," behaviour that is seen as disrespectful. In hospital units where shift reports have been discontinued, staff nurses feel that continuity of care is no longer provided through verbal communication and collegiality decreases.

In addition to respect, thoughtfulness is also valued by staff nurses. Staff are not thoughtful when they are late for a shift, call in sick "to get a day off when they are not really sick" when the unit is short of nurses, or when they are late in returning from lunch. This means that someone has to take care of Nurse X's patients, thus causing workload stress. These behaviours are viewed as thoughtless and not respectful of a peer's time.

The obligation of meeting the work needs of a colleague is related to respecting or caring about another's need. A staff nurse's acknowledgement of a peer's need to eat lunch and returning in time so that the colleague can go to lunch shows thoughtfulness. I use the term "obligational thoughtfulness" when it is related to work issues. On the other hand, attending colleagues' baby showers, for example, relates more to "personal thoughtfulness." The nurses I met during this research felt that thoughtful peers were the ones they could trust. They valued thoughtful behaviour as part of what defines an ideal nurse. Having a peer help them with work when they were busy, listen to their reports, give them feedback, and come to their aid when their patient became very ill were viewed as "good nurse" behaviours.

Under certain circumstances, collegial behaviour among staff nurses in their face-to-face interactions incorporates helpfulness, respect, and obligational thoughtfulness. Whatever the interaction, these nurses have to deal with one another directly over a sustained period. In order to achieve dyad collegiality, an egalitarian system of communication and decision-making at the unit level is important. Behaviours mentioned in this section are important to the staff nurse at the level of the dyad because it is centred around the patient, the needs of the staff nurse, and the work a nurse performs daily. Helping behaviour also encourages the collective feeling of nurses working well together and a sense of collegiality in the unit environment.

Collegiality at the Unit Level

Above the dyad level is the unit level. Staff nurses work as a team twenty-four hours a day to provide patient care. Interactions at the unit level engage more than two individuals. In a nursing unit, staff nurses have different roles to perform. For example, there are charge nurses on each shift, case managers, or team leaders. Some units are staffed with all registered nurses, while others have licensed practical nurses and health care aides. The unit manager also plays a part in the interaction and the culture of the unit. The manager's style of management can affect the culture of the unit. In most acute care units the staff nurses are in the majority, so they are responsible for the culture of the unit. However, it is important to consider the difference in power relationships that exist between staff members and the manager. Behavioural arrangements are more complex at the unit level, and the culture of one unit can be different from another unit within the same hospital. Respondents for this research provided collegiality components for this level. Staff nurses spoke about "encouragement," "supporting each other in times of stress," "a decrease in complaints about each other," and "working together" as supportive behaviours. Survey participants #107 and #62 wrote these thoughts:

> Generally treat each other equally, but at times there is a definite barrier between "junior" and "senior" staff. Otherwise there are the usual personality conflicts that occur in any job. (107)

> Extra helping hands, someone to share ideas and impressions. Someone who is there for support. (62)

Collegial behaviour for staff nurses at the unit level would include:

- acts that have the value of equality; working together
- an absence of barriers or boundaries between staff nurses relating to work
- support for each other in times of stress
- direct communication patterns rather than indirect complaints or gossip about a peer; not gossiping about a co-worker
- a willingness to work together as a team to improve the quality of work and reduce errors
- relationships based on work and not on personalities, race, or ethnicity
- a willingness to speak out and provide support when agreeing with another nurse at a staff meeting

Staff meetings are an opportunity to observe staff nurse collegiality. Respondents complained that at these meetings many of their peers remain silent. They themselves do not participate because (1) they are not listened to, (2) they don't care, (3) they do what they want to do anyway, or (4) they are just doing their jobs. Unit rituals such as staff meetings promote or discourage staff nurses depending on the culture of the unit environment. A negative unit environment does not consistently allow for collegial behaviours or foster open discussions at staff meetings. In fact, a negative unit culture leads to gossip and blaming behaviours, thereby limiting collegial behaviours.

In a nursing unit, staff nurses look for actions that create an equal footing for all and not just for a few staff nurses. Self-scheduling, a system in which staff nurses choose the shifts they will work in a given six weeks, is based on equal sharing. Compromise is necessary for everyone to accommodate people's needs for days off so that nurses who need to go to courses or other appointments can do so. Included in compromise is the notion of sharing and perhaps concern for other staff nurses' needs.

Another behaviour at the unit level is ensuring that each member of the group has a coffee break and a lunch break. These activities are recognized as important to reducing stress in a busy day. There would have to be collegial behaviour to facilitate this type of arrangement at the unit level as management is not involved in the outcome and leave it to the staff nurse group in the unit to work out for themselves. A respondent in an interview and one from the survey said the following:

> I had to have lunch, but the staff who went early took all the time. At 13:00 hours I had to meet with my patient. They just have a long lunch and those of us on second lunch have to take less time. I find my co-workers lack concern. ... (S.G., staff nurse, 1997)

> On my unit, which is surgical, our team works together. We have a very high trust and respect for the knowledge and resources each staff member has. Communication is also very good. (Survey #53)

When communication is good and teams work together, lunch and break times are not usually issues. Most often, breaks are arranged at the beginning of the shift. However, when there is a lack of concern about the needs of colleagues, break times become an issue and a source of tension. One of the resources a staff nurse has to share with team members is time. As discussed earlier in terms of scheduled days, "tension seems to build up when nurses have differences over petty things like time shifts" (Survey #45) or during lunch breaks when staff do not return in time to allow a peer to go for lunch. Depending on how these issues are discussed and handled on a unit, the culture is shaped by the behaviour of the majority. We can state that there is disparity between policy and control over the specifics of implementation. These issues can be discussed at unit meetings with staff nurses participating in unit organization to promote collegial behaviours.

Rules for conduct at the unit level for group work life depends on the staff nurse group. The nursing unit can be viewed as the reference group for the individual. If the nurses in the unit enforce certain rules, such as conduct with regard to time, they create a certain culture in the unit. If another nursing unit does not view these rules as important, it will differ from the unit that does and may not enforce the same rules. Staff nurses also describe an "in group" and "out group" as two types of groups within a unit. Members of the "in group" have power, have the ear of the manager, are sent to conferences, can get time off for classes without difficulty, and receive other perks from management. Members of the "out group," on the other hand, have to struggle to get these same privileges and have described feelings and occurrences of being disenfranchised. They saw those in the "in group" doing favours for each other but not for those outside the group, doing things together outside of work hours, and excluding staff who are not in their group both at a social level and within working life. Members of the "in group" were closer to the manager or to certain physicians. The "in group" had power in the unit while the "out group" saw themselves as having less of everything.

Visible minority nurses said they felt marginalized and were not part of the "inner circle" or the "in group." Even when there are many visible minority staff nurses, nursing units can be divided into what nurses perceive as in and "out" groups. Staff nurses are creators of their environment at the unit level. Unless the "in group" and the "out group" culture is discussed openly as an issue of power, this culture will create non-supportive behaviours. Visible minority staff nurses insist that the rules of the game should be fair and that they not be systematically disadvantaged. The impact of racism affects collegial behaviour at the unit level. Minority nurses would like to look at how race and ethnicity influence how interactions occur. They challenge the system of power that subordinates their world view to that of the dominant view and white privilege in order to have equity and thus collegiality.

Visible minority nurses also voiced concerns that white nurses did not experience the racial abuse they receive from patients, visitors, and even from other staff members. In fact, these issues are not discussed openly in staff meetings. As described by C.G.:

> A patient slapped me in my face, another elbowed me in my ribs. I have been called a nigger, stupid, told to go back to where I come from. One patient told me that he would like to kiss my black lips and even a physician had his hand on my breast. (Medical Unit, 1994)

When asked what her co-workers did, C.G. stated that they would "think it funny" or say it "was not fair" or "tell me to report it." However, the incident was not brought up at staff meetings, nor was an incident report filed even under the Occupation Health and Safety Act. Racial harassment is not uncommon in units and minority nurses said that they do not have either the energy or the time to confront this problem. Minority nurses expressed a feeling of not being heard, and some were targeted by those in power if they spoke out. Although racism was not openly discussed, minority nurses, when talking with other minorities, do talk about being left out of the "old girls" network and held back from higher positions within the nursing profession. They discussed problems about being excessively monitored and marginalized by those in power. Minority nurses also discussed how they are pulled aside by managers and spoken to more often than their white counterparts, even when they had more experience and education than white staff nurses. Another problem these nurses described was a manager taking exception with the "way we speak." Patients understood the nurse, but the manager was derogatory about the nurse's accent. Nurses in focus groups tried to minimize the importance of racial slurs while other nurses pointed out that any type of abuse was not dealt with by those in administration. Perhaps a demonstration of collegiality in this area would be white counterparts speaking up on behalf of visible minorities and making sure that management deals with the offence rather than sweeping it under the rug. This would let visible minority nurses know that there is support for them when they report incidents of this type.

Knowledge and experience are positive resources among unit nurses. Junior nurses benefit from the experience of senior staff nurses through mentoring. This sharing of expertise and experience is viewed as collegial behaviour. Senior nurses also provide newcomers with the history of the unit and the hospital. This sharing of information allows for interaction to occur and helps newcomers to the unit understand the culture of the organization. Staff nurses also function together in times of stress, such as when a cardiac code occurs in a unit, and nurses work together as a team to provide care in such circumstances. This is a tense situation and each staff nurse must support the others for the survival of the patient. Supporting each other and playing a role within the team is considered collegial and professional.

Staff nurses felt supported by a peer when problems with physicians arise. This behaviour is seen as collegial and nurses feel secure when, for example, "a physician becomes verbally abusive," knowing that support is available. Staff nurses also want support from each other when they disagree with management. As E.S. (1997) reported, "they [management] wanted us to write out our reports, tape them and chart as well. We all decided not to do this as it was a waste of time." Solidarity at the unit level against those who have more power is viewed as supportive behaviour. Those staff nurses who support management or befriend senior management are viewed as "spies" or those who "can't be trusted." Gossip and complaints in a unit culture decrease unit collegiality. "Spying" is reported by staff nurses when peers go over their work to find errors, in order to report them to the manager or make them look imperfect. Among many staff nurses, there is an "us" versus "them" mentality when it comes to management. Collegial behaviours include awareness of being a member of the staff nurse group and the needs of this group versus the needs of those in power.

Staff nurses report that managers of each unit also help set the tone in influencing how staff nurses relate to each other, although they do not have complete control over the nurses' behaviour. When a manager favours certain members of the group over others, those left out join a subgroup within the unit. In many units, staff nurses discussed having an "in group," which I mentioned earlier. Conflict arises when there is a perception of inequality, thus creating non-supportive behaviours. When one staff is pitted against another for resources within the manager's control, it creates a unit culture that lacks collegiality. Staff nurses state they want to work with each other and dislike personality conflicts. Some staff nurses informed me that they find it difficult to deal with negative personalities, and report that collegial behaviour includes working together with those "you don't get along with." Many of the nurses interviewed stated that working together was important for good patient care.

Although nurses do not praise each other frequently, they do view complaints as negative behaviour. According to staff nurses, complaints and gossip at the unit level indicate an absence of collegial behaviour and a negative work culture. In a unit where the group uses direct communication, staff nurses deal directly with each other and refrain from going to a third party with their complaints. Collegial behaviour occurs when there is limited distance between experienced nurses and their juniors when working together. This is a product of a collegial dyad. Collegial culture is also possible when relations are not based on gender, race, ethnicity, or class. Awareness that barriers occur on the lines of gender, race, ethnicity, and class comes about not just from diversity conferences and hospital policies but also from constant consideration of policies, problems, and conflicts through these different lenses. Trust must become a component of communications and interactions in the unit, in order for change to occur and for collegial behaviours to be encouraged.

Collegiality at the Hospital Level

When we look from the unit level outwards in Figure 1, we note that the hospital, as well as the profession, has a part in collegiality. The "top-down" version of collegiality is based on formal rules of conduct. There are policies regarding racism and harassment for dealing with employees' unacceptable conduct. According to a nurse administrator, honesty and integrity are the cornerstones of the health profession. These behaviours are viewed as positive changes that institutions have made as policy, but not always adhered to in practice. Collegial behaviour at the hospital level would include the participation of staff nurses on committees. Collegiality at the hospital level would involve:

- staff nurses working at the committee level for the benefit of peers
- staff nurses providing a communication network to inform each other of what is going on in their hospital and within the health care system
- staff nurses from one unit informing staff nurses on other units of what is happening in order to facilitate support and political action
- staff nurses working with their union to promote solidarity for staff nurses within the organization
- staff nurses providing the community with information of their role within the hospital

At the hospital level, there is a shift from interaction among a small number of staff nurses within a specific unit to the large group of staff nurses working within a hospital. Although hospitals are bureaucratic, being heard means being able to participate in the creation of rules. Those nurses involved in committee work provide a voice for their colleagues. This behaviour is collegial, as staff nurses are working on behalf of their peers. The more staff nurses are taken seriously on committees, the more they influence what happens at their level. Many staff nurses lack motivation to participate at this level because of the lack of a relationship and trust with those in administration or because they fear retaliation. They view this activity as part of upward mobility and consider it a waste of time if they do not want to be in management. Staff nurse collegiality could include looking at work factors that contribute to staff nurses' stress and the challenges they face. Issues regarding power and helplessness due to their attitudes toward their jobs could be one topic of discussion. The construction of collegiality becomes dependent on the constructs of other actions in the health care system and in the hospital itself. Staff nurses must be aware of what the union can do and instruct the union leaders to speak on their behalf. If nurses are not satisfied with the union, collegiality would include changing the direction of the union by electing leaders who speak for them and struggle for their needs. At the hospital level, many staff nurses lose interest in change. They believe the union and the administration do not have their best interests in mind.

Collegial behaviour includes bringing back to the unit news of what is occurring elsewhere in the hospital and encouraging peers to support those who are going to committee meetings on their behalf. When those who attend meetings know that they have the backing of their colleagues, they can speak on their behalf. Perhaps collegial behaviours include strategy, planning, and coordinating rather than just reacting to what occurs.

Collegiality at the Professional Level

The professional level comprises staff nurses from every hospital in Ontario who belong to either their union or their professional association. Unlike the hospital level (which is dominated by administrators and physicians), this level is dominated by nurses. Although the professional level was not a major topic of discussion among the staff nurses who provided me with qualitative data (as many did not belong to their professional association), I want to consider how staff nurses can come together at this level to provide the respect and input they seek to have in their profession. These associations must ask themselves why staff nurses view them as irrelevant. Their lack of participation should be a concern. Although staff nurses pay dues, their lack of involvement and dissatisfaction at the union level tells me that the union lacks credibility among the staff nurse group. The failure to address the absence of collegial behaviour at the professional level would leave decision-making to the nurse leaders who currently speak for staff nurses. By reviewing some of the comments made in other areas, I conclude that collegiality at the professional level for staff nurses would lead to the following:

- Staff nurses will seek positions to promote the ideas and needs of the staff nurse. They will speak for staff nurses within the profession by participating in their college, their union, and in their professional association.
- Staff nurses, as the largest group of nurses, could provide a strong voice on issues concerning nursing within the organizations.
- Staff nurses will challenge nursing leadership in ideas that affect the staff nurse's position and job description. This means sharing ideas with each other and coming to an agreement as to what they value in the profession.
- Staff nurses will be involved in the union and work with each other to provide a safe work environment that promotes respect, support, and a caring atmosphere.
- Those who are involved will keep their peers informed of the actions through a network for staff nurses.

Because the professional level is distant from both the unit level and the dyad level, participation is low. However, like the dyad and unit levels, staff nurses can control the agenda if they take action within these organizations rather than avoiding participation. Currently, political action is led by a few nurses from the ranks of leadership. The voices of staff nurses tend not to be heard unless their issues are raised by the union, which may not always be aware of their concerns because of their membership's lack of involvement, even within their locals.

Like the professional association, the union is what the staff nurses make of it. I would not like to give the impression that there is no staff nurse interaction and participation at this level. However, there is a big difference between the participation of staff nurses and the participation of nursing leaders in the professional association. For collegiality to be realized at this level, staff nurses must get out of their circle and participate at the structural level of the profession. Supporting their peers who speak for them becomes a valued behaviour and part of the construct of collegiality.

The Construction of Collegiality in Nursing

Collegiality at the level of the staff nurse has actions and interactions, as shown in Figure 1. It goes from simple interactions to complex actions, which require the time and energy of the individual. Staff nurses are engaged in behaviours to promote collegiality during working hours. The same occurs for unit collegiality. However, at the hospital and the professional levels, staff nurses must take time out of their lives to participate in these arenas.

From the dyad to the professional structural level, it is essential to develop a culture based on collegiality that deals with the issues of those involved. Social distance between staff nurses and the profession can be decreased. Political action is also necessary in order to empower the staff nurse group and enable them to voice their concerns from their perspective. For political action to occur, individual staff nurses must unite and strive for group improvements. Empowerment can occur when staff nurses take control of their organization, rather than avoid relating to those currently in power. Unless staff nurses take action to promote their own interests within the health care system, the bureaucratic organizational structure and its hierarchy will continue to put staff nurses in a subordinate position and make policies on their behalf.

Collegiality, as discussed in this paper, leads to action as well as flexibility. It promotes change, empowerment for the staff nurse, and an understanding of the relationships that currently exist within the profession. As the environment and the dyads change at the unit level, so will the construct of collegiality. Staff nurses do not have a voice in current changes within the health care system and within their own profession. This cuts across race, ethnicity, and class and is about the network of relationships that currently exists for the ruling class within the profession. It is not that the staff nurses or visible minority nurses do not know how to network, but it is that they are rarely allowed to participate within the network or welcomed as equal participants within the power structure. Those staff nurses chosen to participate within the network are those who are groomed for the inner circle within the nursing profession.

In this chapter the comments of staff nurses are used to construct their world view of collegiality. Empowerment can come only from action. This construction of collegiality is about actions that occur and actions that need to occur. Staff nurses (who are mostly women) must understand the struggle and be conscious of their position within the system, construct their vision of the nursing profession, and not leave it to the elites within the profession to determine. After all, staff nurses outnumber those in management and in the professional hierarchy. Until staff nurses realize they have power in numbers, the small yet powerful group of females in nursing will continue to construct and promote their view of the profession and collegiality.

References

Bess, J.L. 1988. *Collegiality and Bureauracy in Modern University*. New York: Teachers College Press.

Beyer, J.E., and J. Marshall. 1981. "The Interpersonal Dimension of Collegiality." *Nursing Outlook* 29 (11): 662–665.

Bingham, S. 1979. *Ministering Angels*. New Jersey: Medical Economics Co. Book Division.

Deutsch, M. 1969. "Conflicts: Productive and Destructive." *Journal of Social Issues* 41: 15–17.

Evans, M. 1978. "The Professional Aspects of Communication with Other Nurses." *The Australian Nurse Journal* 8 (3): 39–51.

Fitzpatrick, J.J., M.L. Wykle, and D.L. Morris. 1990. "Collaboration in Care and Research." *Archives of Psychiatric Nursing* IV (1): 53–61.

Gagnon, L. 1991. "Global Collegiality in Emergency Nursing." *Journal of Emergency Nursing* 17 (1): 3.

Hardy, C. 1996. *The Politics of Collegiality: Retrenchment Strategies in Canadian Universities*. Quebec: McGill-Queen's University Press.

Kirby, S., and K. McKenna. 1989. *Methods from the Margins*. Toronto: Garamond Press.

Levine, M.E. 1974. "Profile" (about Levine). *Nursing* 4 (5): 70.

Mackay, L. 1989. *Nursing a Problem*. Stratford: Open University Press.

McMahon, R. 1990. "Power and Collegial Relations Among Nurses on Wards Adopting Primary Nursing and Hierarchical Ward Management Structures." *Journal of Advanced Nursing* 15: 232–239.

Nolan, M.G. 1976. "Wanted: Colleagueship in Nursing." *Journal of Nursing Administration* 6 (3): 41–43.

Ross, A.D. 1961. *Becoming a Nurse*. Toronto: The Macmillan Co. of Canada.

Roth, R. 1995. "Collegiality in Nursing and All-Pro Football Games." *AORN Journal* 41 (2): 326–328.

Styles, M. 1982. *On Nursing*. St. Louis: The Mobsy Co.

Taunton, R., and D. Otteman. 1986. "The Multiple Dimensions of Staff Nurse Role Conceptions." *Journal of Nursing Administration* 16 (10): 31–37.

Chapter Fourteen

Antiracism Advocacy in the Climate of Corporatization[1]

Rebecca Hagey
Jane Turrittin
Evelyn Brody

"Of all the forms of inequality, injustice in health is the most shocking
and inhumane."

Dr. Martin Luther King

Introduction

While racism is believed to be a negative determinant for achieving health,
there is very little discussion on racism in the health promotion literature,
even where determinants of health are the focus. For example, a recent
four-volume review of Canada's health system, which builds on the
determinants of health, does not deal with racism (NFH, 1997). This may
reflect a denial of the problem of racism in medicine (Essed, 1991) and
nursing (Das Gupta, 1996) as well as a paucity of research on the problem
in the social and behavioural sciences in Canada as compared to other
countries, notably the United States and Britain (Day, 1987).

We will briefly review policy critiques of health promotion policies from
the Thatcherite period in Britain. These point to the two-facedness of the
health promotion movement as it embraces corporatism (Loney, 1986).
Electing not to learn from the British experience, the discourse in Canada
pays mere lip service to the determinants of health, even as equitable health
care and publicly administered prevention services are being dismantled.

The emerging agenda of corporatization appears to have little
commitment to equity or to the employees' right to a healthy work
environment. As evidence, we present one of a growing number of cases in
Canadian Public Health Units where managers are implicated in racial

discrimination, harassment, and reprisals in the workplace, adversely affecting the health and well-being of the individuals involved.[2] We point to the current context of policies derived from the corporate sector, which appear to condone the labour management pattern of targeting people of colour and making equity dispensable. Wilson Head (1986) has shown that the compunction for equity in Canada is related to shortages in the labour market.

Perhaps paradoxically, advocacy, one of the key approaches for promoting health, will be most crucial in offsetting the negative effects of racism as corporatization progresses. Van Dijk (1993) uncovers the link between racialist practices and immoral policies that fail to make racism unacceptable. We suggest an astute antiracist advocacy driven by compassion, forgiveness, and love. Head (1983) has noted that, without pressure, legislation and informal policies are unlikely to change (1983). The Ottawa Charter (1986), which highlights equity, is not explicit about racial equity. In the absence of explicit equity legislation, international agreements such as the North American Free Trade Agreement (NAFTA) contribute to a milieu that requires policies in place agency by agency to assure equity through accountability for practices.

Health Promotion Critique and Corporatization

Commenting on the rise of corporatization in the British health system, B.K. Tones takes issue with social engineering that comes top-down and suggests that this approach is unlikely to implement changes such as those recommended in the Black Report on inequalities in health (Tones, 1986; Townsend et al., 1988). Tones's definition of the term advocacy is: "activities designed to influence political decision-making where representations are made by a change agent on behalf of a client group — especially in the context of community development" (1986:11). According to Tones, because proponents of the corporate agenda in Britain have an unstated policy to ignore the problem of racism and will not take action to end it, advocacy from within local communities will be necessary to combat this rise of corporatism.

We take our understanding of corporatization from Strong (1986) and Ahmad (1993). Strong, commenting on the WHO regional strategy for Europe, cautions that health promotion subject to corporate policy has a Janus face; for example, the governmental encouragement of trade and industry around alcohol and tobacco use. He uncovers a theoretical bias in the health promotion movement that favours: (1) the input of planners rather than clinicians; (2) the concept that the public can frustrate the plan; and (3) the Whiggish optimism that the "road to better health lies in economic development" (Strong, 1986:198).

Ahmad (1993) citing Wilding (1992), argues that changes in the health system in Britain need to be examined in light of the implementation of

Thatcher's policies where: (1) a particular management approach has been imposed onto the world of health and welfare; (2) there is a systematic erosion of powers of local government; (3) there is a loss of many rights of citizens, including the loss of services; and (4) there is an increased burden of citizen responsibilities in the face of a strengthened centralized regulatory apparatus. Ahmad outlines the necessary political activities the Black community will need to undertake to compensate for the new corporatization.

We take our understanding of privatization from Ahmad, who observes that top-down policies favouring corporatization open the public sector to private enterprise by splitting the previously combined function of "purchasing and providing" within the National Health Service. One result of this is that "health authorities consequently have attempted to increase their power in the pseudo-market through joint purchasing arrangements with other health authorities, consortia, mergers and takeovers" (Ahmad, 1993:204), thus opening the door to the vagaries of the market, which is not interested in equity. Ahmad notes difficulties in project management with such instability, as well as the problem that contracts with providers are rarely enforceable and that oftentimes there is no choice of providers. Market power and purchasing authorities continue to be championed with little evaluation. Paton (1991) points to evidence that the outcome may inevitably be higher public spending and marvels that the rhetoric of consumerism continues when the consumer has no real say. A new cadre of bureaucrats — i.e., planners — manage the contracts, and the consumer's needs are modified according to the lowest contract price that can be purchased.

Russel and Gilson (1997) have recently critiqued how the management of user fees fails to provide for access by disadvantaged groups to health care in those countries that have moved toward corporate management practices. This is a shifting of the burden of payments onto the consumers who pay if they can and have little recourse or input if they cannot.

In Ahmad's view, local input is impotent, despite administrative techniques to make it appear otherwise, because local authorities in Britain have their budgets cut if they do not toe the central line (Ahmad, 1993). The centres of power and resource allocation enjoy diminished accountability. In Canada, both the labour market and the health services domain have been restructured directly as a result of NAFTA (Walker, 1997). Marx's definition of free trade still holds: "By free trade they mean the unfettered movement of capital: freed from all political, national and religious shackles" (Marx, 1852; in Walker:325).

Walker points out that under the NAFTA, Canada's

Health, safety and environmental laws and their enforcement, as well as the worker's compensation system, are all under attack.

> Using the mantras of "globalization" and "competetiveness" in the
> context of NAFTA, business leaders cite the need to deregulate and
> privatize Canadian institutions. Harmonization with the United States
> is promoted as a goal. (Walker, 1997:327–29)

The health unit in the case study we present, like every health agency in the
country, was feeling the influence of these and other mantras such as
"efficiency," "excellence," "productivity outcomes," etc. In today's context,
we observe that the centralization of corporate control is still being masked
as decentralization. Local decision-making power with inadequate resources
is being felt as control over misery (King-Hooper & Hagey, 1994). Publicly
under-funded services are becoming dysfunctional, paving the way for middle-
class support for privatization, thus providing opportunities for multinational
health consortia in Canada. For a time there was some discourse opposing
this process.[3]

The national discourse is now appropriating the voices of opposition,
and the message of accommodation is coming through, as for example in
Deber and Swan. By focusing on general practitioners and only those
specialists who are still state-employed in the British system, Deber and
Swan claim there is "no reason to predict any downward spiral" from
privatization of Canada's health system (Deber & Swan, 1997:331). They
ignore the fact that specialists outside the British National Health system
account for two tiers of service, whereby only those who are eligible for
insurance coverage or can afford out-of-pocket specialists services are getting
full benefits, despite the complexities of payment channels arising from
policies outlined by Klein (1996). Saltman (1997) reviews studies that show
that equity (as defined) has been decreasing in Britain since this shift. Ahmad
(1993) lamented the difficulties of implementing equity policy priorities and
showed how this process is further compromised by the purchaser/provider
split — the new roles for planners and the private sector — with potentially
serious consequences of ethnoracial disadvantage in a racist society.

The interest in antiracist policy is the heart of our concern in this paper.
We focus on how racism is played out in a provincially funded public health
department — recently re-named community health department (CHD),
perhaps to give the impression of local accountability. Ironically, perhaps,
the department has been engaged in implementing mandated health
promotion policy initiatives in the metropolitan area it serves (Ministry of
Health of Ontario, 1989). The mayor has recently proclaimed DIVERSITY
to be the city's motto, in perhaps another irony.

First, we wish to present the ambivalent policy context affecting the
health unit in question. Compliance and opposition, turbulence and

accommodation characterize the shift to corporatization. Critiques show issues parallel to those raised by our critical colleagues in Britain. Canadian commentary includes our own insights into the discourse of corporatization and its relation to racism.

Corporatization and the Discourse around Racism

In Canada, at the federal level, there is currently a clean-up initiative underway to normalize the shift to privatization. This shift is being facilitated by centralization and the reflexive rhetoric of corporate management. An example of this is a recent call for letters of intent put out to researchers seeking research funds from the Canadian Health Services Foundation (CHSRF) Open Grants Competition (1999).[4] This appeal expresses concern for "informed public participation in decision making." Note the word "competition," which now appears in the title, as a genuflection to fashionable market ideology.

The document goes on to indicate full awareness of problems accruing from under-funding and uses the euphemism "health reform" to help gloss over those problems. Acknowledgment of the issue of centralization comes out in a section explaining the themes targeted for funding. Section 2.1, titled "Centralization and aggregation of health services," states the centralization theme "was consistently raised as a priority by regional managers trying to overcome historical patterns of health-seeking behaviour, distributions of power and entrenched interests" (CHSRF, 1999:7). It goes on to identify research questions of particular interest; for example:

> Are there circumstances where there are negative repercussions from public participation, for public policy principles guiding the Canadian health system (e.g., equity conditions of the Canada Health Act, single tier system)? How might these be avoided? (CHSF, 1999:8)

This statement can be inspected for its underlying discourse strategy (using van Dijk's [1993] method) to reveal that there is an acknowledgment that the single-tier system is under threat or it would not be topicalized. The threat being named in the passage is from the public, as in the phrase "negative repercussions from public participation." So Strong's observation for Britain (Strong, 1986), that the public can be formulated by government as frustraters of the plan, would appear to hold true for Canada as well, and the term "equity," specified as an example in the question, can work as subliminal advertising toward racial stereotyping.

While the term "equity" can legitimately be seen as tipping investigators off to include visible minority status (Census Canada term) in their proposals, the frame of what critical research is possible has already had its limits set. Researchers have been advised that members of the public are a legitimate problem focus. Normally, researchers carefully examine the wording in the call for letters of intent in order to parrot that wording as closely as possible to improve their chances of getting funded. This is the mechanism by which the dominant message gets recycled without a conspiracy taking place.

The document as it is formed already represents the shift to corporatization, even though it gives the appearance that this matter and the issues raised are going to be researched in the upcoming competition. But the application requires that government funds are matched with corporate funds for this health system research. Thus, corporations having interest in the research called for encroach on the alleged neutrality of the research enterprise. What corporation is going to fund research that is likely to be anti-privatization and defend the single-tier system? Notice, also, that government sponsorship in partnership with corporations has now come under the name "Foundation," which has a private ring to it.

One of the foundations offering matching funds is under the aegis of the province of Ontario. One of the first moves by former Conservative Premier Mike Harris when he took office was to rescind the protection provided to visible minorities in the equity legislation brought in by the previous New Democratic Party (NDP) government. The NDP's employment equity bill was intended to institutionalize social justice principles and was calculated to improve health by narrowing the gap between richest and poorest, since health indicators correlate with the narrowest gap (Sullivan, 1992). The NDP also had an Antiracism Secretariat, which was the darling of numerous minority groups and which produced excellent materials, all terminated by the incoming Conservatives.

Our criticism is not of any particular government but of the entire global strategy, already well under way, as reflected in the WHO strategy for Europe critiqued by Strong above.[5] The NDP government, for example, was not perfect. Panitch and Swartz (1988) have been critical of the way trade unions in Canada have been dismantled by governments making way for privatization, including that of the NDP in Ontario, which legislated unions into wage roll-back and freeze accommodations. We will show in our case study that the union was not paying attention to the problem of racial disadvantaging in the workplace. It is worth noting here that the union itself was under siege, losing thousands of members, due to hospital bed closures and cutbacks.

At a national level, attention has been shifting to intersectoral influences, which feed into the "Whiggish optimism" (Strong, 1986:198), mentioned earlier, favouring economic development and cutting transfer payments to the provinces. No doubt, this has led to a general anxiety within public health departments despite bolstering by the Epp Report, which indicated big tasks ahead for the social marketing of health:

> We must bear in mind that health is not necessarily a priority for other sectors. This means that we have to make health matters attractive to other sectors in much the same way that we try to make health choices attractive to people. (Epp, 1986:11)

And the list is long of unhealthy choices offered in the marketplace, as well as the unhealthy effects of the industrial sector, such as cancer and heart disease noted by Strong, even as Canada's industrial sector has been under threat because of the NAFTA.

A vociferous attack was mounted against the shift to corporatization in the health system by those both within and outside the medical profession, but the myth that racism does not exist in Canada is so strong that even left-leaning analysts have been myopic about the problem.[6] In short, researchers representing virtually all segments of the political spectrum have failed to investigate the surge of racialist decision-making in the recent cut-backs with a disproportionate negative impact on people of colour (Das Gupta, 1996).

Informed by this overview of the more macro critical issues concerning corporatization, we turn now to have a look at the micro level of personnel management to develop a focus on racism and employee health.

The Problem of Institutionalized Racism

According to van Dijk (1993), who attempts to account for the rise in frequency and severity of racism in several European countries and the US, the political right is giving messages of permission to commit racism through many institutional forms: political speeches, media, corporate management practices, educational venues, and policy documents. In Canada avowed racists have been vocal members of the Reform Party, which has since been rechristened the Canadian Alliance Party and is now the country's official Opposition. Van Dijk's research shows that the dynamics produced in this phenomenon begin with a message of denial — "we are not racist" — but at the same time the effect produced is a growth toward normality and naturalness of racist practices and affiliations, together with an unspoken policy that objections to racism are disruptive and irritating (van Dijk, 1993; Wetherall & Potter, 1992).

Under Canadian corporatism — underfunding of health care in the guise of restructuring in order to pave the way for corporate marketeering — the focus on the "employee as a problem" increases with impunity. A "blame the victim" approach can be justified in the name of downsizing. The definition of the situation is always that the institution is under challenge.

Add to that the vulnerability of people of colour in an environment having no equity policy in place and the exacerbation of racism is predictable, especially in a milieu where racism is being normalized insidiously (van Dijk, 1993).

In an attempt to stem the tide of normalization of racism, in 1995, The Congress of Black Women of Canada, Toronto Chapter, organized an important conference: "End the silence on racism in health care: Build a movement against discrimination, harassment and reprisals." Its report, written by Agnes Calliste (1995) was presented subsequently in deposition to the Metro City Council Committee on Anti-Racism, Access, and Equity in a call for resources to investigate the continuing problem of racism in the health care system. In a speech to the conference, June Veecock, educator with the Ontario Federation of Labour, describes the dynamics of the mix of racism and corporate accountability, which has the logic of blaming the person of colour targeted in the downsizing enterprise:

> When we remain silent, what in effect we are doing is contributing to our own oppression. And I know that once you begin to speak, you have to be prepared for what comes. People are accused of making false claims of racism. They are accused of being incompetent and of using racism as an excuse for their incompetence. So that immediately the focus is shifted. The accuser becomes the accused. The victim is then faced with the additional burden of not only having to prove that she is experiencing racism, that this is a racist environment, but also that she is competent ... and enter your union who regrettably, more often that not, pays little attention to the issue of racism and does not pursue the complaint from this angle. And so what happens is that the union finds itself responding to management's agenda, and they, too, are perceived as being on the same side of the issue. I have spoken to many workers when they call my office and I say, "Are you unionized? Go to your union." They say, "June, they are a waste of time. Believe me." And I know that to be the case in many institutions. (Veecock, 1995:60–61)

D.E. Smith has discussed Veecock's observation in the context of theory that critiques administrative practices. Smith notes that the nature of societies organized by documentary practices (research and policy) is that an institution's proxies set up particular relations to protect it/themselves. Individuals who challenge the institution are scrutinized with impunity, because implicitly that challenge is an attack on the institution's right to rule (Smith, 1990).

Currently, the question is whether the "3-D" pecking order, which discounts, discredits, and disadvantages visible minorities, can operate with impunity to target individuals to be forced out under the shift to corporate management, cutbacks, and downsizing — i.e., underfunding of health care and what Martin Luther King called injustice in health. The term injustice can apply to individuals denied services and to those whose health suffers because of harassment in the workplace. See Saltman (1997) for a recent discussion of distributive justice for recipients of health care and Storch (1996) for an examination of the growing tension in Canada between the ethics of social justice and economics, as the forces of centralizing and downloading erode fundamental Canadian values of universal caring, exemplified in the Ottawa Charter, which reads:

> Health promotion is the process of enabling people to increase control over, and to improve, their health. The fundamental conditions and resources for health are peace, shelter, education, food, income, a stable eco-system, sustainable resources, social justice and *EQUITY* ... Health promotion action aims at making these conditions favourable through *advocacy* for health ... *Health promotion focuses on achieving equity in health* [our emphasis]. (Ottawa Charter for Health Promotion, 1986:1)

We believe this declaration applies to those working in health care agencies and calls for racial equity, although it ought to be more explicit. We turn now to show abrogation of these values in a practice setting guided by health promotion policy.

Case Illustration from a Community Health Unit

> "[N]urse administrators must set up organizations that take into account the need to care for and promote caring among nurses ... [T]he nurse acts ultimately to preserve the other's wholeness." (Swanson, 1993:356)

A series of incidents at a provincially funded Community Health Unit (CHU), located in a cosmopolitan Canadian city, illustrate the presence of racism within the climate of the new corporatism characteristic of the business of health promotion in the 1990s.

The CHU celebrated its seventieth year of service delivery in 1994 with 68 employees — 10 management, 17 administrative staff, and others, including public health nurses. Its CEO was a racial minority woman, but there was otherwise little congruence between its staff's ethnic/racial identity and that of the client population: although 85% of the staff were female, three of the unit's seven male employees were managers.[7] Consultants hired in 1994 to examine and make recommendations about the Unit's equity practices described its organization as "very traditional" (Kohli & Thomas, 1995).

Implementation of mandatory guidelines adopted by the province of Ontario in 1989 necessitated a major organizational restructuring in the work of the Unit, transforming the activities of public health nurses and occasioning marked changes in management style. The Unit's nurses, who had formerly functioned autonomously within a "nursing only" hierarchy to deliver services to individuals and families, were now expected to collaborate with non-medical professionals as members of teams responsible for planning strategies to effect change through "such activities as advocacy, policy development, media campaigns, [and] working with large community groups and coalitions" (Director of Adult Health, 1994a). The shift from "Manager" to "Director" to refer to supervisory personnel reveals the increasingly bureaucratic tone characteristic of the Unit's emerging management style. "Director" is a more top-down position than manager, thus reflecting a local shift in attitude toward centralized governance under Thatcherite ideology.

The fact that the Unit was headed in turn by five CEOs and seven Business Administrators between 1984 and 1994 suggests that the period of organizational and policy transition was difficult for both staff and management, due to frequent changes in administrative procedures. Twenty-five employees, 13 of whom had permanent jobs, left in 1993 and 1994. Permanent jobs were offered to only two of the 25 new people hired, and "racial minorities hired ... (all) filled temporary positions"(Kohli & Thomas, 1995).

Though racism had not previously been a serious problem at the CHU, the change in management style resulted in an increasing rift between management and staff, which affected the organization's culture in ways that facilitated the expression of everyday racism. In the early 1990s, incidents in which some managers misused their authority and certain staff made negative comments about non-whites and treated them in condescending ways became more frequent.

The increasingly discriminatory work environment provoked other incidents. Two public health nurses, one of Greek heritage, the other Ukrainian, left with grievances pending. This contributed to a "culture of silencing" (Kohli & Thomas, 1995). Fearing loss of their jobs due to "insubordination," employees critical of discriminatory practices failed to speak out. Others, however, opted to defend their rights and seek redress for unfair treatment by filing grievances charging the administration with discrimination; 13 such grievances were filed between 1991 and 1994. When the administration questioned the professional competence of a sixth-generation Black Canadian nurse, Evelyn Brody, who had been on staff at the CHU since 1978, and imposed a 10-day suspension from work upon her, she challenged their decision by filing a grievance charging them with discrimination. Having resolved to "no longer deny that racism is a part of my everyday experience," Ms. Brody began to publicly speak out against it.[8]

At an in-house transition workshop in 1992, employees identified "communication" and "lack of trust" as significant problems in the health unit. Rather than addressing these problems in an effective way, the administration targeted Ms. Brody as the source of the problem. She was assigned a heavier workload than her colleagues, given an unfair portion of the least valued work assignments (health consultations), and was denied her requests for in-house training. They did not allow her to use sick time for doctor's appointments, as others in her bargaining unit freely did, and, predictably, her health was undermined. (See Ahmad, 1983.) They required her (but not others) to provide regrets in writing when she was unable to attend team meetings. During awards presentations at an annual staff function, Ms. Brody "was the last nurse to be called to the podium" (Ministry of Labour, 1996:8) and "was never honoured by her manager but rather by the Communications Director" (ONA, 1996:4) . All others who had served more than 15 years were duly rewarded.

On more than one occasion, the racism directed toward Ms. Brody undermined administrative procedures. Rules regarding reporting off sick, for example, were applied to Ms. Brody "which had not been implemented and which were not applied to anyone else at that time" (Ministry of Labour, 1996:12).

In her 1994 performance appraisal, Ms. Brody's supervisors wrongly rated her overall performance as "poor" due to their erroneous view that she had a "communication" problem that jeopardized the work of the health unit because it interfered with effective team functioning. Ms. Brody worked on two teams, and her performance on the second team, in which she did not experience harassment, was not in question. To "assist" her to improve her communication style, the director of the team in question required Ms. Brody to undergo a three-month performance review during which her supervisors subjected her to further harassment through over-surveillance and other indignities. She was required to keep a weekly activity log, to meet with her supervisors weekly to discuss comments she made at team meetings (which they had written down), and to prepare and deliver a paper on teamwork. Though Ms. Brody had received letters from several community groups thanking her for presentations she had made to them, the administration argued that:

> the (positive) response of the community to Ms. Brody's work ... has no specific bearing on issues surrounding remedial action ... which

refers to (her) difficulty maintaining effective working relationships with peers, team members and directors in a team-based organization. (Director of Adult Health, 1994b)

Acting to defend her rights in a courageous, professional manner, Ms. Brody informed her supervisors in writing that "the view taken in the performance appraisal was a racist one" and filed still another grievance. While processing her grievance, Ms. Brody's union, the Ontario Nurses Association (ONA), advised her to participate in the performance review and "look as though you are trying to improve."

When Ms. Brody refused to make the oral presentation because, in her expressed view, "a nurse of Anglo Saxon descent would not have to," the Unit's CEO threatened her with dismissal and suspended her from work for 10 days without pay (ONA, 1996:19). Though Ms. Brody eventually made the oral presentation to those responsible for harassing her, her performance review was extended for an additional three months because of her failure to demonstrate to her supervisors' satisfaction that her communication skills were effective.

Then when, for health reasons, Ms. Brody resigned from the CHU, the ONA failed to inform her that within 10 days she should write a letter — a grievance for constructive dismissal — stating that she resigned under duress and needed to be reinstated. Instead, the ONA advised her to pursue a settlement offer from her former employer because she would lose rights to early retirement should she be "terminated." Ms. Brody rejected this option because it exempted the Unit from its obligation to acknowledge discrimination against her. Then the ONA entered into collaboration with the CHU and, in complete disregard of her wishes and without prior discussion of the terms with her, proceeded to settle on her behalf.

So the pattern Veecock outlined appears to fit Evelyn Brody. Having flagged her experience of racial discrimination, Ms. Brody was forced to defend her own competence on one of the teams she worked on. (To reiterate, her work was satisfactory on the other team to which she was assigned in the CHU.)

Ms. Brody's union collaborated with management and made a grave error in withholding information crucial for her job security and control over her employment arrangements; this, as Sullivan points out, can be a determinant of health:

Important gains in the health status of the population can be achieved through gradual public policy changes that increase employment security and the degree of control people have over their employment arrangements. (Sullivan, 1992:9)

Evelyn Brody carefully documented four years of everyday racism in her unit and has become the Malcolm X of Canadian nursing. She has collected a litany of powerful examples and stories; for example:

> Can you imagine how nurses who are supposed to be caring persons could be so insensitive as to arrange for the white nurses to have paid registration at a conference, and then to advise me that I could go but I would have to sneak in without paying?

Brody was successful in receiving, for the mental anguish she suffered, $10,000, the maximum provided under the Ontario Human Rights Code, and of having relevant documents removed from her file. She received no acknowledgment that it was racism that management perpetrated. The board of directors of the CHU, having confidently denied that there was racism at their Unit, hired independent investigators to demonstrate their contention. Basing findings on an objective study of the Unit's equity practices, the research consultants made 44 recommendations for an organizational change process for combating racism and implementing employment equity (Kohli & Thomas, 1995:62–69). Recommendation number one dealt with eliminating reprisals for suggesting that racism could be at issue. In the words of Evelyn Brody, "maybe now the unit will be a safe place to work."

Brody proceeded to file a grievance under the Ontario Occupational Health and Safety Act, which had recently upheld sexual harassment as a violation. Her attorney argued that racial harassment also violated the act, using the Ottawa Charter and health promotion research to establish determinacy, but was denied. Brody, together with Claudine Charley, another nurse who charged her employer with racial discrimination, lobbied the University of Toronto, urging its Faculty of Nursing to conduct research on racism. In recent years, the Faculty, together with the nursing department at McMaster University, received $5 million to study the quality of work life of nurses in Ontario. The problem of racism in the profession and in the health care system has been identified by an historian of nursing in Canada as one of the major challenges facing the profession in this century (McPherson, 1996). The Quality of Work Life unit (since renamed to reflect its focus on effectiveness and outcomes) has not generated even one study on racism in the profession or in the health care system.

Spurred on by Brody and a network called the Centre for Equity in Health and Society, nurses are now documenting their experiences of racism addressed through complaints and grievances with a view to policy recommendations and strategic changes (Collins et al., 1998). One of the participants stated:

I think that you need more nurses that will stand up and do things like this to make changes ... to point out the wrongs that have been done and to point out that racism is a thing that we have to try and eradicate. ... I could have gone maybe further if I had let things slide, but at the same time I came out of it feeling that I did a good job as a nurse. ... I think you have to stand up for what you know is right. (Collins et al., 1998:file #7)

Anti-Racist Organizing Against Institutionalized Racism

Many organizations across Canada realize that, if visible minority groups are going to advocate successfully for equity within the health care system, they will have to mobilize. For example, The Ontario Association of Black Health Care Providers, The Association of Blacks in the Health Sciences, and The Faculty of Medicine, Annual Visiting Lectureship on Aboriginal Health Perspectives have been quietly attempting to raise awareness without triggering guilt responses that in turn produce denial that racism exists (Dominelli, 1989; Calliste, 1996). By contrast, active membership of visible minorities in some of the mainstream professional organizations — such as the Registered Nurses Association of Ontario (RNAO) — is sparse. To its credit, however, the RNAO has put through an anti-racism policy statement and helped to sponsor a documentary film, "Ending the Silence on Racism in Nursing," distributed by Zac Films (zacfilms@sympatico.ca).

There is a growing trend toward organizing nursing associations around race, ethnicity, or culture; for example, there are the Aboriginal Nurses Association of Canada, the Chinese Nurses Association of Canada, the South Asian Nurses Association, the Filipino Nurses Association, the Somali Nurses Association, and numerous others. Wilson Head observed that the Ontario Human Rights Code and the Canadian Charter of Rights and Freedoms would never have come into being without the struggles of numerous minority pressure groups (Head, 1983:9). Evidently, the conditions for visible minorities working in the health care system warrant organizing, as Calliste (1996) has reported.

Hine (1989) and Barbee (1993) have argued that racist ideology accounts for a racially stratified system of nursing workers in the US, with Blacks and other ethnic minorities in the lower levels. Evidence reveals that this holds true for Canada, although formal research has not been done, suggesting massive denial of the problem. Semmes (1996) has located the problem of racism as it affects the health of African Americans within the context of post-industrial society; such a comprehensive study has yet to be undertaken for Canada.

The top nursing political body in Ontario advising the Ministry of Health — the provincial nursing advisory committee — has no visible minority members despite the large proportion of visible nurses on the front line, and there is felt disenfranchisement from the dominant professional associations and regulatory bodies, as reflected in resolutions submitted recently to the Canadian Nurses Association (Resolution to the Canadian Nurses Association Executive Director, July 2002, Toronto, by the Centre for Equity in Health and Society). Das Gupta (1996) has outlined racist management practices in Ontario nursing, including targeting, scapegoating, excessive monitoring, marginalization, seeing solidarity as a threat, infantalization, blaming the victim, bias in work allocation, underemployment and the denial of promotions, lack of accommodation, segregation of workers, co-optation and selective alliances, and tokenism. Explicit anti-racist organizing rather than mild-mannered appeals for "ethnic sensitivity" are called for both in health research and service delivery by Stubbs (1993). McMurray, for example, declares that "advocacy implies cultural sensitivity as well as empowerment," but does not endorse anti-racism (McMurray, 1991:19). See also Fleras and Elliott (1992) for the failure of multiculturalism, which emphasizes cultural differences, not similarities and not antiracism.

Antiracism is interested in commonalities while respecting distinctiveness in a system of shared power. Calliste (1996) and Dei (1996) both call for antiracism advocacy that recognizes the interlocking oppressions and institutions of hegemony.

An extensive antiracism initiative was started by the Ontario Hospital Association together with the previous (NDP) provincial government's Ministry of Health. We offer the definition of diversity from its initial glossary and note that it was criticized because designated group members felt marginalized by it. Others said "partaking in structures" is not the point, "when the game is already fixed like monopoly" as argued by Ahmad (1993). The Report by Collins et al. on grievances and complaints filed by immigrant women nurses of colour states:

> Diversity exists when all communities, including traditionally excluded communities, and all designated groups within communities, can give voice effectively to their issues, and partake equitably in the decision-making structures that determine their lives. (Collins et al., 1998:Transcripts, 3)

The final report of that committee produced important policy recommendations that have been of assistance for those of us doing research related to racism in the health disciplines, by offering formal sanction and encouragement of our work, which is collaborative with ethnoracial communities. Recommendation 9, for example, reads:

That professional associations, regulatory bodies, colleges and universities implement antiracism organizational change and that: 9.1) these organizations distribute, and make available the tools produced by the Ontario Hospital Anti-Racism Task Force, in implementing anti-racism organizational change; 9.2) those organizations involved in promoting and advancing knowledge on health, work in partnership with ethnoracial communities to develop and implement research initiatives on issues related to racism and health. (Joint Policy and Planning Committee, 1996)

The arduous, painful advocacy undertaken by Evelyn Brody in defending her case "in order that others would not have to go through what I went through" is shared by numerous groups working to implement such recommended changes. Organizations such as the Congress of Black Women of Canada and coalitions such as the Centre for Equity in Health and Society link advocates from diverse ethnoracial communities together and are lobbying for change. Their ethics are compassionate, forgiving, and driven by the power of love (Sandoval, 1990). Given the support dimensions of working with individuals who are being devastated by racialist exclusion, marginalization, isolation, problematization, and containment (Essed, 1991), they are over-burdened with the tasks of their commitments to antiracism. Because such groups have little access to resources in comparison to the forces of corporatism, however, the degree to which they can instill choices for greater institutional accountability, to offset the everyday transactions of racism manifest throughout the health system, remains to be seen.

The milieu of corporatization is moving toward privatization in Canada, with private clinics and nursing agencies, and it is anticipated that there will be private hospitals as reported for Australia (White & Colyer, 1998).

Van Dijk (1993) asserts that racialist discrimination and exclusion are immoral and that immoral practices exist because policies permit them. While the Ottawa Charter (1986) defines advocacy as an enabling process and is clear about equity and its links to determining health, it should be more explicit about the infringements on health due to racial inequity. In the absence of explicit equity legislation, international agreements, such as NAFTA, contribute to a milieu that we have seen requires strict personnel policies in place to ensure accountability for equitable management practices.

Notes

1   The authors wish to thank Evelyn Brody for her intellectual collegiality in assembling the facts and documents presented in this article. We thank Corinne Hart for comments on an earlier draft.

2 See Ahmad, 1983; Ordway, 1973; Olson et al., 1986; and Zanna & Olson, 1994.
3 See Armstrong, Choiniere, & Day, 1994; Armstrong, Choiniere, Feldberg, & White, 1995; Armstrong & Armstrong, 1996; and Armstrong et al., 1996.
4 CHSRF is a public not-for-profit corporation. The Foundation's mission is to sponsor and promote applied health systems research, to enhance its quality and relevance, and to facilitate its use in evidence-based decision-making by policy makers and health systems managers.
5 Strong, 1986; WHO, 1980; WHO, 1984; WHO, 1985.
6 See Armstrong, 1994; Armstrong, Choiniere, & Day, 1993; Armstrong et al., 1997.
7 Fifteen percent of the unit's employees were non-white compared to almost 25% in the population at large; 7.5% were disabled, compared to 13% in the general population; no Aboriginal peoples were on staff; and a greater proportion of men than women held full-time positions (Kohli and Thomas 1995:17–18).
8 The number of quotations of Ms. Brody in this article stem from her discussions with the first two authors of this piece during the preparation of the manuscript; they are not taken from her public documents.

References

Ahmad, W.I.U. (1983). Making black people sick: "Race," ideology, and health research. In W.I.U. Ahmad, (Ed), *"Race" and health in contemporary Britain*. Buckingham: Open University Press. 11–33.

———. (1993). Promoting equitable health and health care: A case for action. In W.I.U. Ahmad (Ed)., *"Race" and health in contemporary Britain*. Buckingham: Open University Press. 201–14.

Armstrong, P. (1994). Caring and women's work. *Health and Canadian Society* 2(1).

Armstrong, P., & Armstrong, H. (1996). *Wasting away: The undermining of Canadian health care*. Toronto: Oxford University Press.

Armstrong, P., Armstrong, H., Choiniere, J., Mykholovskiy, E., & White, J.P. (1997). *Medical alert: New work organizations in health care*. Toronto: Garamond Press.

———. (1996). *The promise and the price: New work organizations in Ontario hospitals*. Occasional Paper. Toronto: York University Centre for Health Studies.

Armstrong, P., Choiniere, J., & Day, E. (1994). *Take care: Warning signals for Canada's health system*. Toronto: Garamond.

———. (1993). *Vital signs: Nursing in transition*. Toronto: Garamond Press.

Armstrong, P., Choiniere, J., Feldberg, G. & White, J.P. (1995). *Voices from the ward: A pilot study of the impact of cutbacks on hospital care*. Toronto: York University Centre for Health Studies.

Barbee, E. (1993). Racism in US nursing. *Medical Anthropology Quarterly* 7(4): 346–62.

Calliste, A. (1995). (1996) Antiracism organizing and resistance in nursing: African Canadian women. *Canadian Review of Sociology and Anthropology/RCSA* 33(3): 362–90.

———. End the silence on racism in health care: Build a movement against discrimination, harassment, and reprisals. *Canadian Congress of Black Women Report*. Toronto: Ontario Institute for Studies in Education. 25–26 May.

Canadian Health Services Foundation (CHSRF). (1999). Open Grants Competition: Call for letters of intent.<<http://www.chsrf.ca/english/programs/loi2_et.html>>.

Collins, E., Calliste, A., Choudhry, U., Fudge, J., Guruge, S., Hagey J.R., Henry, S., Lee, R., & Turrittin, J. (1998). *Making racism seeable: Phase I: Complaints and grievances filed by immigrant women nurses of colour*. Final Report. Toronto: Centre for Excellence in Research on Immigration and Settlement.

Das Gupta, T. (1996). *Racism and Paid Work*. Toronto: Garamond Press.

Day, S. (1987). Impediments to achieving equality. In S.L. Martin & K.E. Mahoney (Eds.), *Equality and Judicial Neutrality*. Toronto: Carswell Publishing.

Deber, R., & Swan, B. (1998). Question two (supplementary question): The case of the United Kingdom. In National Forum on Health, *Striking a balance: Health care systems in Canada and elsewhere. Canada Health Action: Building on the Legacy*. Sainte-Foy, QC: MultiMondes.

Dei, G.J.S. (1996). *Anti-racism education: Theory & practice*. Halifax: Fernwood Publishers.

Director of Adult Health. (1994a). Staff performance review. 25 July. On file, Centre for Equity in Health and Society.

Director of Adult Health. (1994b). Letter to Evelyn Brody. 29 June. On file, Centre for Equity in Health and Society.

Dominelli, L. (1989). Racism in a caring profession. *New Community* 15(3): 391–403.

Epp, J. (1986). *Achieving health for all: A framework for health promotion*. Ottawa: Health and Welfare Canada.

Essed, P. (1990). Against all odds: Teaching against racism at a university in South Africa. *European Journal of Intercultural Studies* 1(1): 41–56.

———. (1991). *Understanding everyday racism: An interdisciplinary theory*. London: Sage Publications.

Fleras, A., & Elliott, J.L. (1992). *Multiculturalism in Canada: The challenge of diversity*. Toronto: Nelson.

Head, W.A. (1986). An exploratory study of the attitudes and perceptions of minority and majority health care workers. Commissioned by the Race Relations Division of the Ontario Human Rights Commission.

———. (1983). Race relations today: The state of the art. *Currents* 1(l).

Hine, D. (1989). *Black women in white: Racial conflict and cooperation in the nursing profession, 1890–1950*. Bloomington, IN: Indiana University Press.

Joint Policy and Planning Committee. (1995). *Draft antiracism policy guidelines*. Toronto: Ontario Hospital Association and the Ministry of Health, November.

——. (1996). *Antiracism policy guidelines*. Toronto: Ontario Hospital Association and the Ministry of Health, November.

King-Hooper B., & Hagey, R. (1994). Control issues in Native health care: Perspectives of an urban community health centre. In S. Bolaria & H. Dickinson (Eds.), *Health, illness and health care in Canada*. 2ⁿᵈ ed. Toronto: Harcourt Brace.

Klien, R. (1996). *The new politics of the national health service*. 3ʳᵈ ed. New York: Longman.

Kohli, R. & Thomas, B. (1995). *A time for change: Anti-racism, employment equity, organizational change process*. Toronto: Doris Marshall Institute for Education & Action. October.

Kramuer, & B.S. Brown (Eds.) *Racism and mental health essays*. Pittsburgh, PA: University of Pittsburgh Press. 123–45.

Labonte, R. (1988). World trade and investment agreements: Implications for public health. *Canadian Journal of Public Health* 89(1): 10–12.

Loney, M. (1986). *The politics of greed: The new right and the welfare state*. London: Pluto Press Ltd.

Marx, K. (1852). What is Free Trade? *New York Daily Tribune* 25 August. In Walker (see below), 325.

McMurray, A. (1991). Advocacy for community self-empowerment. *International Nursing Review* 38: 19–21.

McPherson, K. (1996). *Bedside matters*. Toronto: Oxford University Press.

Ministry of Health of Ontario. (1989). *The mandatory health programs and service guidelines: Persuant to section 7 of the Health Protection and Promotion Act 1983*. Toronto: Ministry of Health.

Ministry of Labour, Ontario. (1996). Hearing in the case of Evelyn Brody, on violation of the Occupational Health and Safety Act. October.

National Forum on Health/Forum National sur la Santé (NFH). (1997). Canada health action: building on the legacy. Vol 1. Children and youth; Vol 2: Adults and seniors; Vol. 3: Determinants of health: Settings and issues; Vol 4. Health care systems in Canada and elsewhere; Vol 5: Evidence and information. Sainte-Foy. QC: MultiMondes.

Olson, J., Herman, C. & Zanna, M (Eds.). (1986). *Relative deprivation and social comparison: The Ontario symposium*. Vol. 4. Hillsdale, NJ. Lawrence Erlbaum Associates Publishers.

Ontario Nurses Association (ONA). (1996). Deposition to the Ministry of Labour hearing in the case of Evelyn Brody. May.

Ordway, J. (1973). Some emotional consequences of racism for whites. In C.V. Willie, B.M.

Organization for Economic Cooperation & Development (OECD). (1996). OECD Health Data 96 (on CD-Rom). Paris: OECD Health Policy Unit.

Ottawa Charter for Health Promotion. (1986). World Health Organization International Conference on Health Promotion. Ottawa, Canada. 17–21 November.

Panitch, L. & Swartz, D. (1988). *The assault on trade union freedoms.* Toronto: Garamond Press.

Paton, C. (1991). Myths of competition. *Health Science Journal* 30 May: 22–23.

Russel, S., & Gilson L. (1997). User fee policies to promote health service access for the poor: A wolf in sheep's clothing? *International Journal of Health Services.* 27(2): 359–79.

Saltman, R.B. (1997). Equity and distributive justice in European health reform. *International Journal of Health Services* 27(3): 443–53.

Sandoval, C. (1990). Theorizing white consciousness for a post-empire world: Barthes, Fanon, and the rhetoric of love. In R. Frankenberg (Ed.), *Displacing whiteness.* Durham, NC: Duke University Press.

Semmes, C.E. (1996). *Racism, health and post-industrialism: A theory of African-American health.* London: Praeger.

Smith, D.E. (1990). *The conceptual practices of power: A feminist sociology of knowledge.* Toronto: University of Toronto Press.

Storch, J. (1996). Foundational values in Canadian health care. In M. Stingl & D. Wilson (Eds.), *Efficiency vs. equality: Health reform in Canada.* Halifax: Fernwood Publishing.

Strong, P.M. (1986). A new-modelled medicine? Comments on the WHO's regional strategy for Europe. *Social Science & Medicine* 22(2): 193–99.

Stubbs, P. (1993). "Ethnically sensitive" or "anti-racist?" Models for health research and service delivery. In W.I.U. Ahmad (Ed.), *"Race" and health in contemporary Britain.* Buckingham: Open University Press. 34–47.

Sullivan, T. (1992). Strategic planning for health: How to stay on top of the game. *Health Promotion.* Summer.

Swanson, K. (1993). Nursing as informed caring for the well-being of others. *Image: Journal of Nursing Scholarship* 25(4): 352–57.

Tones, B.K. (1986). Health education and the ideology of health promotion: A review of alternative approaches. *Health Education Research* 1(1): 3–12.

Townsend, P., Davidson, N. & Whitehead, M. (1988). *The Black Report and the health divide: Inequalities in health.* London: Penguin Books.

van Dijk, T.A. (1993). *Elite discourse and racism.* Newbury Park, CA: Sage Publications.

Veecock, J. (1995). Speech. In A. Calliste, *Canadian Congress of Black Women Conference Report.* Toronto: Ontario Institute for Studies in Education. Appendix F: 56–66.

Walker, C. (1997). NAFTA and occupational health: A Canadian perspective. *Journal of Public Health Policy* 18(3): 325–33

Wetherell, M., & Potter, J. (1992). *Mapping the language of racism: Discourse and the legitimation of exploitation*. New York: Columbia University Press.

White, K. & Colyer, F. (1998). Health care markets in Australia: Ownership of the private hospital sector. *International Journal of Health Services* 28(3): 487–510.

Wilding, P. (1992). The British welfare state: Thatcherisms's enduring legacies. *Policy and Politics* 20(3): 201–12.

World Health Organization (WHO). (1984). *Health promotion: A discussion document on the concept and principles*. Geneva: WHO.

——. (1980). A new-modelled medicine? Comments on the WHO's regional strategy for Europe. Thirtieth Session of the Regional Committee for Europe. Fez, Morocco. 7–11 October.

——. (1985). *Strategies for health for all in Europe: Regional evaluation, Copenhagen*. Geneva: WHO.

Zanna, M., & Olson, J. (Eds.). (1994). *The psychology of prejudice: The Ontario symposium*. Vol 7. Hillsdale, NJ: Lawrence Erlbaum Associates Publishers.

Chapter Fifteen

Undertaking Advocacy

Merle Jacobs

Understanding issues around race, class, gender, and age is not enough. We also need to engage in advocacy in order to promote social change. The questions we must ask ourselves are " How do I advocate?" and "Who will listen to me?" These two questions do not have direct answers; however, in order to achieve some level of success we need to build bridges with other like-minded individuals. We also need to develop relationships with individuals in positions of power — especially those within government and business. Our focus is to make such persons aware of our concerns regarding social conditions, policies, and actions that are harmful to the citizenry in general. We may want to make them mindful of the difference between merely understanding discrimination and changing the environment that supports these injustices. Currently, we discuss issues about diversity and racism and then we discuss education, health, and social services. In the discussion of education, health, and social service we have separate silos that allow the status quo to exist. It is in the intersection of race, class, and gender and in the integration of the different institutions that dynamic social action will occur. Structures that support current toxic environments can then be shifted to allow for the production of healthy social relations — for it is through community interaction and advocacy that the web of social relationships are addressed and changed.

Women, work, and society covers a broad area; thus, you will not run out of issues to undertake and strive to change. We can be agents of change or bystanders within the shifting dynamic of society. The following proposals are suggested to help you to address issues of injustice that are part of our everyday lives.

Tactics for Increasing Awareness

- Co-ordinate efforts between other individuals who want change
- Co-ordinate efforts between organizations
- Contact business leaders in your area who may wish to support the issue
- Drop off relevant literature at your MPP's office with your name and telephone number
- Meet with local MP/MPP
- Obtain a commitment from the MP/MPP to take the message to the Minister
- Follow-up with your local MPP
- Take local action, including sending letters and petitions to your MPP
- Call the Premier's office and Minister's office to express your views
- Take local action with the media, including monitoring coverage, writing letters to the editor, and contacting friendly reporters with key messages
- Start a petition/sign a petition and take it to your local MP/MPP and ask him or her to deliver it to the Minister

Your Key Messages: Why Are They Important?

Whenever you converse with business leaders or members of other organizations, or with your political leaders, you must have a message that is consistent and well prepared.

Key messages are the issues that you and your group have put together, and that you wish to get across. Use the research and published articles to create five key messages that you wish to present when advocating for social change. It does not matter if the change is in the area of health, gender, or race discrimination. More than five key messages will be difficult to absorb, so keep things as uncomplicated as possible. This is also important when writing to magazine or newspaper editors.

- **Research is important.** Remember that you are trying to distinguish your organization and your issue from many other worthwhile causes. Prepare yourself for the style as well as the substance of the meeting. Knowing your audience, how they operate, and what they need and want from groups like yours can make a huge difference. The deeper the impression you make, the better the odds are that your cause will be recognized by the MP/MPP and that you will be able to influence his or her actions.
- **A good case contains a clear and simple statement of your issue.** It needs to be well researched, competently analyzed, and

focused on a clear set of issues. It should also present a straightforward conclusion and, where necessary, offer realistic alternatives.

- **Explain your case as a teacher would.** Polish your stories to make a point. Personalize them so that the person to whom you are speaking (MP/MPP) has a powerful tool to take on to other audiences. These individuals want the support of others so that they will not be by themselves in the forefront for change.

- **A persuasive case is simply a good case that has been tailored for specific use in the public arena.** Many public groups stop with a good case. What this type of case most often fails to do is convey the emotional importance of the issue — either your sense of commitment, or its importance to the MP/MPP. Major policy changes occur in government and it is in this area that you must make a tailored case that is persuasive, not only for the individual with whom you are speaking or to whom you are writing, but also so that she or he can take this to their caucus and to their community.

- **There is a difference between a face-to-face meeting and writing a letter.** In both forms of communication, however, remember to prepare, prepare, prepare.

Steps to a Successful Meeting

1. Prepare, prepare, prepare. Set your objectives and develop your strategy and communication plan before you make any phone calls. Key messages are "a must."

2. Research your local MPP's views on what you are presenting. Does he or she have any personal experiences in the area? When meeting with local businesses or other organizations, research their views and their structures.

3. Decide with whom you want to meet. In some cases, the more influential the MP/MPP (i.e., a cabinet minister), the more difficult it will be to schedule a meeting. An initial meeting with a staff person may be a worthwhile first step. However, indicate your desire to meet with the MP/MPP in the future. This also applies to business leaders.

4. Think about timing. Fridays are usually constituency days and therefore good meeting days. In addition, when the legislature is not sitting, MPs/MPPs are often in their constituency offices.

5. Send a letter (by fax, if possible) requesting an opportunity to meet. Follow-up by phone with the staff and ask for a commitment for the meeting date and time. Continue to call once every week until a meeting is scheduled. Remember to ask how much time you have

with the MP/MPP. If the allotted time is insufficient, ask for more. Usually you may get only fifteen minutes and need to prepare for getting your message across within this time-frame.

6. Ask appropriate people to accompany you. Prepare them ahead of time with objectives and key messages. Agree beforehand on who will address what issues.

7. Prepare an information package to be sent one week prior to your meeting. Ask the individual to review the material before the meeting. Include information on the provincial and local organization, relevant statistics, information on your current initiatives, and any national or provincial papers or motions supporting your issue. The meeting will be more productive if both groups are prepared. Include a meeting agenda in the package.

8. Prior to the meeting, decide what types of information and commitment you want to have when you leave the meeting. Be specific. Ask for a reply or action by a specific date. There is a difference between meeting with business leaders and other organizations and meeting with politicians. With the former, you need to discuss issues that they see as important for their membership or consumers. With politicians, they are concerned with issues relating to their responsibility to society and to those who elected them.

9. When meeting with a politician, you may need to have a second meeting before you get any commitment from the MP/MPP. Be persistent. Be prepared with an action that you can suggest to a sympathetic MP/MPP.

10. Start the meeting by stating why you asked for the meeting and what you hope to accomplish. If possible, use hand-outs to help communicate your information. Keep it simple. Remember that these individuals are not specialists on your issue. And keep it relatively brief — the more influential MPs/MPPs have the greatest time pressures and will appreciate a succinct, persuasive presentation.

11. Use references from the research you have done on the MPP's office regarding its position on the issue. Offer ways in which the MP's/MPP's office can benefit from supporting your organization or your issue. For example, your organization could includes the office's name in their newsletter, invite members of the office to speak at monthly meetings, or include the office in community awareness days. Remember that MPs/MPPs are elected and their goal is to stay in that position by being well known, well liked and active in their communities.

12. End the meeting by asking for a commitment from them to respond by a specific date, or schedule another meeting to discuss next steps and the commitment you are seeking. Once again, be specific.

13. Write a follow-up letter outlining the issues discussed and next steps for both groups (if applicable). Send the letter to the MP's/MPP's office within five business days of the meeting and send copies to all of the people who attended.

14. Contact organizations that are supportive to your objectives with the results of your efforts.

Ten Steps to a Successful Letter-Writing Campaign

1. Set your objective for the letter-writing campaign — what outcome do you want? To change or influence policy, etc.?

2. Develop key messages to be included in the letters. The key messages should reflect the focus and objective of the campaign.

3. **Do not use form letters**. Politicians and bureaucrats discount these letters because they appear too staged. Varying each letter allows for the personal importance and emotion of the issue to be communicated. Provide participants in the letter-writing campaign with key messages, names, and addresses so they can create their own letters.

4. Ask for a specific action in the letters you write. For example, ask MPs/MPPs to express their support publicly for your issue or cause, and to seek the support of their colleagues in caucus.

5. Back-up your request with statistics and research to demonstrate the importance of the issue. Don't be afraid to use personal examples. This will ensure that the MP/MPP understands all aspects of the issue.

6. Provide participants in the letter-writing campaign with a deadline for their letters. Ask them to report back when the letters are complete.

7. Send the letters to the MPP's constituency address and make sure that all of the letters are personalized. Send copies of the letters to the Minister and to the Premier.

8. Schedule the letter-writing campaign for greatest effect. A particularly good time is six to twelve months before an election; however, it can be any time that is appropriate. The timing can also reflect local events.

9. Follow-up the letters with phone calls to recipients to ensure that the letters were received. This will increase awareness of the issues and will stress the need for action.

10. Ask for a formal response from the MP/MPP. Report back to the participants on the number and quality of the responses.

Petitioning the Legislative Assembly

Residents of the province have the right to petition their legislators. A petition is a request to the Parliament to take some specific action (or to refrain from taking some action) to redress a public grievance. The action requested must be within the scope of jurisdiction of the Legislative Assembly, and the request must be clear, temperate, proper, and respectful.

Form and Content

A petition must be addressed to either the Parliament, Legislature, or Legislative Assembly of the province. Petitions addressed to "the Government of _____" or to a particular minister cannot be accepted.

Petitions must be written, typewritten, or printed; and it is recommended that the paper be standard letter or legal size.

If a petition consists of more than one sheet of signatures, the text of the petition must appear at the top of *every* sheet. Each person petitioning the Parliament must print his or her name and address and sign his or her name under the text of the petition.

A petition must contain *original* signatures only, written directly on the face of the petition and not pasted or transferred to it. Petitions must be free of erasures or insertions.

Petitioners must be residents of the province. It is acceptable for petitioners to be under the age of majority.

Presentation

A petition may only be presented by a member of the Legislative Assembly, and it must comply with the requirements above, before the member may present it.

It is not the practice in the Ontario Legislature for the Speaker or a minister of the Crown to present a petition. Petitions received by a minister of the Crown are usually presented by the Chief Government Whip.

It is the responsibility of the petitioner(s) to arrange for a member of the Legislative Assembly to present a petition; an MPP cannot be compelled to present a petition, and presentation of a petition by an MPP does not imply that he or she endorses the contents of the petition.

Sample Petition

*I believe that the persons dealing with in Ontario should have access to [what the need is]. As such, I believe that all persons with [insert the issue].

I urge the Ontario Government to provide leadership in this area and change [laws, or government policy].

Name (printed)	**Signature**	**Address**

*The wording at the top must appear on every sheet!

Sample Letter Requesting a Meeting or Detailing an Issue of Concern

Date
MPP's Name
MPP's Address
MPP's Fax

Dear [name of the MPP]:

I am writing to request [that you look into the important issue] (or) [an opportunity to meet with you as soon as possible] regarding [the issue]. As my MPP it is important that you are aware of some of the key issues surrounding [the issue] and policy reform.

[Put in the concerns and the historical data regarding the issue]. I have attached a few articles related to the area of concern.

I will be in touch with you shortly to [set up a meeting, if so desired] discuss this issue with you further and look forward to [speaking or meeting] with you in the near future.

Yours truly,

Sample Follow-up Letter after Meeting

Date
MPP Name
MPP Address

Dear [name of the MPP]:

Thank you for taking the time to meet with me. I appreciate your interest and concern in the key issues surrounding _____.

As we discussed, _____ [the issues you discussed].

I will contact you during the week of _____ to discuss the Minister's feedback on this important issue. Again, thank you for your interest in improving the lives of those individuals experiencing _____ [the issue] in Ontario.

Yours truly,

***

Advocacy is not limited to the few samples provided in this chapter; these samples are included to promote an understanding of the actions needed in advocacy. In addition, they demonstrate that it takes energy and time away from our busy lives to advocate for others and for ourselves. The ideas presented here indicate that individuals and organization members have valuable expertise, and can legitimize their causes through contact with people in positions of power. Critical decisions are made within government without the input or the knowledge of the citizenry, after which it may be too late for action. We need to ensure that we have information about the changes that are occurring around us through the media and other sources.

Given the work of those scholars who have engaged in research on women, work, and society, we now have a wealth of material at our disposal. The reader of this book now needs to move from understanding the problems that face us in society to tackling them. Reform can only occur when we take action; thus, social change and advocacy go hand in hand. The more voices heard, the less likely those in power will be to take actions that are not in the best interests of women and other groups within our society.